THE DEMOCRATIC CONSTITUTION

THE DEMOCRATIC CONSTITUTION

Neal Devins and Louis Fisher

OXFORD
UNIVERSITY PRESS

2004

OXFORD
UNIVERSITY PRESS

Oxford New York

Auckland Bangkok Buenos Aires Cape Town Chennai
Dar es Salaam Delhi Hong Kong Istanbul Karachi Kolkata
Kuala Lumpur Madrid Melbourne Mexico City Mumbai Nairobi
São Paulo Shanghai Taipei Tokyo Toronto

Published by Oxford University Press, Inc.
198 Madison Avenue, New York, New York 10016
www.oup.com

Oxford is a registered trademark of Oxford University Press

Library of Congress Cataloging-in-Publication Data

Devins, Neal
The democratic constitution / by Neal Devins and Louis Fisher.
p. cm.
ISBN-13 978-0-19-517122-8; 978-0-19-517123-5 (pbk.)
ISBN 0-19-517122-5; 0-19-517123-3 (pbk.)
1. Constitutional law—United States.   2. Constitutional law—United
States—Interpretation and construction.   3. United States—Politics
and government.   4. Pressure groups—United States   5. Judicial
process—United States.   I. Fisher, Louis.   II. Title.

KF4550   .D38   2004
342.7302—dc21   2003021076

3 4 5 6 7 8 9

Printed in the United States of America
on acid-free paper

To my sister, Margie.
—Louis Fisher

To my parents, Matt and Dian Dollinger.
—Neal Devins

Preface

Through a series of case studies, our book explains how constitutional law is shaped both by judicial and nonjudicial forces. Instead of concentrating solely on what the Supreme Court or lower courts say about the Constitution, we also examine the contributions by the elected branches, the states, interest groups, and the general public. The result is a richer, more dynamic, and more accurate picture of the way that constitutional law develops.

Our book has a second objective. Not only do we show how constitutional law is shaped by the larger political culture, we argue that it *should* work that way. We think that constitutional law in this broader sense is more stable, more consistent with constitutional principles, and more protective of individual and minority rights.

A number of recent studies have challenged the Court's status as ultimate interpreter of the Constitution. Some scholars argue that Court rulings have played no meaningful role in effectuating social change and, as such, call for the Court to issue "minimalist" decisions—decisions that allow popularly elected government to play a leadership role in defining constitutional norms.[1] More striking, some academics speak either of "constitutional moments" in which the people—through elections and the like—effectively amend the Constitution, or of populist constitutionalist discourse in which the courts would steer clear of constitutional interpretation altogether.[2] We think that these studies often discount the pivotal role that courts can and should play in triggering both social movement and elected government action.[3] Decisions by the Court do matter. But equally important, if not more so, are the reactions of elected officials and the people to Supreme Court decisions and the many constitutional issues that never come to the courts or, when they do, are returned by judges to the political branches for resolution.

Several studies have explained how elected officials and public opinion help define constitutional norms, but they usually consider only one or two subject areas and are often limited to specific historical periods.[4] Some studies speak in generalities or offer theoretical models.[5] Our work is grounded in concrete examples, revealing the work of interest groups, the color of legislative debate, and strategies within the executive branch.[6]

vii

We have published many books and articles that prepare us for this work. Fisher's *Constitutional Dialogues: Interpretation as Political Process* (Princeton, 1988) won the Louis Brownlow Book Award, given by the National Academy of Public Administration. His book *American Constitutional Law* (McGraw-Hill, 1990, 1995; Carolina Academic Press, 1999, 2001, 2003) is also grounded in three-branch interpretation, as is his recent *Religious Liberty in America: Political Safeguards* (University Press of Kansas, 2002). His other books and over three hundred articles explore many of these issues, as do his thirty-eight appearances testifying before congressional committees. In his work with the Congressional Research Service (CRS) over a thirty-year period, he has been personally involved in many of these disputes. The views expressed in this book are personal, not institutional, and do not represent the positions of either CRS or the Library of Congress.

Devins (with Fisher) coauthored *Political Dynamics of Constitutional Law* (West, 1992, 1996, 2001), which provides case studies and documents to illustrate congressional and executive involvements. Devins's *Shaping Constitutional Values: Elected Government, the Supreme Court, and the Abortion Debate* (Johns Hopkins, 1996) is also devoted to three-branch interpretation. Many of his articles in law journals and appearances before congressional committees analyze the role that elected officials play in constitutional interpretation. In 1993, Devins edited *Elected Branch Influences in Constitutional Decisionmaking* (Law and Contemporary Problems). When the House Judiciary Committee held hearings in January 1998 on the role of Congress in constitutional interpretation, both he and Fisher were invited to testify.

In writing this book, we have benefited from the help of a number of people and institutions. Akhil Amar, Lee Epstein, Barry Friedman, Mark Graber, Abner Greene, Sandy Levinson, Chip Lupu, John McGinnis, Bob Nagel, David O'Brien, Suzanna Sherry, Bill Treanor, Mark Tushnet, and Keith Whittington helped to sharpen our ideas by commenting on draft chapters and, more generally, discussing aspects of the project with one or both of us. Through grants, sabbaticals, and the like, we have also benefited from the support of the Smith Richardson Foundation and the College of William and Mary. Felicia Burton and especially Della Harris not only provided word processing support but made the two of us feel that we were working in the same office, not hundreds of miles away from each other. Over the years, several William and Mary law students have provided research support to this and related projects. These students include Mary Sue Backus, Erin O'Callaghan, Keith Finch, Robert Juelke, Chris Shea, Jan Starkweather, Wendy Watson, and Jarrell Wright. Finally, special thanks are owed to our editor at Oxford, Dedi

Felman. Dedi's enthusiasm for the project greatly facilitated the completion of the manuscript. Also, along with Molly Barton, Dedi provided us with extremely valuable commentary on the manuscript. We appreciate very much the careful and thoughtful copyediting by Judith Hoover and the production work by Rebecca Johns-Danes.

Fisher dedicates the book to his sister, Margie, for a lifetime of support and encouragement. Devins dedicates the book to his parents, Matt and Dian Dollinger, for their love, generosity, and inspiration.

Some of the material in this book plays off other works of ours. In particular, portions of chapter 10 were first published in our jointly authored article "Judicial Exclusivity and Political Instability" (84 *Virginia Law Review* 85 (1998)).

September 12, 2003

Contents

THE DEMOCRATIC CONSTITUTION

Introduction

The origins of this book date back to 1987. At that time, the view that Supreme Court interpretations controlled the Constitution's application was not subject to serious challenge. For example, when reporting that six out of ten Americans thought the Supreme Court was the ultimate constitutional arbiter, newspapers simply noted that these six were "correct."[1] Likewise, journalists and academics alike expressed outrage when Attorney General Edwin Meese argued that Supreme Court decisions were not "binding on all persons and parts of government henceforth and forevermore."[2] Even more telling, the Senate Judiciary Committee was sufficiently alarmed by the Meese speech that Supreme Court nominees were asked to comment on it.

But 1987 also marked the end of an era. Social conservatives, who had long complained of judge-made rights, anticipated that Reagan-era judicial appointments would reshape the federal judiciary. Likewise, the left anticipated that Warren Court liberalism would soon fade from view. In short, notwithstanding the attacks on Attorney General Meese, the left could no longer look to the courts to advance their political agenda. With both sides having reason to jettison judicial supremacy, academics began turning their attention to elected government interpretations of the Constitution.

There is another reason that 1987 is important: That is the year we began talking about writing this book. Fisher had just published *Constitutional Dialogues*, a book arguing that constitutional principles emerge from a dialogue among all three branches of government as well as the states and the general public. Devins suggested in a review of this book that the best way to examine the impact and quality of nonjudicial interpretations of the Constitution was through a series of extended case studies.[3]

This book does precisely that. Through a series of case studies, we demonstrate that nearly all landmark Supreme Court decisions cannot be understood without first paying attention to the politics surrounding them. We offer several explanations as to why this is so.

First, Justices pay attention to public opinion when crafting their decisions, whether in desegregating public schools in the Southern states[4] or striking down President Harry Truman's wartime seizure of the steel mills.[5] Likewise, political judgments by Congress can increase the chances for judicial support, such as the decision by Congress to look to the Commerce Clause to require hotels and restaurants to serve minorities and nonminorities alike.[6] Politics is also helpful in assessing Supreme Court doctrine. Any analysis of the Court's decision to approve the internment of Japanese Americans should take into account that the internment was a subterfuge devised by the military and approved by the Justice Department.[7] Legislation enacted in response to the federalism case of *Garcia v. San Antonio Transit* (1985) spoke to whether states are adequately protected in the political process.[8]

Second, politics decides how well a court ruling is implemented. The institutional dynamics that made the legislative veto so popular before the Supreme Court invalidated it in *INS v. Chadha* (1983) explains why the device continues to be used—well over four hundred legislative vetoes have been adopted since that decision.[9] The difficulties in enforcing *Brown v. Board of Education* (where the Court delegated its remedial authority to Southern district court judges) led to mid-1960s elected branch reforms, producing more desegregation by statute than by judicial action.[10]

Populist resistance to Court decision making often prompts the Court to recalibrate its position, reflected in the Court's acceptance of Roosevelt's New Deal initiatives after the so-called switch in time.[11] Public outrage over the persecution of Jehovah's Witnesses pressured the Court to reverse its position on mandatory flag salutes.[12] On abortion and school busing, elected branch disapproval may well have contributed to the Rehnquist Court's moderation of some Burger Court decisions.[13]

Elected officials sometimes conclude that a judicial ruling is in error. Notwithstanding *McCulloch v. Maryland* (1819), President Andrew Jackson decided that Congress lacked authority to establish a national bank.[14] More recently, Court decisions on voting rights, religious liberty, freedom of the press, sovereign immunity, the fairness doctrine, the independent counsel, and homosexual sodomy have either been limited or neutered through state and federal legislation.[15]

Third, elected officials sometimes speak the first and last word on the Constitution's meaning. On impeachment, executive privilege, war powers, and many other issues, courts often steer clear of the issue by invoking one or another jurisdictional limitation.[16] When this happens, political actors control constitutional interpretation. Moreover, there is not one constitution but fifty-one. The fifty state constitutions allow the states to define constitutional law in ways that depart markedly from what the U.S. Supreme Court has said.[17] These multiple decision points give citizens—operating through their state legislatures, governors, and state courts—an opportunity to think independently and creatively about constitutional issues.

In calling attention to the profound role that nonjudicial actors play in shaping constitutional values, we do not argue that the Court plays but a minor role in these disputes. Quite the contrary. We agree that the Court often shapes elected government discourse and explain why the Court must play such a role. These volleys between elected officials, the public, and the Court both make the Constitution more relevant to our lives and improve the quality of constitutional decision making. With each branch checking the other and the people checking government, a dynamic process makes the Constitution more vibrant and stable. Our study, ultimately, is a call for courts, elected officials, and the public to be activist in shaping governmental policy. By arguing that courts can and should play a pivotal role in triggering both social movements and elected government action, we part company with other scholars who have challenged the Court's status as ultimate interpreter of the Constitution. Nevertheless, because newspapers and constitutional law texts typically treat Court interpretations of the Constitution as supreme, much of our study explains why Court decisions are anything but final.

The initial chapters of our book identify some central misconceptions about constitutional law today. It is false to believe that the constitutional values announced to the public by the Supreme Court are final. The famous case of *Marbury v. Madison* (1803) never made that claim, although recent decisions by the Court suggest otherwise. Justice Robert Jackson once said that decisions by the Court "are not final because we are infallible, but we are infallible only because we are final." That, too, is erroneous. The history of American law demonstrates conclusively that the Court is neither final nor infallible. It was not final in the nineteenth century with its slavery decision in the *Dred Scott* case nor when it upheld the "separate but equal" doctrine for race relations. Nor has it been final in the twentieth century on such issues as child labor, abortion, federalism, busing, church-state relations, the death penalty, the legislative veto, and other issues.

Another misconception is the belief that the Court has a special role in safeguarding individual and minority rights, and that such duties cannot be entrusted to the elected branches with their majoritarian base. History teaches a different lesson. From 1789 to the present, Congress and the President have had a better record than the courts in protecting individual and minority rights. For the Court's first century and a half, Justices were more inclined to protect the rights of corporations and government. The Warren Court, for two decades, offered a more progressive model; then, individuals and lobbying groups repeatedly went to the judiciary to vindicate their rights. However, the post-Warren years reveal a return to the customary pattern. Individuals and groups, disappointed with the results of litigation, or even in the expectation of litigation, routinely appeal to the elected branches to redress constitutional wrongs.

Chapters on domestic separation of powers, war powers, and federalism repeatedly show that nonjudicial actors have always dominated the courts in sorting out structural issues. For the most part, structural issues (especially crucial decisions of war) are left to the elected branches. When the Justices do intervene, their decisions are very much tied to signals sent the Court by both lawmakers and the public.

Several chapters focus on individual rights and liberties, explaining how the elected branches play a constructive role. Chapters on race and privacy, for example, show that *Brown v. Board of Education*, *Roe v. Wade*, and other landmark Supreme Court decisions are a point of departure, not an end point, in the nation's struggle over equal educational opportunity and abortion rights. Sometimes (with school desegregation being the most prominent example), the elected branches support Court decision making and, in so doing, encourage the Justices to provide additional constitutional safeguards. At other times, however, the Court yields to public criticism. Witness, for example, the Court's retreat on court-ordered busing and its backtracking on abortion in the face of elected government resistance.

Chapters on race, religion, and speech explain in concrete terms how Congress and the President have taken the initiative, often long before the courts, in protecting rights and liberties. In many cases, after the judiciary has defined rights and liberties in a restrictive manner, the elected branches have returned to the scene to give greater protection. Although this process is sometimes reversed, with elected officials seeking to limit Court decisions protective of individual rights, the prevailing pattern is one of elected branch dominion in the safeguarding of individual and minority rights.

Our book also calls attention to the significant role that interest groups and the general public play in lobbying elected officials. "Liberty," as Learned Hand put it, "lies in the hearts of men and women; when it dies there, no constitution, no law, no court can save it."[18] For this very reason, a potent force in driving three-branch interpretation—often in a constructive direction—are public attitudes and preferences.

Discussing constitutional law solely in terms of cases decided by the Supreme Court puts a burden on the judiciary that it cannot, and should not, carry. Constitutional rights are better protected by a political process that involves all three branches, the states, and the public. It is this process of give and take and mutual respect that allows all parts of government to expose weaknesses, hold excess in check, and gradually forge a consensus on constitutional values. An open process—with many entry points and opportunities for reconsideration, reinforced by a balance between democratic decisions and judicial checks—provides a lasting stability to the Constitution.

Judicial Supremacy as Orthodoxy

To the general public, even the educated public, constitutional law consists of various cases that wend their way to the U.S. Supreme Court, which periodically decides the meaning of the Constitution and communicates that fact to a waiting nation. Advocates of this model occasionally acknowledge that Congress, the President, and the states may participate in constitutional debate at earlier stages, but those activities are considered subordinate and given junior varsity status. According to this account, the authoritative and final voice, regardless of content and reasoning, belongs to the Court.

This picture of constitutional law is not a stereotype. Although several political scientists and legal academics have challenged this model,[1] judicial supremacy nonetheless remains the dominant model taught in undergraduate, graduate, and law schools. Because of this preoccupation with case law and the neglect of nonjudicial actors, Professor Michael Reisman of the Yale Law School has said that there is no "comprehensive course on constitutional law in any meaningful sense in American law schools."[2] But this belief in judicial supremacy is misplaced. The text of the Constitution, the intent of the framers, and the independent interpretations of the Constitution by both the Congress and the White House demonstrate the fallacy of the popular (and scholarly) belief in judicial supremacy. Although Court decisions figure prominently in the shaping of constitutional values, elected officials and the American people also play a defining role in forging new understandings of the Constitution—even if that means challenging unpopular Court decisions.

Roots of Judicial Hegemony

Justice Robert Jackson once said that decisions by the Supreme Court "are not final because we are infallible, but we are infallible only because we are final."[3] A cute turn of phrase, but even the most casual observer of American history knows that the Court has been neither final nor infallible. Justice Byron White was closer to the truth when he said, in 1970, that "this Court is not alone in being obliged to construe the Constitution in the course of its work; nor does it even approach having a monopoly on the wisdom and insight appropriate to the task."[4]

Part of the exaggerated notions of judicial power relies on a famous statement by Charles Evans Hughes: "We are under a Constitution but the Constitution is what the judges say it is."[5] It is generally thought that Hughes made this remark while Chief Justice; however, he said it while governor of New York. A more serious misconception is that Hughes never argued for judicial monopoly on constitutional, or even legal, matters. His speech responded to critics who opposed giving power to a commission to investigate abuses by railroads. He feared that without such powers in the hands of a commission, these divisive issues would flow into the courts and damage the judiciary as an institution. Judicial duties, he said, had to be carefully circumscribed. Any effort to transfer railroad issues to the judiciary "would swamp your courts with administrative burdens and expose them to the fire of public criticism . . . criticism from which they should be shielded and will be shielded if left with the jurisdictions which it was intended they should exercise."[6] Hughes is not calling the judiciary an 800-pound gorilla, capable of taking on all challengers. He advises his listeners to treat the courts as politically vulnerable. Judicial resources and goodwill must not be squandered in a vain show of overreaching.

Nevertheless, the school of judicial supremacy seems to be firmly established. For example, former federal judge Robert H. Bork wrote in 1990, "The Constitution is the trump card in American politics, and judges decide what the Constitution means. When the Supreme Court invokes the Constitution, whether legitimately or not, as to that issue the democratic process is at an end."[7] Indeed, the furor over Bork's nomination to the Supreme Court was largely rooted in a belief in judicial supremacy: that Bork's presence on the Court would play a transformative role in shaping the meaning of the U.S. Constitution. For Bork critic Ronald Dworkin, "The Supreme Court in the last analysis [has] the power to decide for the government as a whole what the Constitution means."[8]

Members of Congress, too, often refer to the Court as the supreme voice on constitutional matters. Although legislators necessarily consider constitutional values and issues throughout the year, sometimes they will carelessly suggest that a constitutional matter is for the courts, not for Congress. In 1997, Senator Arlen Specter called the Court "the ultimate arbiter of determining what the law will be. . . . We know since the [1803] decision of the Supreme Court of the United States in Marbury versus Madison, the Supreme Court of the United States has been the preeminent institution, because the Supreme Court of the United States has the last word."[9]

Such statements from legislators give inadequate credit to Congress, exaggerate the role of the judiciary, distort the holding in *Marbury*, and conflict with what we know about the development of constitutional law over the past two centuries. There are many examples to illustrate how Congress can challenge and reverse Court decisions on both statutory and constitutional questions. When lawmakers find it convenient to seek cover in a Court ruling, however, Congress's willingness to both interpret the Constitution and challenge the Court gives way to political expediency.[10]

Congress also encourages the belief in judicial supremacy when it deliberately ducks a constitutional question. For example, rather than decide for itself whether the measure is constitutional, it includes in the statute an expedited procedure to permit quick challenges in the courts. Congress resorted to that practice four times from 1985 to 1996, and on all four occasions the Court declared the legislation to be unconstitutional.[11] The not-so-hidden message in statutes that contain expedited procedures: We're not sure about the constitutionality of what we have done. But the statute is politically popular and we don't want to figure out whether we bungled it. But don't worry. The Court will set it right.

Presidents, too, encourage a belief in judicial supremacy. Like Congress, the White House sometimes finds it easier to hide behind a Court decision than to take the heat for independently interpreting the Constitution. Witness, for example, President James Buchanan's depiction of slavery as "a judicial question, which legitimately belongs to the Supreme Court of the United States."[12] One hundred years later, President Dwight Eisenhower sounded a similar message in a very different setting. In sending federal troops into Little Rock to enforce *Brown v. Board of Education*, Eisenhower expressed no opinion on whether *Brown* was correctly decided. Rather, he spoke of "the responsibility and authority of the Supreme Court to interpret the Constitution."[13] This practice of depicting Supreme Court rulings as definitive continues.[14]

Journalists and reporters do much to promote judicial supremacy. When the Supreme Court issues a significant decision, newspapers typically treat that ruling as final and definitive. Writing for the *Washington Post* in 1996, Joan Biskupic said that the importance of the Supreme Court is not in the number of its cases: "It is in the court having the last word. The justices are the final arbiter of what is in the Constitution."[15] Curiously, the cases she offers to prove her point hardly support the last-word doctrine: *Dred Scott* (overridden by constitutional amendment), the striking down of New Deal laws (followed by judicial reversal), the desegregation case of 1954 (of limited impact), and *Roe v. Wade* (from which the Court conducted a partial retreat in 1992). In 1998, in describing the struggles of Justices in searching for a resolution, Biskupic concluded that "whatever a majority decides does indeed become *the* answer."[16] *Roe v. Wade* was the answer? *Dred Scott?* The decisions on child labor? At best, the Court provides *an* answer, which becomes one part of the mix of forces that shape the meaning of the Constitution.

Only in recent decades has the Supreme Court laid claim to delivering the final word. The supremacy premise began modestly with *Marbury v. Madison* (1803), when Chief Justice John Marshall declared that it is "emphatically the province and duty of the judicial department to say what the law is."[17] As explained later in this chapter, Marshall was in no position—politically—to dictate to the other branches. By 1857, the Court was sufficiently confident in its authority that Associate Justice John Catron informed President-elect Buchanan that, in the matter of *Dred Scott*, the Court would "decide and settle a controversy which has so long and seriously agitated the country."[18] This assertion of judicial finality will be remembered as a costly self-inflicted injury that still haunts the Court.

Judicial supremacy did not rear its head again until 1958, when the Court, in *Cooper v. Aaron*, repudiated Arkansas Governor Orval Faubus's efforts to stop court-ordered desegregation. By refusing to let black students enter Little Rock's Central High School, Faubus ignored a lower court order. In response, the Supreme Court proclaimed that *Marbury* "declared the basic principle that the federal judiciary is supreme in the exposition of the law of the Constitution."[19] In 1962 and 1969, the Court declared itself the "ultimate interpreter of the Constitution" in controversial decisions concerning reapportionment and the House of Representative's refusal to seat Adam Clayton Powell.[20] The Court's vision of itself "as ultimate interpreter of the Constitution" persists today. In its 1992 decision on abortion rights, the Court argued that when it interprets the Constitution, it "calls the contending sides of a national controversy to end their national division by accepting a common mandate rooted in the Constitution."[21] Similarly, in a 1997 decision on religious liberty, the Court insisted that Congress must accept constitutional rulings by the Court as authoritative and final.[22]

The Court's habit of declaring itself the ultimate interpreter of the Constitution must be read with caution. First, who does the Court say is the final word? Itself. Without being overly skeptical, isn't there a bit of self-interest here, a claim that is patently self-serving? How would we respond if the President said that of all the people in the country it was his considered judgment that he is the most intelligent? Jay Leno and other late-night comics would have a field day.

Second, the Court invariably calls itself the ultimate interpreter when it fears that the political order will ignore its command. That pattern is obvious in the disputes over Little Rock, reapportionment, Adam Clayton Powell, abortion, and the decision in 1997 on religious liberty. In all these cases, the threat of elected official resistance to its orders cast a shadow on the Court's decision making. In the abortion case, for example, the Court spoke ominously of the "profound and unnecessary damage" it would suffer if it "surrender[ed] to political pressure."[23] In other words, the Justices' sweeping declarations of judicial power cloak institutional self-doubt, much as a gorilla pounds his chest and makes threatening noises to avoid a fight.

The Scope of Judicial Review

Judicial supremacy has no basis in the Constitution. The text does not confer upon the Supreme Court the power to declare unconstitutional an act of Congress, the President, or state government. Judicial review is implied in certain language in the Constitution and comments by the framers, but it is largely judicial review against the states, not against Congress and the President. Under Article III, Section 2, judicial power extends to all cases "arising under this Constitution, the Laws of the United States, and Treaties made." In most of the early drafts at the Constitutional Convention, the language "arising under" applied only to laws passed by Congress.[24] On August 27, 1787, William Samuel Johnson moved to insert the words "this Constitution and the" before the word "Laws." James Madison objected, stating that he "doubted whether it was not going too far to extend the jurisdiction of the Court generally to cases arising Under the Constitution, & whether it ought not to be limited to cases of a Judiciary Nature. The right of expounding the Constitution in cases of this nature ought not to be given to that Department."[25] Johnson's motion was agreed to without further discussion, "it being generally supposed that the jurisdiction given was constructively limited to cases of a Judiciary nature."[26]

What do we make of this legislative history? Evidently, the effort to limit the Court's power to cases of a "judiciary nature" implied that the Court had less than a full-scale power of judicial review. At the Virginia ratifying convention and in Alexander Hamilton's *Federalist* No. 80, the intent of the "arising under" language is clarified: It meant judicial review only against the states.[27] Judicial control over Congress and the President was not implied.

Whenever the framers discussed judicial review, they generally referred to it as a means of controlling the states. Madison, concerned about state encroachment, wanted Congress to exercise a veto power over state actions that violated the U.S. Constitution. Roger Sherman thought this congressional power was unnecessary because the state courts would have the power to strike down invalid state laws.[28] Other delegates favored judicial review over state laws. State actions inconsistent with the Constitution "would clearly not be valid," said Gouverneur Morris, and judges "would consider them as null & void."[29]

In October 1788, while commenting on a draft constitution for Virginia, Madison expressed strong opposition to judicial supremacy. He analyzed proposed language for a "Council of Revision," which would have allowed judges and the executive to review bills passed by the Virginia legislature. Either the judges or the executive could object to bills they considered hasty, unjust, or unconstitutional. However, two-thirds or three-fourths of each house could then override the objection. In cases where a bill had a constitutional dimension and the legislature voted to override the council, Madison preferred that the bill be suspended until the next election and require repassage by a two-thirds or three-fourths vote. He did not want the final word left to judges: "In the State Constitutions & indeed in the Fedl one also, no provision is made for the case of a disagreement in expounding them; and as the Courts are generally the last in making [the] decision, it results to them by refusing or not refusing to execute a law, to stamp it with its final character. This makes the Judiciary Dept paramount in fact to the Legislature, which was never intended and can never be proper."[30]

From 1789 to 1803, some precedents set the stage for the Court's declaration in *Marbury* that it could declare acts of Congress unconstitutional. In 1792, federal judges objected to a congressional statute that required them to serve as commissioners on claims settlement. Because their decisions could be set aside by the secretary of war, the courts were essentially issuing "advisory opinions" and serving as subordinates to executive officials. Before the Supreme Court could rule on the constitutionality of the statute, Congress repealed the offending sections and removed the secretary's authority to veto decisions rendered by federal judges.[31]

In 1796, the Court upheld the constitutionality of a carriage tax passed by Congress.[32] If the Court had the power to uphold a congressional statute, presumably it had the power to strike one down. However, Justice Samuel Chase said it was unnecessary "*at this time*, for me to determine, whether this court, *constitutionally* possesses the power to declare an act of Congress *void* . . . but if the court have such power, I am free to declare, that I will never exercise it, *but in a very clear case.*"[33] Thus, almost a decade after the Constitutional Convention, the Justices of the Supreme Court were still uncertain whether they possessed judicial review over Congress. At most, the power appeared to be quite limited and certainly not the freewheeling judicial review of subsequent years.

In 1798, the Court upheld another congressional statute, this time involving the procedure for amending the Constitution.[34] In that same year, several Supreme Court Justices offered a range of opinions on the existence and scope of judicial review. Justice Iredell cautioned that the Court should never invoke judicial review against Congress except in a "clear and urgent case." He particularly objected to striking down laws on such vague grounds as "the principles of natural justice," which were regulated "by no fixed standard" and invited too much judicial lawmaking.[35] As late as 1800, the Court was still unsure about invalidating an act of Congress. Justice Chase said that even if it were agreed that a statute contrary to the Constitution would be void, "it still remains a question, where the power resides to declare it void?" The general opinion, he said, was that the Court could declare an act of Congress unconstitutional, "but there is no adjudication of the Supreme Court itself upon the point."[36] Soon there would be.

The Misunderstood *Marbury* Precedent

Marbury v. Madison, in which the Court declared a portion of the Judiciary Act of 1789 to be unconstitutional, is generally treated as an authoritative basis for judicial supremacy. In fact, it stands for a much more modest proposition. Chief Justice Marshall stated that it is "emphatically the province and duty of the judicial department to say what the law is."[37] So it is, but the authority to say what the law is does not make the Court supreme, other than in that particular case. It also is the province and duty of Congress, in concert with the President, to say what the law is. The Court merely states what the law is on the day the decision comes down. If Congress and the President disagree with that interpretation, the law may change after that.

Did Chief Justice Marshall believe that the Court was so superior to the other branches that it could dictate to them? Obviously not. The Court was in no position in 1803, politically, to issue orders to Congress and the President. The Jeffersonians had captured control of Congress and the presidency in the election of 1800. The Federalist Party remained in control of the judiciary, but that position was tenuous. Marshall knew that he could not strong-arm the other branches.

Federalist appointee William Marbury, nominated by President John Adams and confirmed by the Senate to be a justice of the peace in the District of Columbia, had never received his commission. He wanted the Court, under a provision in the Judiciary Act of 1789, to order President Jefferson or Secretary of State Madison to deliver the commission. Suppose that Marshall decided that the provision was constitutional and he possessed statutory authority to issue a mandamus. Did he think that his order would be obeyed? No. Everyone, including Marshall, knew what would have happened. As Chief Justice Warren Burger has noted, "The Court could stand hard blows, but not ridicule, and the ale house would rock with hilarious laughter" had Marshall issued a mandamus ignored by the Jefferson administration.[38] Marshall avoided this humiliation by holding that the statutory provision was unconstitutional.

The Court's precarious position was underscored by the impeachment proceedings initiated by Jeffersonians. *Marbury* was decided on February 24, 1803. The House impeached John Pickering, a district judge, on March 2, 1803 and the Senate convicted him on March 12, 1804. As soon as the House completed impeachment proceedings against Pickering it turned its guns on Justice Samuel Chase. If that move succeeded, Marshall could have been the next target.

In this perilous atmosphere, Marshall wrote to Chase on January 23, 1805, suggesting that if members of Congress objected to judicial decisions it was not necessary to impeach judges. Instead, Congress could simply review and reverse objectionable decisions through the regular legislative process. Marshall's letter to Chase is somewhat ambiguous. He could have been referring to reversals of statutory, not constitutional, interpretations, but given the temper of the times the latter seems more likely. Here is Marshall's language to Chase: "I think the modern doctrine of impeachment should yield to an appellate jurisdiction in the legislature. A reversal of those legal opinions deemed unsound by the legislature would certainly better comport with the mildness of our character than [would] a removal of the Judge who has rendered them unknowing of his fault."[39]

This is not the language of an arrogant, chest-thumping Supreme Court. It has a nervous tiptoe quality, anxious to survive from day to day in a political climate that was hostile to judicial power. To speak of judicial supremacy in such times is untenable. As political scientist Walter Murphy has written, "For his part, Marshall in *Marbury* never claimed a judicial monopoly on constitutional interpretation, nor did he allege judicial supremacy, only authority to interpret the Constitution in cases before the Court."[40]

The Role of Elected Branches

In the early decades, when there were few decisions by the Supreme Court to light the way, Congress and the President necessarily tackled, on their own, a number of complex constitutional issues. Without guidance from the Court, Congress deliberated for years on such issues as judicial review, the Bank of the United States, congressional investigative power, slavery, internal improvements, federalism, the war-making power, treaties and foreign relations, interstate commerce, and the President's removal power.[41] It was in the elected branches, "not in the courts, that the original understanding of the Constitution was forged."[42] Legislative and executive debate was informed, intense, and diligent. It had to be, given the paucity of direction at that time from the Supreme Court and the lower courts.

Certainly, judicial supremacy would have been alien to the members of the First Congress. During the debate in 1789 on the President's removal power, James Madison saw no reason to defer to the judiciary on the constitutionality of what Congress was about to do. While acknowledging that "the exposition of the laws and Constitution devolves upon the Judiciary," he begged to know on what ground "any one department draws from the Constitution greater powers than another, in marking out the limits of the powers of the several departments?"[43]

Early presidents also believed that each branch of government should act as an independent interpreter of the Constitution. George Washington's first veto was on constitutional grounds. Thomas Jefferson, viewing the Alien and Sedition Acts (which criminalized speech critical of the government) as patently unconstitutional, used his pardon power to discharge "every person under punishment or prosecution under the sedition law."[44] Andrew Jackson announced his own theory of coordinate construction in an 1832 message vetoing legislation to recharter the Bank of the United States. The fact that a unanimous Supreme Court had approved the Bank's constitutionality in *McCulloch v. Maryland* left him unfazed. "The opinion of the judges," proclaimed Jackson, "has no more authority over Congress than the opinion of the Congress has over the judges, and on that point the President is independent of both." Each public official, he said, takes an oath to support the Constitution and "swears that he will support it as he understands it, and not as it is understood by others."[45]

Throughout this period, the Court played a supportive role to constitutional judgments by the elected branches, using the power of judicial review not to invalidate their efforts but to affirm them. Over Justice John Marshall's long career on the Court, which stretched from 1801 to 1835, only in the single case of *Marbury* did he declare a statutory provision unconstitutional. On all other occasions he upheld the statutes passed by Congress and signed into law by the President, sustaining their interpretations of the Commerce Clause and other provisions.

The legislative and executive branches first determine, through independent deliberations and joint efforts, the constitutionality of a measure. They, not the courts, are responsible for first testing the edges of constitutionality and making the hard choices of public policy. Only after that complex and demanding task do the courts, on occasion, exercise the power of judicial review. Judges generally accept and endorse the outcomes of this political process. For the most part, then, courts play a coordinate, not a superior, role.

During the court-packing battle of 1937, proponents of judicial supremacy argued that the courts were guardians of individual and minority rights. The Senate Judiciary Committee, vigorously rejecting the court-packing plan, indulged in hyperbole by stating, "Minority political groups, no less than religious and racial groups, have never failed, when forced to appeal to the Supreme Court of the United States, to find in its opinions the reassurance and protection of their constitutional rights."[46] That same year, however, Henry W. Edgerton (later appointed a federal judge) found a wholly different pattern. After reading Supreme Court opinions from 1789 up to the 1930s and examining them for the proposition that the Court generally protects individual and minority rights, he concluded that they "give small support to the theory that Congress had attacked, and judicial supremacy defended, 'the citizen's liberty.'" He generally found that the Court protected the government rather than the citizen. *Marbury*, in fact, was such a case. William Marbury appealed to the Supreme Court to gain his commission, but the Court, with elaborate reasoning, denied relief.

Edgerton also analyzed *Dred Scott*, where, for only the second time in its history (*Marbury* being the first), the Court declared an act of Congress unconstitutional. Through the voice of its Chief Justice, Roger B. Taney, the Court prohibited Congress from preventing the spread of slavery into the Western Territories because the right to own a slave is "distinctly and expressly affirmed in the Constitution."[47] "Cured by the result of the Civil War,"[48] *Dred Scott* is a fine example of how individual rights, unprotected by the courts, are vindicated by Congress and the President.

Abraham Lincoln refused to accept Court decisions as the last word on the larger questions of public policy. Such issues were to be reserved to the elected branches.[49] His inaugural address in 1861 proclaimed that if government policy on "vital questions affecting the whole people is to be irrevocably fixed" by the Supreme Court, "the people will have ceased to be their own rulers, having to that extent practically resigned their

Government into the hands of that eminent tribunal."[50] Lincoln's Attorney General Edward Bates did not regard himself bound by the *Dred Scott* decision. He released a long opinion holding that neither color nor race could deny American blacks the right of citizenship.[51] For its part, Congress passed legislation in 1862 to prohibit slavery in the territories.[52]

Gatekeeping by the Court

Who participates in litigation depends on judicial doctrines that limit the type of case that may be adjudicated. These principles operate as hurdles, or thresholds, for plaintiffs. Yet they do more than that. They shield judges from cases that might threaten their independence and institutional effectiveness. They ration scarce judicial resources and enable judges to postpone or avoid decisions on politically sensitive issues. As a consequence, legal and constitutional issues are pushed to elected officials and the general public.

The Constitution, by specifying that the "judicial power" extends only to "cases" or "controversies," guards against abstract judicial declarations of policy. The question of distinguishing a concrete dispute from a hypothetical issue remains. To this end, the Court insists that litigants have a personal stake in the controversy (standing) and that their claims be presented in an adversary context (adverseness). Beyond those threshold requirements, the Court recognizes that the Constitution commits some matters to other branches for resolution. Some legal disputes present a nonjusticiable "political question" that is unsuited for the judiciary because of an "unusual need for unquestioning adherence to a political decision already made," "the potentiality of embarrassment from multifarious pronouncements," and the impossibility of judicial resolution "without expressing lack of the respect due coordinate branches."[53]

Political question and justiciability barriers have been used to foreclose judicial resolution of several significant constitutional disputes. Challenges to the constitutionality of the Vietnam War, U.S. recognition of the Vatican as a separate state, the manner in which the Senate conducts impeachment trials, and President Reagan's sending military advisors to El Salvador were all dismissed on political question grounds. Judges, especially Supreme Court Justices, are adept at manipulating threshold requirements. When unprepared to resolve a dispute, these barriers are a principal "avenue of escape." Yet, when the Court decides to settle a dispute, these requirements "will not stand in [the] way."[54] For Alexander Bickel, arguing that "no good society can be unprincipled; and no viable society can be principle-ridden,"[55] the strategic use of threshold requirements is a necessary device for an unelected judiciary to avoid debilitating conflicts and thereby protect its institutional capital. For Gerald Gunther, however, avoiding adjudication through unprincipled reasoning both damages legitimate areas of principle and invites "free-wheeling interventionism."[56]

Noncompliance

In theory, judicial opinions are binding on the public and the other branches of government. In practice, judicial opinions are implemented with varying degrees of fidelity by local and federal officials. Is noncompliance contemptuous of the judicial process? Not necessarily; it depends on the ruling. If the Court misjudges its power and inflates its institutional position, it cannot expect acquiescence from the public and other branches of government. Unintentional violations of court orders may also occur, but they can be relieved by adequate education and clear judicial rulings. In between these two positions are various shades of avoidance and evasion.

Justice Oliver Wendell Holmes understood that law is what society will sustain: "The first requirement of a sound body of law is, that it should correspond with the actual feelings and demands of the community, whether right or wrong."[57] Thomas Corcoran, who clerked for Holmes, recalls that the Justice warned the Court to avoid decisions that require great social changes unless citizens are ready and willing to comply. He said there was "no use talking about a law that will not be willingly obeyed by at least 90 percent of the population."[58]

Noncompliance may result from deliberate evasion, as in the South's "massive resistance" to the desegregation cases. But some of the delay here was attributed to the Court's decision to announce a strong position in *Brown I* and a weaker one in *Brown II*, the implementing ruling a year later. Several phrases in the latter decision—including "practical flexibility," "as soon as practicable," "a prompt and reasonable start," and "all deliberate speed"—gave a green light to obstruction and procrastination.[59]

In 1983, the Supreme Court held that the "legislative veto," used by Congress for fifty years to control executive actions, was unconstitutional.[60] Over the next two decades, however, Congress passed more than four hundred new legislative vetoes, all signed into law by Presidents Reagan, Bush I, Clinton, and Bush II. Although the Court delivered an important case on separation of powers, there has been a wide gap between judicial doctrine and political practice.

Noncompliance sometimes results from poor communication of judicial opinions. Scholars have found that most people do not understand interpretations (often erroneous) provided by the media and local officials.[61] Mistakes and misconceptions by reporters are likely, given the technical nature of many decisions and the deadlines and space limitations imposed by newspapers, magazines, and broadcast services. The risk of public misperceptions is especially great in the final week of the Supreme Court's term, when a large number of important cases are released. Making matters worse, even seasoned reporters often find it difficult to understand what the Court really means.[62] Justices sometimes stray from the case's central issue and add extraneous matter in the form of obiter dicta. Also, concurrences sometimes read like a dissent and cut new ground.[63] As Justice Ruth Bader Ginsburg has noted, "Murky decision-reporting may accurately capture a murky decision."[64] Whatever the explanation, the public cannot accept or approve rulings that are reported inaccurately.

Compliance with Court rulings is also hampered by the sheer force of inertia. Court decisions must pass through the perceptual screens of citizens who believe that current practices can persist with only slight modifications. Four decades after *Engel v. Vitale* (1962), which struck down state-sponsored prayers in public schools, school authorities continue to set aside time during the day for students to say prayers. Local officials may prefer to reinterpret judicial decisions on church-state separation to minimize the level of conflict and dissension within their communities.

Finally, judges in the lower courts have substantial latitude in applying Supreme Court doctrines. After the Supreme Court handed down its desegregation decision in 1954, lower court judges followed different paths in implementing the ruling. Some were faithful; others were defiant or evasive. Many federal judges were torn between the edict of the high court and the sentiments and customs of their local communities. It has been said that the Constitution is what the Supreme Court says it is, but Supreme Court decisions often mean what district courts say they mean.[65]

Justice Thurgood Marshall, after dissenting in a case that reversed the Second Circuit, later met with the judges from that circuit and urged them to read the Court's decision narrowly.[66] In 1985, Justice Brennan said that the Court's rulings on *Miranda*-type cases "have led nearly every lower court to reject its simplistic reasoning."[67] He pointed out that the Court's reasoning "is sufficiently obscured and qualified as to leave state and federal courts with continued authority to combat obvious flouting by the authorities of the privilege against self-incrimination. I am confident that lower courts will exercise this authority responsibly, as they have for the most part prior to this Court's intervention."[68]

Court-Curbing Techniques

Justice Stone once chided his brethren, "The only check upon our own exercise of power is our own sense of self-restraint."[69] That is an important check, but it is by no means the only one. Judges act in an environment that constantly tests the reasonableness and acceptability of their rulings. Courts issue the "last word" only for an instant, for after the release of an opinion the process of interaction begins: with Congress, the President, executive agencies, states, professional associations, and the public at large.

Court-curbing periods often emerge when the judiciary acts by nullifying statutes, particularly those passed by Congress. But the judiciary can also create enemies by *upholding* legislation, such as the broad nationalist rulings issued by Chief Justice John Marshall. To restrain the courts, members of Congress introduce a variety of legislative bills and constitutional amendments. Hearings are held to explore ways to curb the judiciary. State legislatures prepare petitions of protest; state judges pass resolutions of "concern," if not condemnation. To reduce the tension, the federal judiciary may decide to conduct a partial and possibly graceful retreat.

Judicial-congressional confrontations were especially sharp between 1858 and 1869 (reflecting the *Dred Scott* case and congressional efforts to protect Reconstruction legislation), 1935 and 1937 (reacting to the Court's nullification of New Deal legislation), and 1955 and 1959 (triggered by decisions involving desegregation, congressional investigations, and national security).[70] A new round of court-curbing efforts began in the late 1970s to challenge judicial rulings on school prayer, school busing, and abortion, and after 1995, when the Republican-controlled Congress considered measures to limit judicial activism.

The judiciary is most likely to be out of step with Congress or the President during periods of electoral and partisan realignment, when the country is undergoing sharp shifts in political directions while the courts retain the membership and orientation of an age gone by.[71] During earlier periods, attacks on the judiciary generally came from liberal groups: Jeffersonians, Jacksonians, Radical Republicans, LaFollette Republicans, and New Deal Democrats. However, conservatives dominated the 1955–1959 confrontation and have inspired most of the court-curbing efforts since then.

Court curbing is part and parcel of the constitutional design. Writing in the *Federalist Papers*, Alexander Hamilton reminded those who feared a too powerful Supreme Court that the judiciary "may truly be said to have neither FORCE nor WILL, but merely judgment; and must ultimately depend upon the aid of [elected officials]."[72] Implicit in this statement is the belief that the Supreme Court's "legitimacy—indeed, the Constitution's—must ultimately spring from public acceptance, even approval."[73]

When the public cannot accept or approve court rulings, it is hardly surprising that the Court's handiwork will be called into question or, worse yet, ignored. Beyond noncompliance, the Constitution empowers elected officials, among other things, to amend the Constitution, strip the courts of jurisdiction, and alter the number of Justices who sit on the Supreme Court. Congress, of course, may also enact legislation to cast doubt on the efficacy of Supreme Court constitutional interpretations.

Constitutional Amendments

Whenever two-thirds of both houses of Congress deem it necessary, they may propose amendments to the Constitution. Ratification requires three-fourths of the states to accept. Alternatively, two-thirds of the states may call a convention for constitutional amendment, but thus far all successful amendments have been initiated by Congress. The process of amending the Constitution is extraordinarily difficult and time-consuming. On only four occasions has Congress successfully used constitutional amendments to reverse Supreme Court decisions.

Constitutional amendments—the Thirteenth, Fourteenth, and Fifteenth—were used to nullify *Dred Scott*. Senator Charles Sumner argued that the issue of slavery could not be decided merely by reading the Constitution or what the courts had said about it: "Let the people change, and the Constitution will change also; for the Constitution is but the shadow, while the people are the substance."[74] The courts, he said, "will not perform the duty of the hour" to abolish slavery, and had in fact interpreted the Constitution to favor it.[75]

On three other occasions, constitutional amendments were used to overturn the Court.[76] Other amendments, driven by seemingly irresistible political forces, have fallen by the wayside. A successful amendment process requires an extraordinary combination of social, economic, and political forces. If any one of those factors is absent, an amendment may fail. For example, Congress made a concerted effort in 1964 to amend the Constitution to overturn the Supreme Court's decisions in the reapportionment and school prayer cases. Because of delays by House committees and filibusters on the Senate side, those efforts proved fruitless.

Even when Congress reacts against a court decision by clearing an amendment for ratification by the states, the hurdles are immense. After several Supreme Court decisions approving state authority to limit economic opportunities for women, Congress approved the Equal Rights

Amendment (ERA) in 1973 and sent it to the state legislatures for ratification. Prohibiting the denial or abridgement of "equality of rights under the law . . . on account of sex," the amendment was overwhelmingly approved by both the House and the Senate. But ERA supporters were slow in organizing state coalitions and, ultimately, failed to win over three-fourths of the states. In particular, with the National Organization of Women (ERA's principal sponsor) supporting both the amendment and abortion rights, a counteroffensive was launched by "conservative activists [who] saw abortion and the ERA as two prongs of the '[women's] libbers' general strategy for undermining traditional values."[77] Fourteen Southern and Mormon states (along with Illinois) embraced traditionalist arguments and refused to ratify the amendment. In 1982, the ERA expired.

Statutory Reversals

Part of the constitutional dialogue among the three branches involves "statutory reversals," actions by Congress and the President to nullify a decision by the Supreme Court. In addition to its role in interpreting the Constitution, the courts must frequently interpret statutes passed by legislatures. Statutory and constitutional questions can merge. Suppose that Court decisions uphold the constitutionality of government conduct that limit individual rights. Congress may intervene to provide more protection. For example, when the Court ruled that the police may search newspaper offices without first obtaining a subpoena or that the Air Force can forbid an Orthodox Jew from wearing a yarmulke, Congress enacted legislation to supplant judicial policy.[78] Even when legislative reversals involve purely statutory interpretations by the Court, these questions often embody fundamental issues of constitutional magnitude, such as race and gender discrimination. A dominant business of the Court is statutory construction, and through this function it interacts with other branches of government in a process that constantly refines the meaning of the Constitution. By deciding cases on statutory rather than constitutional grounds, the Court invites the other branches to participate and thereby lessens the risk of destructive confrontations.

Members of Congress have little doubt about their authority to overturn statutory interpretations by the Court. Senator Alexander Wiley told a witness in 1946:

> What is being worked out here today is part of the mechanics of our constitutional system of checks and balances. . . . I need hardly point out to my colleagues that the founding fathers contemplated three

strong and independent branches of government—legislative, judicial and executive—each of which was, insofar as possible, to tend to its own knitting. That means that the legislative branch, which is Congress, should do the legislating. When this delicate system of checks and balances is thrown out of balance, as I believe it is [by the decision here,] the very foundation of our Republic is endangered . . . and Congress must reverse the Court.[79]

Congress has resorted to statutory reversals with greater frequency in recent years. A single statute, the Civil Rights Act of 1991, overturned or modified nine Supreme Court decisions. By increasing its staff, Congress can monitor judicial rulings more closely. Interest groups are now better organized to follow court decisions and bring them to the attention of Congress. Finally, the judicial appointments by Republican Presidents Reagan and Bush I from 1981 to 1993 gave the courts a conservative cast, putting pressure on the more liberal Congress at that time to respond with statutory reversals.[80]

Court Packing

Congress has altered the number of Justices on the Supreme Court throughout its history. Congress authorized six Justices in 1789, lowered that to five in the ill-fated Judiciary Act of 1801, returned to six a year later, and increased the number in subsequent years to keep pace with the creation of new circuits. Since 1869 the number of Justices has remained fixed at nine. In none of these instances is the alteration of court size linked so blatantly to changing judicial policy as in FDR's court-packing plan in 1937.

In response to a series of Supreme Court rulings invalidating both his New Deal reforms and his initiatives to gain control of the administrative state, Franklin D. Roosevelt struck back. Following his landslide reelection victory in 1936, he launched a counterattack, proposing that for every Justice over seventy years of age, he be authorized to appoint an additional Justice until the Court's size grew from nine to fifteen. The Senate Judiciary Committee savaged the proposal, "declar[ing] that we would rather have an independent Court, a fearless Court . . . than a Court that, out of fear or sense of obligation to the appointing power, or factional passion, approves any measure we enact."[81] Congress's harsh words for the FDR plan, however, did not encourage continued Court resistance to New Deal initiatives. Shortly after the defeat of the court-packing plan, the Court announced several decisions supportive of New Deal programs.

The failure of the court-packing plan did not end elected branch reprisals against the Court. Dissatisfaction with the Warren and Burger Courts produced a spate of legislative proposals to strip the federal courts of jurisdiction in a number of controversial areas. Those proposals were rooted in Article III of the Constitution, which recognizes Congress's powers to "order and establish" lower federal courts and to make "exceptions" and "regulations" to the Supreme Court's appellate jurisdiction. From 1953 to 1968, more than sixty bills were introduced in Congress to limit the jurisdiction of the federal courts over school desegregation, national security, criminal confessions, and a variety of other subjects.

Typical of these efforts was a bill introduced by Senator William Jenner to withhold the Supreme Court's appellate jurisdiction on such matters as the First Amendment rights of communists.[82] Attorney General William Rogers found the bill a dangerous threat to judicial autonomy. To Rogers, the "natural consequences of such an enactment is that the courts would operate under the constant apprehension that if they rendered unpopular decisions, jurisdiction would be further curtailed."[83] The Jenner proposal and others of this era were eventually defeated, but not without substantial debate as to the scope and meaning of the Article III exceptions clause.

In the late 1970s, a second wave of court-stripping proposals attacked the Burger Court for its decisions on abortion rights and school busing. As described by Harvard's Abram Chayes, federal courts, rather than resolving private disputes between private individuals, are now "asked to deal with grievances over the administration of some public or quasi-public program and to vindicate the public policies embodied in the governing statutes or constitutional provisions. As a result, courts are inevitably cast in an affirmative, political—activist, if you must—role, a role that contrasts with the passive umpireship we are taught to respect."[84]

The Meese Firestorm

During his 1984 confirmation hearing to become attorney general, Edwin Meese characterized these proposals as both "unwise" and constitutionally "impermissible" and claimed that "if confirmed . . . I would recommend a veto" of such legislation.[85] It is revealing that an administration so critical of the Supreme Court would reject the efforts of their conservative bedfellows to exercise democratic control of a judiciary "run amok." Apparently, the Reagan administration thought it at least imprudent (and quite possibly wrong) to attack the integrity of the judicial branch in this manner.

Meese protected the judiciary here, but a 1986 speech at Tulane Law School featured a fundamental challenge to Supreme Court decision making. Meese cited Abraham Lincoln, Supreme Court Justice Felix Frankfurter, and constitutional historian Charles Warren in explaining why the Constitution is distinct from and superior to "what the Supreme Court says about the Constitution."[86] Constitutional interpretation, he said, "is not the business of the Court only, but also properly the business of all branches of government." Each of the three coordinate branches "has a duty to interpret the Constitution in the performance of its official functions."[87]

Meese was careful to say that Court decisions do have a binding quality on the parties in a case and "also the executive branch for whatever enforcement is necessary."[88] Even with this qualification, Meese found himself denounced by journalists, law professors, and interest groups. Eugene Thomas, the president of the American Bar Association, suggested that the adoption of Meese's theory would "shake the foundations of our system."[89] The American Civil Liberties Union denounced Meese for inviting "lawlessness."[90] Laurence Tribe of Harvard Law School said that the Meese position "represents a grave threat to the rule of law because it proposes a regime in which every lawmaker and every government agency becomes a law unto itself, and the civilizing hand of a uniform interpretation of the Constitution crumbles."[91]

What inspired these attacks? Did these critics believe in judicial supremacy to the extent that they would oppose Jefferson's repudiation of court-approved sedition laws and Lincoln's attacks on *Dred Scott*? Hardly. What made the Meese speech seemingly blasphemous was his political position: opposition to Court rulings on abortion, affirmative action, and school prayer. In an editorial titled "Why Give That Speech?" the *Washington Post* made clear that, although Meese's central claim about the propriety of elected branch constitutional interpretation was "self-evident," his remarks were "very troublesome" because of the "subtle, unspoken" message.[92]

The Meese flap spilled over into 1986 and 1987 Supreme Court confirmation hearings. In 1986, Senator Arlen Specter asked Chief Justice – designate William Rehnquist whether the Supreme Court "is the final arbiter, the final decision-maker of what the Constitution means." Rehnquist thought the question deserved a one-word answer: "Unquestionably."[93] Stated Rehnquist, "We rightfully think of our courts as the final voice in the interpretation of our Constitution, and therefore tend to think of constitutional law in terms of cases decided by the courts."[94] One year later, Supreme Court nominee Anthony Kennedy offered a more nuanced response to Specter's question. Noting, "I can think of instances, or I can accept the proposition that a chief executive or a Congress might not accept as doctrine the law of the Supreme Court," Kennedy hypothesized the Supreme Court's overruling its decision according constitutional protection to newspapers and asked Specter rhetorically, "Could you, as a legislator, say I think that decision is constitutionally wrong and I want to have legislation to change it? I think you could, and I think you should."[95]

By 1993, the last-word frenzy had abated. No one raised an eyebrow when Justice Ruth Bader Ginsburg wrote that "judges play an interdependent part in our democracy. They do not alone shape legal doctrine, but . . . participate in a dialogue with other organs of government, and with the people as well."[96] The Senate Judiciary Committee complimented her call for interactive constitutional decision making.[97]

Conclusions

Judicial supremacy finds no support in our legal development. The Court recognizes time and again that constitutional values are hammered out as part of a broader dialogue. Certainly, the Court plays a critical part in this dialogue. But the Court does not stand alone, dictating its views of constitutional truth to an obedient public. Congress and the White House, too, speak of their authority to independently interpret the Constitution. Nor can judicial supremacy be defended by turning to the text of the Constitution and the intent of the framers.

How, then, to explain the persistence of the belief in judicial supremacy? The practice of journalists and editorial writers to depict Court rulings as definitive helps feed the public's belief in judicial supremacy. Moreover, textbooks used in undergraduate and law schools rarely consider the pivotal role played by nonjudicial actors. To borrow a line from Justice Scalia, judicial supremacy appears like a "ghoul in a late-night horror movie that repeatedly sits upon its grave and shuffles about, after being repeatedly killed and buried."[98] But like a horror movie ghoul, judicial supremacy is more ethereal than real. It is there to command us when "we wish it to do so, but we can command it to return to the tomb at will."[99] The next chapter identifies the various nonjudicial actors who share with the courts the task of interpreting and applying the Constitution.

Who Participates?

When the Court interprets the Constitution it has plenty of company. Congress, the White House, government agencies, interest groups, the general public, and the states are all legitimate players. Before a case is ever considered, Congress or the states must enact a law or the executive branch must promulgate a regulation. Once a case is in court, the states, the Justice Department, and congressional coalitions, sometimes as parties to the case and sometimes as amici curiae ("friends of the court"), press their views on the judiciary. After a decision is issued, elected government may seek to expand or limit the holding with a number of techniques, including subsequent statutory action, creative interpretation and enforcement (to the point of nonenforcement), or nullifying the ruling through constitutional amendment. If a court lacks jurisdiction to decide a constitutional issue, the resolution of the dispute is left entirely to elected government.

Elected government influences extend well beyond particular adjudicated disputes. The number of Justices who sit on the Supreme Court and the Court's appellate jurisdiction are both subject to elected branch tinkering. Federal judges depend on presidential nomination and Senate confirmation. They depend on congressional support for their budgets, which must be justified and defended, as with any agency. All of these actions are exposed to the full glare of social and political scrutiny.

Social Pressures

Just as the Supreme Court leaves its mark on American society, so are social forces part of the mix of constitutional law. The Court, frequently regarded as a nonpolitical and independent branch of government, is very much a product of its times. Justice Cardozo reminded us that the "great tides and currents which engulf the rest of men do not turn aside in their course and pass the judges by."[1] In 1905, the Supreme Court remarked that as a result of the general grant of powers expressed in the Constitution, "as changes come in social and political life it embraces in its grasp all new conditions which are within the scope of the powers in terms conferred."[2] At times, those social and political changes are recognized and accepted by the Court; on a number of occasions, they force the Court to make changes in judicial doctrines. As Max Lerner noted, judicial decisions "are not babies brought by constitutional storks, but are born out of the travail of economic circumstance."[3]

Morris Raphael Cohen, one of the early students of legal realism, denied that the law is a "closed, independent system having nothing to do with economic, political, social or philosophical science."[4] It was Lord Radcliffe who counseled that "we cannot learn law by learning law." By this tantalizing phrase he meant that law must be "a part of history, a part of economics and sociology, a part of ethics and a philosophy of life. It is not strong enough in itself to be a philosophy of itself."[5]

Social and political forces affect the process by which a multimember Court gropes incrementally toward a consensus and a decision. In such areas as civil rights, sex discrimination, church and state, abortion, and criminal procedures, the Court moves with a series of half steps, disposing of the particular issue at hand while preparing for the next case. Through installments it lays the groundwork for a more comprehensive solution, always sensitive to the response of society and the institutions of government that must enforce judicial rulings. This social and political framework sets the boundaries for judicial activity and influences the substance of specific decisions, if not immediately, then within a few years. A purely technical approach to the law misses the constant, creative interplay that takes place between the judiciary and society at large.

The Constitution's framers recognized that public opinion would shape constitutional discourse.[6] In particular, Alexander Hamilton and James Madison both recognized that a written constitution could never trump the will of the people. Hamilton, commenting on freedom of the press, said that "whatever fine declarations may be inserted in any constitution respecting it, [it] must altogether depend on public opinion, and on the general spirit of the people and of the government."[7] Madison likewise heralded the power of public opinion, arguing that the "ultimate authority . . . resides in the people alone."[8]

Public debate over the death penalty is instructive in this matter. In 1972, the Supreme Court of California declared the death penalty a violation of the state constitutional ban against cruel or unusual punishments. Within nine months, the voters of California amended the state constitution to reinstate the death penalty.[9] At the national level, in 1972 the Supreme Court abruptly struck down death penalty statutes in Georgia and Texas as cruel and unusual because of the erratic nature of their application. The 5–4 majority focused on the arbitrariness and inequalities in state practices: the increasing rarity of executions and the application of that punishment to blacks more than whites, to men more than women, and to the poor more than the rich.[10] The Court acknowledged that cruel and unusual punishment requires "a flexible analysis that recognize[s] that as public opinion change[s], the validity of the penalty would have to be re-examined."[11] Following that decision, the majority of states immediately reinstituted the death penalty and added new procedures. The Court reviewed the changes in Georgia's statute and upheld, 7 to 2, the new procedures.[12]

Twenty-five years later, when death penalty opponents had won several important political victories, the annual number of executions began to decline.[13] Consistent with this shift in public attitude, the Supreme Court found it unconstitutional both to execute mentally retarded people and to have judges, not juries, impose death penalty sentences.[14] In its ruling on mentally retarded offenders, the Court specifically pointed to "a national consensus" having developed against such executions.[15] It did not look to the text of the Constitution or to the framers' intent, and certainly not to its own decisions.

It is too flippant to accept Mr. Dooley's pronouncement that the Supreme Court follows the election returns, but a number of studies show that the Court generally stays within the political boundaries of its times.[16] When it strays outside those boundaries and opposes the policy of elected leaders or social trends, it does so at substantial risk to its legitimacy. The Court maintains its effectiveness by steering a course that fits within the permissible limits of public opinion.

The judiciary is not a political body in the same sense as Congress and the President, but pragmatism and statesmanship must temper abstract legal analysis. Tocqueville noted in the 1840s that the power of the Supreme Court "is enormous, but it is the power of public opinion. They are all-powerful as long as the people respect the law; but they would be impotent against popular neglect or contempt of the law." Federal judges "must be statesmen, wise to discern the signs of the times, not afraid to brave the obstacles that can be subdued, nor slow to turn away from the current when it threatens to sweep them off."[17]

During his service as a federal appellate judge, William Howard Taft commented on the interplay between judicial decisions and public opinion. He said that the right to publicly criticize judicial action is "of vastly more importance to the body politic than the immunity of courts and judges from unjust aspirations and attack." He added, "Nothing tends more to render judges careful in their decisions and anxiously solicitous to do exact justice than the consciousness that every act of theirs is to be subjected to the intelligent scrutiny of their fellow-men, and to their candid criticism."[18] Some of this criticism would come from "learned text-writers" and law reviews, but Taft also saw the value of scrutiny from the general public. He put it this way: "If the law is but the essence of common sense, the protest of many average men may evidence a defect in a judicial conclusion though based on the nicest legal reasoning and profoundest learning."[19]

Opposition to slavery came from the public, not from judicial, executive, or legislative actions. Individual Americans, untutored in the fine points of constitutional law, viewed slavery as repugnant to fundamental political, moral, and legal principles, especially those embedded in the Declaration of Independence. The essential antislavery documents were private writings and speeches, not court decisions or legislative statutes.[20] Citizens felt a strong duty to express their opinions on constitutional rights. They deferred neither to courts nor to legislatures. Americans of the mid-nineteenth century "were not inclined to leave to private lawyers any more than to public men the conception, execution, and interpretation of public law. The conviction was general that no aristocracy existed with respect to the Constitution. Like politics, with which it was inextricably joined, the Constitution was everyone's business."[21]

The responsiveness of courts to the social community is especially immediate at the local level. District judges have strong ties to their local community. They are selected in part because often they were born and educated in their district, practiced law there, and participated in local politics. These local allegiances affect their decisions in such areas as civil rights, labor relations, and sentencing of Vietnam resisters. As public opinion turned against the Vietnam War, federal district judges responded by handing down lighter sentences against draft resisters.[22] A conference of federal judges in 1961 agreed that public opinion "should not materially affect sentences" and that the judiciary "must stand firm against undue public opinion." Nevertheless, after adding the qualifier "undue," the judges cautioned that "this should not mean that the community's attitude must be completely ignored in sentencing: although judges should be leaders of public opinion, they must never get so far out in front that the public loses sight of them."[23]

Federal judges are appointed for life and are immune from periodic campaigning for electoral office, but they know that the ability to write acceptable opinions depends on sensitivity to the public. This consideration plays into the assignment of opinions. In 1944, Chief Justice Stone initially assigned the Texas "White Primary" case to Justice Frankfurter. Justice Jackson expressed his misgivings to both Frankfurter and Stone, suggesting that because of "Southern sensibilities," it was unwise to have a Vienna-born Jew, raised in New England (the seat of the abolition movement), write the majority opinion striking down a Texas statute governing the election of Democrats. With Frankfurter's knowledge and consent, Stone transferred the case to Stanley Reed, a native-born, Protestant, and old-time Kentuckian. Reed was a Democrat of long standing, whereas Frankfurter's past ties to the Democratic Party were suspect.[24]

New appointments allow the Supreme Court to incorporate contemporary social and political attitudes. So long as judges "are relatively normal human beings," observed Chief Justice William Rehnquist, they cannot "escape being influenced by public opinion."[25] Consequently, a judge who decided "to seal himself off hermetically from all manifestations of [current] public opinion . . . would [nevertheless] be influenced by the state of public opinion at the time he came to the bench."[26] Although Justices sometimes object that precedents are too easily abandoned and the principle of stare decisis ignored, new Justices bring fresh ideas and philosophies to the Court. In a dissent, Justice Black complained in 1971 that constitutional protections "should not be blown around by every passing political wind that changes the composition of this Court."[27] No doubt he was frustrated by policy shifts from the Warren Court to the Burger Court, yet Black himself had been part of the Roosevelt appointees in the late 1930s and early 1940s who helped chart a new course in constitutional interpretation and broke sharply with conservative doctrines.

Justice Jackson, using characteristically blunt language, recognized that changes in the Court's composition enable it to stay abreast of contemporary views. He denied that this capacity did violence to the notion of an independent, nonpolitical judiciary: "Let us not deceive ourselves; long-sustained public opinion does influence the process of constitutional interpretation. Each new member of the everchanging personnel of our courts brings to his task the assumptions and accustomed thought of a later period. The practical play of the forces of politics is such that judicial power has often delayed but never permanently defeated the persistent will of a substantial majority."[28]

While proponents of judicial supremacy pay homage to the Court's power to strike down elected government action, it is a mistake to think of judicial review in a purely negative sense, as the act of nullifying the acts of Congress, the President, and the states. This treatment overlooks the more important and more frequent process where the Court affirms and legitimates the actions of the elected branches. Charles L. Black Jr. has explained the way this works: "The prime and most necessary function of the Court has been that of *validation*, not that of invalidation. What a government of limited powers needs, at the beginning and forever, is some means of satisfying the people that it has taken all steps humanly possible to stay within its powers. . . . The Court, through its history, has acted as the legitimator of the government."[29]

Individual and Group Lobbying

Public attitudes and preferences are often funneled through individuals and groups that press their constitutional agendas on Congress, the executive branch, and the courts. In a speech in 1969, Justice Thurgood Marshall emphasized the importance of public participation: "No matter how solemn and profound the declarations of principle contained in our charter of government, no matter how dedicated and independent our judiciary, true justice can only be obtained through the actions of committed individuals, individuals acting both independently and through organized groups."[30]

One of these "committed individuals," Belva Lockwood, completed her legal studies and was admitted to the bar of the District of Columbia in 1873. However, she was denied the right to practice in the federal courts solely because she was a woman. She "immediately laid siege" to Congress and by "energetic lobbying" was able to secure the passage of legislation in 1879 permitting women to practice in the federal courts.[31] For her efforts, she became the first woman admitted to practice before the U.S. Supreme Court. Lockwood's experience shows that the courts are hardly the last word on constitutional law, nor are they reliable guardians of individual and minority rights. With no opportunity to gain satisfaction in the courts, which had regularly denied women the right to practice law, she was able to convince Congress—an all-male body—to give her the appropriate relief.[32] For those who believed that the issue of practicing law should be left to the courts, Senator George Hoar strongly disagreed: "With the greatest respect for that tribunal, I conceive that the lawmaking and not the law-expounding power in this Government ought to determine the question what class of citizens shall be clothed with the office of advocate."[33]

At the turn of the twentieth century, the National Consumers' League channeled its resources to win important protections for factory workers, both legislatively and through the courts. For example, after successfully lobbying the Oregon legislature to limit a woman's workday to ten hours, National Consumer League general counsel (and later Supreme Court Justice) Louis Brandeis set about defending the law in court. By incorporating into his brief facts assembled by experts regarding women's hours of labor, he convinced the Court that long hours of work threatened the health and well-being of women workers.[34] In response, the American Liberty League was organized by conservative businessmen to challenge new forms of economic regulation by government.[35]

The National Association for the Advancement of Colored People (NAACP), created in 1909, set up a Legal Defense and Educational Fund in the 1930s to make litigation a more systematic tool for gaining important new rights for the black community. Starting in 1935, the Legal Defense Fund launched a calculated assault against segregation. A generation later, with its victory in *Brown v. Board of Education* (1954), the Fund found itself at "the 'cutting edge' of all the complex social and political forces that were at work to produce desegregated America."[36] Beyond race relations, the Legal Defense Fund's practice of systematically thinking through what battles could be won and what battles ought to be deferred became a model for other interest groups, especially those promoting environmental and women's interests, in their campaigns to use courts to advance social policy objectives.

Witness the efforts of the American Civil Liberties Union (ACLU) to expand constitutional guarantees for gays and lesbians. In launching a "test case" challenge to Georgia's antisodomy statute, the ACLU waited five years for a case in which an individual was arrested in his home.[37] Correspondingly, in challenging the military's "Don't ask, don't tell policy," the ACLU sought to frame the issue before the courts, arguing that the policy was about status (equality) not conduct (rights).[38]

Through the publication of articles, books, and commission reports, interest groups publicize their findings and conclusions about important public matters. Reliance on this body of literature concerned many legislators who feared that the courts might be giving indiscriminate credence to "unknown, unrecognized and nonauthoritative text books, law review articles, and other writings of propaganda artists and lobbyists."[39] The author of this statement, Congressman Wright Patman, complained in 1957 that the Supreme Court had turned increasingly for guidance to private publications and studies promoted by the administration. The research was designed, he said, not to study an issue objectively but to advance the particular views of private groups trying, through the medium of publication, to influence the judiciary's disposition of public policy questions. Experts have pointed out that the members of these study committees and commissions are aware that lawyers will cite the reports in their briefs "and that the real impact of this might very well be in the decisions made by courts and administrative agencies."[40]

The practice of judges citing professional journals goes back at least to Justice Brandeis in the 1920s. Other Justices, including Cardozo and Stone, also adopted this technique as a way of keeping law current with changes in American society. The opinions by Brandeis gave new meaning to the word "authority." He believed that a judicial opinion "derives its authority, just as law derives its existence, from all the facts of life. The judge is free to draw upon these facts wherever he can find them, if only they are helpful."[41]

The use of litigation in the 1940s and 1950s to shape social policy led to broader public participation and produced fundamental changes in the amicus curiae brief. Originally, such briefs permitted third parties, without any direct interest in the case, to bring certain facts to the attention of the court to avoid judicial error. The purpose was to identify cases not known to the judge. Courts welcomed such assistance, as "it is the honor of a court of justice to avoid error."[42] Over the years the amicus brief lost this innocent quality and became an instrument used by private groups to advance their cause. Amicus representations in court were similar to group representations before congressional committees: "Just as group participation injects a more popular and majoritarian characteristic into the legislative process, it does the same for the judicial process."[43] The amicus curiae brief moved "from neutrality to partisanship, from friendship to advocacy."[44]

Today, amicus briefs are filed in close to 85 percent of all cases.[45] Moreover, with twenty organized interests participating in the typical amicus case (a case where at least one amicus brief is filed), it is not unusual for eighteen hundred organizations to sign on to at least one Supreme Court brief each term.[46] With Justices frequently citing amicus briefs in their decisions, interest groups will continue to lobby the Court through amicus filings.[47] In a 1989 abortion case, over four hundred organizations and thousands of individuals signed on to one of seventy-eight amicus briefs.[48]

Lobbying before the Supreme Court, of course, represents but a small part of interest group efforts to shape constitutional values. Interest groups, such as the Southern Christian Leadership Conference, the National Organization of Women, and the Christian Coalition, are a guiding light of social movements—movements that affect public discourse and shape constitutional norms. Organized interests also speak as experts and, in so doing, affect constitutional discourse. For example, by repudiating its earlier finding that homosexuality is a psychopathic condition, the American Psychiatric Association paved the way for increasing societal acceptance of homosexuality.[49]

More tellingly, Congress, the White House, and state officials pay close attention to interest groups. Whether the issue is gun control, flag burning, physician-assisted suicide, or other controversies, interest groups play a key role in affecting public policy.[50] Interest group representatives regularly present before Congress constitutional arguments at legislative hearings and, more important, work closely with lawmakers in the crafting of legislation. Presidents, too, go to great lengths to win over interest groups. When Ronald Reagan announced his pro-life regulatory agenda, for example, he did so before a group of right-to-life leaders. Beyond legislation and regulation, interest groups also work closely with the President in the selection of both judicial and agency appointees and the Congress in assessing these appointments.

A particularly vivid example of the power of interest groups to shape constitutional decision making is the effort of state and local officials to push their views before Congress and the White House. Whether the issue is unfunded mandates, welfare reform, or the applicability of fair labor standards, state and local officials play a prominent role in affecting Washington's willingness to embrace policy arguments grounded in the Tenth Amendment and other federalism protections.[51]

An incident in President Clinton's second term underscores the capacity of state and local organizations to protect their interests. In 1998, Clinton issued an executive order on federalism, setting forth a number of principles to define the boundaries between the national government and the states. Unlike earlier executive orders (including one Clinton issued in 1993), the 1998 order specified instances in which federal preemption is warranted without any references to the traditional boundaries of state and local authority. The National Conference of State Legislatures, the National Governors Association, the U.S. Conference of Mayors, the National Association of Counties, the National League of Cities, and several other groups issued a sharp protest. Within two months these organizations had helped persuade the Senate to adopt language urging Clinton to repeal the executive order and reissue one issued by Reagan that was more favorable to the states.[52] Initially, the Clinton White House promised to rewrite the executive order but later agreed to withdraw it and start over, this time working in concert with state and local organizations.[53]

Independent Jurors

Millions of citizens are called to sit on grand juries and regular juries. In deciding to indict or convict their fellow citizens, for the most part they follow the law as explained by prosecutors and judges. On some occasions, often highly important ones, jurors rely on their own conscience to decide what is constitutional and proper. In their own way, jurors sense and articulate what is due process, equal protection, free speech, unreasonable searches and seizures, and cruel and unusual punishments. In exercising independent judgment, jurors at various times have represented the best and the worst of democracy.[54]

The concept of an independent juror, free under some circumstances to reject a judge's instruction of what the law is, has deep roots in America. In a diary entry in 1771, John Adams spoke about the difficulty that juries have in determining questions of law, which are frequently expressed in Latin and French. It was reasonable to expect the judge to instruct on the law and for juries to decide questions of fact. And yet, Adams asked, "is it not an absurdity to suppose that the law would oblige them to find a verdict according to the direction of the court, against their own opinion, judgment, and conscience?" It was not only a juror's "right, but his duty" to find a verdict "according to his own best understanding, judgment, and conscience, though in direct opposition to the direction of the court."[55] Thomas Jefferson wrote in 1789:

> It is left therefore to juries, if they think the permanent judges are under any biass [sic] whatever in any cause, to take upon themselves to judge the law as well as the fact. They never exercise this power but when they suspect partiality in the judges, and by the exercise of this power they have been the firmest bulwarks of English liberty. Were I called upon to decide whether the people had best be omitted in the Legislative or Judiciary department, I would say it is better to leave them out of the Legislative.[56]

In 1793, President George Washington issued his neutrality proclamation to prevent Americans from siding militarily in the war between France and England. When citizens were prosecuted for violating the proclamation, jurors would acquit because they refused to convict someone for a crime established only by a proclamation. With no statute to cite, the government dropped other prosecutions.[57] Juries decided that criminal law was left to Congress and the legislative process, rather than allow the President to fix criminality by decree. President Washington appealed to Congress to consider legislation that would authorize effective prosecution. Congress passed the Neutrality Act the next year, giving the administration the firm legal footing it needed to prosecute violators.

In the early years of the American republic, judges found it difficult to dictate the law to skeptical frontier jurors. One foreman told a judge that "the jury want to know whether that *ar* what you told us, when we first went out, was *raly* the law, or whether it was *only jist* your notion."[58] During the nineteenth century, jurors objected to legislation that mandated the death penalty not only for murder but for treason, piracy, arson, rape, robbery, burglary, and sodomy. Without the opportunity to vote for a lesser penalty, many jurors voted to acquit. Legislatures

w·n pressured to add sentencing discretion to the process, such as
al juries to decide between the death penalty and life imprison-
m stead of jurors complying with the law, they exercised indepen-
d ment to challenge the law and force greater flexibility.

·r crimes, jurors can be hostile to the underlying criminal law.
I· ught against individuals for violating laws regarding hunting,
g·nd liquor (during the Prohibition Era), jurors would often
a· se they regarded the laws as unreasonable or too severe. No
n· evidence prosecutors offered, jurors were likely to rebel.[60]
h· ome prosecutors decided not to waste time with futile cases
a· s were forced to rewrite or repeal the unpopular laws.

also acquit when they decide that law enforcement officers
· eir powers and offended basic liberties. In some early cases,
· nts were not represented by counsel, jurors would acquit
· mental unfairness. One juror told a judge, "Until the state
· ic defender, he would let everyone go free."[61] Under these
· s and the federal government were compelled to provide
· nsel not only for capital crimes but for other offenses as
· ·ide that the government has used heavy-handed tactics
· vidual and helped manufacture a crime that would not
· ithout the government's manipulation, acquittal may
· secutors that they have violated basic constitutional
· draw a line around permissible governmental behavior,
· islators enact, prosecutors bring, or judges decide.

· t in basic questions of constitutional law is evident
· rnography and obscenity. In these areas, the Supreme
· if not incomprehensible, guidelines. Jurors are sup-
· hether the average person, applying contemporary
· would find that the work, taken as a whole, appeals
· t; (2) whether the work depicts or describes, in a
· sexual conduct specifically defined by the applica-
· hether the work, taken as a whole, lacks "serious
· ·l, or scientific value."[62] Prurient means inclined
· ut what is lascivious? It means inclined to lust;
· s lust, wantonness, and lewdness? These words
· d, jurors will decide for themselves whether a
· or music performance is harmful to their home
· controversial cases in 1990, juries in Cincinnati,
· , Florida, decided that an art gallery and the
· not guilty of obscenity charges. The constitu-
· ·ds more on the conscience, intuition, taste,
· jurors than Supreme Court doctrines.

Jury nullification remains a controversial issue. The term *that*
jurors may acquit even when they are convinced that the *int is*
guilty as charged: Jurors refuse "to be bound by the fac *case*
or the judge's instruction regarding the law. Instead, the *es its*
conscience."[63] At times, this tactic is used by a minority to *jority*
policy: "Considering the costs of law enforcement to the b *unity*
and the failure of white lawmakers to devise significant *rative*
responses to black antisocial conduct, it is the moral resp *black*
jurors to emancipate some guilty black outlaws."[64] But *phy of*
jury nullification is broader than black protest. In the *study,*
juries "might be the last outpost of a skeptical citizen *of too*
much power in the hands of public officials, and null *duces a*
degree of unpredictability that requires prosecutor *ember*
who has the last word about who is punished."[65]

The Congressional Presence

hases of
Congress participates in constitutional decisio *approval*
the lawmaking process, from the enactment *d depart-*
of constitutional amendments to the oversig *ipated in*
ments and agencies. In recent decades, Cong *dividual*
litigation both in its own name and throu *tters that*
members. Finally, when it comes to impea *Congress*
the Supreme Court deems unreviewable *pretation,*
speaks the first and last word on the Co *ed govern-*
The pervasiveness and significance *cipal alle-*
combined with the Supreme Court's will *"Congress*
ment, has led numerous interest grou *ause there*
giance to the Congress, not the courts. *milar vein,*
is increasingly asked to look at these *tion of the*
is nobody else. It is now the court *resentation*
the National Abortion Rights Actio *Some legal*
constitutional right to choose "dep *interpreta-*
in Congress responding to the wil *ld be "freer*
academics join in this support for *, and a freer*
tion. For example, Robin West *ndered, not*
to envision, and then to realize, *
individual and collective life" b *tional inter-*
furthered, by judicially crafte *olars, signals*
This growing call for congr *
pretation, especially from left

a dramatic shift in perceptions. In 1979, Owen Fiss wrote that legislators "are not ideologically committed or institutionally suited to the search for the meaning of constitutional values," but see their primary function in terms of registering the preferences of the people, "what they want and what they believe should be done."[69] In 1983, federal appeals court judge and former congressman Abner Mikva blasted Congress for its "superficial and, for the most part, self-serving constitutional debate." Noting that Congress "is a reactive body unable to enact legislation until the problem at hand reaches crisis proportions" and that "the constitutional principles involved in a bill, unlike its merits, are generally abstract, unpopular, and fail to capture the imagination of either the media or the public," Mikva perceived that "regardless of the rhetoric that emanates from Congress, the legislature has for the most part . . . left constitutional judgments to the judiciary."[70] Stanford's Paul Brest echoed these sentiments in his 1986 broadside on Congress's "capacity and commitment to engage in constitutional interpretation," concluding that "until and unless Congress develops trustworthy procedures for determining constitutional issues, it must abstain from contradicting judge-made decisions."[71]

Congress's ascendancy as constitutional interpreter has much to do with criticism of Supreme Court rulings in recent decades. Yet, earlier attacks on Congress were overstated, for they were premised on the notion that the courts were a more vigorous guardian of the Constitution than the Congress. The truth lies somewhere in between. Congress can perform "an essential, broad, and ongoing role in shaping the meaning of the Constitution," but it is a coordinate role, part of a "continuing colloquy" between courts and Congress in which constitutional principle is "evolved conversationally not perfected unilaterally."[72] The record of congressional constitutional interpretation supports this proposition. Before, during, and after adjudication, the courts and Congress engage coequally in a constitutional dialogue with each other and with the executive branch.

Before legislation is enacted, Congress undertakes a constitutional review of the measure. Legislators and their staff assess a bill's constitutionality, assisted by the Congressional Research Service, the Office of General Counsel in the House, the Senate Legal Counsel, and the General Accounting Office. Through formal legislative hearings and informal requests, constitutional scholars, Justice Department and other government officials, and interest groups offer their views of a measure's constitutionality.

Congress's consideration of constitutional questions in lawmaking, as well as oversight, often hinges on which committee the matter is before. In 1963, for example, Senate leadership insisted that the Commerce Committee take charge of landmark civil rights legislation out of fear that the more conservative Judiciary Committee would block civil rights reform.

Congress wanted to prohibit discrimination by restaurants, hotels, and other public accommodations. In the wake of hearings raising doubts about Congress's authority to ground this provision in the Fourteenth Amendment's equal protection guarantee, Congress invoked its commerce power as an alternative support. By framing the statute this way, the Supreme Court was able to uphold the measure on commerce grounds without ever having to consider the Fourteenth Amendment issue.[73]

Aside from framing issues for judicial resolution, Congress and its members also participate in the litigation process. Sometimes, the Supreme Court invites the House, the Senate, or individual members to present an amicus brief and participate in oral arguments. Amicus briefs, most notably in abortion and separation of powers disputes, have been filed at the initiative of the Senate, the House, and their individual members. For example, a coalition of more than two hundred members of Congress filed an amicus brief in *Harris v. McRae* (1980), defending Congress's right to fund or not fund abortions as it sees fit.

On rare occasions, individual members file lawsuits challenging the constitutionality of congressional or White House action. The courts typically refuse to resolve these disputes because they represent disputes within Congress, with one faction at odds with another. As illustrated by war power cases and other matters, judges are apt to tell legislators: Use your own institutional powers to protect yourself. Don't come to the courts for relief. That was basically the message in 1997 when the Court rejected standing for Senator Robert Byrd and his colleagues, who complained that the Line Item Veto Act of 1996 was unconstitutional.[74] When Congress has exhausted its institutional powers, the courts may grant relief. For example, Senator Edward Kennedy successfully challenged President Nixon's use of the "pocket veto" during a 1972 recess.[75]

Congress is forced to participate in litigation when the Justice Department refuses to defend a statute's constitutionality. In cases involving the constitutionality of the bankruptcy court and the legislative veto, for example, congressional and executive branch interests collided.[76] In both cases, congressional and Justice Department lawyers fought each other at oral argument and through briefs filed before the Supreme Court.

Once the Supreme Court decides a case, Congress may use a wide variety of powers to signal its approval or disapproval. On constitutional questions, Congress hardly ever pursues alternatives such as stripping the Court of jurisdiction or reenacting a statute that the Court struck down. But there are many opportunities for Congress to pass legislation that contains constitutional values that differ from what the Court has just decided.

Constitutional amendment proposals, requiring two-thirds approval from both houses of Congress and ratification by three-fourths of the states, are rarely successful. But these initiatives may drive judicial decision making. In response to the Court's failure to invalidate gender classifications, Congress approved and sent to the states for ratification a proposed Equal Rights Amendment (ERA) prohibiting the abridgement of "equality of rights . . . on account of sex." The amendment, never ratified, proved influential. During debate in October 1971, Representative Martha Griffiths said that the whole purpose of the ERA was to tell the Court "Wake up! This is the 20th Century."[77] A month later, a unanimous Court struck down an Idaho law that preferred men over women in administering estates.[78] Within a few years, Court decisions became "fully compatible with arguments made by leading mainstream ERA proponents in such documents as Congressional committee reports and hearings records on the ERA, and in testimony in the Congressional Record by leading ERA sponsors."[79]

Congress has often been successful in reversing Supreme Court decisions that legislators believe insufficiently protect individual rights. In 1976, the Supreme Court held that law enforcement officials could subpoena a bank and obtain records without the depositor's knowledge. The Court treated the materials as business records of a bank, not private papers of a person. Within two years Congress passed the Right to Financial Privacy Act, requiring either knowledge on the part of a depositor that a subpoena has been served, or supervision by the courts.[80] Thus, safeguards to Fourth Amendment rights that were unavailable from the courts were secured by legislative action.

Executive Branch Interpretations

Executive power in constitutional decision making is extraordinarily broad. The executive appoints Supreme Court Justices, recommends legislation and constitutional amendments, exercises the veto power, promulgates regulations, and uses the bully pulpit. In each of these ways, the executive interprets the Constitution and shapes constitutional values. Indeed, in its day-to-day administration of the law and management of the federal government, there is little doubt that the executive branch interprets the Constitution more often than the courts: "Whenever a federal law enforcement officer decides whether there is probable cause for an arrest, the executive branch has interpreted the Fourth Amendment;

whenever federal employees are disciplined for statements they made, the executive branch has interpreted the First Amendment."[81]

Two agencies in the Justice Department are particularly active in constitutional interpretation: the Office of Legal Counsel (OLC), which advises the attorney general on pending and enrolled legislation and the legality of presidential initiatives, and the Office of Solicitor General, the government's lawyer before the Supreme Court. These two offices are often a stepping-stone to the Supreme Court. Chief Justice Rehnquist and Justice Scalia previously served as head of OLC. Justices Thurgood Marshall, Robert H. Jackson, Stanley Reed, and Chief Justice Charles Evans Hughes were former solicitors general. The White House Counsel's Office has emerged as the President's lawyer, providing him "access to legal advice that is not filtered through the institutional biases or political preoccupations of the Justice Department."[82]

The President participates in the lawmaking process by sharing with Congress his views on the constitutionality of proposed legislation, including busing, abortion, flag burning, and school prayer. Executive lawmaking authority includes the veto power. When the President concludes that an act of Congress is unconstitutional, the last word on that dispute typically rests with the executive (unless two-thirds of both the House and Senate can overturn the veto). President George H. W. Bush helped maintain strict abortion funding restrictions by successfully vetoing five bills that allowed some federal funding of abortion. Even the threat of a veto is often sufficient reason for Congress to revise or remove contested language in a bill.

Curiously, the President sometimes signals constitutional objections to legislation through signing statements. When Bush I signed flag protection legislation in 1989, he expressed "serious doubts that it can withstand Supreme Court review."[83] Reagan was equally troubled about "a violation of the system of separation of powers carefully crafted by the framers of the Constitution"[84] when he signed the Gramm-Rudman deficit control bill. In both instances, constitutional objections were pushed aside because the President embraced these measures' underlying policies. Along the same lines, signing statements sometimes claim that statutory provisions won't be enforced because the President thinks they are unconstitutional. From Ronald Reagan to George W. Bush, Presidents have all contended that they would not comply with congressionally enacted legislative veto provisions enacted after the Court, in *INS v. Chadha* (1983), had ruled them unconstitutional. Yet at the agency level, executive officials are likely to find it prudent and necessary to live with these legislative controls.[85]

Beyond its lawmaking authority, the executive frames constitutional disputes through its regulatory authority. Although rule making is supposed to implement congressional intent, there is sufficient ambiguity in many statutes for executive officials to push in one direction or another depending on their constitutional beliefs. In 1991, the Supreme Court refused to overturn Reagan administration regulations that prohibited federally funded abortion counseling because of the substantial deference it felt was owed to executive branch statutory interpretations.[86] When Congress subsequently sought to overturn these regulations through legislation, Bush I successfully vetoed the bill. One of Clinton's first acts as President was to reverse Reagan's regulation. One of Bush II's first acts as President was to reverse Clinton's policy of using federal funds to support groups that offer abortion counseling overseas.

The executive regularly litigates constitutional disputes both as a party and as an amicus. The decision to support or oppose Supreme Court review, as well as the preparation of briefs and oral arguments, is entrusted to the solicitor general. He is the only litigant who has a right to participate in Supreme Court litigation without first seeking the Court's permission. An OLC opinion states that the solicitor general "protects the Court's docket by screening the Government's cases and relieving the Court of the burden of reviewing unmeritorious claims."[87] The Court helps to perpetuate this gatekeeper image, granting review (certiorari) at a rate of between 75 to 90 percent of the time in cases presented to them by the solicitor general.[88] The Court often leans heavily on solicitor general arguments in its decision making. The solicitor general's brief in *Brown*, for example, played an instrumental role in convincing the Court of the political unacceptability of segregation.

Government arguments before the Supreme Court, however, are not the exclusive province of the solicitor general; occasionally, the White House will direct solicitor general filings. Modern accounts of such intervention include Eisenhower's drafting of portions of the government's brief in *Brown v. Board of Education*[89] and the Carter White House's reversal of the solicitor general's preliminary position in *Regents v. Bakke*,[90] an affirmative action case.

The solicitor general is not always the only government voice before the Court. When an independent agency is a party to a dispute, the agency is sometimes allowed to file a brief or argue before the Court. As a result, there are several instances when a federal agency and the solicitor general have openly disagreed with each other before the Supreme Court. Consider the following two cases involving the Federal Communications Commission (FCC). In *FCC v. Pacifica Foundation* (1978), the FCC successfully argued that certain words could be kept off the airwaves for most broadcasting hours and thereby withstood the solicitor general's challenge to the FCC orders as overbroad because the FCC did not consider "the context in which the offending words were used."[91] In *Metro Broadcasting v. FCC* (1990), the FCC and the solicitor general locked horns over race preferences, with the FCC arguing that the "promotion of diversity in broadcast programming" is a "compelling" governmental interest, while the solicitor general characterized preferences as impermissible "racial stereotyping."[92] In this square-off the FCC prevailed again.[93]

Executive branch participation in constitutional adjudication does not end when the Supreme Court hands down its ruling. The executive may seek to affect further court action through judicial appointments, constitutional amendment proposals, and much more.

The Political Impact of Appointments

Elected government's most direct link to judicial decision making is the overtly political process of selecting and approving federal judges. Article II of the Constitution authorizes the President to nominate federal court judges "with the Advice and Consent of the Senate." This selection process enables the President and Senate to advance their respective judicial philosophies (or, at least, to reject unacceptable judicial philosophies).

Appointments to the Supreme Court "are highly political appointments by the nation's chief political figure to a highly political body."[94] Reform proposals to take politics out of the process of selecting federal judges are hopeless. From an early date, senators wielded considerable power in choosing nominees for federal courts. Members of the Supreme Court (especially Chief Justice Taft) have well-earned reputations for lobbying successfully for candidates. Other sectors of government are also active. An unusually candid judge remarked, "A judge is a lawyer who knew a governor."[95]

A review of judicial appointments makes clear that the Supreme Court's constitutional decision making is very much related to this political nomination-confirmation process. In 1870, a seven-member Court, along strictly partisan lines, invalidated legislation seeking to discharge Civil War debts by treating paper money as legal tender, with all four Democratic Justices in the majority and all three Republicans in dissent. Fifteen months later, after Republican President Ulysses Grant filled two Supreme Court vacancies, the Court immediately overturned its decision, now declaring the Legal Tender Act constitutional.[96] Grant had reason to believe that his two nominees would sustain the statute: William Strong, as a member of the Supreme Court of Pennsylvania, had already sustained the Legal Tender Act; Joseph P. Bradley appeared to be no less sympathetic.[97] A similar feat was accomplished by FDR's New Deal appointees. These Justices assured the death of the *Lochner* era by, among other things, reversing the Court's 1918 declaration that Congress cannot regulate child labor under its commerce power.

Also dramatic was President Eisenhower's appointment of Earl Warren as Chief Justice in 1953. Without Warren, the Court may well have upheld *Plessey*'s "separate but equal" doctrine. The Supreme Court was set to decide that issue in its 1952 term with Chief Justice Fred Vinson at the Court's helm. After briefs were filed (including an important brief filed by the Justice Department in the last month of the Truman administration that argued that racial segregation undermined America's stature as leader of the free world) and oral arguments were heard, the Court redocketed the case so that it also could decide the constitutionality of segregated education in the "federal city," Washington, D.C.

At this time, the Justices were divided; their December 1952 conference suggested a 5–4 opinion (to uphold!) segregated education. As Justice William O. Douglas wrote in his autobiography, "It was clear that if a decision had been reached in the 1952 Term, we would have had five saying that separate but equal schools were constitutional, that separate but unequal schools were not constitutional, and that the remedy was to give the states time to make the two systems of schools equal."[98] Douglas's claim is subject to question, but there is little doubt that the Vinson Court would have exacerbated the conflict over segregated schools by issuing an opinion from a deeply divided Court. In 1953, however, Vinson died and Warren became Chief Justice, an occurrence prompting Justice Felix Frankfurter to exclaim, "This is the first solid piece of evidence I've ever had that there really is a God."[99] A year later, the Court issued its unanimous ruling in *Brown* that "separate educational facilities are inherently unequal."

The direction of Court decision making was also altered by the confirmation of Warren Burger to succeed Warren as Chief Justice. In 1971, the Burger Court limited Warren Court rulings that had protected individuals from having their citizenship stripped, prompting Justice Hugo Black to complain (in dissent) that the equal protection guarantee should not be "blown around" by new appointments to the Court.[100] Likewise, in a 1974 dissent, Justice Stewart objected that two recent Nixon appointees provided the difference in overturning a 1972 decision: "A basic change in the law upon a ground no firmer than a change in our membership invites the popular misconception that this institution is little different from the two political branches of the government."[101]

Justice Stewart's lament is, to put it mildly, strained. Supreme Court appointments are inherently political. They always have been. Judicial decisions are part of the policymaking process. The White House and the Senate have good reason to pay attention to the likely voting patterns of judicial nominees. Presidents try to select candidates to further their political agenda; senators are entitled to do the same. Admittedly, it is nearly impossible to predict with confidence how a nominee will decide once given the life tenure of a federal judgeship. Some Justices behave in unexpected ways. Earl Warren, Harry Blackmun, and David Souter are some prominent examples.

The role of ideology in the President's judicial selections, particularly in recent years, has resulted in vigorous Senate review of judicial nominees, especially Supreme Court appointments. Of the 145 presidential nominations to the Supreme Court, 27 have been rejected by the Senate. This rejection rate, close to 20 percent, is higher than that of any other post requiring Senate confirmation. Aside from exercising its veto power by turning down nominees, the Senate also shapes the judicial selection process by "advising" the President whom he should and should not nominate. Benjamin Cardozo's 1932 nomination to the Court, for example, was partly the result of assiduous lobbying by Senator William Borah.[102] Senator Warren Rudman was a strong (and successful) advocate for David Souter. Stephen Breyer's 1994 nomination by Bill Clinton came in the wake of growing Senate opposition to Clinton's apparent first choice, Interior Secretary Bruce Babbitt. Breyer had been a former chief counsel of the Senate Judiciary Committee.

The Senate also seeks to shape judicial decision making through its jawboning of nominees throughout the confirmation process. "Members of the Judiciary Committee," according to a 1993 study by Stephen Wermiel, "have learned to shape the constitutional dialogue in the confirmation hearings to make clear to nominees that a willingness to profess belief in some threshold constitutional values is a prerequisite for the job."[103] Beginning with the 1981 nomination of Sandra Day O'Connor, "these threshold values have included a commitment to the existence of unenumerated rights protected by the Constitution, including the right to privacy, and respect for *stare decisis*."[104]

The battleground over Supreme Court nominations reveals that the President and Senate both recognize that the best way to shape outputs (Court rulings) is to control inputs (who sits on the Court). This principle also applies to other positions where presidential nomination and Senate confirmation are required, such as lower court judgeships and high-ranking executive branch positions.

State Interpretations

Constitutional decision making involves much more than the three branches of the federal government. State judges and officials take an oath "to support and defend the Constitution" and to put this oath into effect through interpretations of both the U.S. Constitution and their state constitution. In many instances, independent state interpretations can provide broader individual rights protections than those mandated by the Supreme Court. With that said, states have also pursued policies that restrict rights and liberties.

The most conspicuous example of restrictive state practice was the decision of Southern states to adopt a policy of massive resistance to the Court's decision in *Brown v. Board of Education*. In contrast, most state efforts to limit *Roe v. Wade* raised issues that the Court had not explicitly considered: Spousal consent, parental consent and notification, waiting periods, informed consent requirements, and the like were not addressed in *Roe*. From 1973 to 1989, nearly all of these efforts failed, but the steady stream of legislation (306 antiabortion measures were passed during this period) kept the abortion issue before the Supreme Court and certainly provided it with countless opportunities to expand state authority in this area.

In sharp contrast to state legislative campaigns against *Brown* and *Roe*, states often provide for greater protections of individual rights than is available under the U.S. Constitution. Witness, for example, lawmaker efforts to expand First Amendment religious liberty and Establishment Clause protections. During the nineteenth century, in response to religious conflict between Catholics and Protestants, several states adopted so-called Blaine Amendments, prohibiting public support for church schools. Starting in the 1980s, moreover, state lawmakers have responded to court decisions rejecting claims by fundamentalist Christian educators that they could raise their children as they see fit by enacting laws expanding the rights of religious parents.[105] State courts, too, have played a leadership role in expanding constitutional protections. So long as state courts base their decisions on "bona fide separate, adequate, and independent grounds," the Supreme Court will not stand in the way of their efforts to expand individual rights protections.[106] In short, the last word on state constitutional law rests with state courts.

That states would see their constitutions as independent charters, providing for additional freedoms beyond the U.S. Constitution, is hardly surprising. State constitutional interpretation, as Wisconsin Supreme Court Justice Shirley Abrahamson observed, must take account of the "peculiarities" of the state, "its land, its industry, its people, its history."[107] The Texas Supreme Court, for example, explained why its state constitution provides for particularly broad free speech protections by referring to the "experiences and philosophies" of the state's founders, whose views were shaped by "years of rugged experience on the frontier."[108] For the Alaska Supreme Court, a generous interpretation of state privacy rights is necessitated by the state's tradition of being "the home of people who prize their individuality."[109]

Many of the so-called innovations by the U.S. Supreme Court were established first at the state level. The Warren Court was praised for issuing *Gideon v. Wainwright* (1963), which granted indigent defendants the right to counsel provided by the government. Yet many states had already recognized that right. The Supreme Court of Indiana in 1854 stated that "a civilized community" could not prosecute a poor person and withhold counsel. In 1859, the Wisconsin Supreme Court called it a "mockery" to promise a pauper a fair trial but tell him he must employ his own counsel. Congress passed legislation in 1892 to provide counsel to represent poor persons.[110]

Each state, according to the Court, has the "sovereign right to adopt in its own constitution individual liberties more expansive than those conferred by the Federal Constitution."[111] Depicting the "rediscovery by state supreme courts of the broader protections afforded their own citizens by their state constitutions . . . [as] probably the most important development in constitutional jurisprudence in our time," Justice William Brennan in 1986 encouraged "state courts to step into the breach."[112] Indeed, disappointed Justices often remind their state counterparts that they may reach an opposite result under state constitutional law. As Chief Justice Burger once remarked, "For all we know, the state courts would find this statute invalid under the State Constitution."[113]

A search and seizure case illustrates the freedom of states to develop greater constitutional protections for individuals. In 1980, the Supreme Court of Washington held that a police officer had exceeded his authority in seizing incriminating evidence in a student's room. The U.S. Supreme Court reversed the decision, using its "plain view" doctrine to uphold the seizure, and sent the case back to the state court. On the next go-round the Supreme Court of Washington, basing its opinion solely on the constitution and laws of the state, concluded that it was right the first time and found the officer's actions impermissible.[114]

Holdings such as these have become increasingly commonplace. The Rehnquist Court's reluctance to expand constitutional protections already has resulted in interest groups turning their attention to state courts and state legislatures. During 1990, for example, state supreme courts hinged more than 140 pro–civil liberties rulings on state protections of rights.[115] From 1950 to 1969, there were only ten such cases. From 1970 to 1986, there were approximately three hundred such cases.[116] This ongoing flurry of activity in state government and state courts on abortion and other questions therefore is more than a harbinger of things to come. It demonstrates the fundamental role played by the states in shaping constitutional values.

Conclusions

The Supreme Court is but one of several players that interpret the Constitution. Congress, the White House, government agencies, the states, the general public, and interest groups all play critical interdependent roles in shaping constitutional values. The sweep and influence of these interactions are broad and pervasive. Indeed, unlike the courts, whose role in constitutional decision making is confined to resolving "cases or controversies," elected government and interest group influences occur before, during, and after litigation. Through the resolution of constitutional conflicts not subject to judicial action, matters of profound constitutional significance are the exclusive province of elected government.

Chief Justice Warren believed that the operations of the Supreme Court could be easily distinguished from the work of Congress and the executive. Progress in politics, he said, "could be made and most often was made by compromising and taking half a loaf where a whole loaf could be obtained." He insisted that the "opposite is true so far as the judicial process [is] concerned." In the operation of the courts, "and particularly in the Supreme Court, the basic ingredient of decision is principle, and it should not be compromised and parceled out a little in one case, a little more in another, until eventually someone receives the full benefit."[117] Yet the record of the Court in such areas as school desegregation, sex discrimination, criminal procedure, church and state, just compensation, and other constitutional issues is precisely one of piecemeal action. No criticism of the Court is intended by this observation, for the Court shares with Congress and the executive the need to confront the world with measured steps.

Compromise, prudence, expediency, half-loaves, and ad hoc actions are a part of the process by which the Court functions, and the media must function in this environment as best it can. Justice Potter Stewart, reflecting on the Court's handiwork in deciding what evidence could be introduced into the courtroom, said that decisions on the exclusionary rule were "a bit jerry-built—like a roller coaster track constructed while the roller coaster sped along." Justices were in no position to think in terms of a whole loaf or uncompromised principle: "Each new piece of track was attached hastily and imperfectly to the one before it, just in time to prevent the roller coaster from crashing, but without the opportunity to measure the curves and dips preceding it or to contemplate the twists and turns that inevitably lay ahead."[118]

Limitations on judicial authority do not deny the Court's profound power in constitutional decision making. The Court remains a power, but it is a power constantly checked by other legitimate institutions. As Justice Robert Jackson put it, "The Constitution-makers left the Court in vital respects a dependent body."[119] Courts prevail when their decisions are persuasive to elected officials and the public. When decisions fall short of that standard, the door remains open to further interpretations until a consensus emerges.

Federalism

The meaning of federalism has been determined more by Congress, the President, and the political process than by judicial rulings. The two political branches determine the balance between states and the national government whenever they exercise the spending power, the taxing power, and the Commerce Clause to direct state activities. These constitutional judgments are generally affirmed by the courts and in many cases never challenged. On those occasions when federal courts impose their views of federalism and choose to strike down congressional statutes, the judicial doctrine will prevail only if it is supported by Congress and the American people. Otherwise, the regular political process will force a correction.

Through the President's power to nominate Justices and the Senate's power to confirm, the Court necessarily is affected by the election returns. That is how President Franklin D. Roosevelt secured judicial approval of New Deal measures. More recently, with the appointment of four Justices by Presidents Reagan and Bush I, the Court has begun to place new limits on what Congress may do under the Commerce Clause and other national powers. While the creative energy in defining federalism remains with Congress and the President, social and political forces continue to define the reaches of federal power.

The Federal-State Balance

Federalism is one way of allocating and dispersing power. By dividing political authority and sovereignty between the national government and the states, federalism provides a structural check on national power, protecting not only states' rights but individual rights. The framers, with their distrust of power, tried to create a balance between the central government and the states. That balance has changed over time, prodded more by political and economic imperatives than by judicial rulings.

After America declared its independence from England in 1776, thirteen states operated independently without a central government. The Articles of Confederation, drafted in 1777 and ratified in 1781, allowed each state to retain "its sovereignty, freedom and independence" with the exception of a few powers expressly delegated to the national government. Because of inadequate authority at the top, the states chose delegates to meet in Philadelphia in 1787 "to devise such further provisions as shall appear to them necessary to render the constitution of the Federal Government adequate to the exigencies of the Union."

When the draft Constitution circulated, critics objected that it created a national government instead of a federal form (a confederation of sovereign states). In *Federalist* No. 39, James Madison conceded that some features of the Constitution gave it a national character, but other provisions vested power directly in the states. The framers had created something new, something in between. Madison concluded that the Constitution "is, in strictness, neither a national nor a federal Constitution, but a composition of both."

The delegates needed to strengthen the national government without sacrificing the separate identity and functioning of the states. What model would work? The French theorist Montesquieu believed that republican government could flourish only in small countries. He reasoned that as the size of a country increased, popular control would have to be surrendered, requiring aristocracies for moderate-size countries and monarchies for large countries. In *Federalist* No. 10, Madison turned this theory on its head by arguing that republican government was unlikely to survive in a small territory because a dominant faction would oppress the smaller ones. "Extend the sphere," however, "and you take in a greater variety of parties and interests; you make it less probable that a majority of the whole will have a common motive to invade the rights of other citizens."

Subdividing this large territory into distinct states would add another safeguard. In *Federalist* No. 28, Alexander Hamilton argued that the national government and the states could check usurpations from each other: "The people, by throwing themselves into either scale, will infallibly make it preponderate. If their rights are invaded by either, they can make use of the other as the instrument of redress." This formulation depends on the regular political process as the remedy, not on litigation and court rulings.

Among the enumerated powers of Congress is the authority to "regulate Commerce with foreign Nations, and among the several States, and with the Indian Tribes." When the scope of the Commerce Clause reached the Court in 1824, Chief Justice John Marshall read it broadly to give Congress the power to regulate economic life in the nation to promote the free flow of interstate commerce, including actions within state borders that interfered with that flow.[1] Typical of Marshall's attitude about national power is the controversy over the U.S. Bank.

Creating a U.S. Bank

McCulloch v. Maryland (1819), which upheld the constitutionality of the U.S. Bank, vividly illustrates how Congress, the President, executive officials, and courts engage in three-branch interpretation. The political branches performed the spade work and heavy lifting of constitutional analysis; their inquiry and balancing of values were later blessed by the Court.

A central constitutional question in *McCulloch* was whether Congress could establish a national bank in the absence of express authority in the Constitution. Was there some "implied power" that might justify a national bank? Some of those issues had been thrashed out earlier, in 1781, when the Continental Congress debated the merits of a national bank. Robert Morris, superintendent of finance (forerunner to the secretary of the treasury), proposed a national bank and a committee further explored the idea. Congress decided that a national bank would be both proper and advantageous.[2] Nine states supported the plan, one state (Massachusetts) voted against it, and one state (Pennsylvania) was divided. Of the four delegates from Virginia, Madison was the only one to vote against the bank. He objected that the Articles of Confederation contained no express authority for a national bank.[3] A decade later, he used the same argument to oppose a national bank under the U.S. Constitution.

There had been little discussion about a national bank at the Constitutional Convention of 1787. As part of Article I, regarding the power of Congress to establish post offices and post roads, the delegates considered giving Congress power to grant charters of incorporation necessary for the United States. Rufus King of Massachusetts worried that Congress might use this power to establish a national bank, reviving the political warfare that had taken place in the Philadelphia and New York banking communities over fears that Congress would charter a competing banking institution. The delegates decided to remove the language on incorporation.[4]

The issue resurfaced in 1790 when the House of Representatives asked Secretary of the Treasury Alexander Hamilton to prepare a report on creating a national bank.[5] Debate the following year focused primarily on the constitutional authority of Congress to act in this area. Madison noted that the power of establishing an incorporated bank was not among the powers vested in Congress by the Constitution. Several members challenged his analysis, some pointing out that Madison had argued strongly in 1789 that the President had the power to remove executive officials even though that power is not specifically stated in the Constitution.[6] Others remarked that Madison, in one of his essays in *The Federalist*, had repudiated the doctrine of enumerated powers.[7] After extensive debate, the House voted 39 to 20 to create the bank. Madison was the most prominent opponent.

With the bill now heading to the President, George Washington asked his Cabinet to advise him on the constitutionality of the bank. Attorney General Edmund Randolph and Secretary of State Thomas Jefferson concluded that Congress had no authority to create a bank. Randolph argued that governments with written constitutions are circumscribed by the powers specified for them.[8] Jefferson said that the Tenth Amendment meant that all powers not *expressly* delegated to the federal government were reserved to the states or to the people.[9] However, the legislative history of the Tenth Amendment shows conclusively that the qualifier "expressly" was deliberately excluded on the ground that there "must necessarily be admitted powers by implication, unless the Constitution descended to recount every minutiae."[10] The author of that insight was James Madison.

Hamilton's analysis was by far the most penetrating of the three Cabinet members. Having drafted the bank bill, he could hardly claim detachment and objectivity, but the other major players—Madison, Jefferson, and Randolph—also started with strongly held opinions. Hamilton argued forcefully that the doctrines promoted by Jefferson and Randolph "would be fatal to the just & indispensable authority of the United States."[11] Persuaded by Hamilton's analysis, Washington signed the bill.[12]

When a case challenging the constitutionality of the U.S. Bank was brought before the Supreme Court, Hamilton's arguments carried the day. With the War of 1812 fueling nationalist sentiment, Chief Justice Marshall acted on his Federalist leanings and wrote an opinion in *McCulloch* that embraced an expansive view of Congress's powers. Marshall borrowed wholesale from Hamilton's interpretation of implied powers, sovereignty, and the Necessary and Proper Clause. The creative and constructive role of interpreting the Constitution thus belonged to Congress and the executive branch.

The controversy about the U.S. Bank continued into the 1830s, when President Andrew Jackson waged a personal war against the Bank. Congress tried to renew the Bank in 1832, but Jackson was ready with a veto. Although previous Congresses and Presidents had regarded the Bank as constitutional, and despite the Court's reasoning in *McCulloch*, Jackson relied on his own independent judgment that the bill was unconstitutional. He insisted that each branch must be guided by its own opinion of the Constitution. That interpretation of the veto power has been followed ever since.

When Congress Is Silent

The dialogue between the courts and elected officials on the meaning of federalism is revealed in other ways. If Congress does not exercise its commerce power, that authority is called silent or dormant, and the Supreme Court may decide that a state action is forbidden by the Commerce Clause. At that point, if Congress enacts legislation to authorize the state action, the courts will acquiesce to the legislative judgment.

This pattern was established in 1852, when the Court held that the height of a bridge in Pennsylvania, constructed under state law, made it "a nuisance"; it was so low that it obstructed navigation. Congress quickly passed legislation declaring the bridges at issue to be "lawful structures" and the Court, on a second go-round, ruled that the bridge was no longer an unlawful obstruction.[13]

In dissent, Justices McLean, Grier, and Wayne expressed dismay that a Court decision could be set aside by Congress. How could Congress reopen an issue that had been adjudicated? Wasn't a court ruling final and binding? Said McLean: "The congress and the court constitute coordinate branches of the government; their duties are distinct and of a different character. The judicial power cannot legislate, nor can the legislative power act judicially."[14]

The positions by McLean and his colleagues have remained a minority view. The Court noted in 1946, "Whenever Congress' judgment has been uttered affirmatively to contradict the Court's previously expressed view . . . this body has accommodated its previous judgment to Congress' expressed approval."[15] More recently, a concurrence by Justices Kennedy and O'Connor conceded that "if we invalidate a state law, Congress can in effect overturn our judgment."[16]

State Controls over Incoming Liquor

In the nineteenth century, the Supreme Court developed the doctrine of exclusive jurisdictions: Whatever fell under national control was excluded from state control, and vice versa. As the Court noted in 1876, "The powers which one possesses, the other does not."[17] This doctrine was never that crisp, as evidenced by the earlier dispute over the dormant Commerce Clause. Congress could always intervene and give states power that the Court had denied.

The theory of mutually exclusive powers produced a head-on collision between the Court and Congress in 1890. The Court ruled that a state's prohibition of intoxicating liquors from outside its boundaries could not be applied to original packages or kegs. Only after the original package was broken into smaller packages could the state exercise control. The power of Congress over interstate commerce, said the Court, trumped state police powers and local options. The Court hedged its opinion: States could not exclude incoming articles "without congressional permission."[18]

After the Court's decision, imaginative entrepreneurs opened up "original-package saloons," making it impossible for the states to exercise any control. Brewers and distillers from outside the state could package their goods "even in the shape of a vial containing a single drink."[19] Within a matter of months, Congress considered legislation to overturn the decision. The irreverent attitude in Congress is reflected in the remarks of Senator George Edmunds of Vermont, who said that the opinions of the Supreme Court regarding Congress "are of no more value to us than ours are to it. We are just as independent of the Supreme Court of the United States as it is of us, and every judge will admit it." If the Court made an error with its constitutional analysis, "are we to stop and say that is the end of the law and the mission of civilization in the United States for that reason? I take it not." The Court's word was not final. Further consideration by Justices might produce a different result: "As they have often done, it may be their mission next year to change their opinion and say that the rule ought to be the other way."[20]

Congress overturned the decision by passing legislation that made intoxicating liquors, upon their arrival in a state or territory, subject to the police powers "to the same extent and in the same manner as though such liquids or liquors had been produced in such State or Territory."[21] On the distribution of power between the national government and the states, Congress had the final word. A year later, the Court upheld this statute.[22]

Regulating Child Labor

The same dialogue between Congress and the Court, with the legislative branch having the last word, occurred with child labor legislation. In attempting to prohibit the transport of goods that had been produced by children—goods that were themselves entirely harmless—Congress was asserting a significantly new national power. Writing in 1908, soon-to-be-President Woodrow Wilson opposed child labor legislation, as did William Howard Taft, President from 1909 to 1913.[23]

By 1916, however, both the Democratic and Republican Party platforms advocated child labor legislation.[24] In that year, Congress passed a bill to prevent the products of child labor from being shipped interstate, basing the statute squarely on the national power to regulate commerce. No producer, manufacturer, or dealer could ship or deliver for shipment in interstate or foreign commerce any article produced by children within specified age ranges. The House Labor Committee concluded that "the entire problem has become an interstate problem rather than a problem of isolated States and is a problem which must be faced and solved only by a power stronger than any State."[25] Wilson, breaking ranks with his previous association with states' rights Democrats, signed the bill. His advisors warned that the vote in the November elections would be close and that "women will vote in a large number of states."[26]

Two years later, the Supreme Court, by the narrow margin of 5 to 4, struck down the statute as unconstitutional. It argued that the production and manufacture of goods were not part of commerce and could not be regulated by Congress.[27] Within a matter of days, members of Congress introduced new measures to regulate child labor, this time relying on the taxing power. An excise tax would be levied on the net profits of persons employing child labor within prohibited ages.[28] Senator Robert L. Owen was particularly combative. His bill on child labor legislation, based entirely on the Commerce Clause, contained language that was anything but subtle: "Any executive or judicial officer who in his official capacity denies the constitutionality of this act shall ipso facto vacate his office."[29] He rejected the idea that the Court had a supreme or exclusive role in interpreting the Constitution:

> It is said by some that the judges are much more learned and wiser than Congress in construing the Constitution. I can not concede this whimsical notion. They are not more learned; they are not wiser; they are not more patriotic; and what is the fatal weakness, if they make their mistakes, there is no adequate means of correcting their judicial errors, while if Congress should err the people have an immediate redress; they can change the House of Representatives almost immediately and can change two-thirds of the Senate within four years, while the judges are appointed for life and are removable only by impeachment.[30]

The child labor amendment to the tax bill passed the Senate by a healthy margin (50 to 12), was accepted by the House, and became law.[31] But a federal district court in North Carolina declared the excise tax unconstitutional. When the issue was taken to the Supreme Court, Solicitor General James M. Beck prepared a brief that defended the tax. He cautioned the Court to exercise political prudence when reviewing, and possibly overturning, the considered efforts of its coequal branches, Congress and the President. The belief that the judiciary is fully empowered to judge the motives or objectives of the other branches "is a mischievous one, in that it so lowers the sense of constitutional morality among the people that neither in the legislative branch of the Government nor among the people is there as strong a purpose as formerly to maintain their constitutional form of Government." If the Court would announce that in the field of child labor legislation there was no judicial review, and that any remedy must lie with the people, "the people will themselves protect their Constitution." The idea that the Court was "the sole guardian and protector" of the Constitution inevitably led to an impairment of what Beck called "the constitutional conscience." In his judgment, the Constitution "will last in substance as long as the people believe in it and are willing to struggle for it."[32]

This time the Court struck down the child labor tax 8 to 1. Taft, now sitting as Chief Justice, wrote for the majority, objecting that Congress had passed not a provision but a "mere penalty." Although courts are generally reluctant to speculate about legislative motives, the Court stated that it "must be blind not to see that the so-called tax is imposed to stop the employment of children within the age limits prescribed."[33]

Congress responded by passing a constitutional amendment in 1924 to give it the power to regulate child labor. However, the amendment never attracted sufficient support. By 1937, only twenty-eight of the necessary thirty-six states had ratified it. Congress returned to the Commerce Clause a year later when it included a child labor provision in the Fair Labor Standards Act of 1938.[34] Thus, Congress revived the very constitutional power that had been denied it by the Court in 1918: the commerce power. This may appear to be asking for another rebuff, but the Court of 1938 was not the Court of 1922. Because of new appointments after the court-packing fight of 1937, the Court was more receptive to the power of Congress to regulate child labor. The statute of 1938 was challenged, taken to the Court, and upheld unanimously.[35]

Over these two decades, the Court decided to return to the doctrines of Chief Justice Marshall, who had given generous support to the power of Congress to regulate commerce. Congress refused to accept the narrow judicial construction adopted by the Court in the child labor cases. Legislators persevered and won. The Court later admitted that "the history of judicial limitation of congressional power over commerce, when exercised affirmatively, had been more largely one of retreat than of ultimate victory."[36]

Packing the Court

The fight over child labor was one of many federalism battles between the Justices and elected officials. In a series of bold rulings, the Supreme Court struck down several New Deal statutes in the 1930s intended to cope with the Great Depression. For example, the Court in 1935 invalidated the National Industrial Recovery Act (NIRA), which had invoked the Commerce Clause to create industrial codes to regulate economic activities.[37] The Court held the statute unconstitutional in part because Congress had failed to provide adequate standards to guide the executive branch, but President Roosevelt knew that the question of delegating legislative power was less important than the Court's narrow definition of the Commerce Clause. He lashed out at the Court for taking the country back to the "horse-and-buggy" days.[38]

In 1936, Roosevelt won reelection by an overwhelming margin. He bided his time until early the next year, at which point he unveiled a plan to "reorganize" the federal judiciary. Claiming that the Supreme Court was unable to function effectively, he proposed that for every Justice over seventy years of age, he be empowered to appoint an additional Justice until the number of Supreme Court Justices reached fifteen. He asked for similar powers to appoint judges in the appellate and trial courts. At face value, the purpose seemed to be a desire to improve the efficiency of the courts by dealing with the problem of "aged or infirm judges."

In an address on March 9, 1937, Roosevelt was more candid. He described the national government as "a three horse team" of Congress, the President, and the courts. Two of the horses "are pulling in unison; the third is not." Roosevelt accused the Supreme Court of acting "as a policy-making body" by invalidating federal and state statutes. The problem was no longer mere inefficiency: "We must take action to save the Constitution from the Court and the Court from itself." Roosevelt promised to appoint additional Justices "who will not undertake to override the judgment of the Congress on legislative policy."

Opponents of the plan quickly marshalled their forces. On March 21, Chief Justice Hughes released a letter to Senator Burton K. Wheeler, explaining that the Court "is fully abreast of its work." By denying that the Court was overworked or in need of additional Justices, Hughes helped pull the plug on the bill by spotlighting Roosevelt's political agenda.[39] Gallup polls, moreover, revealed that most voters opposed restrictions on the Court.[40] Fearing the central planning and executive supremacy associated with the totalitarian governments of Hitler and Mussolini, voters strongly opposed a radical transformation of the balance of power among the three branches of government.

Nevertheless, the bill picked up some support. Democrats in Congress may not have liked the scheme, "but they could not justify frustrating the President while the Court persisted in mowing down legislation."[41] On "White Monday," March 29, the Court gave these Democrats a way out. Approving state and federal reform initiatives, including its reversal of a ten-month-old decision that New York's minimum wage law was unconstitutional, the Court signaled its willingness to uphold Roosevelt's New Deal initiatives.[42] Over the next few weeks, the Court signed off on both the Social Security Act and the National Labor Relations Act.[43] In the words of one of Roosevelt's close associates, "The Court, with no change of its Justices . . . convinced the Court of Public Opinion that the sentence of reorganization proposed by the court bill might safely be suspended, at least during a period of probation."[44]

On June 7, the Senate Judiciary Committee issued a report opposing the reorganization plan. Probably at no time in history has a presidential proposal been so savaged by a congressional report. The committee exposed Roosevelt's real purpose: to use force against the judiciary. Using blunt and powerful language, the committee ripped the proposal with such unsparing thoroughness that no President has repeated Roosevelt's plan. The report chastised the bill "as a needless, futile, and utterly dangerous abandonment of constitutional principles. It was presented to the Congress in a most intricate form and for reasons that obscured its real purpose."[45] Proclaiming "We are not the judges of the judges. We are not above the Constitution," the report concluded with the admonition that "it is far better that we await orderly but inevitable change of personnel than that we impatiently overwhelm them with new members."[46]

Although the Senate trashed the court-packing bill, Congress completed action on a bill to provide full pay for Supreme Court Justices who retired. The retirement bill shot through both houses and was enacted on March 1.[47] After a decent interval, Justice Van Devanter announced his retirement to take advantage of the benefits. Roosevelt nominated Senator Hugo Black for the position. On January 5, 1938, Justice Sutherland announced his intention to retire. To replace Sutherland, Roosevelt picked Solicitor General Stanley Reed. Justice Cardozo died on July 9, 1938, giving Roosevelt a third opportunity to appoint a Justice. This time he turned to a close friend, Felix Frankfurter. Justice Brandeis retired on February 13,

1939 and was replaced by William O. Douglas, who had served in the Roosevelt administration as chairman of the Securities and Exchange Commission. Justice Butler died on November 16, 1939; Frank Murphy, after filling several positions in the Roosevelt administration, including attorney general, took Butler's place.

Having gone four and a half years without a chance to name anyone to the Court, within a little over two years Roosevelt had now appointed five Justices. Later, in evaluating the court-packing episode, Roosevelt said he lost the battle but won the war. The Court read the Commerce Clause more generously to uphold presidential initiatives and congressional legislation.[48] Owen Roberts was one of the conservative Justices who rethought his position on the Commerce Clause. After retiring, he explained the force of public opinion that beat against the Court: "Looking back, it is difficult to see how the Court could have resisted the popular urge for uniform standards throughout the country—for what in effect was a unified economy."[49]

Access to Public Accommodations

Federalism was at stake in 1875 when Congress passed legislation to guarantee blacks equal access to public accommodations. With this statute, Congress attempted to impose national values on the states. Although the Civil War amendments elevated blacks to the status of citizen, in many states they were denied access to theaters, restaurants, inns, and other public facilities. Congress attempted to redress this injustice, but the Court struck down the statute in 1883. The dialogue between legislators and judges resumed almost a century later, in 1964, when Congress passed similar legislation. This time the Court unanimously upheld the congressional view of federalism.

The statute in 1875 attempted to close the gap between the Declaration of Independence and the Constitution. The preamble announced, "It is essential to just government we recognize the equality of all men before the law."[50] All persons in the United States were now entitled "to the full and equal enjoyment of the accommodations, advantages, facilities, and privileges of inns, public conveyances on land and water, theaters, and other places of public amusement." The statute did not specifically identify the part of the Constitution that empowered Congress to act. The Thirteenth Amendment, ratified in 1865, had abolished slavery. It could have been argued that any denial of equal accommodation functioned as a "badge of slavery." The Fourteenth Amendment, ratified in 1868, prohibited states from abridging the privileges or immunities of citizens, from depriving persons of life, liberty, or property without due process of law, or denying any person the equal protection of the laws. It, too, provided potential grounds for acting against states that denied equal accommodation.

The legislative debate in 1875 revealed an eloquent commitment to support basic constitutional rights that were not protected by some of the states. One of the sponsors, Congressman Benjamin Butler, forcefully rejected the claim that the bill was an attempt to impose a national standard of "social equality" among blacks and whites:

> Social equality is not effected or affected by law. It can come from the voluntary will of each person. Each man can in spite of the law, and does in spite of the law, choose his own associates.
>
> . . . There are many white men and white women whom I should prefer not to associate with who have a right to ride in the [rail] cars. That is not a question of society at all; it is a question of a common right in a public conveyance.
>
> And so in regard to places of amusement, in regard to theaters. I do not understand that a theater is a social gathering. I do not understand that men gather there for society, except the society they choose to make each for himself. So in regard to inns. Inns or taverns are for all classes of people.[51]

Butler denounced opposition to the bill as "an illogical, unjust, ungentlemanly, and foolish prejudice." The objection, he said, was not association between black and white. Whites in the Southern states enjoyed their association with blacks, provided it was on an unequal plane: "There is not a white man [in] the South that would not associate with the negro—all that is required by this bill—if that negro were his servant. He would eat with him, suckle from her, play with her or him as children, be together with them in every way, provided they were slaves. There never has been an objection to such an association. But the moment that you elevate this black man to citizenship from a slave, then immediately he becomes offensive."[52]

This statute was declared unconstitutional by the Supreme Court in the *Civil Rights Cases* (1883).[53] The Court did not find in the Thirteenth or Fourteenth Amendment adequate support for the legislation. Section 5 of the Fourteenth Amendment empowered Congress "to enforce, by appropriate legislation, the provisions of this title," but the Court decided that Congress could regulate only "state action," not actions by the private parties who operated inns and hotels, railroads and other public conveyances, theaters and other places of public amusement. The Court also denied that the exclusion of blacks from public accommodations represented a badge of slavery subject to regulation under the Thirteenth Amendment.

Having rejected the Civil War amendments as possible bases for the statute, the Court hinted that Congress might have found leverage through the Commerce Clause, especially with regard to transportation from one state to another: "And whether Congress, in the exercise of its power to regulate commerce amongst the several States, might or might not pass a law regulating rights in public conveyances passing from one State to another, is also a question which is not now before us, as the sections in question are not conceived in any such view."[54]

There the matter lay for eighty years, until 1963, when President John F. Kennedy advocated equal access for blacks to public accommodations. In recommending legislation, he cited both the Commerce Clause and the Fourteenth Amendment as constitutional authorities. American society, he said, had become more mobile and economic life increasingly interdependent: "Business establishments which serve the public—such as hotels, restaurants, theatres, stores and others—serve not only the members of their immediate communities but travelers from other States and visitors from abroad." This flow of interstate commerce underscored the responsibility to provide equal access and service to all citizens.[55]

A month later his brother, Attorney General Robert F. Kennedy, appeared before the Senate Commerce Committee to present the legal case for the public accommodations title. The legislation relied on both the Commerce Clause and the Fourteenth Amendment. Although the *Civil Rights Cases* of 1883 had rejected the latter and was still "good law," Kennedy believed that "much of the force of that decision had disappeared. State regulation of private business has increased . . . [and consequently] views of what action may be attributed to the State have changed."[56] Rather than take an unnecessary risk, the administration relied primarily on the Commerce Clause.[57]

By offering the Court two constitutional grounds, the administration hoped to avoid an unnecessary confrontation between the elected branches and the judiciary. Congress adopted the same strategy. In reporting the bill, the Senate Commerce Committee argued forcefully that the Commerce Clause provided sufficient constitutional authority for the statute.[58] While some senators favored the Fourteenth Amendment because "the integrity and dignity of the individual should not be placed on lesser grounds such as the commerce clause,"[59] the Senate committee followed the constitutionally safer course and relied on the clause. The House Judiciary Committee justified the public accommodations provision on both "state action" (Fourteenth Amendment) and the commerce power.[60] In two unanimous opinions, the Supreme Court relied on the commerce power to uphold the public accommodations title.[61]

Twice over a century Congress considered legislation to give blacks equal access to public accommodations. In the end, the political branches—not the courts—served as the guardians of minority rights and constitutional liberties. The persistence and ingenuity of Congress and the President prevailed over judicial obstacles. The creative work of imparting meaning to federalism lay with legislators and executive officials, driven by public pressures.

Floating/Puncturing a Judicial Doctrine

In 1976, the Supreme Court announced a novel theory of federalism. Divided 5–4, it struck down a congressional statute that extended federal wage-and-hour provisions to almost all state employees. The Court reached its decision by distinguishing between "traditional" and "nontraditional" governmental functions, but few judges in the lower courts had any success in applying this doctrine. Nine years later, split again 5–4, the Court abandoned its theory of federalism. The protection of states, it said, would depend largely on the political process operating within Congress.

The 1976 case concerned the impact of federal minimum wage standards on the states. The Fair Labor Standards Act of 1938 had expressly exempted states and their political divisions from federal minimum wage and overtime provisions. In 1966, Congress extended federal minimum wages and overtime pay to state-operated hospitals and schools. Two years later, the Court agreed that Congress had a rational basis for the legislation, pointing to the effect on interstate competition and the avoidance of labor disputes and strikes.[62]

In the same year as the Court's decision, President Nixon's election moved federalism front and center. A nationwide address on August 8, 1969, announced the basic tenets of a "New Federalism in which power, funds, and responsibility will flow from Washington to the States and to the people."[63] When Congress in 1973 passed legislation extending minimum wage and maximum hour provisions to cover almost all employees of states and their political subdivisions, Nixon vetoed the bill, calling it "an unwarranted interference with State prerogatives."[64] Congress passed new legislation the following year, reaching a compromise with Nixon by stretching out the minimum wage increases but still applying them to state and local government. Nixon signed this bill.[65] Meanwhile, he hoped his appointments to the Supreme Court—Warren Burger, Harry A. Blackmun, Lewis F. Powell Jr., and William H. Rehnquist—would make it more supportive of states' rights.

The National League of Cities brought an action to declare the 1974 amendments unconstitutional. The case was argued twice before the Supreme Court. During the second argument, an exchange between Solicitor General Robert H. Bork and Justice Powell raised questions about the constitutionality of the 1974 amendments. If the Court upheld that statute, Powell wondered what limits would remain on the commerce power:

> I am concerned with whether or not, if we decide this case in favor of the Government, there will indeed be any limitation as to how far the Federal Government can go in regulating the affairs of the state and localities themselves. Give me the power of purse, give me the power to decide what you are paying—I control you. I think that is inevitable. . . . I am thinking about the long-time doctrine of Federalism that seems to me to be on the verge of being destroyed by vesting in the Federal Government, the power to put floors under and ceilings over the wages of Federal and State employees.[66]

Powell's concern flavored the Court's decision, which struck down the 1974 amendments because they "directly displace the States' freedom to structure integral operations in areas of traditional governmental functions."[67] The Court's effort to draw a line between traditional and nontraditional governmental functions proved to be illusory, with judges unable to apply the Court's doctrine either with confidence or consistency. District and appellate courts would find a function to be "traditional," and thus within the area of state sovereignty, but the Supreme Court would reverse by calling the function nontraditional and outside the protection of the 1976 ruling.[68] By 1983, some Court watchers decided that little life remained in the 1976 doctrine. Linda Greenhouse of the *New York Times* wrote about the dynamic process of constitutional law: "If there is a lesson here, it is not one to comfort those who cherish the illusion of the Constitution as revealed truth. For it reveals constitutional adjudication as a fitful, fragile, human process."[69]

One of the curious features of the 1976 decision is that when the Supreme Court remanded the case to a three-judge district court, instead of the district court's determining the difference between traditional and nontraditional functions, it said to the Department of Labor: You figure it out. In December 1979, Labor identified the nontraditional governmental functions that would be subject to federal minimum wage and overtime provisions. It also listed traditional functions; in addition to those mentioned by the Court in 1976, Labor could think of only two others: libraries and museums.[70]

Labor's list of nontraditional functions included local mass transit systems. William T. Coleman Jr., representing the interests of the American Public Transit Association, wrote to Secretary of Transportation Neil Goldschmidt, protesting Labor's interpretation of mass transit.[71] Goldschmidt requested a meeting of high-level representatives of the Departments of Justice, Labor, and Transportation and the White House to discuss the government's posture in the case.[72] Just as the courts were divided on the distinction between traditional and nontraditional functions, so was the executive branch.

Lawyers in the White House wanted to rethink Labor's analysis. The OLC in the Justice Department also examined the issue, agreeing with Labor that mass transit was not a traditional governmental function.[73] Having lost the internal debate, the Transportation Department participated in a "working group" with Labor to minimize the economic costs for local mass transit authorities.

The dispute was now on its way to the Supreme Court. The San Antonio Metropolitan Transit Authority (SAMTA) filed an action in district court, objecting to Labor's characterization of local mass transit as nontraditional. On the same day, several SAMTA employees brought suit against the transit authority for overtime pay under the Fair Labor Standards Act. In 1983, the district court concluded that municipal ownership and operation of a mass transit system was a traditional governmental function and thus exempt from the Fair Labor Standards Act. Three federal appellate courts and one state appellate court reached the opposite conclusion: that transit systems in the past had been owned and operated by private businesses; states became involved in mass transit only because of funding received from the federal government.[74]

With confusion swirling in the lower courts, the Supreme Court held two oral arguments in 1984. It specifically asked the parties whether the 1976 ruling should be reconsidered and possibly overturned. Legal advisors in the Reagan administration were torn. On the one hand, the administration was committed strongly to federalism and the general philosophy of the Court's ruling in 1976. President Reagan, for example, instructed his Cabinet that "uncertainties regarding the legitimate authority of the national government should be resolved against regulation at the national level," and ultimately reinforced that instruction with an executive order on federalism.[75] At the same time, administration officials did not disagree with Labor's conclusion.

During the second oral argument, the Court indicated that it was prepared to overturn its 1976 ruling and shift to Congress the basic responsibility for monitoring and defending federalism.[76] The 1976 ruling was overruled in 1985, when Justice Blackmun switched sides. Although initially voting in conference to reaffirm, he reversed course because he "ha[d] been able to find no principled way in which to affirm."[77] Writing for a 5–4 majority, Blackmun said that the essential safeguard for federalism was not the judiciary but the political dynamics operating within Congress.

Blackmun's decision threatened the states with massive costs. Most state employees were already receiving at least the minimum wage, but the financial burden of meeting the overtime provisions of the Fair Labor Standards Act could have soared to several billion dollars. To protect the states, Congress passed legislation to postpone the effective date of Blackmun's decision (decided February 19, 1985) to April 15, 1986. It also permitted the use of compensatory time as a substitute for paying overtime.[78] Legislative action emphasizes the role of Congress in making constitutional interpretations about federalism and the Commerce Clause. Senator Howard Metzenbaum claimed that the bill "vindicates the Supreme Court's faith . . . that the proper protection for the sovereign interests of States and their political subdivisions lies not in directives issued by the Federal Judiciary but rather the give-and-take of our federal system—especially the role of the States and cities in the political process."[79]

The nationwide debate from 1976 to 1985—in the courts, Congress, and the executive branch—illustrates the broad forces that interact to shape the meaning of federalism. The Court's effort in 1976 to establish a new legal doctrine to strengthen states' rights proved to be unworkable, leading to the eventual overruling in 1985. In so doing, the Court returned to Congress the principal responsibility for defining federalism.

The Court Strikes Back

The Court's decision in 1985 did not remove the judiciary as an arbiter of federal-state conflicts. In selected areas, the Court continues to monitor the boundaries between national and state power, while Congress and the executive branch press their own independent interpretations of federalism.

In 1991, the Court reviewed a provision in Missouri's constitution that requires most state judges to retire at age seventy. It held that this provision did not violate the federal Age Discrimination and Employment Act

(ADEA). The Court reasoned that Missouri, as an independent state, has a range of action that is protected by the Tenth Amendment and the Guarantee Clause of Article IV, Section 4.[80] Despite references to the Tenth Amendment, the Guarantee Clause, and state independence, the decision recognized that Congress could reenter the dispute and have the last word.

The Court was more assertive a year later when it rejected, 6 to 3, Congress's demand that states come up with a way to dispose of low-level radioactive waste by 1996 or be forced to become the owners of it. Concluding that this policy "would 'commandeer' state governments into the service of federal regulatory purposes," the Court invalidated the legislation on Tenth Amendment grounds.[81] By 1992, the composition of the Court had changed dramatically. Four of the six members of the majority were appointed by Presidents Reagan and Bush I after the 1985 ruling: Antonin Scalia, Anthony Kennedy, David Souter, and Clarence Thomas. Along with Sandra Day O'Connor (an earlier Reagan appointee) and William Rehnquist (elevated to Chief Justice by Reagan), the new Justices were less inclined to defer to Congress and the political process.

In many ways, the law on radioactive waste seemed a model of federal-state cooperation. Rather than ram a national policy down the throats of the states, Congress encouraged the states to discover a solution. The bill had been drafted by the National Governors' Association to find a nationwide remedy for the problem of low-level radioactive waste storage. In defending the statute's constitutionality, Solicitor General Kenneth Starr argued, "In light of the origin of the problem as a dispute among the States, the requests of the States for a state-oriented solution and the assiduous care Congress displayed in attending to the interests and concerns of the several States, the Act is a constitutionally permissible example of cooperative federalism designed to preserve, rather than pre-empt, state authority."[82] In dismissing these arguments, the Court returned the issue to Congress. The decision had little impact on public policy. Instead of trying to draft another statute to correct problems identified by the Court, Congress merely relied on the existing compacts that states had formed to dispose of radioactive waste.

In a closely watched decision in 1995, the Court in *United States v. Lopez* struck down a congressional statute that banned guns within 1,000 feet of a school. Divided 5 to 4, the Court ruled that Congress had exceeded its authority under the Commerce Clause and specifically rejected the Clinton administration's claim that Congress had "ample basis . . . to conclude that disruption of the educational process would have substantial deleterious effects on the national economy."[83] The Court held that the statute had nothing to do with commerce or any sort of economic enterprise.[84] To the Court, Congress had intruded into two areas traditionally associated with state and local control: schools and crime.

Some commentators treated the decision as one of the most important rulings in recent decades because it limited the power of Congress under the commerce power. However, it may have been a case where Congress simply failed to present adequate findings to show an interstate commerce link with guns on school playgrounds. Within two months of the decision, a Senate subcommittee held a hearing on the federal role of guns in schools. Legislation was introduced to make the requisite findings. The sponsor of this bill, Senator Herbert Kohl, testified, "Almost every gun is made from raw material from one State, assembled in a second State, and transported to the schoolyards of yet another State. . . . One 14-year-old Madison, WI, gang member told the Wisconsin State Journal that the older leaders of his gang brought carloads of guns from Chicago to the younger gang members." Walter Dellinger, head of OLC, testified to the same point.[85]

On the basis of this hearing, Congress passed new legislation in 1996, finding that crime at the local level "is exacerbated by the interstate movement of drugs, guns, and criminal gangs," that the occurrence of violent crime in school zones has resulted in a decline in the quality of education, and that it has the power under the Interstate Commerce Clause to enact the legislation. Furthermore, to protect the bill from constitutional attack, Congress invoked its power to regulate articles of commerce that have moved across state lines. The statutory language provides that "it shall be unlawful for any individual knowingly to possess a firearm that has moved in or that otherwise affects interstate or foreign commerce at a place that the individual knows, or has reasonable cause to believe, is a school zone."[86] There has been no litigation to challenge this statutory language. Unless there is, the last word on this policy belongs to Congress.

In another 5–4 ruling, the Court in 1997 applied its understanding of federalism to strike down a key portion of the 1993 Brady gun control law. That statute required state and local law enforcement officers to conduct background checks on prospective handgun purchasers. Relying heavily on its 1992 decision on radioactive waste, the Court held that state legislatures "are *not* subject to federal direction."[87] Citing the Tenth Amendment as ground for invalidating the statutory provision, the Court ruled that Congress may not "command" state officers to administer a federal regulatory program.[88] The Court's decision did not have a substantial effect on governmental policy. Most states already require background checks, and beginning on November 30, 1998, gun dealers were required to check the names of prospective buyers against a computerized list of offenders prepared by the FBI.

Another blow to congressional power came in 2000, when the Court held that a provision in the Violence Against Women Act (VAWA) of 1994 could not be sustained under the Commerce Clause or Section 5 of the Fourteenth Amendment.[89] The provision permitted victims of rape, domestic violence, and other crimes "motivated by gender" to sue their attackers in federal court. Unlike the Guns in the Schoolyard Act, Congress had amassed findings and compiled a record to demonstrate that domestic violence and sexual assault cost the economy $5 to $10 billion a year. Split along political lines, the majority consisted of the conservative-moderate wing (Rehnquist, O'Connor, Kennedy, Scalia, and Thomas), and the dissents came from the moderate-liberals (Stevens, Souter, Ginsberg, and Breyer).

The VAWA decision had limited reach. All states have laws prohibiting violence against women. The decision, though certainly limiting Congress, does not foreclose Congress from making use of different sources of federal power to regulate violence against women. In another 2000 ruling, the Court, in a rare unanimous decision involving federalism, upheld a congressional statute (the Driver's Privacy Protection Act of 1994) that prohibited states from disclosing the personal information that drivers provide when obtaining a license.[90] As a result of the legislation, states may not sell addresses, telephone numbers, and other information included in the license application.

The fact remains, however, that Congress can no longer expect the Court to support efforts to expand federal power. In addition to its narrowing constructions of the Commerce Clause and the Tenth Amendment, the Rehnquist Court has also breathed new life into the state sovereignty protections of the Eleventh Amendment and has limited the reach of Congress's powers to regulate the states under Section 5 of the Fourteenth Amendment. For example, through a trio of 5–4 decisions in 1999, the Court held that legislation enacted pursuant to the Fourteenth Amendment could not override state sovereign immunity under the Eleventh Amendment.[91] Moreover, by limiting Congress's Section 5 powers to the remedying of pervasive discrimination by the states, the Court struck down parts of the Religious Freedom Restoration Act (1997), the ADEA (2000), and the Americans with Disabilities Act (2000).[92]

Federalism was very much at stake in 2000, when the Court reversed the Supreme Court of Florida's order for a manual recount to decide the presidential election. Although critics accused the majority of inconsistently championing states' rights in most matters but not in this one, the Court was faced with interpreting national law as expressed in Article II, Section 1, Clause 2 of the Constitution and Title 3, Section 5 of the U.S. Code. Chief Justice Rehnquist and Justices Scalia and Thomas noted in their concurrence that the Court's "inquiry does not imply a disrespect for state *courts* but rather a respect for the constitutionally prescribed role of state *legislatures*."[93]

Writing for the *New York Times,* Linda Greenhouse remarked that "the fault line that runs through the current Court as an all but unbridgeable gulf has to do not with the higher-profile issues of race, religion, abortion or due process, but with federalism."[94] With the election of George W. Bush, that fault line may widen. By appointing Justices who value states' rights arguments, Bush appointees will likely strengthen the resolve of the Rehnquist Court. In other words, the pace and scope of Rehnquist Court decisions striking down federal statutes (thirty-one from 1995 to 2003) may well increase over the next several years.

Contract with America

The Rehnquist Court's increasing willingness to limit congressional power came on the heels of the 1994 elections and the Republican "Contract with America," which pledged a smaller federal government and a larger role for the states. The Republican victory in the elections gave them control of both houses of Congress, converting the "Contract" into a blueprint for legislative action. The Republicans proposed far-reaching legislation in 1995 to shift power and duties to the states, including proposals for welfare, medical care, and economic regulation. Riding the crest of this renewed commitment to federalism, Reagan and Bush I appointees found it easier to validate states' rights claims.

The "Contract" was fueled by widespread populist disapproval of Congress. Opinion polls revealed that Americans thought that the federal government was not trustworthy, that members of Congress cared more about making themselves look good than making the country better, and that people elected to Congress quickly lost touch with the people.[95] Responding to these populist signals, the "Contract" guaranteed "the first ever vote on a constitutional amendment" to establish term limits for members of Congress. Republicans wanted to eliminate the "lifetime job" for members and convert Congress into a "citizen legislature." Clearly, the purpose was to punish the national legislature for being "out of touch" with Middle America and to return political power to states and localities. In 1995, however, the U.S. House of Representatives turned down several proposed constitutional amendments to limit representatives and senators to a certain number of terms.[96]

The "Contract" also promised to do away with the practice of the federal government's imposing expensive mandates on the states without providing federal funds. Legislation was enacted into law on March 22, 1995, but it did not terminate unfunded mandates. Many of the mandates concerning civil rights, the disabled, and other categories were specifically exempted. For the mandates that are covered, the statute merely requires the Congressional Budget Office (CBO) to flag any bill that creates an unfunded mandate on the states of $50 million or higher. On the basis of these CBO estimates any member of Congress may make a point of order, but the point of order can be overridden by simple majority vote. Although the legislation may make Congress more sensitive and responsive to the issue of unfunded mandates, previous mandates can continue and new ones can be added.

By the 1996 elections, much of the "Contract with America" had fizzled in the face of Senate skepticism and Clinton veto threats. At the same time, Democrats and Republicans alike increasingly embraced the call to downsize government. In 1998, Congress pressured the Clinton administration to strengthen state prerogatives in an executive order on federalism.[97] In 1999, legislation (H.R. 2245) was introduced to require Congress and executive officials to follow new procedures when the federal government intends to preempt state powers. Federalism impact assessments would be necessary. The bill went nowhere because some powerful interest groups, like the U.S. Chamber of Commerce, argued that one-size-fits-all national laws are less costly for businesses. Similarly, many labor and environmental groups would rather work through a single Congress than fifty states.[98]

The Court's willingness to impose its view of federalism over that of Congress may have something to do with how individual Justices regard the work of Congress on constitutional matters. In a speech on April 18, 2000, Justice Scalia said that Congress "is increasingly abdicating its independent responsibility to be sure that it is being faithful to the Constitution." Whereas the Court in the past had routinely presumed the constitutionality of congressional legislation, Scalia warned that "if Congress is going to take the attitude that it will do anything it can get away with and let the Supreme Court worry about the Constitution . . . then perhaps that presumption is unwarranted."[99] Obviously, Scalia's statement does not adequately explain the series of judicial rebuffs to Congress on federalism issues, because there are usually four Justices who want to uphold the challenged statute. But if Congress is developing the reputation of being inattentive to constitutional limits and careless in drafting legislation, there is added incentive for the judiciary to flex its muscles.

Congress has encouraged the Court in other ways. In the wake of recent rulings limiting congressional power, there has been no talk of stripping the Court of jurisdiction, of amending the Constitution, or of enacting legislation at odds with these decisions. The precedential effects of Court decisions limiting federal power are hardly ever mentioned in the *Congressional Record*. With the exception of Court rulings invalidating the VAWA and the Religious Freedom Restoration Act, there are few comments about the wisdom of any of the Court's federalism-related decisions.[100] Furthermore, Congress has shown relatively little interest in rewriting these statutes. When Congress does revisit its handiwork, lawmakers pay close attention to the Supreme Court's rulings, limiting their efforts to revisions the Court is likely to approve.[101] The seeming disinterest of the contemporary Congress to preserve its power as a coequal interpreter of the Constitution emboldens the Court to see itself as the ultimate arbiter of constitutional truth.

Conclusions

Federalism has changed over the past two centuries because of profound structural changes in the U.S. economy. Areas in which state and local government were once virtually supreme—including agriculture, mining, manufacturing, and labor—eventually gave way to federal controls when transportation systems and economic markets assumed a national character. Over time, much of intrastate commerce became interstate commerce. The federal taxing power, magnified by the Sixteenth Amendment and the income tax, ushered in hundreds of federal grant programs. More than 20 percent of the budgets of state and local governments comes from federal funds.

Issues long identified with local government (education, health, welfare, and law enforcement) are now largely a matter of federal-state cooperation. On questions of civil rights and social justice, moreover, Congress has persevered in the face of both state and Supreme Court resistance. Following the Supreme Court's rejection of child labor and public accommodations legislation, for example, Congress eventually prevailed. More recently, Congress has begun responding to Rehnquist Court decisions limiting, among other things, federal efforts to expand religious liberty protections and to sanction violence against women.

Litigation, although helping to define federal-state relations, operates largely at the margins. Over time, court doctrines designed to restrict congressional control over the states have failed because they have been vague, unworkable, or washed away by economic and political developments. The Court continues to be an important player, but does not dominate federal-state relations.

4

Separation of Powers

The framers adopted a system of separated powers to avoid the kind of centralized authority that threatens individual liberty. By separating power among three branches, they hoped that checks and balances would restrain political abuse and preserve republican government. The great bulk of separation of power controversies are handled by the elected branches, not the courts.

Nevertheless, law reviews carry hundreds of articles that examine with microscopic precision judicial rulings on separation of powers. The net result is a mixture of inconsistent and incoherent theories, ranging from pragmatic solutions to purist formulations. How does the federal government function in the face of this doctrinal confusion? The short answer is that government does fairly well because most of the principal disputes involving separation of powers are resolved outside the courts. The great majority of these collisions never reach the courts or, if they do, are quickly pushed back to the executive and legislative branches for nonjudicial remedies. Complex and delicate arrangements are fashioned regularly outside the courtroom, forcing legislators and executive officials to discover midground solutions that satisfy the needs of both institutions.

Inconsistent Judicial Rulings

Under the best of conditions, the Supreme Court offers limited help in resolving basic disputes over separation of powers. There are simply too many conflicts over issues that are not easily addressed in court. Moreover, during recent decades, the Court has slipped back and forth in its search for principles, sometimes embracing a functional and pragmatic approach and switching later to a strict, formalistic model. With this confusion, the executive and legislative branches operate under unusual pressure to fend for themselves.

The functional approach appears in the Supreme Court's decision in 1974 rejecting President Nixon's claim of an absolute power to withhold the Watergate tapes and to dictate the limits of executive privilege. Instead, the Court emphasized checks and balances and the need for a "workable government."[1] The President's generalized need for executive privilege could not trump the particularized need of federal courts for evidence. Separation of powers entered the Court's equation only in the sense of preserving "the essential functions of each branch."[2] There was no effort to establish rigid boundaries and disallow the slightest intrusion.[3]

Three years later, in a case involving Nixon's papers in the National Archives, the Court again viewed separation of powers in practical terms. It denied that the three branches of government must remain "entirely free from the control or coercive influence, direct or indirect, of either of the others"[4] and endorsed the "more pragmatic, flexible approach" of James Madison and Justice Story.[5] This approach permitted some sharing and overlapping of power.

Within a few years, however, the Court began to advance a strict notion of separate powers. In 1982, it upheld an absolute immunity for the President in civil cases, expressing concern about the "dangers of intrusion on the authority and functions of the Executive Branch."[6] A highly formalistic model of separate powers continued with *INS v. Chadha* (1983), which invalidated the legislative veto. The Court dismissed as irrelevant the usefulness of this instrument for settling executive-legislative disagreements: "Convenience and efficiency are not the primary objectives—or the hallmarks—of democratic government."[7] The Court insisted that the Constitution divided government into "three defined categories, Legislative, Executive, and Judicial," and that it was a duty of the Court to resist the "hydraulic pressures inherent within each of the separate Branches to exceed the outer limits of its power."[8] As explained later in this chapter, *Chadha* did not settle the legislative veto dispute.

The Court persisted with doctrinaire formulations in the Gramm-Rudman case, *Bowsher v. Synar* (1986), which involved an effort by Congress to deal with escalating budget deficits. The Court rejected the statutory assignment of executive duties to the comptroller general because he is subject to removal by a joint resolution of Congress. In reaching that judgment, the Court claimed that the framers provided for "a separate and wholly independent Executive Branch."[9] "Subject only to impeachment proceedings," the Court argued, the President was responsible not to the Congress but to the people, and "once Congress makes its choice in enacting legislation, its participation ends. Congress can thereafter control the execution of its enactment only indirectly—by passing new legislation."[10] No one reading newspapers for a week (in 1986 or now) could believe that. The Court itself has acknowledged the power of Congress to investigate the executive branch, issue subpoenas, and hold executive officials in contempt.[11]

A few years later, the Court jettisoned the rigid doctrines of *Chadha* and *Bowsher*. In 1988, it upheld the power of Congress to authorize federal judges to appoint an independent counsel to prosecute high-ranking officials in the executive branch. Although the attorney general could remove the independent counsel only for "good cause," the Court concluded that the good cause standard did not "unduly trammel" executive authority.[12] The President's need to control the independent counsel was not "so central to the functioning of the Executive Branch" as to require that the independent counsel serve at the pleasure of the President.[13] The Court now stated that "we have never held that the Constitution requires that the three Branches of Government 'operate with absolute independence.'"[14]

A year later, the Court again embraced a pragmatic, functional attitude when it upheld the U.S. Sentencing Commission. This agency was challenged on a number of separation of powers grounds: judges sitting on the Commission exercised nonjudicial functions, and the Commission could "make law" unless their recommendations were disapproved by Congress. In rejecting these charges, the Court noted that "the Framers did not require—and indeed rejected—the notion that the three Branches must be entirely separate and distinct."[15] The Court explicitly adopted a "flexible understanding of separation of powers."[16]

It should not be surprising that in the midst of these conflicting rulings the executive and legislative branches would be put on notice to figure out separation of powers disputes by themselves. And so they have.

Jurisdictional Barriers: Covert Spending

Federal courts use a number of doctrines to sidestep separation of powers disputes. Through such threshold tests as standing, courts play virtually no role in defining the allocation of power between Congress and the President on such issues as the Statement and Account Clause, impeachment, and the Incompatibility and Ineligibility Clauses.

The Statement and Account Clause provides that a "regular Statement and Account of the Receipts and Expenditures of all public Money shall be published from time to time."[17] The phrase "from time to time" suggests that the framers allowed for some secrecy—not total secrecy to keep the public forever in the dark, but limited secrecy. Beginning with the Central Intelligence Act of 1949, however, Congress has chosen to rely on secret spending without ever giving an accounting to the public. By 2003, Congress used covert methods to provide the Central Intelligence Agency, the National Security Agency, and other parts of the intelligence establishment with approximately $40 billion a year. The money is hidden in appropriations accounts and no public accounting is made.

This practice conflicts with the intention of the framers. In 1788, Robert Livingston told his colleagues at the New York ratifying convention that the Statement and Account Clause operated as a check against popular corruption: "Congress are to publish, from time to time, an account of their receipts and expenditures. These may be compared together; and if the former, year after year, exceed the latter, the corruption may be detected, and the people may use the constitutional mode of redress."[18] James McHenry, a member of the Constitutional Convention, advised the Maryland House of Delegates in 1787 that "the People who give their Money ought to know in what manner it is expended."[19] In his *Commentaries*, Joseph Story emphasized that Congress "is made the guardian of this treasure; and to make their responsibility complete and perfect, a regular account of the receipts and expenditures is required to be published, that the people may know, what money is expended, for what purpose, and by what authority."[20]

Since these statements were made, however, federal judges have made it clear that the meaning of the Statement and Account Clause is to be left to elected officials, not to the courts. In 1974, a federal taxpayer's effort to have the CIA budget disclosed failed before the Supreme Court. Without disputing the lower court's assertion that the framers "deemed fiscal information essential if the electorate was to exercise any control over its representatives and meet their new responsibilities as citizens of the Republic,"[21] the Supreme Court ruled that the taxpayer lacked standing to sue.[22] In a dissent, Justice Douglas expressed surprise that the Court would refuse to adjudicate the case and toss it back to the political branches: "Congress of course has discretion; but to say that it has the power to read the clause out of the Constitution when it comes to one or two or three agencies is astounding."[23]

Another private citizen, attempting through the Freedom of Information Act (FOIA) to gain access to CIA documents detailing legal bills and fee arrangements of private attorneys retained by the Agency, was unsuccessful when a federal appellate court decided in 1980 that the CIA documents were exempt from disclosure under FOIA. When the plaintiff tried to argue that the FOIA exemption violated the Statement and Account Clause, the court ruled that the plaintiff lacked standing to raise this constitutional challenge against secret appropriations and expenditures for the CIA.[24]

Thus, the meaning of the Statement and Account Clause depends on Congress and executive officials to flesh out this particular part of the Constitution. In the 1974 case, the Court said that this subject matter "is committed to the surveillance of Congress, and ultimately to the political process."[25] In a case brought by a member of Congress, a federal appellate court noted that the Statement and Account Clause "is not self-defining and Congress has plenary power to give meaning to the provision."[26]

In 1997, under pressure of a lawsuit, the CIA released a figure of $26.6 billion for the budget of the intelligence community. Of that amount, the CIA portion was about $3 billion. In 1998, the CIA voluntarily released a figure of $26.7 billion for the community's budget, but in 1999 it again refused to disclose the aggregate budget and it has remained secret since that time. A lawsuit to obtain the budget total by invoking the FOIA was dismissed in 1999.[27] Litigation efforts continue, and Congress remains under political pressure to release the budget of the intelligence community.

Impeachment

The Constitution provides that the President, Vice President, and all civil officers of the United States shall be removed from office upon "Impeachment for, and Conviction of, Treason, Bribery, or other high Crimes and Misdemeanors." The House impeaches by a majority vote; a two-thirds vote of the Senate is needed for conviction. Other than making the Chief Justice the presiding officer in the Senate after a President has been impeached, the framers excluded the judiciary and the courts have not tried to carve out a role. In 1993, the Supreme Court turned aside a challenge to the impeachment of federal judge Walter Nixon, dismissing the case as a nonjusticiable political question.[28]

Legislators decide many key issues, such as the burden of proof. Should it be clear and convincing evidence? Preponderance of the evidence? Beyond a reasonable doubt? Lawmakers are at liberty to select whatever test they are comfortable with. The two chambers, moreover, determine crucial procedural issues, including the right of the accused to confront and cross-examine witnesses and the opportunity of house managers to call witnesses. Legislators make judgments to accept or exclude evidence and determine issues of relevance and materiality, while senators decide whether deliberations at the end of the trial should be open or closed.

What are the grounds for impeachment? Treason is defined in Article III, Section 3, of the Constitution, and bribery is generally understood to mean the giving, offering, or taking of rewards as payment for favors. However, there is continuing disagreement about the meaning of "other high Crimes and Misdemeanors." Does the word "crimes" apply only to actions indictable in the courts (statutory offenses), or did the framers have in mind something broader, covering abuse of office and "political crimes" against government and society? "Other" suggests that high crimes and misdemeanors are of the same order as treason and bribery, but precisely what this clause means is left to the individual interpretations of lawmakers, not courts.

During the impeachment of President Richard Nixon, House Judiciary Committee staff, including future first lady Hillary Rodham, concluded that impeachment "is a constitutional remedy addressed to serious offenses against the system of government," and, consequently, criminality is not essential to impeach and remove a federal official.[29] Likewise, members of Congress may conclude that a federal official, although guilty of a crime, ought not to be removed from office. During the vote on the removal of President Bill Clinton, for example, several senators announced that he was guilty as charged (of perjury and obstruction of justice) but that the nature of the offenses did not justify removal.[30]

The Clinton impeachment is instructive for other reasons. Throughout the process, several members hinged their votes on matters having nothing to do with the specific allegations made against the President. Democrats, for example, attacked Independent Counsel Kenneth Starr for "twist-[ing] and warp[ing] his task from . . . find[ing] the truth to . . . get[ting] the President."[31] Democrats spoke about the wrongness of "overturn[ing] the results of a national election" and the need to "listen to the people of America. They do not believe impeachment is a proper remedy for President Clinton's misbehavior."[32]

What, then, of a congressional resolution of censure as a substitute for impeachment and removal? Although Congress is authorized by the Constitution to censure its members for "disorderly behavior," the act of censuring officials outside the legislative branch raises serious questions of separation of powers.

Some guidance on this issue comes from the Senate's adoption of a resolution in 1834 censuring President Andrew Jackson for assuming "authority and power not conferred by the Constitution, but in derogation of both." This resolution responded to Jackson's decision to remove a secretary of the treasury for refusing to transfer the government's deposits from the central U.S. Bank to state banks. Jackson, outraged by the censure resolution, complained that "without notice, unheard and untried, I thus find myself charged on the records of the Senate, and in a form hitherto unknown in our history, with the high crime of violating the laws and Constitution of my country."[33] Jackson argued that if Congress wanted to charge him with constitutional violations, it had to act through the impeachment process. Three years later, the Senate ordered the censure resolution expunged from its record.

In December 1998, during the impeachment debate on Clinton, the House prevented a vote on a censure resolution offered by Democrats. Echoing Jackson's claims, Speaker-elect Bob Livingston said that censure "is out of the realm of responsibility of the House of Representatives. We have a constitutional responsibility to charge or not charge, impeach or not impeach."[34] Efforts on the Senate side to adopt a censure resolution also failed.

With the rejection of these resolutions, censure no longer appears a viable substitute for impeachment. Although there is no consensus governing what constitutes a "high crime and misdemeanor," lawmakers understand that they cannot seek cover in a judicial opinion. Instead, legislators must decide for themselves the degree to which partisan and political factors should define the procedures and standards governing the impeachment and removal of federal officials.

Incompatibility and Ineligibility Clauses

Although the framers did not intend a pure separation of powers, they added to the Constitution two provisions designed to keep the executive and legislative branches at a certain distance. The Constitution prohibits members of either house from holding any other civil office (the Incompatibility Clause) and prohibits members of Congress from being appointed to any federal position whose salary has been increased during their term of office (the Ineligibility Clause).[35] Judicial reliance on jurisdictional barriers has ensured that the meaning of those two clauses has been developed almost entirely by the executive and legislative branches.

The framers included the Incompatibility and Ineligibility Clauses to prevent the executive from using the appointment power to corrupt legislators.[36] The English Crown had used appointments to undermine the independence of Parliament.[37] The Incompatibility Clause has existed for two centuries without any definition or application by federal courts. When the clause reached a district court in 1971, in a case involving the right of members of Congress to hold a commission in the armed forces reserves, the judge remarked that the "meaning and effect of this constitutional provision have never before been determined by a court."[38]

Three years later, the Supreme Court held that the plaintiffs lacked standing to bring their case.[39] In response to the objection that if courts fail to resolve the issue of the Incompatibility Clause, as a practical matter no one can, the Court replied, "Our system of government leaves many crucial decisions to the political processes."[40] In 1977, when the Justice Department examined the issue of whether members of Congress may hold commissions as officers in the armed forces reserves, it concluded that the "exclusive responsibility for interpreting and enforcing the Incompatibility Clause rests with Congress."[41]

As to the Ineligibility Clause, interpretations by Congress and the executive branch have far outweighed contributions from the courts. Opinions by attorneys general from 1882 to 1895 held that members of Congress were ineligible under the Constitution to accept appointment to an executive position.[42] Later, however, the executive branch reached a settlement with Congress to nominate a member of Congress who was ineligible under a literal reading of the Constitution. In 1909, President William Howard Taft wanted Senator Philander Knox to serve as secretary of state, even though the salary of that office had been increased during Knox's term. As a way of removing part of the constitutional problem, the Senate passed legislation to reduce the compensation of the secretary of state to the previous level.[43] That did not satisfy the express language of the Ineligibility Clause, but it appeared to take away the appearance of gain and corruption.

Although the bill passed the Senate without debate and without a recorded vote, substantial opposition developed in the House. Congressman James B. (Champ) Clark, who would serve as speaker from 1911 to 1919, strongly objected to the nomination: "We all know that this bill is an attempt to make a man eligible as Secretary of State who is ineligible under the Constitution of the United States. [Applause.] This bill is simply an effort to override the Constitution by statute. . . . It is a question of the construction of the Constitution. It is a question of understanding plain English."[44]

Congressmen Oscar W. Gillespie and Edwin Y. Yates agreed, insisting that the provisions of the Constitution in question "are plain, they are emphatic, they are unequivocal," and that "it is clear to even a layman as to what the clause in the Constitution says and means." Nevertheless, the House passed the bill by the vote of 173 to 116, largely on the ground that the President had a right to select who he wants for the Cabinet and that the bill satisfied the spirit of the Ineligibility Clause.[45] The bill, providing for the repeal of the increase in salary for the secretary of state, was enacted. [46]

The Ineligibility Clause has been cited to challenge the appointment of some judges. Senator Hugo Black was nominated to the Supreme Court in 1937, although a retirement system for the judiciary had been enacted that year while Black served in the Senate. In response to a case raising the constitutional issue, the Court held that the plaintiff lacked standing to bring the suit.[47] More recently, the nomination of Congressman Abner Mikva to the D.C. Circuit was challenged on the ground that the salaries of federal judges had been increased during his term in Congress. Once again, the suit was tossed out because of lack of standing.[48] A district court said that Mikva's opponents had an opportunity to defeat the nomination; senators on the losing side could not then ask the judiciary to reverse the Senate's action.[49] The Justice Department concluded that Mikva's appointment to the D.C. Circuit was not barred by the Ineligibility Clause, reasoning that the scheduled salary increase had not taken effect at the time of Mikva's nomination, and that if it had, a bill could be enacted providing for the repeal of the increase.[50]

A similar situation developed in 1973, when President Nixon wanted to nominate Senator William Saxbe to be attorney general, even though the salary of that office had been increased during Saxbe's term as senator. The Justice Department concluded that Saxbe would be eligible if Congress passed legislation setting his salary for attorney general at the level established before the increase.[51] After lengthy and contentious debate, the bill passed the Senate, 75 to 16.[52] With less debate, the House passed the bill 261 to 129 and it became law.[53]

Following the precedents established for Saxbe and others, Congress passed legislation in 1980 to permit Senator Ed Muskie to become secretary of state in the Carter administration. The salary of that office was reduced to its previous level.[54] In 1993, to allow President Clinton to select Senator Lloyd Bentsen as secretary of the treasury, Congress passed comparable legislation.[55] Although subject to academic attack, including an article aptly titled "Why Lloyd Bentsen is Unconstitutional,"[56] standing barriers prevented a successful lawsuit challenging Bentsen's appointment.

Given the Court's record of avoiding many of the disputes between Congress and the President and its failure to develop a consistent, coherent, and reliable theory of separated powers, it is not surprising that the meaning of separation of powers is developed for the most part outside the courts. The actual substance of various clauses and provisions in the Constitution are largely the result of compromises and accommodations crafted by legislators and executive officials.

The Veto Power

If the President decides to withhold his signature from a bill, he is directed by Article I, Section 7, of the Constitution to return it "with his Objections to that House in which it shall have originated, who shall enter the Objections at large on their Journal, and proceed to reconsider it." If "two thirds of that House" agree to pass the bill, it is reconsidered by the other house, and if approved by two-thirds of that house, "it shall become a Law." The ambiguities of this language were first clarified by congressional precedents, and those legislative judgments were later sustained by the courts.

Must Congress *immediately* proceed to reconsider a veto? Initially, that was the practice under the early Presidents, when vetoes were rare. President Washington exercised his first veto on April 5, 1792. The House of Representatives resolved that the bill be reconsidered the next day, when it sustained the veto.[57] Washington's second veto, on February 28, 1797, was sustained a day later, on March 1.[58]

There were no vetoes by Presidents John Adams or Jefferson. When President Madison vetoed a bill on February 21, 1811, members of the House of Representatives debated at great length the propriety of referring a veto message to a select committee for initial review. Some believed that the Constitution required immediate consideration. Others insisted that each house had a right to refer a vetoed bill to a select committee for closer study. The override effort took place two days later, with the House sustaining the veto.[59]

President Jackson's fourth regular veto set the precedent for no action at all by Congress: the veto was unchallenged. The Senate concluded that the constitutional requirement of "proceed to reconsider" was satisfied by laying the veto message on the table without moving to either a debate or a vote.[60] Jackson's last regular veto was sent to the Senate on Friday, June 10, 1836. An unsuccessful effort to override did not occur until fourteen days later (Sundays excluded).[61]

Later vetoes experienced even longer delays.[62] Today it is established practice that if the President vetoes a bill, Congress may schedule an override vote at any time during the two years of a Congress. This constitutional question is not litigated. It is left to the rules and procedures of the two houses of Congress.

What is meant by "two thirds of that House" for an override vote? Two-thirds of the total membership of each house, or merely two-thirds of a majority present? The House of Representatives early decided on two-thirds of the members present, provided they formed a quorum.[63] That ruling was liberalized in 1912, when Speaker Champ Clark announced that an override required two-thirds of the members present *and voting*.[64] On this particular override attempt there were 174 yeas and 80 nays, with 10 members voting present. Although the 174 fell short of two-thirds of the 264 present, it did constitute two-thirds of the 254

voting; the override therefore carried.[65] Building on these legislative precedents, in 1919 the Supreme Court decided that two-thirds of a quorum
sufficed for an override.[66]

May a President sign a bill after the final adjournment of a Congress?
For much of U.S. history, Presidents believed that they were a constituent
part of Congress with respect to the lawmaking process and therefore
could sign legislation only while Congress remained in session. Consistent
with that belief, Presidents would come to a special room in the Capitol
and sign hundreds of bills in the final days of a Congress. President Grover
Cleveland challenged that practice and refused to go to the Capitol, but
relented a year later on the advice of his attorney general.[67] In 1920 and
again in 1931, two attorneys general argued that the President had constitutional authority to sign a bill after the final adjournment of Congress.[68]
In 1932, the Supreme Court agreed with that assessment.[69] Once again, the
political branches paved the way in interpreting constitutional language.

Presidents typically exercise two types of vetoes: the regular (or return)
veto, and the pocket veto. For regular vetoes, after a bill passes Congress
the President may return it with his objections, requiring two-thirds of
each chamber for an override. That type of veto power is therefore qualified or conditional. In the case of pocket vetoes, however, the veto power
is absolute whenever a congressional adjournment "prevents" the return
of a bill.[70] Although some court rulings have established important param-
eters for the pocket veto, there has not been a definitive judicial ruling
to clarify the President's power. As a result, the scope of the pocket veto
has been left largely to practice and to political understandings developed
by the executive and legislative branches.

The Supreme Court did not decide a pocket veto dispute until 1929,
when it held that a five-month adjournment of Congress in 1926 "prevented" the President from returning a bill to Congress.[71] In 1938, the
Court held that a brief recess of three days by the Senate did not prevent
the President from returning a bill to Congress, particularly when Congress had authorized legislative agents to receive veto messages during
the recess.[72] There were no further decisions by federal courts until the
early 1970s, when Senator Ted Kennedy successfully challenged a pocket
veto by President Nixon during a short adjournment.[73] The Senate was
absent for four days and the House for five. Unlike the 1929 case, Nixon's
action involved a short adjournment *during* a session rather than a lengthy
adjournment at the end of a session.

As a result of this litigation, Presidents Ford and Carter entered into
an accommodation with Congress, pledging not to use the pocket veto
except at the end of a Congress; they would not use the pocket veto in

the middle of a session or between the first and second sessions. Several actions by President Reagan reopened the pocket veto controversy when he experimented with pocket vetoes between the first and second sessions. One of these pocket vetoes was challenged by Congressman Mike Barnes, who lost in district court but prevailed in the D.C. Circuit.[74] Just when it appeared that the pocket veto issue might be resolved judicially, in 1987 the Supreme Court held that the dispute was moot because the bill in question had expired by its own terms.[75]

The scope of the pocket veto was now back in the hands of the elected branches. From 1989 to 2001, Presidents Bush I and Clinton exercised a pocket veto between sessions or in the middle of a session, but instead of treating the pocket veto as an absolute veto, they returned the bill to Congress for a possible override. They thus created a third variant, or hybrid: a *returned pocket veto*! For example, on August 5, 2000, President Clinton vetoed the Marriage Tax Relief Reconciliation Act, claiming that the summer break of Congress (from July 27 to September 5) "prevented my return" of the bill within the meaning of the Constitution as interpreted by *The Pocket Veto Case*. Yet he added this qualification: "In addition to withholding my signature and thereby invoking my constitutional power to 'pocket veto' bills during an adjournment of the Congress, to avoid litigation, I am also sending H.R. 4810 to the House of Representatives with my objections, to leave no possible doubt that I have vetoed the measure."[76] Similarly, on August 31, he pocket vetoed the Death Tax Elimination Act and appended the same explanation.[77]

On September 6, the House treated the two veto messages as return vetoes, not pocket vetoes.[78] On September 7, the House voted 274 to 157 to override the veto of the death tax bill, short of the two-thirds needed.[79] During the debate, no one referred to Clinton's action as a pocket veto. On September 13, the House took up the veto of the marriage tax bill, and again no member regarded Clinton's disapproval memo as a pocket veto. The vote of 270 to 158 fell short of the necessary two-thirds.[80]

This odd arrangement of returned pocket vetoes reflects a mix of federal court decisions and executive-legislative accommodations. It illustrates how, at times, the meaning of the Constitution is decided partly by federal courts and partly by imaginative arrangements created by the elected branches. It appears unlikely that a judicial decision or enactment of legislation will clarify this confusing and unsettled practice. Congress and the President seem fairly comfortable with the present arrangement, and there is no obvious litigant who might bring a case to resolve once and for all this constitutional dispute.

Recess Appointments

Congressional recesses and adjournments invite another separation of power disagreement: the power of the President to make recess appointments. The framers realized that the Senate would not always be in session to give its advice and consent to presidential nominations. To cover those periods of absence, the President "shall have Power to fill up all Vacancies that may happen during the Recess of the Senate, by granting Commissions which shall expire at the End of their next Session."[81] A determination by the President to exploit this power to the fullest would undermine the Senate's constitutional power over confirmations.

The reach of the power to make recess appointments has been defined primarily by the legislative and executive branches, not by the courts. An early issue involved the meaning of "happen." Does that mean only the vacancies that "happen to take place" during a recess, or the broader reading of any vacancy that may "happen to exist" at the time of a recess? A long list of opinions by attorneys general favored the latter interpretation.[82] Those opinions opened the door to possible abuse by the President, relying on recess appointments instead of the regular process requiring Senate approval. In the face of executive interpretations, Congress responded with statutory restrictions.

In a report issued in 1863, the Senate Judiciary Committee rejected the opinions of attorneys general. Interpreting the constitutional language "may happen during the Recess of the Senate" to include what happened before the recess seemed to the Committee "a perversion of language."[83] Such reasoning by the administration tilted the balance of power toward the President and placed inordinate weight on the need to fill a vacancy, all at the cost of excluding the Senate. Unless Congress placed some constraint on the power to make recess appointments, an "ambitious, corrupt, or tyrannical executive" could nullify the Senate's constitutional role.[84]

To protect the prerogatives of the Senate, Congress decided to invoke its power of the purse. Legislation in 1863 prohibited the use of funds to pay the salary of anyone appointed during a Senate recess to fill a vacancy that existed "while the Senate was in session and is by law required to be filled by and with the advice and consent of the Senate, until such appointee shall have been confirmed by the Senate."[85] This statute proved to be far too rigid. In some cases, officers had to serve without pay (relying on savings and loans) until the Senate consented to the nomination, prompting Congress to pass special statutes to compensate people who served for long periods as a recess appointee and were not entitled to a salary.[86] To eliminate some of the harsh effects of the existing law on recess appointments, legislation in 1940 permitted payment of salaries (1) if the vacancy arose within thirty days prior to a Senate adjournment, (2) if, at the time of adjournment, a nomination was pending before the Senate (other than a nomination for someone appointed during the preceding recess of the Senate), and (3) if a nomination was rejected by the Senate within thirty days prior to an adjournment and a person (other than the one rejected) receives a recess commission.[87]

In addition to executive branch appointments, the use of recess appointments to place men and women on the federal courts is especially sensitive, for these individuals remain on the bench for a year or more and must face confirmation after their recess appointment ends. In 1959, after President Eisenhower placed Earl Warren, William J. Brennan Jr., and Potter Stewart on the Supreme Court as recess appointees, the House Judiciary Committee prepared a report that was highly critical of this practice and the damage it inflicted on the independence of the courts.[88]

In 1960, a Senate resolution also challenged this practice.[89] The Senate did not want to confirm a recess appointee who had already sat on the bench and issued decisions. Should senators take into account those decisions when they act to confirm? Would a judge decide cases with an eye toward the President's having to later nominate that person for a life term, followed by confirmation hearings and Senate vote? Were litigants given short change in court by pleading their cases before an unconfirmed judge?

Although the Senate resolution is legally nonbinding, no President since Eisenhower has made a recess appointment to the Supreme Court. The power exists, technically, but a President who defied the resolution would risk having the nominee, after serving a year or so as a federal judge, rejected decisively by the Senate to protect its institutional prerogatives. Furthermore, the executive and legislative branches appear to understand that judicial recess appointments pose a substantial risk to the independence and integrity of the judiciary and to the constitutional rights of litigants. Although the President's authority to make recess appointments to the federal courts was upheld by the Second Circuit in 1962,[90] and again in 1985 by the Ninth Circuit,[91] the final word on whether it will be done lies exclusively with the President and the Senate. The fact that the federal courts have sanctioned the use of judicial recess appointments does not require the political branches to accept the practice as constitutionally correct.

After President Carter made a recess appointment to a federal district court, leading to the 1985 ruling by the Ninth Circuit, no President used the recess appointment power for Article III judges until President Clinton, in his last month in office, appointed Roger Gregory on a recess basis to the Fourth Circuit. The selection was highly controversial because Gregory would be the first black to serve on that circuit. When President George W. Bush took office, he had a choice of letting Gregory serve out his recess appointment and nominating someone else to replace him, or renominating him for a life term. As part of a political accommodation with Senate Democrats, he chose to nominate Gregory for a permanent seat to the Fourth Circuit and Gregory was then confirmed by the Senate.

The Power to Investigate

There is no explicit power in the Constitution for Congress to investigate the executive branch, but members of Congress acted as though that power existed long before any court ruling gave a judicial blessing. When the House of Representatives learned in 1792 of heavy losses by the troops of Major General St. Clair in an Indian attack, it first considered a resolution to request the President to institute an inquiry.[92] Congressman Hugh Williamson objected that there was no reason to defer to the President on this occasion. Claiming that "an inquiry into the expenditure of all public money was the indispensable duty of this House," he proposed that the House create a select committee to investigate.[93] After defeating the initial resolution 35 to 21, the House passed a resolution to empower a committee to inquire into the causes of the military failure and "to call for such persons, papers, and records, as may be necessary to assist their inquiries."[94] According to the account of Thomas Jefferson, at that time serving as secretary of state, President Washington convened his Cabinet to consider whether the House had constitutional authority to request such papers. After debating the issue, the Cabinet agreed

> first, that the House was an inquest, and therefore might institute inquiries. Second, that it might call for papers generally. Third, that the Executive ought to communicate such papers as the public good would permit, and ought to refuse those, the disclosure of which would injure the public: consequently were to exercise a discretion. Fourth, that neither the committee nor House had a right to call on the Head of a Department, who and whose papers were under the President alone; but that the committee should instruct their chairman to move the House to address the President.[95]

The Cabinet concluded that there was not a paper "which might not be properly produced." Congress received papers and accounts furnished by the Treasury and the War Departments and heard explanations from the heads of those departments and from other witnesses. General St.

Clair supplied the congressional committee with written remarks on the expeditions. The Cabinet's belief that the House could call on the heads of departments only through the President was an artificial formality quickly abandoned.

Although Congress exercised the investigative power on many occasions after 1792, it was not until *McGrain v. Daugherty* (1927) that the Supreme Court got around to acknowledging the constitutional power of Congress to investigate activities in the executive branch.[96] The Court had no alternative. It could not at that time, or even earlier, deny the existence of such a power. It could merely affirm a power long recognized as legitimate by Congress and the President.

A number of cases decided by the Court have checked excesses of congressional investigations, especially the procedures adopted by legislative committees.[97] Other decisions have given broad support to congressional investigations.[98] Most of these separation of power disputes, however, are handled by accommodations between the political branches. In particular, speaking of an "implicit constitutional mandate to seek optimal accommodation [through bargaining]," the federal courts almost always steer clear of information access disputes between the executive and legislative branches.[99]

When executive officials refuse to comply with a congressional request for information, one of the legislative instruments of coercion is the contempt power. Individuals who refuse to testify or produce papers are subject to being cited for contempt of Congress, leading to fines and imprisonment. That power has been exercised many times. In 1980, President Carter threatened to withhold documents concerning his oil import fee. Secretary Charles W. Duncan Jr., with a contempt citation hanging over his head, surrendered the documents to a House committee. A year later, Energy Secretary James B. Edwards narrowly escaped a contempt citation by agreeing to provide information on the synthetic fuels program to a House committee.[100]

Interior Secretary James Watt withheld documents from a House subcommittee in 1981, provoking a committee subpoena for the documents and a recommendation that he be cited for contempt; several weeks later, Watt made the documents available to the subcommittee.[101] When EPA Administrator Anne Gorsuch Burford refused to turn over "sensitive documents found in open law enforcement files" concerning EPA's enforcement of the "Superfund" program designed to clean up hazardous waste sites, the House voted 259 to 105 to hold her in contempt.[102] After an initial skirmish in court,[103] the Reagan administration agreed to release the documents to Congress. In 1991, the Bush I administration averted a potential contempt action against the Justice Department by allowing lawmakers to review a legal opinion that gave FBI agents authority to kidnap fugitives in foreign nations.[104]

Congress has other points of leverage. In 1986, President Reagan invoked executive privilege to deny to the Senate certain internal memos that Chief Justice–designee William H. Rehnquist had written while serving in the Justice Department from 1969 to 1971. Democrats on the Senate Judiciary Committee began rounding up votes to subpoena the papers. Later, they selected an even tougher sanction. As Senator Ted Kennedy explained succinctly in an op-ed piece: "Rehnquist: No Documents, No Senate Confirmation."[105] Reagan agreed to a narrowed request by the Committee to read twenty-five to thirty documents that Rehnquist had written during his career in the Justice Department.[106] A few days later, the Committee requested and received additional documents prepared by Rehnquist while in the Department.[107] With the deadlock broken, Rehnquist's nomination went forward.

There are many other legislative tools to pry loose documents in the executive branch. The informal practice of imposing "holds" allows any senator to stop floor action on legislation or nominations. The majority leader may then decide whether to honor the hold. In 1993, Senator John Warner announced that he would release his hold on the intelligence authorization bill after receiving assurance from the CIA that it would search its files for information on Defense Department nominee Morton Halperin. CIA Director James Woolsey had planned to brief Republican members of the Senate Armed Services Committee but was ordered not to do so by White House Counsel Bernard Nussbaum.[108] In 1999, Senator Charles Grassley placed a hold on the nomination of Richard Holbrook to be U.S. ambassador to the UN because he objected to the State Department's treatment of Linda Shenwick, who worked at the U.S. mission to the United Nations. After giving Congress information on mismanagement at the UN, she was threatened with a suspension and transfer to another job. Grassley explained that if lawmakers did not protect agency whistleblowers, "a valuable source of information to Congress will likely dry up."[109] After being reassured that Shenwick would not be punished by the State Department, Grassley lifted his hold on Holbrooke.

Federal courts can help to resolve executive-legislative disputes, but more by nudging them toward an acceptable middle-ground position than by imposing a solution. During the Ford administration, a House subcommittee issued a subpoena to obtain from the American Telephone and Telegraph Company information on "national security" wiretaps by the administration. The D.C. Circuit helped the subcommittee and the administration negotiate an accommodation that would satisfy their institutional interests. Each branch, wrote the D.C. Circuit, "is most likely to meet their essential needs and the country's constitutional balance" by working out a compromise with the other.[110]

With federal courts generally refusing to play a hands-on role in information access disputes, the dance that now takes place between legislative and executive interests will persist. Armed with the powers of contempt, the purse, and the confirmation of presidential appointments, Congress is well positioned to bargain with the executive. Indeed, it is only in rare cases that the executive will object to congressional requests for information. And though some Justice Department officials complain that agency heads are too willing to turn over privileged information to their congressional overseers, the White House prefers the current system of accommodation to one in which the President's agenda is jeopardized by protracted executive privilege fights with Congress.[111]

The Legislative Veto

The Supreme Court in *INS v. Chadha* (1983) declared that legislative vetoes were an invalid form of congressional control. From the early 1930s, Congress had used legislative vetoes—one-house vetoes, two-house vetoes, and even committee vetoes—to approve or disapprove executive actions. The Court held that legislative efforts to control the executive branch had to comply with bicameralilsm and presentation of a bill to the President.

In so doing, the Court announced a strict doctrine of separation of power and encouraged the belief that Congress exists for the sole purpose of passing legislation, with no opportunity to influence the implementation of a bill once it has been enacted. Nevertheless, from the moment the Court announced its decision, Congress continued to rely on the legislative veto to control agency actions. From 1983 to 2004, Congress created more than four hundred new legislative vetoes and they were signed into law by Presidents Reagan, Bush I, Clinton, and Bush II. These statutory provisions require agencies to obtain the approval of congressional committees and subcommittees.

What accounts for the gap between what the Court said and what the two political branches do? Why has there been so little compliance with this "epic" decision on separation of powers? Is it a matter of congressional contempt for the judiciary? A better explanation is that the Court reached too far and failed to understand the practical needs that led Congress and the executive branch to adopt the legislative veto in the first place. Those needs existed before *Chadha* and they continued after the Court's decision.

Legislative vetoes were created in the 1930s not because Congress wanted to meddle with administrative details but because President Herbert Hoover wanted to "make law" without congressional action. In 1929, he asked Congress to delegate to him broad authority to reorganize the executive branch, subject to some form of congressional approval. He suggested that the President be allowed to act "upon approval of a joint committee of Congress."[112] Hoover was willing to tolerate the legislative veto because the regular legislative process for reorganizing government contained too many uncertainties, including the prospect of Congress's ignoring a President's request or placing unwanted amendments on his proposal. Hoover finally received reorganization authority in 1932, subject to a one-house legislative veto.[113]

President Franklin D. Roosevelt initially thought that the legislative veto in the reorganization statute was unconstitutional, and that any congressional action short of a bill or joint resolution would merely represent "an expression of congressional sentiment" and would have no legally binding effect.[114] Members of the House of Representatives balked at his interpretation, realizing that disapproval by bill or joint resolution would mean that Congress would need a two-thirds majority in each house to override the expected presidential veto. Recognizing that Congress would never grant him reorganization authority without reserving to itself a control short of a public law, Roosevelt reversed his constitutional position within a matter of days and supported an amendment that allowed Congress to reject his reorganization plans by a concurrent resolution.[115] The reorganization bill passed in 1939 with the two-house veto, and Roosevelt signed it into law.[116] When Congress extended the President's reorganization authority in 1949, it tightened legislative control by resorting to a one-house veto.[117]

The legislative veto continued to spread to other areas. Legislation in 1940 authorized the attorney general to suspend deportation of an alien, subject to a two-house veto (later changed to a one-house veto).[118] This procedure appealed to both Congress and the President, for otherwise, they could grant relief to aliens in hardship cases only through the passage of hundreds of private bills.[119]

Executive-legislative relations experienced new strains in the 1970s, when Congress decided to extend the legislative veto to such areas as the war power, national emergencies, impoundment, presidential papers, federal salaries, and selected agency regulations. By the late 1970s, Congress even considered applying the legislative veto to control regulations issued by every agency of government. The legislative veto now appeared to be more of an offensive weapon of congressional micromanagement than a defensive check against broad delegation.

The Carter Justice Department sought Supreme Court review to kill the legislative veto once and for all. By the time the Court took up the matter, however, Reagan had been elected president. Viewing the legislative veto as a check on excessive regulation, the Reagan administration seemed inclined to defend the veto in *Chadha*, but Attorney General William French Smith disagreed. "I pointed out," wrote Smith, "that the Republicans had controlled the presidency for one-half the time since 1952, but had controlled both houses of Congress only two years during that period. Why then sacrifice executive power for legislative power?"[120] This argument, thanks to a direct appeal to the President, ultimately prevailed.

Shortly after the administration "won" the case, it recognized that a rigid insistence that Congress control agency activities only by passing another public law would backfire on the executive branch by depriving it of needed flexibility and discretion. For example, when President Reagan signed an appropriations bill in 1984 for the Department of Housing and Urban Development and independent agencies, he stated that the provisions requiring executive agencies to seek the prior approval of the Appropriations Committees were invalid under *Chadha*.[121] His signing statement implied that the committee veto provisions would be regarded by the administration as legally nonbinding. Under this reading, agencies could notify their review committees and then do precisely as they wished without obtaining the committees' approval.

The House Appropriations Committee knew how to respond. It threatened to repeal legislation that allowed the National Aeronautics and Space Administration (NASA) to exceed its spending caps subject to committee approval. Because of Reagan's statement, the committee told NASA that it could exceed its caps only through the enactment of supplemental legislation, requiring approval from both houses of Congress and presentment to the President. Not surprisingly, NASA head James M. Beggs much preferred the limited legislative veto check to the onerous demand that NASA obtain formal positive law approval before it exceeds its spending caps. Beggs successfully pleaded his case to Congress, seeking "an informal agreement" and promising "not to exceed amounts for Committee designated programs without the approval of the Committee of Appropriations."[122]

In addition to informal legislative vetoes, Congress continues to put committee vetoes in public laws, and agencies comply out of self-interest. They know that any attempt on their part to defy committee control is likely to produce the kind of backlash seen in the NASA dispute. Executive agencies have to live with their review committees year after year and have a much greater incentive to make accommodations and stick by them. Presidents and their legal advisors can indulge in dramatic confrontations with Congress on these issues; agencies, however, do not want bloody dogfights with the committees that authorize their programs and provide funds.

To lessen the chance of a self-inflicted wound, the Supreme Court usually abides by the prudential course of not formulating "a rule of constitutional law broader than is required by the precise facts to which it is to be applied."[123] The Court ignored that fundamental guideline in *Chadha* by issuing a decision that not only reached beyond the immigration statute at question but exceeded the Court's understanding of executive-legislative relations. Through an endless variety of formal and informal agreements, congressional committees will continue to exercise control over administration decisions. By misreading the history of legislative vetoes and failing to comprehend the subtleties of the legislative process, the Court directed the executive and legislative branches to adhere to procedures that would be impracticable and unworkable. Neither Congress nor the executive branch wanted the static model of government offered by the Court. The predictable and inevitable result of *Chadha* is a system of lawmaking that is now more convoluted, cumbersome, and covert than before. In many cases, the Court's decision simply drove underground a set of legislative and committee vetoes that used to operate in plain sight.[124]

Independent Counsel

The Reagan administration's victory in *Chadha* whetted the appetite of political appointees in the Justice Department, the White House, and the Office of Management and Budget (OMB). They began to press for a "unitary executive" model in which the President would have total control over all executive agencies. Headed for extinction under that model were the independent commissions (Interstate Commerce Commission, Federal Trade Commission, Securities and Exchange Commission, etc.) that Congress had created to be somewhat autonomous from presidential control. A measure of independence was granted by restricting the President's power to remove the commissioners, giving them lengthy terms (longer than the President's four-year term) and other statutory protections. The Reagan administration lost the battle for subordinating independent commissions to the President, but its strategy and objectives colored the lawsuits contesting the constitutionality of the independent counsel (called special prosecutor in earlier years).

The special prosecutor statute originated in the politics of Watergate. What began as a bungled attempt to burglarize the Democratic national party headquarters on June 17, 1972, quickly blossomed into a crisis that engulfed the Nixon administration. As a result of congressional investigations, impeachment inquiries, and decisions handed down by courts, President Nixon was forced to resign, and many top officials, including Attorney General John Mitchell, received prison sentences. When the magnitude of the scandal became apparent, Attorney General Elliot Richardson (with Nixon's support) appointed Archibald Cox to investigate the affair. Nixon later fired Cox, resulting in the resignation of Richardson and Deputy Attorney General William Ruckelshaus, all part of the "Saturday Night Massacre."

From the Ford to the Reagan administrations, the Justice Department's position on the independent counsel varied. In response to Watergate, Congress considered a bill to establish a permanent office of special prosecutor. Attorney General Edward H. Levi testified in 1976 that the office was of "questionable constitutionality." He particularly disliked the proposal to place the power of appointment in a body of federal judges.[125] Michael M. Uhlmann, an assistant attorney general, also testified that the proposal was unconstitutional, especially because the duty to enforce a criminal law was "the very core of 'executive functions.'"[126]

Nevertheless, President Carter supported a special prosecutor who would be appointed by federal judges and subject to removal by the attorney general. The office of special prosecutor had a statutory life of five years. When it was reauthorized in January 1983 for another five years, President Reagan signed the legislation and indicated no constitutional misgivings about the office. At that time, other than special prosecutors to investigate such officials as Hamilton Jordan, Timothy Kraft, and Raymond Donovan, there had been little experience with the statute. The 1983 extension changed the office from special prosecutor to independent counsel and altered the ground for removal by the attorney general from "extraordinary impropriety" to "good cause."[127]

On June 23, 1983, the Supreme Court handed down *Chadha*. Three years later, in *Bowsher v. Synar*, the Court employed formalistic rhetoric to forbid a legislative actor (the comptroller general) from performing an executive act (putting into effect the deficit reduction targets of Gramm-Rudman). Those two decisions gave the Justice Department grounds to believe that a successful legal challenge could be mounted against the independent counsel. After years of support from two administrations, the Reagan administration began to actively oppose the office of independent counsel in 1987. By that time, the office had become a thorn in the side of the Reagan administration. It had been used to investigate the Iran-Contra affair and to investigate major figures in the White House, including Michael Deaver and Edwin Meese III.

Yet, because a veto at that point would have been too easily interpreted as an effort to conceal administration misdeeds, Reagan signed the reauthorization bill but expressed "strong doubts" about its constitutionality. Charles Fried, solicitor general under Reagan, explained the reluctance to challenge the independent counsel statute: "Many conservatives thought the Independent Counsel law was an outrage, but the politics were such that we were scared to challenge it. The challenges would have come most naturally in Iran-Contra and in respect to Attorney General Meese's own involvement with the Wedtech scandal. But these were terrible cases in which to challenge a law that the public was told guaranteed impartial justice."[128]

When the constitutionality of the independent counsel was litigated, the Reagan administration filed an amicus brief that presented a number of arguments pointing to constitutional defects in the statute. But unlike the legislative veto and Gramm-Rudman, there was no congressional involvement with the independent counsel. By strictly limiting its own role and expanding attorney general removal power, Congress took seriously its responsibility for passing legislation that would satisfy constitutional requirements and the scrutiny of the courts. Paul Gewirtz noted that the independent counsel law was upheld "because Congress did something that legislatures often fail to do. Rather than pass the buck to the courts, Congress carefully considered possible constitutional objections at the time it adopted the legislation."[129]

The independent counsel statute was scheduled for reauthorization in 1992, but by that time the investigation by Independent Counsel Lawrence E. Walsh into the Iran-Contra affair had so angered the Republicans that they blocked the reauthorization bill. Yet, with the election of Bill Clinton that year, Republicans reversed course and supported reauthorization as a way of scrutinizing his investment in an Arkansas land development venture (Whitewater Development Co.). Because the independent counsel statute had lapsed, Attorney General Janet Reno relied on her own authority to name a special prosecutor, Robert B. Fiske Jr., to investigate Whitewater. When the independent counsel law was enacted in 1994 for another five-year period, the federal court panel decided against Fiske in favor of a replacement: former Republican Solicitor General Kenneth W. Starr.

Just as Republicans had denounced Walsh for investigating Reagan and Bush, so Democrats now pummeled Starr for his probe of Clinton. Matters reached a crescendo when Starr reported to Congress that Clinton might have committed impeachable offenses. By 1999, the political atmosphere was so poisoned that Congress decided against reauthorizing the independent counsel statute. When the Senate Judiciary Committee held hearings that year, not only did Reno recommend against reauthorization, but so did Starr. Reno testified that although she had supported the statute in 1993, she now concluded that the independent counsel law was "structurally flawed and that those flaws cannot be corrected within our constitutional framework."[130] In trying to ensure independence, the statute "creates a new category of prosecutors who have no practical limits on their time or budgets."[131] Starr agreed that the statute was not worth extending, particularly when the Justice Department uses its "raw power to refuse to provide assistance [to an independent counsel] or to drag its feet."[132] He pointed out that the Justice Department has incentives "to come to the aid of a U.S. Attorney, or a regulatory Independent Counsel, [but] has no incentive to help a statutory Independent Counsel. With no institutional defender, Independent Counsels are especially vulnerable to partisan attack."[133] By "regulatory Independent Counsel," Starr was referring to the type of special prosecutor that an attorney general can appoint.

Although the political climate turned against reauthorization, the institutional problem persists: How can the Justice Department, given its conflict of interest, credibly investigate the President and other high-ranking executive branch officials? In her testimony in 1999, Reno said she continued to believe "that there are times when an Attorney General will have a conflict of interest," and that in such times, "to keep the public's faith in impartial justice," it would be necessary for someone other than the attorney general to be put in charge of the investigation.[134] Unless Congress and the President agree on a successor to the independent counsel statute, the two branches will have to look for other remedies. Thus, the creative task of seeking constitutional solutions to conflict of interest problems within the Justice Department will fall again to the elected branches, not to the judiciary.

Conclusions

This chapter underscores the degree to which the meaning of the Constitution depends on nonjudicial interpretations by the executive and legislative branches. Many of the major separation of powers disputes are resolved nonjudicially through trade-offs and compromises reached by the President and Congress. The rough-and-tumble character of political debate lacks some of the amenities and dignity of the judicial process, but executive officials and legislators are well informed and often take their responsibilities seriously. Their contributions to defining separation of powers have much greater impact than the few decisions (some of them contradictory) issued by the courts.

Correspondingly, the frequent interplay between Congress and the executive on separation of powers makes the federal courts ill-suited to play a preemptive, activist role. Political accommodations between the branches can redefine or even undo the substantive impact of a judicial opinion. The branches have no choice but to react to and make accommodations with each other—and perhaps articulate new constitutional positions—in the shadow of the implementation of the law. This dynamic process cannot and should not be constrained by rigid judicial pronouncements. Otherwise, a static vision of the Constitution's division of powers will vitiate the bargaining process that takes place between lawmakers and the White House.

5

The War Power

The constitutional boundaries of the war power are determined only marginally by court decisions. The principal forces that define military activities are nonjudicial: presidential decisions to initiate force, congressional decisions to acquiesce or resist, and public pressure for and against military actions. The momentous decision to commit the nation's blood and deplete its treasury takes place almost exclusively outside the courts. This pattern is evident throughout U.S. history.

Courts are ill-equipped to decide questions about the initiation of war and perform only a modest task in supervising the scope of military operations once underway. If members of Congress fail to assert their prerogatives over war and peace, federal judges have been unwilling to fill the breach left open by lawmakers. Consequently, the content of the Constitution's war-making provisions are largely defined by executive and legislative branch interpretations. For the first century and a half, Congress had the dominant role in initiating war, but ever since 1950, presidential power has widened dramatically. These fundamental changes in constitutional doctrine have occurred without constitutional amendment or defining judicial decisions.

Taming the Dog of War

The framers of the U.S. Constitution studied models of government in Europe that placed the war power securely in the hands of the monarch. Breaking decisively with that tradition, they deliberately transferred the power to initiate war from the executive to the legislature. As the framers were completing their labors at the Constitutional Convention, Thomas Jefferson wrote to his friend James Madison, "We have already given in example one effectual check to the Dog of war by transferring the power of letting him loose from the Executive to the Legislative body, from those who are to spend to those who are to pay."[1]

The overriding principles endorsed by the framers were collective judgment, shared power in foreign affairs, and "the cardinal tenet of republican ideology that the conjoined wisdom of many is superior to that of one."[2] However, those values have been challenged, especially in the years following World War II, by some scholars who would vest in the President an independent power to commit forces into hostilities.[3]

In deciding on the allocation of the war power, the framers reviewed— and rejected—the models of John Locke and William Blackstone. Locke's *Second Treatise on Civil Government* (1690) spoke of three branches of government: legislative, executive, and federative. The last consisted of "the power of war and peace, leagues and alliances, and all the transactions with all persons and communities without the commonwealth." For Locke, the federative power (what we call foreign policy today) was "always almost united" with the executive. Separating the executive and federative powers, he warned, would invite "disorder and ruin."[4]

A similar model appears in Blackstone's *Commentaries* (1771). He defined the king's prerogative as "those rights and capacities which the king enjoys alone." Some prerogatives were "rooted in and spring from the king's political person," including the right to make war or peace. The king could also make "a treaty with a foreign state, which shall irrevocably bind the nation," and issue letters of marque and reprisal (authorizing private citizens to undertake military actions), a prerogative "nearly related to, and plainly derived from, that other of making war." The king was "the generalissimo, or the first in military command," with "the sole power of raising and regulating fleets and armies."[5]

When America declared its independence from England in 1776, the framers vested *all* executive powers in the Continental Congress; they did not provide for a separate executive. The ninth article of the first national constitution, the Articles of Confederation, provided: "The United States, in Congress assembled, shall have the sole and exclusive right and power of determining on peace and war." The single exception to that principle lay in the sixth article, which allowed states to engage in war if invaded by enemies or when threatened with invasion by Indian tribes.

The debates at the Philadelphia convention underscore the framers' intention that monarchical war prerogatives would have no home in America. On June 1, 1787, Charles Pinckney said he was for "a vigorous Executive but was afraid the Executive powers of [the existing] Congress might extend to peace & war &c which would render the Executive a Monarchy, of the worst kind, to wit an elective one." John Rutledge wanted the executive power placed in a single person, "tho' he was not for giving him the power of war and peace." James Wilson also preferred a single executive, but "did not consider the Prerogatives of the British Monarch as a proper guide in defining the Executive powers. Some of these prerogatives were of a Legislative nature. Among others that of war & peace &c."[6]

Edmund Randolph worried about executive power, calling it "the foetus of monarchy." The delegates to the Philadelphia convention, he said, had "no motive to be governed by the British Government as our prototype." Wilson agreed that the British model "was inapplicable to the situation of this Country; the extent of which was so great, and the manners so republican, that nothing but a great confederated Republic would do for it." James Madison later remarked, "The constitution supposes, what the History of all Govts demonstrates, that the Ex. is the branch of power most interested in war, & most prone to it. It has accordingly with studied care, vested the question of war in the Legisl."[7]

Fear that the President would lead the nation into war "in order to achieve personal glory" figured prominently in the framers' thinking.[8] In *Federalist* No. 4, John Jay cautioned that "absolute monarchs will often make war when their nations are to get nothing by it, but for purposes and objects merely personal, such as a thirst for military glory, revenge for personal affronts, ambition, or private compacts to aggrandize or support their particular families or partisans."

Although the President was made commander in chief, it was left to Congress to raise and regulate fleets and armies. The extent of the break with Locke and Blackstone is set forth clearly in *The Federalist Papers*. In *Federalist* No. 69, Hamilton explained that the President has "concurrent power with a branch of the legislature in the formation of treaties," whereas the British king "is the *sole possessor* of the power of making treaties." The royal prerogative in foreign affairs was deliberately shared with Congress, he noted. Hamilton contrasted the distribution of war powers in England and in the American Constitution. The power of the king "extends to the *declaring* of war and to the *raising* and *regulating* of fleets and armies."

The Constitution grants to Congress a number of specific powers to control war and military affairs: to declare war; to grant letters of marque and reprisal; to raise and support armies and to provide and maintain a navy; to make regulations of the land and naval forces; to call forth the militia; and to provide for organizing, arming, and disciplining the militia. Moreover, because commercial conflicts between nations were often a cause of war, the Constitution vests in Congress the power to regulate foreign commerce, an area directly related to the war power.

The framers recognized that in emergency situations the President might have to use military force to repel sudden attacks without first obtaining authority from Congress. The early draft empowered Congress to "make war." Pinckney objected that legislative proceedings "were too slow" for the safety of the country in an emergency; he expected Congress to meet but once a year. Madison and Elbridge Gerry moved to insert "declare" for "make," leaving to the President "the power to repel sudden attacks." Their motion carried 7 to 2. After Rufus King explained that the word "make" would allow the President to conduct war, which was "an Executive function," Connecticut changed its vote and the final tally was 8 to 1.[9]

The President's war power here was defensive, not offensive. Reactions to the Madison-Gerry amendment reinforce the narrow grant of authority to the President. Pierce Butler wanted to give the President the power to make war, arguing that he "will have all the requisite qualities, and will not make war but when the Nation will support it." Roger Sherman objected: "The Executive shd. be able to repel and not to commence war." Gerry said he "never expected to hear in a republic a motion to empower the Executive alone to declare war." George Mason spoke "agst giving the power of war to the Executive, because not <safely> to be trusted with it. . . . He was for clogging rather than facilitating war."

Similar statements were made at the state ratifying conventions. In Pennsylvania, James Wilson expressed the prevailing sentiment that the system of checks and balances "will not hurry us into war; it is calculated to guard against it. It will not be in the power of a single man, or a single body of men, to involve us in such distress; for the important power of declaring war is vested in the legislature at large."[10] In North Carolina, James Iredell pointed out that the king of Great Britain had the power to raise fleets and armies and to declare war, whereas the U.S. Constitution vested those powers "in other hands."[11] In South Carolina, Charles Pinckney assured his colleagues that the President's powers "did not permit him to declare war."[12]

The title commander in chief implies the duty to repel sudden attacks, but beyond that responsibility the President had to await congressional authority. The title also represents an important method for preserving civilian supremacy over the military. The person leading the armed forces would be the civilian President, not a military officer. Attorney General Edward Bates explained in 1861 that the President is commander in chief not because he is "skilled in the art of war" but to keep the army "subordinate to the civil power."[13]

The constitutional framework adopted by the framers is clear in its basic principles. The authority to initiate war lay with Congress; the President could act unilaterally only in one area: to repel sudden attacks. Over the next two centuries, however, a number of incidents were invoked by Presidents and their supporters to expand the President's potential for *making* war over the formal power of Congress for *declaring* war.

Precedents from 1789 to Lincoln

Presidential use of force during the first few decades after the Philadelphia convention conformed closely to the expectations of the framers: The decision to go to war or to mount offensive actions rested with Congress, and Presidents accepted that principle for all wars, declared or undeclared.

The first exercise of the Commander in Chief Clause involved actions by President Washington against certain Indian tribes, actions explicitly authorized by Congress. On September 29, 1789, Congress passed legislation "for the purpose of protecting the inhabitants of the frontiers of the United States from the hostile incursions of the Indians." To provide that protection, Congress authorized the President "to call into service from time to time, such part of the militia of the states respectively, as he may judge necessary for the purpose aforesaid."[14] In 1790 and again in 1791, Congress passed new authorizations to protect the inhabitants in the frontiers.[15]

The executive branch understood that its military operations against Indians were limited to defensive actions. Secretary of War Henry Knox wrote to Governor William Blount on October 9, 1792, "The Congress which possess the powers of declaring War will assemble on the 5th of next Month—Until their judgments shall be made known it seems essential to confine all your operations to defensive measures."[16] Writing in 1793, President Washington said that any offensive operations against the Creek Nation must await congressional action.[17]

The Whiskey Rebellion of 1794 marks the first time a President called out the militia to suppress a domestic insurrection. President Washington acted expressly under authority delegated to him by Congress. Legislation in 1792 provided that whenever the United States was invaded or in imminent danger of external or internal threats, the President could call forth the state militias to repel invasions and suppress insurrections.[18] The statute introduced a novel check on presidential power. If federal laws were obstructed in any state, the President would have to be first notified of that fact by an Associate Justice of the Supreme Court or by a federal district judge. Only then could the President call forth the militia.[19] In 1794, Justice James Wilson certified to President Washington that a rebellion in western Pennsylvania had rendered ordinary legal means insufficient to execute national law.[20] Washington called forth the militias of four states to put down the rebellion.

It is sometimes argued that Congress has the power to declare war but that the President may engage in undeclared wars. In a major legal defense of the Vietnam War, the State Department in 1966 remarked, "Since the Constitution was adopted there have been at least 125 instances in which the President has ordered the armed forces to take action or maintain positions abroad without obtaining prior congressional authorization, starting with the 'undeclared war' with France (1798–1800)."[21] The reference to the war against France is false. Congress debated the prospect of war openly and enacted a number of bills to put the country on a war footing. President John Adams never believed that he could, on his own authority, go to war against France. He asked Congress to prepare the country for war by passing "effectual measures of defense."[22] Congress enacted several dozen measures to prepare for war. During the debates in 1798, Congressman Edward Livingston considered the country "now in a state of war; and let no man flatter himself that the vote which has been given is not a declaration of war."[23]

The quasi-war with France underscored the prerogatives of Congress over war and the deployment of military force. In 1800 and 1801, the Supreme Court recognized that Congress could authorize hostilities either by a formal declaration of war or by statutes that authorized an undeclared war, as had been done against France. In the first case, Justice Samuel Chase noted, "Congress is empowered to declare a general war, or congress may wage a limited war; limited in place, in objects, and in time." In the second case, Chief Justice John Marshall wrote for the Court, "The whole powers of war being, by the constitution of the United States, vested in congress, the acts of that body can alone be resorted to as our guides in this inquiry."[24]

Recent studies by the Justice Department and statements made during congressional debate in 1994 imply that President Jefferson took military measures against the Barbary powers without seeking the approval or authority of Congress.[25] In fact, in at least eleven statutes, Congress explicitly authorized military action by Presidents Jefferson and Madison.[26] Jefferson informed Congress that he had sent a small squadron of frigates to the Mediterranean to protect against attacks from the Pasha of Tripoli, but then asked Congress for further guidance, explaining that he was "unauthorized by the Constitution, without the sanction of Congress, to go beyond the line of defense." It was up to Congress to authorize "measures of offense also."[27]

No doubt, Jefferson's message to Congress omitted many details of what happened in the Mediterranean.[28] The essential legal point is that he went to Congress to seek statutory authority; he did not claim an independent and exclusive power to go to war. In 1805, when conflicts arose between the United States and Spain, Jefferson spoke plainly about constitutional principles: "Congress alone is constitutionally invested with the power of changing our condition from peace to war."[29]

After two decades of congressionally authorized military actions against Indians, internal rebellions, France, and the Barbary pirates, Congress declared its first war in 1812. Much like President John Adams had done in the quasi-war with France, President Madison submitted a message to Congress on November 5, 1811, alerting it to a number of hostile and discriminatory actions by England that required Congress to prepare for war.[30] The commitment to war was to be done by statute, not presidential fiat. Congress responded by raising additional military forces, organizing a volunteer military corps, and augmenting the navy.[31]

Madison's message to Congress on June 1, 1812, identified other "injuries and indignities" committed by England. Although these practices amounted to what Madison called "a state of war against the United States," he deferred to Congress on whether to declare war, "a solemn question which the Constitution wisely confides to the legislative department of the Government."[32] Congress declared war on June 18, 1812.

The power of commander in chief is at its low point when there is no standing army, for the President cannot deploy troops until Congress raises them. But when a standing army does exist, ready to move at the President's command, the balance of power can shift decisively. The capacity of the President to plunge the nation into war is illustrated by President James Polk's decision in 1846 to order General Zachary Taylor to occupy disputed territory on the Texas-Mexico border. The order provoked a clash between U.S. and Mexican soldiers, allowing Polk to tell Congress on April 11 that "war exists."[33] Although Polk took the decisive initiative, he never argued that he could independently take the country to war; he knew he had to come to Congress to seek authority. Congress declared war on May 13.

Polk's action was censured by the House of Representatives in 1848 on the grounds that the war had been "unnecessarily and unconstitutionally begun by the President of the United States."[34] One of the members voting for the censure was Abraham Lincoln, who later wrote to a friend:

> Allow the President to invade a neighboring nation, whenever he shall deem it necessary to repel an invasion, and you allow him to do so, *whenever he may choose to say* he deems it necessary for such purpose— and you allow him to make war at pleasure. . . . This, our Convention understood to be the most oppressive of all Kingly oppressions; and

they resolved to so frame the Constitution that *no one man* should hold the power of bringing the oppression upon us.[35]

Lincoln's decision to censure Polk may appear to be hypocritical, for during his own years as President he exercised military force during the Civil War without first obtaining authority from Congress. In April 1861, with Congress in recess, he issued proclamations calling forth the state militias, suspending the writ of habeas corpus, and placing a blockade on the rebellious states. However, there are crucial differences between their actions. Polk's initiatives helped precipitate war with a foreign nation; Lincoln confronted a genuine internal emergency of civil war. Polk had some discretion over his actions; Lincoln was compelled to use force to put down an internal rebellion. Even so, Lincoln had genuine doubts about the legality of his actions, particularly the suspension of the writ of habeas corpus. When Congress returned, he explained that his actions, "whether strictly legal or not, were ventured upon under what appeared to be a popular demand and a public necessity, trusting then, as now, that Congress would readily ratify them." He conceded that he had probably exercised "the constitutional competency of Congress."[36] Congress debated Lincoln's actions and gave retroactive effect to them on the explicit assumption that he had acted illegally.[37]

Lincoln's suspension of the writ of habeas corpus was opposed by Chief Justice Roger Taney, sitting as circuit judge. Taney ruled that because the President had no power under the Constitution to suspend the writ, the prisoner, John Merryman, should be set free. When Taney attempted to serve a paper at the prison to free Merryman, prison officials refused to let Taney's marshal perform his duty. Avoiding a direct confrontation with Lincoln, which the judiciary could not afford, Taney merely noted, "I have exercised all the power which the constitution and laws confer upon me, but that power has been resisted by a force too strong for me to overcome."[38]

In the *Prize Cases* of 1863, the Supreme Court spoke clearly about the President's authority to conduct defensive but not offensive actions. Justice Grier said that President Lincoln had authority to take military action in a civil war "without waiting for Congress to baptize it with a name," but carefully stated that the President "has no power to initiate or declare a war either against a foreign nation or a domestic state."[39] The executive branch took exactly the same position in that case. During oral argument, Richard Henry Dana Jr., representing the United States, said that Lincoln's action in responding to the Civil War had nothing to do with "the right *to initiate a war, as a voluntary act of sovereignty*. That is vested only in Congress."[40]

Presidential Power Expands

Aside from Polk's initiatives in Mexico and Lincoln's emergency actions during the Civil War, the power of war in the nineteenth century remained basically in the hands of Congress. Presidents recognized the rule of legislative supremacy in matters of going to war. Congress declared war against Spain in 1898 and again in World War I and World War II.

In 1936, the Supreme Court issued *United States v. Curtiss-Wright Corp.*, a decision that did much to elevate the President as an independent force in foreign affairs. The Court was asked to decide whether Congress could delegate more broadly when legislating for international affairs. The issue was never the existence of independent presidential power. But the author of *Curtiss-Wright*, Justice George Sutherland, decided to use a delegation case to discover inherent powers for the President. He claimed that the exercise of presidential power does not depend solely on an act of Congress because of the "very delicate, plenary and exclusive power of the President as the sole organ of the federal government in the field of international relations."[41] The magic term "sole organ" suggests that when it comes to foreign policy, the President is the exclusive policymaker. The language carries special weight because John Marshall used it in a speech in 1800 while serving in the House of Representatives.

In fact, Sutherland wrenched Marshall's statement from context to imply a position Marshall never advanced. The full context of the debate in 1800 makes clear that Marshall argued that foreign policy is formulated and announced through a collective effort by the executive and legislative branches (by treaty or by statute), and only after that point does the President emerge as the "sole organ" in *implementing* national policy. It was here that Marshall said that the President "is the sole organ of the nation in its external relations and its sole representative with foreign nations."[42] The President merely *announces* policy; he does not *make* it.

Even though Sutherland's opinion is filled with historical and conceptual inaccuracies, *Curtiss-Wright* became a popular citation for Court decisions upholding presidential power in foreign affairs. The case is frequently cited to support not only broad delegations of legislative power to the President but even the existence of independent, implied, and inherent powers for the President.[43]

Shortly after *Curtiss-Wright*, President Franklin D. Roosevelt took steps to lead the country from a state of neutrality to one of war. In June 1940, when France requested additional assistance from the United States, he pledged continuing assistance but cautioned, "I know that you will understand that these statements carry with them no implication of military commitments. Only the Congress can make such commitments."[44] However, when Prime Minister Winston Churchill pressed Roosevelt for used destroyers, Roosevelt announced on September 3, 1940, an agreement to exchange fifty "over-age" destroyers with Britain in return for the right to use bases on British islands in the Atlantic and the Caribbean.[45] Made solely by executive agreement, the destroyers/bases deal circumvented congressional control. Attorney General Robert Jackson defended the constitutionality of the agreement, relying in part on Sutherland's opinion in *Curtiss-Wright*.[46]

The Korean Conflict

The constitutional meaning of the war power changed abruptly in June 1950, when President Harry Truman took the initiative to involve the nation in war in Korea. He acted solely on his interpretation of presidential power, seeking no authority from Congress. The legality of his action has been debated ever since. What is not debatable is the fact that the President, for the first time, had committed U.S. troops abroad to a major conflict on what he considered to be adequate executive authority. He acted without a declaration of war or specific authorization from Congress. Unlike Lincoln, he did not express uncertainty about the legality of his actions and seek retroactive authority from Congress.

For legal footing, Truman cited resolutions passed by the United Nations Security Council. But how could the UN machinery serve as a legal substitute for congressional action? The history of the UN makes it clear that all parties in the legislative and executive branches understood that the decision to use military force through the UN required prior approval from both houses of Congress.[47] Much of the Senate debate in 1945 on the UN Charter centered on whether U.S. troops could be sent to the UN solely by presidential action or would require congressional consent. In the midst of this debate Truman wired a note to Senator Kenneth McKellar, making this pledge: "When any such agreement or agreements are negotiated it will be my purpose to ask the Congress for appropriate legislation to approve them."[48] With that understanding, the Senate approved the UN Charter by a vote of 89 to 2.

Having approved the Charter, Congress now had to pass additional legislation to implement it and to determine the precise constitutional mechanisms for the use of force. The UN Charter called for each nation to ratify agreements to lend military support "in accordance with their respective constitutional processes." The specific procedures for the United States are included in Section 6 of the UN Participation Act of 1945. Without the slightest ambiguity, this statute requires that the agreements "shall be subject to the approval of the Congress by appropriate Act or joint resolution."[49] Statutory language could not be more clear.

With these safeguards supposedly in place to protect congressional prerogatives, how could Truman act unilaterally in ordering U.S. air and sea forces to give South Korea assistance? The short answer is that he ignored the special agreements that were the vehicle for assuring congressional approval in advance of any military action by the President. Congressional reaction to Truman's usurpation of the war power was largely passive. Rather than express outrage, some members offered the weak and historically inaccurate justification that "history will show that on more than 100 occasions in the life of this Republic" the President had ordered American troops to do certain things without seeking congressional consent.[50] These precedents for unilateral presidential action do not come close to the magnitude of the Korean War. As Edward S. Corwin noted, the list consists largely of "fights with pirates, landings of small naval contingents on barbarous or semi-barbarous coasts, the dispatch of small bodies of troops to chase bandits or cattle rustlers across the Mexican border, and the like."[51]

Truman was eventually checked, but by the Supreme Court rather than by Congress. In the midst of a nationwide strike in 1952, President Truman ordered the seizure of the steel mills to help prosecute the war in Korea. He decided to forgo the statutory option available to him: a cooling-off period of eighty days. That procedure had been included in the Taft-Hartley Act of 1947, a measure vetoed by Truman.

The legality of his action was immediately challenged by some members of Congress, who pointed out that in 1951 Congress had specifically considered granting a President seizure authority and chose to reject that course.[52] Newspapers from around the country published editorials that condemned Truman's theory of inherent and emergency power. The editorials ripped him for acting in a manner they regarded as arbitrary, dictatorial, dangerous, destructive, high-handed, and unauthorized by law.[53]

At a news conference, Truman was asked by reporters whether he could also seize newspapers and radio stations. He replied, "Under similar circumstances the President of the United States has to act for whatever is for the best of the country. That's the answer to your question."[54] That definition of executive power so offended the public that he soon found himself backtracking, acknowledging various legal and constitutional limits that operate on the President. He pointed out that Congress could act legislatively to check his action.[55] Congress refused to bite. Truman had gotten himself out on a limb and Congress felt no obligation to either rescue him or saw him down. He continued to dangle.

The steel companies took the matter to court, where the Justice Department presented a remarkable argument that the judiciary had no power to constrain the President. According to Justice, only two checks operated on the President: impeachment and the ballot box.[56] In response, District Judge David A. Pine wrote a blistering opinion that repudiated this theory of inherent presidential power. In holding Truman's seizure of the steel mills to be unconstitutional, Pine admitted that a nationwide strike could do extensive damage to the country, but believed that a strike "would be less injurious to the public than the injury which would flow from a timorous judicial recognition that there is some basis for this claim to unlimited and unrestrained Executive power, which would be implicit in a failure to grant the injunction."[57]

Pine's opinion resonated with the nation. A Gallup poll taken afterward showed dwindling support for the seizure. "This popular reaction . . . as a practical matter became an important element in the legal decision-making process."[58] In a 6–3 ruling, the Supreme Court declared the seizure unconstitutional. With Congress and the nation opposing the seizure, the Court had little difficulty in rejecting Truman's assertion of plenary war-making authority.[59]

One of the law clerks on the Supreme Court at that time was William Rehnquist. In terms of legal precedents, he thought that the administration would prevail. Decades later, sitting now on the Supreme Court, Rehnquist reflected on that decision and came to realize the extent to which the political climate influenced the Court. Truman's definition of presidential power disturbed the country, and a strong negative public sentiment pressed on the Court. Rehnquist remarked, "I think that this is one of those celebrated constitutional cases where what might be called the tide of public opinion suddenly began to run against the government, for a number of reasons, and that this tide of public opinion had a considerable influence on the Court."[60]

Eisenhower and Vietnam

The Korean War helped put an end to twenty years of Democratic control of the White House. "Korea, not crooks or Communists, was the major concern of the voters," writes Stephen Ambrose.[61] The high point of the 1952 campaign came on October 24, less than two weeks before the election, when Dwight D. Eisenhower announced that he would "go to Korea" to end the war. Dissatisfaction with the war destroyed Truman's popularity and had much to do with Eisenhower's victory.

Although Eisenhower initially believed that Truman's decision to intervene in Korea was "wise and necessary,"[62] he came to realize that it was
a serious mistake—politically and constitutionally—to commit the nation
to war in Korea without congressional approval. Eisenhower thought that
national commitments would be stronger if entered into jointly by both
branches, stressing the importance of *collective* action by Congress and
the President.

In 1954, when Eisenhower was under pressure to intervene in Indochina
to save beleaguered French troops, he refused to act unilaterally. He told
reporters in a news conference, "There is going to be no involvement of
America in war unless it is a result of the constitutional process that is
placed upon Congress to declare it. Now, let us have that clear; and that
is the answer."[63] Eisenhower told Secretary of State John Foster Dulles
that in "the absence of some kind of arrangement getting support of
Congress," it "would be completely unconstitutional & indefensible" to
give any assistance to the French.[64] (Eisenhower's attitude about covert
operations was different. On a number of occasions he approved covert
actions in Iran, Guatemala, and Cuba without seeking congressional support or authority.)

For overt actions, Eisenhower's theory of government invited Congress
to enact area resolutions that would authorize presidential action. He did
that with Formosa and in the Middle East. In 1954, conditions in the
Formosa Straits threatened to deteriorate into a military confrontation
between the United States and China. In a memorandum, Secretary Dulles
noted that "it is doubtful that the issue can be exploited without Congressional approval."[65] One issue was whether Eisenhower could order an
attack on the airfields in China. He said that would require "Congressional
authorization, since it would be war. If Congressional authorization were
not obtained there would be logical grounds for impeachment. Whatever
we do must be in a Constitutional manner."[66]

The next year, Eisenhower appealed to Congress for joint action. He
believed that the situation merited "appropriate action of the United Nations," but unlike Truman, he did not go to the UN and exclude Congress.
Quite the opposite. Instead of waiting for the UN to act, he urged Congress
"to participate now, by specific resolution, in measures designed to improve the prospects for peace." The resolution would contemplate the
use of U.S. armed forces "if necessary to assure the security of Formosa
and the Pescadores."[67] Congress responded quickly, the House passing
the resolution 410 to 3 and the Senate supporting it 85 to 3.[68] Eisenhower
followed the same process in 1957 with an area resolution for the Middle
East to forestall Soviet ambitions. He emphasized the importance of executive-legislative coordination: "I deem it necessary to seek the cooperation

of the Congress. Only with that cooperation can we give the reassurance needed to deter aggression."[69] Again the resolution was enacted.[70]

In his memoirs, Eisenhower explained the choice between invoking executive prerogatives and seeking congressional support. On New Year's Day in 1957 he met with Secretary Dulles and congressional leaders of both parties. House Majority Leader John McCormack asked Eisenhower whether he, as commander in chief, already possessed authority to carry out actions in the Middle East without congressional action. Eisenhower replied that "greater effect could be had from a consensus of Executive and Legislative opinion, and I spoke earnestly of the desire of the Middle East countries to have reassurance now that the United States would stand ready to help. . . . Near the end of this meeting I reminded the legislators that the Constitution assumes that our two branches of government should get along together."[71]

Eisenhower's position on the war power was extremely perceptive. He knew that lawyers and policy advisors in the executive branch could always identify a multitude of precedents to justify unilateral presidential action. It was his seasoned judgment, however, that a commitment by the United States would have much greater impact on allies and enemies alike because it would represent the collective judgment of the President and Congress.

Eisenhower's experiment with interbranch cooperation was short-lived. Unlike Eisenhower, President John F. Kennedy was prepared to act during the Cuban missile crisis solely on his own constitutional authority. At a news conference on September 13, 1962, Kennedy warned of a communist buildup (with Soviet assistance) in Cuba. A series of "offensive missile sites," he said, were in preparation.[72] However, he did not request a joint resolution from Congress. Under his power as commander in chief he claimed to have "full authority now to take such action" militarily against Cuba.[73] The Cuba Resolution, passed by Congress on October 3, did not authorize presidential action; it merely expressed the support of Congress to resist "the Marxist-Leninist regime in Cuba."

By the time Lyndon Johnson entered the White House, three U.S. Presidents had taken decisive steps to involve the nation in Vietnam. Truman and Eisenhower provided substantial economic and military assistance to aid the French in Indochina. Under Truman, the United States paid for between 33 and 50 percent of the cost,[74] and aid climbed to about 75 percent during the Eisenhower years. Eisenhower made the first commitment of soldiers, sending 200 military personnel to assist the French.[75] Under Kennedy, the number of military advisors rose from 700 to 16,000.

On August 3, 1964, President Lyndon B. Johnson ordered the Navy to take retaliatory actions against the North Vietnamese for their attacks in the Gulf of Tonkin.[76] He acted following an attack on the U.S. destroyer *Maddox* by communist PT boats. An August 4 report provided further details on the incident and described a second attack, this one against two U.S. destroyers; subsequent studies indicate that this second attack probably never occurred.[77]

Johnson met with the leaders of both parties in Congress and asked for a resolution making clear "our determination to take all necessary measures in support of freedom and in defense of peace in southeast Asia."[78] Congress spent little time debating the resolution. Senate debate started on August 6 and concluded the next day, endorsing the resolution by a margin of 88 to 2. The House passed the measure on August 7 without a single dissenting vote, 416 to 0. The Tonkin Gulf Resolution approved and supported the determination of the President, as commander in chief, to take "all necessary measures to repel any armed attack against the forces of the United States and to prevent further aggression."[79]

Neither house bothered to independently verify what happened in the Gulf of Tonkin. In the midst of a presidential election year, only two members of Congress were willing to challenge the President. One of the dissenters in the Senate, Wayne Morse, displayed an uncanny gift for prophecy: "Unpopular as it is, I am perfectly willing to make the statement for history that if we follow a course of action that bogs down thousands of American boys in Asia, the administration responsible for it will be rejected and repudiated by the American people. It should be."[80] Four years later, after heavy casualties in a war that seemed to have no end and no possible victory, Johnson was driven from office.

Richard Nixon, elected in 1968 to end the war in Vietnam, actually widened it to include Cambodia and Laos. His "incursion" into Cambodia in 1970 triggered nationwide protests and provoked Congress to enact restrictive amendments in 1971 to forbid the introduction of U.S. ground combat troops or advisors into Cambodia.[81] By denying funds for all combat activities in Southeast Asia in 1973, Congress finally brought the war to an end.

In 1975, at the conclusion of the Vietnam War, Secretary of State Henry Kissinger observed that "comity between the executive and legislative branches is the only possible basis for national action" and that "foreign policy must be a shared enterprise."[82] Like Eisenhower before him, Kissinger understood that the President needs the support and cooperation of Congress to successfully fight a war; otherwise, as was true with Vietnam, divisions at home will strengthen the resolve of enemies.

The War Powers Resolution

After years of hearings and lengthy debate, Congress passed the War Powers Resolution in 1973 in an effort to limit presidential war power. Under the resolution, the President is to consult with Congress "in every possible instance," and after introducing forces into hostilities is required to report to Congress within forty-eight hours. Congress anticipated that the President could use military force without congressional authorization for sixty days (with the option of extending this period to ninety days), but longer military engagements would require legislative approval.

The resolution, reflecting a mix of House and Senate provisions, was vetoed by Nixon on the ground that it encroached upon the President's constitutional responsibilities as commander in chief. He told Congress that the "only way in which the constitutional powers of a branch of the Government can be altered is by amending the Constitution—and any attempt to make such alterations by legislation alone is clearly without force."[83] Both houses overrode the veto, though the House narrowly managed the two-thirds necessary (284 to 135); the Senate vote (75 to 18) was more comfortable.

Although the War Powers Resolution overcame a veto, it did not survive doubts about its quality, effectiveness, and motivation. Some of the congressional support relied on party politics: efforts to score some short-term political points at the cost of long-term institutional and constitutional interests. Many legislators took comfort in the resolution's symbolic value rather than its contents. Consider the voting record of fifteen members of the House.[84] Initially, they voted against the House bill and the conference version because they thought the legislation transferred legislative power to the President. To be consistent, they should have voted to sustain Nixon's veto to prevent the bill from becoming law. Instead, they switched sides and delivered the decisive votes for enactment.

These members reversed course for several reasons. Some feared that a vote to sustain the veto would lend credence to the views of presidential power advanced in Nixon's veto message;[85] others thought that an override might be a step toward impeaching Nixon. Representative Bella Abzug voted against the House bill and the conference version because they expanded presidential war power. As she noted during debate on the conference report, "[It] gives the President 60 to 90 days to intervene in any crisis situation, or any pretext, while Congress merely asks that he tell us what he has done."[86] Yet she strongly supported a veto override: "This could be a turning point in the struggle to control an administration that has run amuck. It could accelerate the demand for an impeachment of the President."[87]

The thought of overriding a Nixon veto was tempting. Eight times during the 93rd Congress he had vetoed legislation; eight times the Democratic Congress came up short on the override. Some legislators regarded the override vote on the War Powers Resolution an essential means of reasserting congressional power, particularly in the midst of the Watergate scandals.[88] The Saturday Night Massacre, which sent Special Prosecutor Archibald Cox, Attorney General Elliot Richardson, and Deputy Attorney General William Ruckelshaus out of government, occurred just four days before Nixon's veto of the War Powers Resolution. Ten days before the Saturday Night Massacre, Vice President Spiro Agnew's resignation in disgrace further heightened the cry for partisan and institutional blood.

The partisan climate did not prevent some members of Congress from recognizing that the conference product tilted power dangerously toward the President. William Green, Democrat from Pennsylvania, remarked that the War Powers Resolution "has popularly been interpreted as limiting the President's power to engage our troops in war." Yet a careful reading of the bill indicated that it "is actually an expansion of Presidential warmaking power, rather than a limitation."[89] Other legislators also saw that the bill represented an abdication of congressional power.[90] Senator Thomas Eagleton, a principal sponsor of the Senate bill, denounced the version that emerged from conference as a "total, complete distortion of the war powers concept."[91] Instead of the three narrowly defined exceptions specified in the Senate bill, the conference product gave the President carte blanche authority to use military force for up to ninety days.

Even those who continued to support the War Powers Resolution and urged the override of Nixon's veto admitted the broad sweep of presidential power conferred by Congress. Senators Jacob Javits and Ed Muskie, in a "Dear Colleague" letter distributed to other legislators, conceded that nothing in the bill would have prevented President Nixon from sending U.S. troops to the Middle East to assist Israel against Egyptian threats. The bill, they said, "would have required the President only to report to the Congress within 48 hours in writing with respect to the deployment of U.S. Armed Forces in foreign territory, airspace and waters."[92] The President could commit troops to the volatile Middle East with no nod to Congress other than have aides prepare a written report. Eagleton confessed to being "dumbfounded." With memories so fresh about presidential extension of the war in Southeast Asia, "how can we give unbridled, unlimited total authority to the President to commit us to war?" He charged that the bill, after being nobly conceived, "has been terribly bastardized to the point of being a menace."[93]

Military Initiatives from Ford to Clinton

The War Powers Resolution has failed to achieve the basic purpose announced in Section 2(a): "to fulfill the intent of the framers of the Constitution of the United States and insure that the collective judgment of both the Congress and the President will apply to the introduction of United States Armed Forces into hostilities, or into situations where imminent involvement in hostilities is clearly indicated by the circumstances." In fact, the resolution undermines the intent of the framers and has not ensured collective judgment. Instead, it gives a green light to unilateral presidential action.

From Ford through Clinton, Presidents have used military force on numerous occasions by citing their power as commander in chief. Although they have challenged the constitutionality of the War Powers Resolution, the record since 1973 has been fairly uniform. Presidents have acted unilaterally when using force for short-term operations in areas of the world that are relatively isolated, with little chance of the conflict's spreading. For military operations in regions that pose extreme danger of involving other nations, such as in the Middle East, they have sought congressional approval in advance (without fully admitting that they needed it). This pattern changed abruptly with President Clinton's multiyear, unilateral commitment of ground troops to Bosnia and his air war against Yugoslavia.

During the first few years after enactment of the War Powers Resolution, under Presidents Gerald Ford and Jimmy Carter, the executive branch did little to flex its muscles in war making. Both men understood the need to heal the wounds from the Vietnam War. But the record from Ronald Reagan to Bill Clinton reveals an increasing use of presidential war power, with Congress progressively marginalized. Reagan introduced U.S. troops into Lebanon, invaded Grenada, carried out air strikes against Libya, and maintained naval operations in the Persian Gulf. In none of these actions did he ask Congress for authority. Congress eventually passed legislation in the fall of 1983 to authorize military action in Lebanon for a period of eighteen months.

In 1989, President Bush I relied on independent executive power to invade Panama, and only at the last minute did he come to Congress for support in acting offensively against Iraq. Clinton used military force repeatedly without congressional authority: launching missiles against Baghdad in 1993, carrying out combat operations in Somalia, threatening to invade Haiti, conducting air strikes in Bosnia followed by the dispatch of twenty thousand ground troops, authorizing repeated air strikes against Iraq, sending cruise missiles into Afghanistan and Sudan, and initiating an air war against Yugoslavia. At no point did he feel obliged to obtain authority from Congress.

Instead of challenging these military initiatives and reclaiming legislative power, members of Congress generally defended presidential prerogatives. This pattern prevails regardless of whether the President is from the legislator's party or not. In backing Clinton, for example, Bob Dole, John McCain, and Newt Gingrich, all Republicans, all invoked the President's "authority under the Constitution" "regardless of what Congress does," for the "daily leadership [of the military] has to be an executive function."[94]

Further limiting lawmaker prerogatives, Presidents have seized on a glaring deficiency in the War Powers Resolution. The resolution is written in such a way that the sixty-to-ninety-day clock begins ticking only if the President reports under a very specific section of the statute: Section 4(a)(1). Not surprisingly, Presidents do not report under 4(a)(1). They report, for the most part, "consistent with the War Powers Resolution." The only President to report under 4(a)(1) was Ford in the rescue of the U.S. merchant ship *Mayaguez*, which had been seized by Cambodians. But his report had no substantive importance because it was released after the operation was over. The true meaning of the War Powers Resolution, then, was that Presidents could unilaterally use military force against other countries for as long as they liked, until Congress got around to adopting some kind of statutory constraint.

One of the by-products of the War Powers Resolution is the frequency with which legislators turn not to their colleagues to challenge the President, through the many institutional powers that are available, but to the courts. On four occasions during the 1980s, members of Congress went to court to charge President Reagan with violations of the War Powers Resolution. The position of the legislators was weakened by two facts: They came as a small group unable to represent what Congress intended as an institution, and they were often opposed by another group of legislators who defended the President. Standing in the middle of this crossfire, federal judges essentially told the legislators complaining of executive aggrandizement, Don't come in here and expect us to do your work for you.[95] Because Congress would not stake out an institutional position contrary to the President's, the courts saw no reason to defend a Congress that was unwilling to defend itself. As then appellate court judge Ruth Bader Ginsburg put it, Congress "has formidable weapons at its disposal—the power of the purse and the investigative resources far beyond those available in the Third Branch. But no gauntlet has been thrown down here by a majority of the Members of Congress."[96]

A more interesting case occurred in 1990, when members of Congress challenged Bush I's contemplated use of military force against Iraq. A district judge ruled that the issue was not ready for judicial determination, but decisively rejected many of the sweeping claims for presidential war-making prerogatives advanced by the Justice Department. The court concluded that if Congress confronted the President, and the President refused to accept a statutory restriction, the issue might be ripe for the courts.[97] Of particular significance, the court dismissed the Justice Department's claim that the President could engage in any type of offensive military operation so long as it was not "warmaking." For the court, this reasoning marked an exercise in semantics that would leave the war power in the hands of the President.[98]

After Clinton began bombing Yugoslavia, Congressman Tom Campbell and several other members of the House of Representatives brought a suit in district court seeking a declaration that Clinton had violated the War Powers Clause of the Constitution and the War Powers Resolution. The court held that the lawmakers lacked standing because the injury they identified was not sufficiently concrete and particularized. The fact that Congress had not confronted Clinton with statutory restrictions was crucial: "If Congress had directed the President to remove forces from their positions and he had refused to do so or if Congress had refused to appropriate or authorize the use of funds for the air strikes in Yugoslavia and the President had decided to spend that money (or money earmarked for other purposes) anyway, that likely would have constituted an actual confrontation sufficient to confer standing on legislative plaintiffs."[99]

The D.C. Circuit agreed that Campbell lacked standing.[100] The decision by the appellate court is interesting because it presents radically different positions on the competence of federal courts to decide war powers cases. In a concurrence, Judge Silberman said that "no one" is able to bring a challenge of "a President's arguably unlawful use of force" because of the lack of "judicially discoverable and manageable standards" for analyzing such claims.[101] Judge Tatel disagreed that the case posed a nonjusticiable political question. The question raised is "whether the President possessed legal authority to conduct the military operation," and on such questions he considered courts capable of determining the proper allocation of power among the branches of government.[102]

Military Action after 9/11

Following the terrorist attacks of 9/11, President George W. Bush came to Congress to seek statutory authority for a military response. In requesting congressional authority, he broke ranks with Truman, Bush I, and Clinton, all of whom claimed they could order large-scale military operations in Korea, Iraq, and Yugoslavia without requesting authority from Congress. The result of negotiations between the executive and legislative branches in 2001 was the Use of Force Act, which authorized the President to use "all necessary and appropriate force against those nations, organizations, or persons he determines planned, authorized, committed, or aided" the 9/11 attacks. On the basis of that statute, Bush used military force against terrorist structures in Afghanistan.

A year later, Bush considered military action against Iraq. Initially, the administration concluded that Bush did not need authority from Congress. The White House Counsel's office gave a broad reading to the President's power as commander in chief, and argued that the 1991 Iraq Resolution provided continuing military authority to the President, passing the authority neatly from father to son.[103] The White House also claimed that Congress, by passing the Iraq Liberation Act of 1998, had already approved U.S. military action against Iraq for violations of UN Security Council resolutions.[104] However, by its explicit terms, the statute did not authorize war.[105] Other legal arguments from the White House Counsel's office were strained and unconvincing.[106]

For one reason or another, Bush decided in early September 2002 to seek authorization from Congress. Unlike the situation in 1990, Congress was expected to act *before* the November elections. In 1990, after Iraq had invaded Kuwait, the administration first went to the Security Council to request a resolution authorizing military operations, and only in January 1991, after the elections, did lawmakers return to debate and pass legislation to authorize war. In 2002, the White House pressured Congress to pass the authorizing bill before members returned home for reelection.

During this compressed time period, lawmakers heard conflicting claims on whether a connection existed between Iraq and al Qaeda and whether Iraq possessed weapons of mass destruction. Some legislators, such as Senator Robert C. Byrd, did not find the threat from Iraq "so great that we must be stampeded to provide such authority to the president just weeks before an election."[107] And yet Congress chose to vote under partisan pressure with inadequate information, to pass an authorizing resolution.[108] As with the Tonkin Gulf Resolution, Congress acted hurriedly in the middle of an election without the information it needed. The Iraq Resolution did not decide either for or against military action; it left that decision solely with the President, exactly what the framers hoped they had avoided.

Six members of Congress, along with soldiers and parents, filed a lawsuit to challenge Bush's legal authority to wage war under the Iraq Resolution.

A district court in Massachusetts held that the dispute involved political questions beyond the authority of the judiciary to resolve: "Absent a clear abdication of this constitutional responsibility by the political branches, the judiciary has no role to play."[109] Only if the political branches were "clearly and resolutely in opposition as to the military policy to be followed by the United States" would the issue pose a question that could be resolved by the courts.[110] Whatever the ambiguity of the Iraq Resolution, "it is clear that Congress has not acted to bind the President with respect to possible military activity in Iraq."[111]

When this decision was appealed, the lawsuit had the support of twelve members of Congress. The First Circuit affirmed the district court ruling, but not on the political question doctrine, which it found "famously murky."[112] Instead, it based its analysis on ripeness: "Diplomatic negotiations, in particular, fluctuate daily. The President has emphasized repeatedly that hostilities still may be averted if Iraq takes certain actions."[113] Although the First Circuit agreed that the "amalgam of powers" involved in war envisage "the joint participation" of Congress and the President in determining "the scale and duration of hostilities,"[114] it found no evidence that the President acted "without apparent congressional authorization, or against congressional opposition."[115]

After receiving statutory authority for Iraq, the Bush administration prosecuted a successful military campaign but failed to plan adequately for the occupation. Questions were raised about the quality of information from U.S. intelligence agencies and whether Bush had been forthcoming with the public about the length and cost of the war. U.S. casualties continued to mount after Bush on May 1, 2003 declared "mission accomplished." As with Vietnam, the administration discovered that military victories do not assure political success.

Conclusions

The drift of the war power from Congress to the President after World War II is unmistakable. Instead of building a multinational force with UN backing, the Bush administration found itself almost solely responsible for occupying and pacifying Iraq, resulting in heavy financial costs, casualties, and uncertain goals.[116] The framers' design, deliberately placing in Congress the decision to expend the nation's blood and treasure, has been radically transformed. Over time, because of expectations that have developed about the President's responsibilities in the areas of foreign affairs and the war power, presidential eminence seems defined by the willingness to unilaterally order military strikes. Presidents now regularly claim that the Commander in Chief Clause empowers them to send U.S. troops anywhere in the world, including into hostilities, without first seeking legislative approval. Instead of seeking authority from Congress, Presidents are likely to appeal to international and regional institutions for support, particularly the United Nations and the North Atlantic Council.[117]

The record is not simply one of executive aggrandizement. In the face of repeated presidential initiatives, Congress has failed to protect its prerogatives. The shift of war power from Congress to the President belies a core belief by the framers that each branch would protect its interests; a powerful motive of institutional self-defense would supposedly safeguard the system of separation of powers. Instead, "unwilling to take responsibility for setting foreign policy," Congress almost always "prefer[s] to leave the decision—and the blame—with the president."[118]

Congress's ever diminishing role in war powers comes at substantial cost to the nation and the Constitution. The system of checks and balances applies as much to military policy as to domestic policy. We cannot expect foreign policy and national security to be formulated well in the hands of an unchecked executive. Congressman Lee Hamilton, pointing to the value of joint action by Congress and the President, put it this way: "I believe that a partnership, characterized by creative tension between the President and the Congress, produces a foreign policy that better serves the American national interest—and better reflects the values of the American people—than policy produced by the President alone."[119]

The constitutional position of Congress has deteriorated for a number of reasons. One is the volunteer army. During the Vietnam War years, citizens protested by burning their draft cards, refusing induction, fleeing to Canada, and participating in mass demonstrations. In the current volunteer army, the passions and outlets for civil disobedience are muted. College campuses, once hotbeds of opposition to the Vietnam War, are now largely silent. As Joseph Califano has noted, an all-volunteer army "relieves affluent, vocal, voting Americans of the concern that their children will be at risk of going into combat."[120]

Second, military technology now enables Presidents to wage wars with few casualties. During the four days of bombing Iraq in December 1998, not a single U.S. or British casualty resulted from seventy hours of intensive air strikes involving 650 sorties against nearly one hundred targets.[121] The following year, President Clinton waged war for eleven weeks against Yugoslavia without a single NATO combat casualty.

Third, the growing cost of running for office means that legislators have less time to tend to their institutional and constitutional duties. As Congressman Hamilton explained in 1998, "Members today must spend a disproportionate amount of time fund-raising, which means less time with constituents discussing the issues and less time with colleagues forging legislation and monitoring federal bureaucrats."[122] Less time in Washington, D.C., means less time understanding legislative prerogatives, less time working with colleagues on like-minded issues, and less time forging alliances to fight off executive encroachments.

In surrendering its powers to the President, Congress has little reason to expect assistance from the courts. For good cause, judges are reluctant to intervene unless and until Congress has joined the issue by invoking its institutional powers. With no meaningful resistance to presidential initiatives, the Constitution's war-making provisions have given way to a political dynamic that clearly favors the executive. But White House supremacy comes at a cost. In war making, as with other areas, supremacy in any one branch makes the Constitution less relevant, less durable. When it comes to war, the nation is better protected when the executive and legislative branches act jointly and present a united front.

Privacy

The Constitution explicitly protects a range of individual rights from governmental intrusion. In defending those core values, all three branches make important contributions. Privacy rights are not mentioned in the Constitution. Instead, they are defined by agency regulation, congressional statute, or court decision, with no branch having the final say. Increasingly, state legislatures, governors, and state courts are advancing their own concepts of privacy, drawing from different provisions in state constitutions. The driving force behind these governmental actions, whether at the national or state level, comes from individuals and groups pressing their privacy interests.

In recent decades, the Supreme Court has adopted sweeping notions of fundamental rights (on contraception and abortion). But under the pressure of public condemnation, reaching to core questions of judicial abuse and illegitimate power, the Justices had to carve out a more modest role while recognizing a larger function for elected branches and the states. Today, abortion, gay rights, and the right to die dominate the privacy wars. State and federal officials have played an instrumental role in shaping privacy, sometimes limiting and at other times expanding the availability of privacy rights.

The Specter of *Lochner*

The recognition of implied rights to check legislative action raises questions about the judiciary's role in a democratic society. "Judicial review expresses," as Alexander Bickel observed, "a form of distrust of the legislature."[1] The greater the protection accorded unenumerated rights, the greater the judiciary's countermajoritarian role and the greater the friction between the Court and elected officials.

The judicial tradition that serves as a backdrop to privacy issues is the *Lochner* era, a period from 1905 to 1937 in which the Court shoehorned laissez-faire economics into the Due Process Clause to strike down roughly two hundred social and economic laws. By empowering itself to strike down laws that it deemed to be "arbitrary," "capricious," or "unreasonable," the Court functioned as self-appointed czar over social and economic legislation.[2]

What the Court did in *Lochner* was to embrace a "liberty of contract" nowhere found in the Constitution.[3] A bare 5–4 majority converted the general right to make a contract into a bar against any law that interfered with the freedom of employees and employers to agree to terms. Laws on maximum hours, minimum wages, and working conditions were routinely invalidated by the courts. In his dissent in *Lochner*, Justice Holmes accused the Court of embracing a particular economic theory (laissez-faire) that is not found in the text of the Constitution or the intent of the framers. *Lochner* symbolized judicial overreaching for many.

Congress, the President, labor unions, the press, and a host of social and economic groups openly challenged the Court. Most striking, with the claim that the Supreme Court was unable to function effectively, Franklin Roosevelt proposed legislation that would allow him to appoint an additional Justice for every Justice over seventy years of age until the number on the Court reached fifteen.[4] Although this plan was rejected, a judicial veto over economic legislation was put to rest by Roosevelt's landslide victory in the 1936 election, combined with the repudiation of *Lochner*'s free market philosophy by the enduring Depression.

Yet *Lochner* had a second life. The debate about judicial lawmaking again took center stage with *Griswold v. Connecticut*, a 1965 Supreme Court decision invalidating a Connecticut statute that criminalized the use by married persons of any drug or medicinal article to prevent conception. Writing for the Court, Justice William O. Douglas (a Roosevelt loyalist) wanted to uphold the privacy rights of married couples without appearing to revive the discredited *Lochner* philosophy. In particular, Douglas's disdain for *Lochner* compelled him to ground his decision in constitutional protections, not natural law theories. He argued that a "zone of privacy [was] created by several fundamental constitutional guarantees," including the "penumbras, formed by emanations" of the First, Third, Fourth, Fifth, and Ninth Amendments.[5]

Griswold, while reinvigorating privacy, did not suggest that a constitutional right to abortion was on the horizon. Birth control pioneer Margaret Sanger, in explaining her opposition to Connecticut's anticontraception law, emphasized that the advocates of birth control did not favor abortion; they wanted only to prevent the beginning of life.[6] When the Court heard *Griswold*, Planned Parenthood attorney and Yale law professor Thomas Emerson argued that the invalidation of the anticontraception law would not create a right to abortion.[7] In the Court's private deliberations of *Griswold*, moreover, Earl Warren went out of his way to distinguish the Connecticut statute from antiabortion measures, "implying that he thought such laws were valid."[8]

But in 1973, the Supreme Court issued its decision *Roe v. Wade*.[9] Holding that a woman's right to terminate her pregnancy in the early months outweighed state interests in maternal health and fetal protection, the Court struck down a Texas law permitting abortions only to save the life of the mother. The Court concluded both that the state's interest in potential human life is not compelling until the third trimester of pregnancy (once the fetus becomes viable) and that during the first trimester, the abortion decision is left to the woman (in consultation with her physician).

By valuing a woman's right to privacy over potential human life and by imposing a trimester standard that reads like a legislative abortion code, *Roe* became a lightning rod for critics of judge-made rights. William Rehnquist's dissent analogized *Roe* to *Lochner* and condemned the trimester standard as little more than "judicial legislation." Byron White, in his dissent, likewise spoke of "raw judicial power." Many legal academics, some of whom supported abortion rights, deemed *Roe* an illegitimate, unprincipled, and offensive exercise of judicial power. As John Hart Ely put it, "The Court continues to disavow the philosophy of *Lochner*. Yet . . . it is impossible candidly to regard *Roe* as anything else."[10] While the Court may have tried to tiptoe quietly through *Roe*, it found itself—fully aware of the *Lochner* debacle—back in the soup.

Reagan Nominates Bork

With the 1980 election of Ronald Reagan, judicial activism was again under attack. In 1980 and again in 1984, presidential candidate Reagan pledged to appoint judges who would return "non-essential federal functions . . . to the States and localities . . . who respect traditional family values and the sanctity of innocent human life."[11] The most visible mechanism for putting this philosophy of "judicial restraint" into action was administration attacks on Supreme Court decisions on privacy.

Attorney General William French Smith summarized the administration's position on privacy, arguing that the judiciary is wrong to "discern such an abstraction in the Constitution, arbitrarily elevate it over other constitutional rights and powers by attaching the label 'fundamental,' and then resort to it as, in the words of one of Justice Black's dissents, a 'loose, flexible, uncontrolled standard for holding laws unconstitutional.'"[12] With respect to *Roe v. Wade*, Reagan often spoke of the need to "affirm the humanity of the unborn child in our society" and criticized *Roe* as an unjustified "usurpation of the role of legislatures and State courts."[13]

The defining moment in the Reagan administration's attack on judicial theories of privacy was the July 1987 nomination of Robert Bork to the U.S. Supreme Court. Bork would replace judicial moderate Lewis Powell, the swing vote on a sharply divided Court and the Justice who often stymied much of the "Reagan revolution" through decisive votes on abortion, affirmative action, and church-state matters. The Bork nomination, then, threatened to alter fundamental doctrines of the Court. Indeed, Senate Judiciary Committee Chairman Joseph Biden suggested that the Bork controversy was more about the loss of Justice Powell than about Bork himself, remarking that if "Bork were about to replace Rehnquist or . . . Scalia, this would be a whole different ball game."[14]

Bork's attack on *Griswold*, calling it "an unprincipled decision" that "fails every test of neutrality,"[15] was not lost on his opponents. Although their principal concern was abortion, the Block Bork Coalition feared that using the confirmation hearings to debate abortion would be too divisive and contentious. The solution was to "pluck the heartstrings of [the] middle class" by having abortion subsumed into the larger issue of privacy.[16] This strategy was implemented in a full-page ad that appeared in the *Washington Post* and other newspapers on September 14, 1987. Planned Parenthood warned that the stakes of the Bork nomination were "decades of Supreme Court decisions uphold[ing] your freedom to make your own decisions about marriage and family, childbearing and parenting" and that "if the Senate confirms Robert Bork, it will be too late. Your personal privacy, one of the most cherished and unique features of American life, has never been in greater danger."[17]

Competing reports prepared by the White House and Chairman Biden served as an opening volley in this debate. But the real battle began on September 15, 1987, when Bork and members of the Senate Judiciary Committee went head-to-head on the privacy issue. Senator Biden pressed Bork on his assertion that "the economic gratification of a utility company is as worthy of as much protection as the sexual gratification of a married couple, because neither is mentioned in the Constitution." Senator Edward Kennedy told Bork that he had "serious questions . . . about placing someone on the Supreme Court that . . . find[s] some rationale not to respect [privacy rights]." Bork responded that the founders "banked a good deal upon the good sense of the people [and their elected representatives]" and asked rhetorically, "Privacy to do what[?] . . . to use cocaine in private? Privacy for businessmen to fix prices in a hotel room?"[18]

The Senate Judiciary Committee voted 9 to 5 against Bork's nomination. In explaining why Bork was unacceptable, the majority report emphasized his "narrow definition of liberty" being at odds with "the image of human dignity [which] has been associated throughout our history with the idea that the Constitution recognizes 'unenumerated rights.'"[19] Although senators such as Robert Dole labeled this privacy attack "unfair" and "absurd," the Senate defeated the Bork nomination 58 to 42, in large measure because of the privacy issue.

After Bork, it seems unlikely that a judicial nominee will challenge privacy in such a direct manner. In the wake of Bork's defeat, Anthony Kennedy quickly embraced privacy at his confirmation hearings, noting that "the concept of liberty in the due process clause is quite expansive, quite sufficient, to protect the values of privacy that Americans *legitimately* think are part of their constitutional heritage."[20] The first question asked of David Souter at his confirmation hearing concerned his views on *Griswold*, to which he replied, "I believe that the Due Process Clause of the 14th Amendment does recognize and does protect an unenumerated right of privacy."[21] Even Clarence Thomas told Senator Biden on the first day of his hearings, "My view is that there is a right to privacy in the Fourteenth Amendment."[22] Needless to say, Clinton nominees Ruth Bader Ginsburg and Stephen Breyer embraced privacy rights at their confirmation hearings as well.

Abortion and American Politics

While the Reagan administration invoked judicial restraint in explaining why *Roe* should be overturned, it defended *Griswold* in court and declined to involve itself in nonabortion privacy cases, including *Bowers v. Hardwick* (homosexual sodomy) and *Michael H. v. Gerald D.* (unwed fathers). When asked about its failure to participate in these cases, Solicitor General Charles Fried said that administration actions were "*not* an attack against privacy." He further stated that the Reagan administration and the Department of Justice felt "no particular concern about privacy in general." Their concern about privacy, he said, came only from a desire to narrow its scope in regard to *Roe v. Wade*.[23]

By overturning forty-six state abortion laws, *Roe* triggered unprecedented legislative and administrative activism at both the federal and state level. *Roe* also helps explain the rise in the number of legal abortions from 586,800 in 1972 to 1,553,900 in 1980.[24] Moreover, by freeing the market (especially in authorizing nonhospital abortions), *Roe* spurred changes in access to abortion in the most restrictive states (due to increased availability) and among poor women (due to increased affordability).[25] By increasing the number of legal abortions and the delivery of abortion services, the decision helped catalyze pro-life efforts to overturn *Roe*. Although the Court thought that *Roe* would end the abortion dispute, its decision intensified the battle.

The Court did not take into account the inevitable backlash from elected government and the public at both the state and federal level. "Judges," as Justice Ginsburg has remarked, "play an *interdependent* part in our democracy. They do not alone shape legal doctrine but . . . they participate in a dialogue with other organs of government, and the people as well." Indeed, Ginsburg went so far as to suggest that *Roe* "prolonged divisiveness and deferred stable settlement of the [abortion] issue" by short-circuiting early 1970s legislative reform efforts.[26] Although her claim has been challenged, there is no doubt that *Roe* is a starting point, not a final point, in studying the constitutionality of abortion.

Congress Responds to Roe

Congress has repeatedly shied away from extreme positions on abortion. It rejected "human life" legislation and a proposed constitutional amendment, each of which would have defined the beginning of life as conception and treated fetuses as persons for Fourteenth Amendment purposes. Congress refused to strip federal courts, including the U.S. Supreme Court, of jurisdiction in abortion cases. It also rejected pro-choice absolutism. Efforts to enact freedom of choice legislation—to statutorily codify *Roe v. Wade*—stalled after the Supreme Court's decision in *Planned Parenthood v. Casey* (1992). *Casey* adopted a moderate stance that better reflected the beliefs of Americans than did the absolutist Freedom of Choice Act (FOCA). On one hand, *Casey* reaffirmed *Roe*'s guarantee of the right to choose an abortion; on the other hand, *Casey* substituted a deferential "undue burden" test for the rigid trimester test embraced in *Roe*. Two Gallup polls taken in December 1991 and January 1992, for instance, indicated that 64 percent of Americans would not want *Roe* overturned, but a larger majority, ranging from 70 to 86 percent, favored some restrictions on the abortion right.[27] By making FOCA look extremist by comparison, *Casey* caused a great many pro-choice lawmakers to abandon FOCA after the Court's decision.

Yet Congress agreed to pass legislation limiting funds for abortion. Starting in 1976, Congress, through the Hyde Amendment, has allowed the use of Medicaid funds only for certain types of abortions.[28] Congress also used its appropriations powers to set abortion-related restrictions on programs involving family planning, foreign aid, legal services, military hospitals, the Bureau of Prisons, and the Peace Corps. It limited the use of federal and local funds for abortions in the District of Columbia.

Congress's heavy reliance on appropriations-based policymaking is quite understandable. Because appropriations must be enacted every year, antiabortion forces, through a simple floor amendment, were able to compel a majority to vote up or down on Medicaid funding. Unlike proposals that sought to nullify *Roe*, moreover, a ban on public funding leaves the individual's right to abortion intact and hence appears to be more moderate. Congress has approved a handful of measures that affect abortion rights outside the context of federal funding prohibitions. It encouraged alternatives to abortion by passing the Adolescent Family Life Act (AFLA).[29] This legislation, better known as the "chastity act," offered religious organizations federal funds to promote sexual abstinence as a method of birth control among teenagers. More striking, the Freedom of Access to Clinic Entrances Act nullified a 1993 Supreme Court decision by making it a federal crime for pro-life groups to obstruct the entrance to an abortion clinic.[30]

Through its participation in litigation, Congress also seeks to shape the abortion debate. When the Supreme Court upheld the constitutionality of the Hyde Amendment, for example, a bipartisan coalition of over two hundred congressional amici argued that "to tamper with [the inviolable and exclusive power of the purse] is to tamper with the very essence of constitutional, representative government."[31] More recently, pro-choice and pro-life legislators have lined up on opposite sides of state regulation cases. These filings, although principally symbolic, are nonetheless instructive in measuring legislative attitudes. In a 1986 case, eighty-one pro-choice legislators publicly scolded Solicitor General Charles Fried for having "taken an extraordinary and unprecedented step" in calling for *Roe*'s reversal.[32]

Ever since the 1981 nomination of Sandra Day O'Connor to the Supreme Court, the Senate Judiciary Committee has made a nominee's views on abortion the sine qua non of the confirmation process. Starting with the Carter administration, presidential appointees for such positions as secretary of health and human services, surgeon general, attorney general, solicitor general, and director of the Office of Personnel Management have had their track record on abortion scrutinized by the Senate.

Congressional decision making is highly visible, widely observed, and much criticized. For example, although the Hyde Amendment was subject to prolonged, fierce, and emotional debate, discussion of the amendment's constitutionality were rare and never rose above the level of conclusory rhetoric.[33] Likewise, Congress paid scant attention to the constitutionality of the AFLA. Indeed, when AFLA was reauthorized in 1984, a Senate subcommittee dismissed a serious constitutional challenge against the measure as something "the courts will have to decide."[34]

Constitutional concerns did, however, pervade the attacks on *Roe* that occurred in the early 1980s. In 1981, the Senate Judiciary Committee actively considered human life legislation, court-stripping proposals, and constitutional amendment proposals. In each case, extensive hearings featured the views of constitutional law experts. Committee and subcommittee reports too were replete with citations to this expert testimony as well as Supreme Court decisions and law review articles.

More recently, in considering Congress's authority to punish individuals who frustrate parental notification laws by transporting minors across state lines, the House and Senate Judiciary Committees called on constitutional law experts.[35] Likewise, when considering partial-birth abortion legislation, lawmakers examined whether Congress was constrained by a 2000 Supreme Court decision overturning a state ban on this procedure. By finding that "partial-birth abortion is never necessary to preserve the health of a woman," an April 2003 House Judiciary Committee report concluded that Congress could outlaw this procedure.[36]

Pro-choice legislators also paid careful attention to constitutional concerns in 1990s reform efforts. The FOCA was amended in 1992 to shore up its constitutional foundations. Freedom of access legislation was also modified in the face of constitutional attacks.

Presidential Initiatives

Before the election of Ronald Reagan, abortion was an important but not front-burner issue for the executive. Prior to *Roe*, the White House saw abortion as a states rights issue and left it alone. After *Roe*, abortion was too potent a national issue to be ignored by the White House. In the 1976 election, both Ford and Carter spoke out against public funding of abortion.[37] Neither played an activist role in the abortion dispute, however. Abortion did not figure prominently in their judicial appointments; neither asked the courts to either affirm or disavow *Roe*; legislation and constitutional amendments were not proposed; regulatory initiatives were modest in scope and sweep.

The 1980 election of Reagan changed all that. By advancing a pro-life agenda through spiritual leadership, regulatory reform, judicial appointments, arguments in court, and legislative and constitutional amendment proposals, "the Reagan administration not only fundamentally changed the national debate over abortion but set the stage for how the controversy [would] play out in the 1990s."[38] Once in office, as Charles Fried put it, "the Reagan administration made *Roe v. Wade* the symbol of everything that had gone wrong in law, particularly in constitutional law."[39] In Reagan's view, *Roe* was as divisive and as wrong as *Dred Scott*.[40]

Unable to push through a pro-life legislative agenda, Reagan turned to administrative remedies, the most controversial of which was the so-called "gag rule." The story begins in 1970, when Congress added to a comprehensive family planning statute (Title X) an explicit prohibition against appropriating funds "where abortion is a method of family planning."[41] The Carter administration interpreted the funding ban narrowly, mandating that Title X recipients provide "non-directive counseling" on "pregnancy termination." The Reagan administration chose to limit the use of federal funds for family planning activities and for abortion counseling.

The Supreme Court approved the Reagan scheme because "substantial deference is accorded" to the executive in its interpretation of statutes.[42] The Reagan, and later the Bush I, administration invoked its regulatory authority to advance a pro-life agenda. Policies on fetal tissue research, U.S. AID grant recipients, the importation of the abortifacient RU-486, and restrictions on abortions in military hospitals were all promulgated pursuant to the executive's authority to implement the laws.

Another significant presidential weapon is the veto power, which can be used in two ways. First, the President can block congressionally supported programs that he disfavors. Bush's vetoes in 1992 of legislative efforts to reinstate fetal tissue research and suspend the gag rule fit this category. Second, the veto power can sometimes be used to force Congress to adopt a presidentially supported program. That is precisely what occurred in 1989, when Congress passed the D.C. spending bill to allow the use of city funds to pay for abortions. Bush vetoed the bill and demanded that Congress reinsert the city funding prohibition. After two vetoes of the D.C. funding bill, Congress ultimately capitulated and reinserted the prohibition of both federal and city abortion expenditures.[43]

Abortion's continuing relevance in presidential politics is tellingly revealed by the remarkable speed and vigor with which the Clinton administration put its pro-choice policies into effect. On January 22, 1993, two days after his inauguration, Clinton dismantled the pro-life regulatory initiatives of the Reagan and Bush administrations. Speaking of the national "[goal] to protect individual freedom" and his vision "of an America where abortion is safe and legal, but rare," Clinton lifted the ban on fetal tissue research, suspended limits on the ability of family planning programs to mention abortion, permitted privately funded abortions at military hospitals, suspended the moratorium on the importation of RU-486, and suspended limitations on the use of private funds by pro-choice organizations that also receive AID funds. Clinton later advanced his pro-choice agenda through legislative initiatives, court filings, vetoes, and judicial appointments. For example, in a bitter battle with the Republican Congress, Clinton repeatedly vetoed legislation outlawing partial-birth abortions.

When President George W. Bush took office in 2001, he began to reverse some of the Clinton policies on abortion. One of his first actions, on January 22, was to reimpose a ban on federal aid to international organizations that perform or "actively promote abortion" as a method of family planning.[44] He thus restored the "Mexico City policy" that was in effect under his father. Bush also backed state and federal efforts to ban partial-birth abortions. In February 2002, his Justice Department filed a brief defending an Ohio law banning all but medically necessary partial-birth abortions. In November 2003, he spoke of "the unalienable right to life" when signing the Partial Birth Abortion Ban Act of 2003.[45]

Independent State Action

The states have been as prominent as the federal government in shaping the abortion dispute. Prior to *Roe*, abortion battles were the nearly exclusive province of the states. Since *Roe*, the states have taken advantage of "multiple opportunities for thwarting compliance with, or implementation of [*Roe*]."[46]

Although setting in motion the contemporary abortion dispute, *Roe* was not decided in a political vacuum. Actions in the 1960s by the American Law Institute, American Medical Association, and various religious organizations spurred nineteen states to liberalize their criminal statutes governing abortion. Only three states (Louisiana, New Hampshire, Pennsylvania) prohibited all abortions. In the early 1970s, although thirty-four states had rejected reform initiatives,[47] more dramatic change seemed possible. The National Conference on Commissioners on Uniform State Laws drafted a Uniform Abortion Act, which would have placed no limitations on abortion during the first twenty weeks of pregnancy.

The Court in *Roe* sought to extend these reform efforts. State responses to *Roe*, however, reveal that the nation was not prepared to tolerate a Court decision that appeared little more than judicial legislation. From 1973 to 1989, 306 abortion measures were passed by forty-eight states.[48]

Too much should not be read into state resistance to *Roe*. Many elected officials were quietly pleased by the *Roe* decision. John Hart Ely spoke of "the sighs of relief as this particular albatross was cut from the legislative and executive necks."[49] That an avalanche of abortion restrictions were enacted may mean only that legislators saw no downside in catering to pro-life interest groups, for pro-choice organizations were content to seek judicial relief.

Most states, moreover, are unwilling to play a leadership role in enacting stringent abortion laws. Instead, they wait to see if the courts will approve the antiabortion initiatives of one of a handful of "challenger" states. Furthermore, most of these challenges are not clearly at odds with court decisions, but rather test the limits of these decisions. For example, *Roe* did not explicitly address parental or spousal consent, public funding, hospital-only abortions, or waiting periods. State action on those subjects engages the judiciary in a dialogue on the sweep of abortion rights.

Just as *Roe* transformed state abortion politics in 1973, a 1989 decision signaled a new era in abortion politics. On the brink of overturning *Roe*, the Court declared "the rigid *Roe* framework" unworkable and opened the door to antiabortion legislation by approving, among other things, second trimester fetal viability tests.[50] Following this decision, pro-choice and pro-life interest groups predicted an avalanche of antiabortion legislation.

From 1989 to 1992, only fourteen state statutes were enacted, nine pro-choice and five pro-life. Many legislators would have preferred that the Court retain control over abortion and not return the issue to elected government. But because of the 1989 decision, pro-choice advocates could no longer count on the judiciary. Knowing that pro-choice forces were "going to take names and kick ankles,"[51] the 1989 decision made pro-life initiatives less likely to succeed.

In *Planned Parenthood v. Casey* (1992), the Court adopted a middle-ground approach that supported both abortion rights and broad state regulatory authority, further stabilizing state abortion politics.[52] According to Alan Guttmacher Institute studies, "antiabortion legislators [have] heeded . . . [*Casey*] and curtailed their attempts to make abortion illegal."[53] The one exception to this relative placidity is partial-birth abortion. Following President Clinton's vetoing of a nationwide ban on this procedure, right-to-life activists turned to the states. With only 7 percent of Americans supporting third trimester abortions, state lawmakers have gladly answered this call. In 1997 alone, fifteen states outlawed partial-birth abortions; in eighteen other states, lawmakers considered enacting a ban on this procedure. By 1999, thirty states had enacted a ban. In its first major ruling on abortion since *Casey*, the Court held that Nebraska's partial-birth abortion statute violated the Constitution as interpreted in *Casey* and *Roe*.[54]

State abortion politics is also the story of the often pivotal role played by state court judges. Before *Roe*, several state courts struck down antiabortion laws.[55] After the Supreme Court concluded that a congressional prohibition on the use of Medicaid funds for abortions did not violate the Equal Protection Clause, state courts in California, Connecticut, Massachusetts, New Jersey, and Oregon interpreted their own constitutions to protect the right of indigent women to a state-funded abortion. The New Jersey Supreme Court pointed out that "state Constitutions are separate sources of individual freedoms and restrictions on the exercise of power by the Legislature. . . . Although the state Constitution may encompass a smaller universe than the federal Constitution, our constellation of rights may be more complete."[56]

Ten states' constitutions contain explicit privacy provisions and several others contain clauses that have been interpreted to protect the right to privacy. Some state courts have applied these provisions to protect abortion rights. In 1997, for example, the California Supreme Court struck down a law requiring pregnant minors to secure parental consent or judicial authorization before obtaining an abortion. For the court, the fact that the U.S. Supreme Court had approved an identical law was simply beside the point. Citing language from one of its earlier decisions, the court noted, "Our state Constitution has been construed to provide California citizens with privacy protections encompassing procreative decisionmaking—*broader, indeed, than those recognized by the federal Constitution.*"[57]

Victories in state court, moreover, do not end the political struggle. Instead, the state legislature and voters engage state courts in a dialogue over the meaning of the state constitution. Take the case of California. In 1981 the California Supreme Court declared that the legislature cannot restrict state funding for abortions for indigent women, yet, over the next ten years, the legislature passed laws restricting the funding. And each year, the courts struck down the laws and reinstated the funding. Conservatives resorted to the ballot box to remove liberal judges. California Chief Justice Rose Elizabeth Bird and two other justices were ousted in 1986 when conservatives targeted them for electoral defeat (more because of their position on the death penalty than abortion). Following this ouster, a 5–2 conservative majority dominated the court, but it still issued rulings protective of a woman's right to choose.[58]

Constitutional Dialogues
and the Abortion Dispute

After three decades of elected branch responses to *Roe* and its progeny, it is hard to imagine the issue of abortion not playing a prominent role in a Supreme Court appointment, a Medicaid appropriation, agency regulations, a presidential or gubernatorial campaign, or a host of other policy issues. That the abortion dispute will persist is beyond cavil. All the same, the prospects of interbranch equilibrium on the abortion issue seem better today than at any time since the modern abortion controversy emerged in the 1960s. Rhetoric about judicial overreaching no longer dominates the debate over abortion. At the federal level, no branch of government is at war with another and public policy generally matches public opinion. State action, although more variable, is generally stable. With few exceptions, states have stayed within the prevailing norms of public opinion, symbolically codifying abortion rights and/or enacting parental notification provisions and partial-birth abortion prohibitions.

The Supreme Court seems quite comfortable with (and is, in part, responsible for) the current state of affairs. Court doctrine has both shaped and been shaped by elected branch decision making. Commenting on this "dynamic dialogue between the Court and the American people," Justice O'Connor observed, "No one . . . considers the Supreme Court decision in *Roe v. Wade* to have settled the issue for all time." For O'Connor, "such intense debate by citizens is as it should be. A nation that docilely and unthinkingly approved every Supreme Court decision as infallible and immutable would, I believe, have severely disappointed our founders."[59]

Gay Rights

All three branches, at the state as well as the national level, have been involved in defining the privacy rights of homosexuals. Through prohibitions in several states regarding same-sex marriage, homosexual sodomy, and homosexual adoption as well as limitations on the rights of homosexual parents to obtain custody of or visit with their children, gays have faced significant roadblocks when seeking to form families or to define their own sexuality. Nevertheless, after the U.S. Supreme Court declined in *Bowers v. Hardwick* (1986) to invalidate a state sodomy law, a number of states repealed or nullified those statutes by legislative or judicial action. In Vermont, moreover, a 1997 lawsuit challenging the state's prohibition of same-sex marriage culminated in legislation, enacted in April 2000, allowing gays to form a "civil union," which gives them the same benefits, protections, and responsibilities granted to spouses in a marriage. Three years later, the Supreme Court overturned *Bowers* in *Lawrence v. Texas*. Following *Lawrence*, state and federal officials continue to reexamine the appropriate scope of governmental power over same-sex couples.

In 1791, when the Bill of Rights was adopted, eleven of the thirteen states explicitly outlawed sodomy, with three states singling out sexual acts between men for special condemnation.[60] Government opposition to homosexual conduct extended to restrictions on government employment.

In 1953, for example, President Eisenhower issued an executive order calling for the investigation and possible dismissal of government employees engaged in "sexual perversion."[61]

Efforts to reform sodomy laws began in 1955, when the American Law Institute considered proposals to decriminalize private homosexual conduct. With the emergence of gay rights groups in the mid-1960s, calls for the repeal of sodomy laws escalated. Inspired by the impressive advancements made by Martin Luther King Jr. and other civil rights leaders, leaders in the gay community began suggesting that homosexuals take a "vigorous civil-liberties, social-action approach" to end the criminalization of their behavior.[62]

Reform efforts increased in the wake of a violent police raid of the Stonewall Inn, a gay bar in New York City. After Stonewall, the lobbying and litigation efforts of newly formed gay interest groups paid off. In 1973, the American Psychiatric Association removed homosexuality from its list of mental disorders. More significant, from 1969 to 1975, sodomy laws were either legislatively repealed or judicially invalidated in almost half the states. None of these states, however, was below the Mason-Dixon line.[63]

Bowers v. Hardwick

On August 3, 1982, Michael Hardwick was arrested for violating Georgia's sodomy statute. Unlike nearly all sodomy arrests (which are made in parks or other public places), Hardwick was arrested for committing sodomy with a consenting adult male in the privacy of his bedroom. Although the state decided not to prosecute him, the American Civil Liberties Union contacted Hardwick and told him that his "was a perfect test case" to challenge the Georgia law. Hardwick then filed suit against Michael Bowers, Georgia's attorney general. At first, this ACLU strategy paid off. A federal appeals court struck down the Georgia statute.[64]

When the Justices met in conference to discuss the case, a bare five-member majority emerged to strike down the Georgia law. The critical fifth vote was that of Lewis Powell. Within a week of conference, however, Powell changed his position. For Powell, who confided to one of his law clerks, "I don't believe I've ever met a homosexual," it was impossible to find in the Constitution a right to engage in sexual practices that he could not comprehend.[65] The majority's decision in *Bowers* did not reveal Powell's ambivalence. Instead, wanting to avoid the mistakes of *Lochner* and *Roe*, the Court boldly pronounced that it "is most vulnerable and comes closest to illegitimacy when it deals with judge-made constitutional law."[66]

Immediately after its decision, the Court became the focal point of a fierce national debate among academics, executive branch officials, members of Congress, and Supreme Court Justices. In Congress, *Bowers* was alternately vilified as a "distressing setback" for individual liberties and applauded for "boldly reaffirm[ing] society's right to enact morals statutes."[67] Academic commentary was "voluminous" and "almost universally negative."[68] For example, after leaving his post as Reagan's solicitor general, Charles Fried wrote, "Unless one takes the implausible line that people generally choose their sexual orientation, then to criminalize any enjoyment of their sexual powers by a whole category of persons is either an imposition of very great cruelty or an exercise in hypocrisy inviting arbitrary and abusive applications of the criminal law."[69] Three years after his retirement, Justice Powell described his vote in *Bowers* as "a mistake. . . . When I had the opportunity to reread the opinions . . . I thought the dissent had the better of the arguments."[70]

For gay rights litigants, *Bowers* was "the nail in the coffin" for those who looked to federal courts for protection.[71] *Bowers*, however, also "galvanize[d] a field of legal debate" and proved to be "a shot in the arm for gay intellectuals as well as activists."[72] The Gay and Lesbian Task Force, the Lambda Legal Defense and Education Fund, and other gay rights interests initially turned their attention to the states. In Nevada, Rhode Island, and the District of Columbia, legislatures repealed existing sodomy statutes.[73]

Numerous state courts have also struck down sodomy laws. The Georgia Supreme Court overturned the sodomy statute that the U.S. Supreme Court upheld in *Bowers*. Concluding that "unforced, private, adult" sexual activity "is at the heart of the Georgia Constitution's protection of the right to privacy," the court rejected the state's claim that only "the General Assembly of Georgia" could change the sodomy ban.[74] Other states that have looked to state law or state constitutions to strike down sodomy statutes include Arkansas, Kentucky, Michigan, Montana, and Tennessee.[75] Some state courts, however, have upheld their criminal sodomy statutes, including Louisiana and Missouri.[76]

Gay Rights in the Age of Clinton

The 1992 election of Bill Clinton gave gay rights interests renewed hope for reforms at the federal level. Although Clinton promised the gay and lesbian community that he would "stand with you in the struggle for equality for all Americans," that promise was only partially fulfilled.[77] While lifting restrictions on federal civilian employment and supporting legislation to extend most employment discrimination protections to sexual orientation discrimination,[78] Clinton neither vetoed congressional efforts to limit gay rights nor participated, through his solicitor general, in Supreme Court litigation challenging Colorado's exclusion of sexual orientation discrimination from state and local antidiscrimination measures.

Witness, for example, Clinton's record on gays in the military. Facing opposition both from the Joint Chiefs of Staff and Sam Nunn, Democratic chair of the Senate Armed Forces Committee, Clinton backtracked from his campaign pledge to lift the ban on gays in the military.[79] Under the policy of "Don't ask, don't tell, don't pursue," homosexual conduct was recognized as a ground for discharge, but the Pentagon was not supposed to ask military personnel to disclose their sexual orientation.

With its new policy in hand, the Clinton Justice Department, citing *Bowers v. Hardwick*, argued in court that the military is free to discriminate on the basis of homosexual conduct or status. In the meantime, Congress legislated on the issue, establishing conditions for gays in the military that are more stringent than the Clinton policy. Specifically, the statute, while codifying most of the "Don't ask, don't tell" compromise, allows for the discharge of gay service members unless they can also show that they neither engage in, intend to engage in, nor have a propensity to engage in homosexual acts.[80] Clinton approved this measure and, ironically, six years after his policy took effect, military discharge of gay and lesbian troops increased.[81] In 1999, Clinton described his policy on gays in the military as "out of whack now" and not being implemented "as it was announced and as it was intended."[82]

Clinton also signaled the gay rights community that he would not resist antigay social and political forces when he signed the Defense of Marriage Act (DOMA).[83] Under DOMA, states may refuse to recognize same-sex marriages performed in other states. Moreover, through a provision prohibiting federal recognition of same-sex marriage, gay couples (from states that recognize same-sex unions) cannot file joint tax returns or gain access to spousal benefits under Social Security and other federal programs. For Congress, perceiving "the effort to redefine 'marriage' to extend to homosexual couples [as] a truly radical proposal that would fundamentally alter the institution of marriage," DOMA was depicted as essential in promoting "the sure foundation of all that is stable and noble in our civilization."[84]

Following the enactment of DOMA, gay rights interests continued their campaign to convince state courts and lawmakers to legalize same-sex unions. Although succeeding in Vermont, the Clinton-era campaign for same-sex marriage has faltered. No other state has sought to repeal or tone down their prohibition of same-sex marriage. Instead, lawmakers and voters in several states have signaled their disapproval of same-sex marriage by either amending their constitution or enacting legislation. In 2000, antigay marriage initiatives appeared on the ballots of sixteen states. By August 2000, thirty-three states had adopted explicit prohibitions of same-sex marriage.

Lawrence v. Texas

In its June 2003 *Lawrence v. Texas* decision, the Supreme Court ruled in favor of gay rights. By overturning *Bowers v. Hardwick*, the Court validated popular and elected government's increasing approval of homosexual rights. At the time of *Bowers*, twenty-five states criminalized sodomy; by 2003, only thirteen states carried criminal penalties. When *Bowers* was decided, Americans were evenly divided on whether homosexual activity should be legal between consenting adults; in 2003, 62 percent of Americans thought it should be legal.[85] More striking, nine of ten Americans think that homosexuals should have equal rights in terms of job opportunities. Relatedly, most of the nation's largest employers have bans on discrimination on the basis of sexual orientation (and close to half offer insurance benefits to partners of gay and lesbian employees).[86] For its part, the Supreme Court has become a gay-friendly workplace.

Against this backdrop, it is little wonder that six of the nine Justices would reject Texas's practice of criminalizing homosexual (but not heterosexual) sodomy. For five of the Justices, the solution was to extend a right of privacy to gay relations and, in so doing, overrule *Bowers*. Finding that "[gays] are entitled to respect for their private lives," the Court ruled that the "State cannot demean their existence or control their destiny by making their private sexual conduct a crime."[87]

Following the Court's *Lawrence* decision, Republican Senate Majority Leader Bill Frist announced his support for a constitutional amendment to ban gay marriage. At the same time, the Bush administration has tried to reach out to an estimated four million gay voters and moderates who support gay rights. The chair of Bush's 2004 campaign, Marc Racicot, met with gay leaders in March 2003. Bush also pushed California Republicans to soften their views on social issues in an effort to win back voters.[88] Moreover, Bush left in place a Clinton executive order protecting gays and has appointed gays to several government posts. Also, even though he strongly backed the Texas sodomy statute when he was that state's governor, Bush had no comment on the *Lawrence* decision, claiming it was a state law issue.

Following a February 2004 Massachusetts Supreme Court decision ordering legislative approval of same sex marriage, however, Bush signaled his willingness to support a constitutional ban on gay marriage. Rejecting the court's interpretation of the Massachusetts Constitution, Bush said that "marriage is a sacred institution between a man and a woman. If activist judges insist on redefining marriage by court order, the only alternative will be the constitutional process."[89]

Notwithstanding this denouncement of same sex marriage, gay rights seems to be gaining momentum. Young Americans overwhelmingly support gay rights: 72 percent of eighteen- to twenty-nine-year olds think that homosexual relations should be legal and 59 percent of college freshman support same-sex marriage.[90] Over time, these shifting attitudes may result in more far-reaching changes than those embraced by the Supreme Court in *Lawrence*. What is clear is that the battle over gay rights has been and will be principally defined by political action.

The Right to Die

In recent years, the Court has wrestled with a new privacy question: Is there a constitutional right to die for the terminally ill and for patients who survive solely because of life-support systems but with no hope of recovery? In 1990, the Court suggested that although a competent adult has a right to refuse medical treatment, a state may require "clear and compelling" evidence that an individual has expressed a wish to refuse medical treatment or otherwise terminate life-support systems.[91] Instead of dictating a national standard, as with *Roe*, the Court left it to the states to decide such matters. More telling, in two 1997 cases the Court rejected a privacy right to physician-assisted suicide.[92] Unwilling to disrupt the "earnest and profound debate [taking place throughout the nation] about the morality, legality, and practicality of physician-assisted suicide,"[93] the Court left it to elected officials to sort out whether and when individuals can hasten their own death.

Claims of a right to die, though just making their way to the Supreme Court, date back to antiquity. Plato, for example, criticized the medical profession in his *Republic* for "educating diseases . . . and inventing lingering death."[94] At the same time, it is a basic premise of medicine that doctors, if they cannot cure, should do no harm. When they take their Hippocratic oath they promise, "I will give no deadly medicine if asked, nor suggest any such counsel." Consistent with this tradition, most states, starting with colonial and early state legislatures, have consistently punished the act of assisting suicide.

In critical respects, however, this debate is of modern vintage. It was not until the 1950s that there emerged antibiotics to fight infection and technology that allows individuals to live in a persistent vegetative state. As methods for maintaining life became increasingly available, the question of when life is worth saving and whether individuals should be able to exercise substantial control over their death became more commonplace and more vexing. Needless to say, with the Supreme Court embracing privacy rights in abortion and other settings, the Hemlock Society and other right-to-die advocates turned their attention to the courts.

Witness, for example, the case of Nancy Cruzan. Five years after a 1983 car accident left her in a persistent vegetative state, her parents sought to terminate the life-support systems of their then thirty-two-year-old daughter. But in Missouri, a state with a strong pro-life tradition, clear and compelling evidence had to be introduced before the termination of life support. Without a living will, state officials refused to defer to Cruzan's parents.

Before both the Missouri and U.S. Supreme Courts, the state prevailed. Unwilling to expand the privacy rights of parents who desire to control the upbringing of their children past the age of majority, the Justices, siding with arguments made by state officials and Bush I Solicitor General Kenneth Starr, ruled that Missouri was within its power to place the sanctity of life ahead of family desires.

Cruzan did not sit well with the public, and, through the Patient Self-Determination Act, Congress sought to limit the decision's reach. Pointing to the disconnect between the number of Americans who have living wills (fewer than 10 percent) and public opinion polls suggesting that nearly all Americans support patient self-determination, Congress searched for a way to limit the number of patients who receive unwanted medical treatment. Under the act, health care providers (as a condition of Medicare and Medicaid participation) must inform patients of state law governing their right to refuse medical or surgical treatment, including their right to formulate advance directives through a living will.[95]

Even more than patient self-determination, the public is deeply divided over the question of physician-assisted suicide. A 1996 *Washington Post* poll found 50 percent in support of physician-assisted suicide, 40 percent opposed, and 10 percent undecided.[96] Also, although nearly every state outlaws this practice, one in five doctors and nurses say they have helped their patients commit suicide.[97]

The public, however, seems unwilling to sanction physician-assisted suicide. With the medical profession and religious organizations strongly lined up against assisted suicide, state referendums have yielded next to no reform. Only Oregon voters, by a narrow 51 to 49 percent margin, have approved an assisted-suicide measure. Correspondingly, from 1995 to 1997, thirty different bills in the states to weaken assisted suicide bans were introduced but none was enacted. In contrast, legislation intended to limit physician-assisted suicide has been approved. For example, Congress and the Clinton White House, in response to a 1996 federal appeals court decision finding that physician-assisted suicide is part of the right to privacy, approved the Assisted Suicide Funding Restriction Act of 1997. This statute bars the use of federal funds in assisting or supporting physician-assisted suicide.[98]

When the Supreme Court agreed to review the 1996 appeals court decision, the American Medical and Hospital Associations, which had lined up with the Cruzan family and against the state of Missouri, argued that although patient self-determination is "among the most important rights that the law affords each person," any assistance to intentionally take the life of a patient "is antithetical to the central mission of healing that guides both medicine and nursing."[99] Along the same lines, a coalition of seventeen state attorneys general urged the Court to respect state sovereignty and, with it, the long-standing practice of nearly every state to outlaw assisted suicide.[100] For its part, the Clinton administration explained why "overriding state interests justify" the assisted-suicide ban.[101]

Against this backdrop, it is little wonder that a unanimous Supreme Court concluded that the public and their elected representatives, not judges, should decide this issue. Unlike abortion, where public opinion, the medical community, and some states favored reform, proponents of physician-assisted suicide could not ride the crest of social and political forces. Instead, these proponents asked the Court to buck majoritarian preferences and create a right to physician-assisted suicide out of whole cloth.

The years following the Court's 1997 decisions saw very little change. Oregon's "death with dignity" referendum in November 1997 has had limited effect. In its first five years of operation, 129 Oregonians used drugs prescribed under the law to commit suicide.[102] Nevertheless, right-to-life interests in Congress and the Bush II Justice Department took aim at the Oregon measure. In Congress, legislation was introduced that banned the use of federally controlled prescription drugs for physician-assisted suicide. Although the House passed this bill in 2000, the Senate never voted on it.[103] With the election of Bush, however, the Justice Department attempted to void the Oregon measure as violative of existing federal controlled-substances law. Attorney General John Ashcroft threatened some doctors with prosecution by concluding that assisted suicide is not a "legitimate medical purpose" for prescribing or handing out drugs.[104] In April 2002, federal district judge Robert E. Jones rejected this Ashcroft initiative.[105]

Notwithstanding this high-stakes, emotionally pitched battle, other states are not likely to follow Oregon's lead. With Compassion in Dying and other assisted-suicide proponents bemoaning the "shortcomings of the initiative process," it is more likely that these reformers will increasingly turn their attention to state courts.[106] Whether some state judges, as they did with abortion, will expand privacy rights in this area remains to be seen. What appears certain is that, after three decades of elected government resistance to *Roe v. Wade*, the Supreme Court will not lightly second-guess state determinations of whether and when individuals should be able to determine the terms and conditions of their death.

Conclusions

Just as the judiciary leaves its mark on society, so does society drive the agenda and decisions of the courts. The transformation of the right to privacy underscores the pivotal role that social and political forces play in shaping constitutional values. When *Roe* was decided, the Court thought that it would definitively settle the abortion issue. Thanks to persistent elected government resistance, like the Roosevelt-era attacks on the *Lochner* doctrine, judicial hubris gave way to a healthy respect for democratic institutions. Today, as the 1997 assisted-suicide decisions reveal, the Justices may well think that "the best and most peaceful solution to a contentious moral conflict is not to adopt a sweeping principle and reject the other position,"[107] but to allow lawmakers and the people to engage in an open and honest debate. At the same time, the Court appears willing to strike down governmental prohibitions at odds with contemporary social and political norms. This is the apparent lesson of the Court's overruling of *Bowers* in *Lawrence v. Texas*.

The Court is not the exclusive or even dominant institution on these questions. It is part of the dialogue. The emerging equilibrium on abortion, for example, required all branches and all levels of government to stake out strong positions and do battle with each other. Abortion is simply too divisive for either pro-choice or pro-life absolutism to rule the day.

Changing circumstances demand that constitutional meaning not be too inflexible. As Justice Ginsburg rightly observed at her confirmation hearing, our system is one where "courts do not guard constitutional rights alone. Courts share that responsibility with Congress, the president, the states, and the people."[108]

Race

We are accustomed to looking to the Supreme Court to resolve issues of racial discrimination, but the Court's record in this area over the past two centuries has been modest. More often than not, elected officials have shaped the national discourse over race relations. The Court's voice has been an important one, but it has been far from dominant. In many instances, the Court takes its cues from social and political forces. And when the Court and elected officials disagree with one another, lawmakers have been willing to countermand the Court by enacting legislation at odds with its decisions.

In fact, the widespread belief that the Supreme Court has brought civil rights to national attention is grossly overstated. The Court occasionally serves as a catalyst in a national conversation about race, but elected officials, not judges, are the principal engine of civil rights reform. Judicial rulings to perpetuate slavery, frustrate Reconstruction, and validate the wartime internment of Japanese Americans underscore that the Court's reputation as guardian of minority rights is misplaced. Even during the past half century, with major decisions in school desegregation, affirmative action, and racial districting, the Court has been anything but a steadfast beacon for minority rights. Still, neither the Supreme Court nor elected government dominates equality decision making. Instead, the search for racial equality is marked by vigorous interchanges between the courts and elected government.

From Slavery through Reconstruction

The Constitution, as Justice Thurgood Marshall aptly remarked on the occasion of its bicentennial, "was defective from the start, requiring several amendments and a civil war."[1] By allowing each of the thirteen states the right to import slaves until 1808, the framers allowed states to exclude blacks from citizenship. Slaves were counted as three-fifths of a free person when apportioning legislative districts, and states were required to return those "held to Service or Labour in [another] State, under the Laws thereof."[2] The Founding Fathers also left to states the power of determining voting qualifications. At the time of the Constitutional Convention many states limited voting rights to white landholders; indeed, the state constitutions of Connecticut, Delaware, Kentucky, Maryland, New Jersey, North Carolina, Tennessee, and Virginia excluded blacks from voting. By the time of the Civil War, only Maine, New Hampshire, Vermont, Rhode Island, and Massachusetts allowed free blacks to vote.[3]

If anything, the Supreme Court stood as a roadblock to elected government efforts to stop the spread of slavery. Rather than serve as the "guardian of the powerless in our society," willing to "run counter to shifting political winds" (images invoked by Senators Edward Kennedy and Patrick Leahy at Justice Clarence Thomas's confirmation hearings),[4] the Court vigorously defended the interests of white slave owners. With *Dred Scott v. Sandford* (1857),[5] the Court rejected congressional efforts to exclude slavery from certain parts of the country, holding that a slave owner has a right to transport his "property" as he sees fit, and denied that blacks could exercise the rights of citizens.

By 1862, *Dred Scott* was effectively eviscerated by legislative and executive actions. Acting through the regular legislative process, Congress passed a bill to prohibit slavery in the territories.[6] For its part, the executive branch concluded that the decision did not bind it. Attorney General Bates issued an opinion in which he determined that blacks had been citizens in the past and could be in the future.[7]

Following the Civil War, Congress set out to change the status of blacks in American society. The Thirteenth Amendment formally nullified part of *Dred Scott* by outlawing slavery. The remainder of the decision was rejected by the Fourteenth Amendment, which granted citizenship to all persons born or naturalized in the United States. Black suffrage was the subject of the Fifteenth Amendment's prohibition against denying or abridging the right to vote "on account of race, color, or previous condition of servitude." All three Reconstruction amendments granted to Congress the power to enforce these provisions "by appropriate legislation."

Another effort to correct past injustices against blacks came from race-specific measures approved by the Reconstruction Congress to assist former slaves to become "freedmen." Remarkably, Congress's 1866 debates over these measures are strikingly similar to today's affirmative action debates.[8] Opponents called the measures "class legislation" and argued that rather than promoting "equality before the law," they "overleap the mark and land on the other side."[9] For opponents, the effect of the bill was to make minorities "superior" and give "them favors the poor white boy in the North cannot get."[10] Proponents argued that it would be a "cruel mockery" "not [to] provide for those among us who have been held in bondage all their lives" and that therefore the "true object of [such race-specific legislation] is the amelioration of the condition of the colored people."[11]

The Reconstruction Congress also pushed through legislation guaranteeing blacks equal access to public accommodations. Although blacks were citizens as a result of the Civil War amendments, in many states they were denied access to theaters, restaurants, inns, and other public facilities. Congress thought that the legislation was a necessary response to "illogical, unjust, ungentlemanly and foolish prejudice."[12] However, the Supreme Court concluded that Congress's power to enforce the Fourteenth Amendment's guarantee of equal protection was limited to "state action."[13]

Supreme Court hostility to Reconstruction also reared its head in *Plessy v. Ferguson*, an 1896 decision upholding Louisiana's power to prevent blacks from traveling in the same rail car as whites. In support of its holding, the Court did little to disguise its biases. Concluding that "legislation is powerless to eradicate racial instincts or to abolish distinctions based on physical differences," the Court ruled that "if one race be inferior to the other socially, the Constitution of the United States cannot put them upon the same plane."[14]

The Japanese American Cases

During World War II, the Supreme Court backed the government's internment of Japanese Americans. Although military officials claimed that the internment policy was necessary to the war effort, the undeniable source of the internment policy was America's long history of anti-Asian prejudice. Following the Civil War, immigrants from China and Japan were prohibited from becoming U.S. citizens.[15] By 1882, West Coast states pushed through the enactment of legislation suspending Chinese immigration altogether. But the need for cheap farm labor and railroad workers triggered the immigration of 127,000 Japanese into the United States between 1901 and 1908.[16]

Like the Chinese before them, the Japanese quickly became the target of discrimination. Starting in 1901, California's Republican and Democratic parties had anti-Japanese planks in their platforms. In 1905, the San Francisco School Board established a separate school for Japanese students so that "our children should not be placed in any position where their youthful impressions may be affected by association with pupils of the Mongolian race."[17]

On December 7, 1941, Japan attacked Pearl Harbor, devastating the U.S. Pacific fleet. Within a few weeks of the assault, Japanese Americans, linked by color and culture to a treacherous enemy and lacking political power, became an easy target for wartime frustration. Witness, for example, the pivotal role that California Attorney General Earl Warren (later to be Chief Justice of the United States) played in the relocation of West Coast Japanese. A member of the anti-Oriental Native Sons of the Golden West, Warren, in the immediate aftermath of Pearl Harbor, dubbed the "Japanese situation" the "Achilles' heel of the entire civilian defense effort."[18] In testimony before Congress, he claimed that "when we are dealing with the Caucasian race we have methods that will test the loyalty of them . . . when we deal with the Japanese we are in an entirely different field and we cannot form any opinion that we believe to be sound. Their method of living, their language, make for this difficulty."[19] This racial xenophobia and stereotyping came to typify federal policy toward the West Coast Japanese.

The military, too, pushed for evacuation. Responding to calls for a full-scale evacuation, General John L. DeWitt, commander of the Western Defense Command, called for the evacuation of both Japanese aliens and Japanese Americans. In his recommendation to Secretary of War Henry Stimson, DeWitt explained, "The Japanese race is an enemy race . . . [and it therefore] follows that along the vital Pacific Coast over 112,000 potential enemies, of Japanese extraction, are at large today."[20] Although Department of Justice attorneys raised constitutional objections to the proposed evacuation, President Franklin Delano Roosevelt was not "plagued" by these difficulties. "The Constitution," as Roosevelt Attorney General Francis Biddle observed, "has never greatly bothered any wartime President. That was a question of law . . . and meanwhile . . . we must get on with the war."[21]

In February 1942, Roosevelt issued an executive order empowering the military to "prescribe Military areas" and "determine from which any or all persons may be excluded."[22] One month later, Congress enacted legislation ratifying the executive order.[23] Pointing to "evidence that a tightly knit fifth column exists in the United States," members of Congress uniformly supported the legislation, approving it with little debate in either the House or the Senate.[24]

But the evidence Congress pointed to—War Department "findings"—did not exist. A report prepared by General DeWitt intentionally and incorrectly stated that ethnic Japanese in Hawaii significantly aided the Pearl Harbor attack, that West Coast Japanese were involved in ship-to-shore signaling to enemy submarines, that FBI seizures of arms and contraband supported espionage claims, and that the Japanese community was isolated and might therefore uniformly harbor pro-enemy attitudes.

The Justice Department nevertheless concealed these misrepresentations from the Supreme Court. In an ambiguously worded footnote, it asked the Court to "take judicial notice" of the War Department report for "the facts relating to the justification for the evacuation" and nothing else.[25] For its part, the American Civil Liberties Union sought to transform this footnote into a Justice Department declaration of War Department misdeeds. "This singular repudiation of General DeWitt's testimony on the military necessities," claimed the ACLU in its amicus brief, "obviously . . . [shows] the existence of reliable conflicting information from other sources."[26]

In the end, allegations of race prejudice and inconsistencies in the War Department report were not enough. Although the divide among the Justices was sharp enough to prompt Frank Murphy to confide to his law clerks, "The Court had blown up on the Jap case,"[27] the Court deferred to the judgment of the "war-making branches of the Government," concluding that "hardships are a part of war" and that "citizenship has its responsibilities as well as its privileges."[28]

Eighteen years later, a principal player in the affair, Earl Warren, reflected on the Court's decision. Speaking now as Chief Justice of the United States, Warren saw the internment decision as proof positive that there are some circumstances in which the Court will not reject executive claims of military necessity: "The consequence of the limitations under which the Court must sometimes operate in this area is that other agencies of government must bear the primary responsibility for determining whether specific actions they are taking are consonant with our Constitution."[29]

Warren's message proved prophetic. Starting with President Ford's 1976 declaration that the evacuation was "wrong," elected government efforts to remedy this injustice reveal an encouraging self-awareness and humility in popular government. In 1982, the Commission on Wartime Relocation and Internment of Civilians issued a scathing report outlining government misconduct toward Japanese Americans. In 1988, legislation was enacted to provide restitution to Japanese victims of officially sanctioned racism. At the signing ceremony for the legislation, President Reagan remarked, "No payment can make up for those lost years. So what is important in this bill has less to do with property than honor, for here, we admit a wrong. Here we reaffirm our commitment as a nation to equal justice under the law."[30]

Governmental conduct toward Japanese Americans during the course of World War II is instructive in understanding both the frailty of the presumptive invalidity of racial classifications and the disinclination of the judiciary to combat military excess.[31] Chief Justice Rehnquist may go too far in contending that this episode demonstrates that "it is neither desirable nor remotely likely that civil liberty will occupy as favored a position in wartime as it does in peacetime,"[32] but the fact remains that the safeguard for pernicious racial line drawing does not rest exclusively with the judiciary. Indeed, recent executive and legislative efforts are a striking counterpoint to wartime failures, highlighting elected government's ability to correct past abuses of racial line drawing.

School Desegregation

From the nation's founding through the Japanese American cases, the Supreme Court has contributed to racial divisions.[33] Nevertheless, in the 1930s, civil rights interest groups still saw a possible ally in the courts. In particular, the NAACP Legal Defense and Education Fund, headed by Thurgood Marshall and Jack Greenberg, sought to work within the confines of *Plessy* to overturn segregation in education and elsewhere. For these lawyers, "segregation was illegal because, as practiced, it never provided equality for Negroes."[34] From 1938 to 1950, the NAACP succeeded in painting *Plessy* into an ever narrowing corner, eventually convincing the Justices that "separate but equal" has no place in higher education.[35] In so doing, Legal Defense Fund lawyers, through a strategy of gradualism both in the cases it selected to litigate and in the arguments it made, laid the groundwork for the Court's outlawing of segregation in elementary and secondary education.[36] By 1954, the Court, striking at the heart of Jim Crow, declared in *Brown v. Board of Education* that "separate educational facilities are inherently unequal."[37]

Today, it may seem inconceivable that *Brown*'s basic declaration of racial equality would trigger complaints about judicial power. When *Brown* was decided, however, segregation was so ingrained in the South that the outlawing of dual school systems promised social turmoil and massive resistance. These deep feelings were not lost either on the Court or on the Department of Justice. In an effort to temper Southern hostility, Chief Justice Warren sought to craft a unanimous opinion of limited reach and the Justice Department recommended that the Court *not* specify a remedy in the case. Accordingly, the Court did not issue a remedy when it declared segregation to be unconstitutional.

The Justice Department also called attention to the ways racial segregation undermined America's stature as a world leader. Starting with a 1948 case involving restrictive covenants, "the Truman administration stressed

to the Supreme Court the international implications of U.S. race discrimination . . . [including] the negative impact on American foreign policy
that a pro-segregation decision might have."[38] In *Brown*, the administration left no doubt that the cold war imperative of defeating communism
was undermined by racial segregation. "The United States," according
to the Justice Department brief, "is under constant attack in the foreign
press, over the foreign radio, and in such international bodies as the
United Nations because of various practices of discrimination against minority groups in this country."[39]

When the Truman administration brief was filed in December 1952, the
Court was set to decide *Brown* with Chief Justice Fred Vinson at its helm.
But the Court redocketed *Brown* so that it could also decide the constitutionality of segregated education in the "federal city," Washington, D.C.
At this time, the Court was sharply divided; the December 1952 conference
suggested that five Justices would *uphold* segregated education.[40] The
division was attributable, in part, to the uncertain history of the Fourteenth Amendment. Chief Justice Vinson observed that, although District
of Columbia public schools were segregated when the Fourteenth Amendment was adopted, Congress failed to enact proposed legislation barring
such segregation. In 1953, Vinson died and Warren became Chief Justice.
He was able to construct a unanimous opinion that segregation in education was unconstitutional. After another year, in which the public had
time to contemplate a desegregated country, the Court issued *Brown II*,
declaring that desegregation remedies must proceed with "all deliberate
speed."[41]

The Court's bifurcation of its merits and remedies holdings, as well as
the absence of judgmental rhetoric in its segregation decisions, reveals
that the Justices sought to improve the acceptability of their decision by
speaking in a single moderate voice. In particular, rather than require
Southern systems to take concrete steps to dismantle dual systems, the
Court recognized in *Brown II* that "varied local school problems" were
best solved by school authorities, that district court judges were best
suited to examine "local conditions," and that delays associated with
"problems related to administration" were to be expected.[42] For this reason, Justice Robert Jackson deemed that *Brown* was more politics and
sociology than law.[43]

The Court was correct in anticipating a hostile response to its opinion.
After ordering that desegregation proceed "with all deliberate speed,"
one hundred Southern congressmen called the Court's action "a clear
abuse of judicial power . . . and [an] encroach[ment] upon the reserved
rights of the States and the people."[44] Moreover, many states sought to
subvert *Brown* by replacing public school systems (subject to equal pro-

tection demands) with state-funded private school systems. Finally, some school systems simply disregarded *Brown*. The most notorious example of this phenomenon occurred in Little Rock, Arkansas, where President Eisenhower was compelled to send in armed troops to force compliance with *Brown*.

Initially, the Eisenhower administration seemed reluctant to participate in *Brown*.[45] Indeed, President Eisenhower was so hesitant to speak out on the segregation question that he took the unusual step of amending the government's brief in *Brown I* to encourage the Court to devise orderly plans that would take into consideration the fact that the segregated life-style had been sanctioned by the Supreme Court for over fifty years.[46] Furthermore, the President sought to publicly distance himself from the issue. Asked whether he agreed with the Court's decision, the President responded, "It makes no difference whether or not I endorse [*Brown*]. The Constitution is as the Supreme Court interprets it."[47] In an address to the nation in 1957 concerning Little Rock, Eisenhower likewise pointed to his duty to carry out the decisions of federal courts and not the legal or moral correctness of *Brown*.[48]

One year after Eisenhower addressed the nation, the Supreme Court formally declared Arkansas Governor Oval Faubus's efforts to block school desegregation unconstitutional. The Court also proclaimed itself "supreme in the exposition of the law of the Constitution."[49] But this declaration mattered little to Southern school officials. For these officials, there was no reason to openly defy the Court. *Brown II*'s emphasis on local conditions suggested that the Supreme Court would tolerate tokenism and delay. Indeed, Southern newspapers heralded the remedial order, especially because the Court entrusted the implementation of its decision to "our local judges [who] know the local situation."[50]

From 1954 to 1964, the Court's only foray into school desegregation was its Little Rock decision. Indeed, well aware of the "momentum of history" and the "deep feeling" people had about school segregation, the Court refused to hear a 1955 challenge to Virginia's miscegenation law. The state court's conclusion that the law was necessary to prevent "a mongrel breed of citizens" may well have offended the Justices,[51] but the Court wasn't about to touch this issue, particularly after critics of *Brown* warned that integrated schools would produce a "mongrelization" of the white race. In this way, the Warren Court sidestepped an explosive confrontation with Southern segregationisits rather than risk "thwarting or seriously handicapping" its decision in *Brown* and, with it, its institutional prestige.[52]

This ambivalence on school desegregation, miscegenation, and other vestiges of Jim Crow spanned most of the Warren Court's sixteen-year life. Remarkably, one decade after *Brown*, only 2 percent of black children attended biracial schools in the eleven Southern states. In the 1965–1966 school year, however, the percentage of black children in biracial schools rose to 6. The turning point here was not hyped-up judicial enforcement; instead, the principal impetus to meaningful school desegregation was rooted in elected branch action.

By 1964 there was a growing recognition on Capitol Hill that "we must simply face the fact that the decisions of the Supreme Court are not being carried out . . . and that unless we are to make a mockery of them . . . Congress must act to put the strength of the National Government behind them."[53] At this time, the judiciary likewise recognized the limits of court-centered approaches to school desegregation. The Supreme Court spoke of there being "entirely too much deliberation and not enough speed" in enforcing *Brown*,[54] and a federal appellate court aptly noted that a "national effort, bringing together Congress, the executive, and the judiciary may be able to make meaningful the right of Negro children to equal educational opportunities. *The courts acting alone have failed.*"[55]

The solution was the 1964 Civil Rights Act, which, among other things, authorized Justice Department participation in school desegregation litigation (Title IV) and demanded that federal grant recipients be nondiscriminatory (Title VI). More significant, the implementation of the Elementary and Secondary Education Act of 1965, coupled with the issuance and enforcement of guidelines for Title VI of the Civil Rights Act of 1964, marked a significant shift in federal power over state education systems. With Title VI's demand that federal grant recipients be nondiscriminatory, Congress became willing to pump billions of dollars of aid into the compensatory education of educationally deprived children. These billions of dollars were sufficient incentive for many school systems to comply with federal nondiscrimination standards.

It was against this backdrop of increasing federal involvement in school desegregation that the Warren Court stepped up its own involvement, declaring in 1964, "The time for mere 'deliberate speed' has run out."[56] This parallelism should come as no surprise. With Congress and the White House both making equal educational opportunity a national priority and envisioning an increasing judicial role, political opposition no longer concerned the Court. Judicial involvement, instead, was consistent with initiatives taken by the elected branches and public opinion. In this way, the task of educating the nation and producing bipartisan support for enforceable civil rights fell not to the judiciary but to Congress and the President.

From the Great Society
to the Southern Strategy

The 1960s civil rights reforms extended well beyond school desegregation. Initiatives were also launched to ensure racial justice in housing, employment, and voting. All part of Lyndon Johnson's "Great Society," these reforms were part of a "major assault on poverty in behalf of a more equitable, color-blind system of economic distribution."[57]

The 1965 Voting Rights Act illustrates the impact of elected government on constitutional rights. The story begins in Selma, Alabama. On March 7, 1965, a peaceful group of six hundred protesters marched against the continuing denial of black voting rights, only to be tear-gassed and attacked "with clubs, whips, and ropes" by state troopers as white spectators cheered.[58] With television bringing pictures of this brutality into millions of homes, the Selma protest prompted a national outcry and immediate call for comprehensive voting rights legislation.

A week after the protest, on March 15, President Johnson spoke to a joint session of Congress about the need for more effective voting rights legislation. The Emancipation Proclamation, Johnson said, was a promise of equality to black Americans: "A century has passed since the day of promise. And the promise is unkept."[59] Calling for immediate action to stop state officials from circumventing the Fifteenth Amendment, Johnson introduced his voting rights bill. The bill marked a dramatic restructuring of the existing voting system, shifting authority away from state governments to the federal government. States could no longer use literacy tests and other methods to disenfranchise blacks. Moreover, to prevent discriminatory voting practices from taking effect, most Southern states had to have changes to their voting laws "precleared" by the Department of Justice or the D.C. Circuit.

The bill sharply increased minority registration and voting. In the targeted Southern states, the percentage of black registered voters increased from 29 in 1964 to over 56 in 1972. The number of elected black officials also increased, from well under a hundred in 1964 to 963 in 1974.[60]

The Warren Court supported elected-branch initiatives. In 1966, the Court upheld Department of Justice preclearance authority as well as the literacy test prohibition.[61] In 1969, the Court again sided with Justice in rejecting Mississippi efforts to dilute minority votes by changing county elections from a single-district scheme (where each district, including predominantly minority districts, would choose a representative) to an at-large scheme where voters pick and choose among competing slates of candidates in one countywide election, with the candidates receiving the most votes filling all available seats (so that majority voters can block the election of minority candidates).[62]

The Warren Court did more than simply bless the civil rights initiatives of Congress and the White House. The Court also stepped up its pursuit of racial justice. In 1967, for example, the Justices agreed to hear a challenge to Virginia's miscegenation law. With the principle of desegregation well established, the Court concluded that "restricting the freedom to marry solely because of racial classifications violates the central meaning of the Equal Protection Clause."[63] The foundation for that ruling lay not in judicial decisions but in the political groundwork developed by the elected branches.

By 1969, however, Lyndon Johnson, Earl Warren, and other Great Society reformers had vanished from the political scene. That year also marked a sea change both at the White House and on the Supreme Court. On January 20, Richard Nixon became President. Nixon's presidential campaign prominently featured a "Southern Strategy" in which candidate Nixon promised, through administrative initiatives and judicial appointments, to ease pressure on Southern school districts to end desegregative practices. For example, with Warren having announced his retirement before the 1968 election, Nixon attempted to reshape the direction of the Court through his appointment of Warren Burger as Chief Justice. Although federal court decisions continued to challenge local school policies and practices on questions of race, the "rare historic moment when the President, congressional leadership, and the public all recognized that protection of the rights of black Americans was the fundamental [social and educational] issue" had passed.[64]

The Politics of Forced Busing

By the end of the 1960s, the efforts of the federal government had dramatically eroded Southern school segregation. For example, between 1963 and 1968, the percentage of black children in all-black schools in the South dropped from 98 to 25.[65] Nevertheless, the elected branches' endorsement of *Brown*'s simple nondiscrimination demand was, from the start, tempered by opposition to forced busing. A provision of the Elementary and Secondary Education Act, enacted during the Great Society's heyday, prohibits the use of federal funds for "the assignment or transportation of students or teachers in order to overcome racial imbalance."[66] Adding fuel to this opposition, President Nixon opposed "buying buses, tires, and gasoline to transport young children miles away from their neighborhood schools"[67] and instructed the Office of Civil Rights (OCR), as well as the Department of Justice, that "they are to work with individual school districts to hold busing to the minimum required by law."[68]

Opposition to busing intensified after the Supreme Court, in 1971, decided in *Swann v. Charlotte-Mecklenburg* that court-ordered busing was an appropriate technique to desegregate the nation's schools.[69] In approving the use of black-white pupil ratios and mandatory student reassignments as "starting point[s] in the process of shaping a remedy," the Court recognized that, to eliminate all vestiges of an unconstitutional dual school system, desegregation remedies might have to be "administratively awkward, inconvenient, and even bizarre."[70]

Immediately after *Swann*, several members of Congress issued strong bully pulpit statements rebuking the Court. More striking, Nixon delivered a national address on the evils of busing. Noting that concerned parents "do not want their children bused across the city to an inferior school just to meet some social planner's concept of what is considered to be the correct racial balance,"[71] he submitted legislative proposals that would have Congress designate a hierarchy of remedies in school desegregation lawsuits.[72]

Congress ultimately rejected the Nixon proposals, claiming that the Court's status as coequal branch warranted legislative respect to its constitutional holdings. In place of the Nixon proposals, Congress enacted, as Title VII of the 1972 Education Act amendments, restrictions on both federal financial support of mandatory busing and federal advocacy of busing "unless constitutionally required."[73]

Congress's hesitancy here is revealing. Although it may well possess the power to limit the Court's remedial authority under either the Exceptions Clause or its authority to enforce the Fourteenth Amendment, Congress generally views these powers as too heavy-handed. Consequently, legislative responses to judicial excess often take the form of funding restrictions. For example, starting in 1972, Congress has repeatedly enacted legislation limiting the use of federal funds by OCR to require busing and instructed federal courts that busing should be a remedy of last resort.[74]

Elected government's antibusing stance represented a serious threat to the Burger Court. In particular, the Court appeared reluctant to break significant new doctrinal ground on behalf of civil rights interests. The Court explicitly favored local control over equal educational opportunity by refusing to include overwhelmingly white suburban school systems in a city's school desegregation plan.[75] Likewise, the Burger Court removed school finance from judicial scrutiny, holding that a state need not equalize gross differences in per-pupil expenditures among school districts. In reaching this conclusion, the Court emphasized "the wisdom of the traditional limitations on this Court's function."[76] In short, decisions about school funding would be left to state political decisions.

By placing local control of education ahead of the interests of civil rights plaintiffs, the Burger Court paid close attention to the signals sent from both the White House and Congress. In particular, President Nixon, who campaigned against judicial activism and for states' rights as part of his Southern Strategy, helped transform the Court by nominating William Rehnquist, Lewis Powell, Harry Blackmun, and Warren Burger. For these Justices, the judiciary's self-interest in having its orders enforced as well as respect owed Congress warranted a diminished role for the courts.

In other areas of civil rights, the Burger Court also hesitated to contradict elected government. Witness, for example, the Court's flip-flop on the question of numerically based proofs of discrimination. Immediately before *Swann*, the Court went well beyond statutory language to allow civil rights plaintiffs to challenge employment practices that have a disproportionate racial impact, such as the need to have a high school or college degree.[77] Rather than build on this landmark, however, the Burger Court rejected impact-based proofs of discrimination in voting rights and other constitutional cases.[78]

The Burger Court's civil rights legacy, though ambiguous, is easily understood in the context of social and political forces. At the time of both its busing and employment discrimination decisions, Warren Burger "was anxious to appear to be the Court's leader, like his strong-willed predecessor."[79] Indeed, Burger voted with the majority in these decisions, in part, so that, as Chief Justice, he could assign to himself the task of writing these landmark decisions.[80] By using black-white population ratios as a justification for court-ordered busing, however, the Court brought much woe unto itself. Widespread opposition to *Swann*, including threats to strip the Court of jurisdiction, highlighted the risks of unpopular rulings. With its institutional prestige challenged, the Court could not ignore the necessary link between popular support and successful implementation of its rulings.

Starting in 1991, the Rehnquist Court issued several decisions signaling the end of court-ordered desegregation. Pointing to "considerations based on the allocation of powers within our federal system" and extolling local control's virtues in "allow[ing] citizens to participate in decision making, and allow[ing] innovation so that school programs can fit local needs,"[81] the Court has made it clear that federal courts should be willing to terminate desegregation orders.

The Rise of Affirmative Action

Following its failed experiment with forced busing, the Burger Court proved itself unable to help define the debate over race preferences. Rather than speak coherently (let alone decisively) about preferences, none of its first three affirmative action rulings yielded a majority decision. In sharp contrast, Congress and White House decision making was anything but indecisive. Starting with Lyndon Johnson's June 1965 Howard University commencement address and up until the 1980 election of Ronald Reagan, elected government support of race preferences was unambiguous.

In his commencement address, Johnson spoke of the devastating effect of long years of slavery and pledged "not . . . just to open the gates of opportunity" but to see to it that "all our citizens . . . have the ability to walk through those gates."[82] This speech transformed civil rights policy from a focus on individualized fair treatment objectives to an emphasis on group claims for proportional representation. By arguing that equality of opportunity was not enough, Johnson set the stage for his administration's efforts to withhold federal contract awards from employers with inadequate minority representation. For example, pursuant to its 1965 Executive Order 11,246 demand that government contractors make adequate use of minorities, Johnson's Department of Labor issued its "Philadelphia Plan," withholding government contracts in Philadelphia and other selected cities until contractors submitted pledges to hire minority workers.

These efforts were expanded by the Nixon administration. Between March 1969 and October 1971 Nixon issued three executive orders to "help establish and promote minority business." The creation of the Office of Minority Business Enterprise within the Department of Commerce and the call for increased representation of minority business enterprises within federal departments and agencies were the by-products of these executive orders. For the Nixon administration, "the unique historical experience of . . . disadvantaged minorities . . . cannot be ignored in shaping a national effort to produce substantial new entrepreneurial activity."[83]

The Nixon administration successfully defended the Philadelphia Plan in court, threatened to veto legislative efforts to rescind the plan, and extended the plan to nineteen other cities. Ironically, the Nixon White House supported expanding the Philadelphia Plan, in part, to encourage political strife. Specifically, Nixon realized that the plan created a political dilemma for the Democrats, namely, the division of two traditional Democrat constituencies: labor unions and civil rights groups.[84]

The Carter administration took Nixon and Johnson initiatives one step further by strengthening existing affirmative action programs and launching numerous race- and gender-conscious initiatives. Carter initiatives included efforts to demand adequate minority student representation in tax-exempt private schools, the granting of preferences to minority broadcasters, the establishment of a minority business enterprise set-aside for Department of Transportation highway programs, and Equal Employment Opportunity Commission (EEOC) efforts to racially balance the workplace.[85] For the 1980 Democratic Platform, "an effective affirmative action program is an essential component of our commitment to expanding civil rights protections."[86]

Reagan campaigned against this vision of numerical racial justice. The 1980 Republican Party platform declared that "equal opportunity should not be jeopardized by bureaucratic regulations and decisions which rely on quotas, ratios, and numerical requirements to exclude some individuals in favor of others."[87] Echoing this sentiment, Reagan's first and only Civil Rights Division head, William Bradford Reynolds, decried racial preferences as "[just as] offensive to standards of human decency today as [they were] some 84 years ago when countenanced under *Plessy v. Ferguson*" and, accordingly, told Congress that the Justice Department would oppose "the use of quotas or any other numerical or statistical formula designed to provide to nonvictims of discrimination preferential treatment."[88]

Three extraordinary policy blunders made by Reagan at the urging of the Department of Justice severely damaged his affirmative action counterrevolution. First, Reagan's ostensible commitment to simple nondiscrimination was undermined when his administration sought in 1982 to restore the tax-exempt status of racially discriminatory private schools.[89] Second, in the midst of this fiasco, Reagan announced his opposition to provisions of the 1982 Voting Rights Act amendments which make disparate racial impact an important evidentiary tool in voting rights cases.[90] Third, in 1983, Reagan sought to remove Mary Frances Berry and two of her colleagues from the U.S. Commission on Civil Rights. In their stead, Reagan had hoped to appoint to the Commission individuals who "don't worship at the altar of forced busing and mandatory quotas" and "don't believe you can remedy past discrimination by mandating new discrimination."[91]

Congress and the courts successfully resisted these counterinitiatives. By an 8–1 vote, the Supreme Court concluded that racist schools could not receive tax breaks.[92] The courts likewise blocked Reagan's dismissal of Berry, forcing the administration to cut a deal with Congress that kept her and other liberals on the Commission.[93] Finally (and most significant), with 62 senators and 389 representatives cosponsoring the bill, Congress had little difficulty pushing through voting rights legislation.[94]

Contrary to the Reagan administration's claim that the proposed legislation would result in quotas, the Senate Judiciary Committee report concluded that the Supreme Court, in requiring proof of discriminatory intent in voting rights cases, placed "an unacceptably difficult burden on plaintiffs."[95] Ten years later, thirteen blacks and five Hispanics were elected from eighteen newly created, predominantly minority districts. By 1995, the House of Representatives had thirty-eight black members (including seventeen from the South), up from twenty-six in 1990 (with five from the South).[96] In 2002, there were thirty-nine black members.

For its part, the Rehnquist Court has issued conflicting opinions on race-conscious redistricting. In 1993, the Court called into question the constitutionality of racial gerrymandering. Rejecting Clinton administration claims that the principle of the color-blind constitution must yield to "the unfortunate fact that racial block voting occurs,"[97] the Court concluded that racial gerrymandering is subject to the same standard of strict scrutiny review as other racial classifications.[98] By 1999, however, the Court made clear that lawmakers may take political affiliation into account when drawing district lines "even if it so happens that the most loyal Democrats happen to be black Democrats and even if the State were *conscious* of that fact."[99]

Efforts to Dismantle Affirmative Action

Following its defeat on voting rights, the Reagan administration shied away from costly battles with civil rights interests. Consequently, although some kamikaze pilots at the Department of Justice were allowed to continue their mission, neither the White House nor other agencies gave them assistance. Before the Supreme Court, Department of Justice efforts to dismantle affirmative action received a mixed reception. But even if the Court had embraced Justice arguments, the meaning and reach of its affirmative action decisions likely would have been controlled by elected officials. Decisions in 1986 and 1989 illustrate the transformative role of social and political influences.[100] By striking down affirmative action plans under some form of heightened review, these cases were, in important respects, victories for the Reagan Justice Department. In the end, however, these decisions were severely limited by strong state and federal government support for affirmative action programs.

State and local officials worked around the 1989 decision and its demand that affirmative action programs be "narrowly tailored" to serve "a compelling governmental interest" (strict scrutiny review). The decision prompted a slew of "disparity studies" to prove the likelihood of continuing discrimination in public contracting.[101] Furthermore, public contracting schemes, rather than employ rigid set-asides, now treat race or ethnicity as a "plus factor."[102] Reaction to the 1986 ruling is equally striking. Although it invalidated a school board's practice of laying off nonminority employees ahead of less senior minority employees, the decision was hailed by major newspapers as "a significant victory for civil rights groups" because it "left the way clear for employers to adopt affirmative action programs in the workplace."[103]

By staking out a hard-line position and pursuing it with reckless abandon, the Civil Rights Division weakened the Department's position with Congress and within the Reagan administration. The most telling example of the Department's lack of political clout within the administration was its failed attempt to persuade the White House to modify Executive Order 11,246, which required 325,000 government contractors to adopt affirmative action plans. Although Brad Reynolds claimed that the "[11,246] program is broken and . . . needs to be fixed in a way that brings it back in line with the principle of non-discrimination,"[104] pragmatists within the Administration, such as Labor Secretary Bill Brock, thought it "politically unacceptable" for the White House to expend further political capital in this area.[105] Brock ultimately prevailed; in August 1986, the White House killed the proposal "because of recent Supreme Court decisions upholding some affirmative action plans."[106]

The White House saw these decisions as a significant political rebuke to the Department's campaign to eliminate affirmative action, which was considered too entrenched to oppose. Under Reagan, affirmative action proved to be so pervasive "that the very government agencies of an administration that opposes quotas and goals report to the Equal Employment Opportunity Commission on their progress toward meeting affirmative action numerical goals!"[107] The administration, moreover, did not alter either the Small Business Administration's or other executive-initiated set-aside programs or EEOC guidelines providing for an inference of adverse impact whenever the utilization of women and minorities is less than 80 percent of their availability.

Civil Rights under Bush I

Like Reagan, Bush I granted broad discretion to the Department of Justice to oppose affirmative action, while other parts of his administration vigorously supported race and gender preferences. Indeed, rather than seek to reshape the civil rights landscape, the Bush administration engaged in damage control to distance itself from Reagan-era aftershocks.

In his first month in office, Bush emphasized his "commit[ment] to affirmative action" and, with it, his desire "to see a reinvigorated Office of Minority Business in Commerce."[108] He also sought to cool the fires of the Reagan FCC's opposition to affirmative action. In the summer of 1989, he appointed three FCC commissioners who expressly supported the granting of race preferences to minority broadcasters. Before the Supreme Court, these appointees turned their words into deeds by vigorously (and successfully) defending diversity preferences.[109]

In deliberations between Congress and the White House over the 1991 Civil Rights Act, the Bush administration also sought to work with civil rights interests. The Supreme Court began to backtrack from its previous positions on civil rights and issued five decisions in 1989 that made it more difficult to prove discrimination under Title VII (employment discrimination) and other statutes.[110] Congress and civil rights interest groups went to work on legislation that would both nullify these decisions and make it easier for civil rights plaintiffs to bring lawsuits. After an imbroglio over whether disparate-impact proofs of discrimination would unduly pressure employers to hire by the numbers to stave off costly litigation prompted a presidential veto and several rounds of marathon negotiations, Bush pressured his negotiators to meet with civil rights leaders and to find a way for him to sign the bill. Ironically, although dissatisfaction with the Supreme Court prompted this legislation, the key to the compromise was to delegate to the courts the task of specifying standards of proof governing disparate-impact cases.

The 1991 Civil Rights Act forever shattered the post–New Deal Supreme Court's image as civil rights heroes. While civil rights interests persistently turned to the Warren and Burger Courts, the advent of the Rehnquist Court has signaled a growing divide between the Supreme Court and the civil rights establishment. With the 1991 Civil Rights Act overturning nine Rehnquist Court interpretations, elected government became the civil rights establishment's "Court of Last Resort."

Social and Political Forces Dominate

In its June 1995 ruling in *Adarand Constructors, Inc. v. Pena*, the Supreme Court cast doubt on the constitutionality of affirmative action. By a 5–4 vote, the Court refused for the first time to uphold a congressionally approved set-aside program. Ruling that federal affirmative action plans were subject to the same standard of strict scrutiny review as state and local government programs, *Adarand* tightened the standards governing affirmative action. At the same time, *Adarand* sought to "dispel the notion that strict scrutiny is 'strict in theory, but fatal in fact.'"[111]

Even before its release, *Adarand* had been largely overtaken by social and political forces. For example, in the spring of 1995, Congress was considering a bill introduced by Senator Jesse Helms entitled the "Act to End Unfair Preferential Treatment"; the White House was in the midst of an extensive review of federal affirmative action programs; announced and prospective presidential candidates—including Bob Dole, Phil Gramm, Jesse Jackson, Arlen Specter, and Pete Wilson—had made affirmative action one of the centerpieces of their presidential bids; and a citizen-sponsored ballot initiative in California threatened to do away with most state affirmative action programs. By May 1995, "the question of the hour" was not whether the Supreme Court would settle the affirmative action controversy, "but simply whether it will stand aside and let the nation sort through these problems on its own."[112]

Over the next few years, the pendulum had turned again. Several key Republican legislators, motivated both by a desire "to craft a positive message for minorities" and a corresponding fear that a catfight over affirmative action would slow down their pursuit of the "Contract with America" and other reforms, pushed affirmative action to the back burner.[113] For this reason, Republicans in both the House and the Senate have voted against proposals to roll back federal affirmative action programs.[114]

For its part, the Clinton administration limited *Adarand*'s reach. In a 1995 speech on affirmative action, Clinton emphasized that the decision "actually reaffirmed the need for affirmative action."[115] Moreover, through a White House–conducted "Affirmative Action Review," the Clinton administration concluded that nearly all affirmative action programs are responsive to discrimination, do not unduly burden nonminorities, and accomplish their objectives of increasing opportunities for minorities and women.[116]

With affirmative action solidly entrenched within the Washington, D.C. beltway, opponents of affirmative action shifted their attention to the states. In particular, from 1995 to 1998, California has played a leadership role in dismantling affirmative action. On July 20, 1995, one day after President Clinton addressed the nation on affirmative action, the University of California Regents heeded Republican governor and presidential candidate Pete Wilson's claim that racial preferences "threaten to infect the nation with 'the deadly virus of tribalism'" and voted to eliminate affirmative action hiring and admissions.[117]

More significant, in 1996, the citizens of California passed a state constitutional amendment that banned affirmative action. Proposition 209 provides that the state "shall not discriminate against, or grant preferential treatment to, any individual or group on the basis of race, sex, color, ethnicity or national origin in the operation of public employment, public education, or public contracting." Although a federal district court issued an injunction preventing implementation of the amendment, the Ninth Circuit Court of Appeals approved the amendment. In a bow to the force of public opinion, the Ninth Circuit remarked, "A system which permits one judge to block with the stroke of a pen what 4,736,180 state residents voted to enact as law tests the integrity of our constitutional democracy."[118]

California, though leading the charge in the populist revolt against affirmative action, did not stand alone. In November 1998, Washington voters approved a similar initiative. With opinion polls showing widespread support for California-like measures and with the financial support of the American Civil Rights Institute, state initiative fights, not judicial rulings, seemed ready to become the focal point in the battle over preferences.[119]

By 2000, however, the initiative movement had lost steam. In the wake of Proposition 209, a backlash against the initiative resulted in California Republicans losing majority control of the California Assembly. In Florida, Governor Jeb Bush vigorously and successfully opposed a ballot initiative. Claiming that the proposed initiative violated state law, Bush went to court to block a vote on it.[120] Following their defeat in Florida, the American Civil Rights Institute backed away from its populist campaign against affirmative action. At that time, opponents of affirmative action had little recourse but to turn to the courts.

Grutter v. Bollinger

In a June 2003 ruling, the Supreme Court denied affirmative action opponents the victory they could not obtain in the political process. By a 5–4 vote, the Justices upheld efforts by the University of Michigan Law School to make sure that a "critical mass" of minority students were admitted each year. Although the Court also invalidated the university's practice of awarding a set number of points to *all* undergraduate applicants from designated races, the law school decision, *Grutter v. Bollinger*,[121] made clear that colleges and universities could treat race as a "plus factor" in admissions.

Social and political forces help explain the Court's ruling. Federal and state officials were almost unanimous in their support of affirmative action. Briefs defending the Michigan program were filed by 23 states, 124 members of Congress, and 13 senators. No member of Congress formally opposed the Michigan policy, and only one state (Florida) filed a brief attacking the Michigan plan. For its part, the Bush II administration sought to carve out a compromise position. While embracing racial diversity in education as "important and entirely legitimate," the administration condemned Michigan's race-conscious policies because "a variety of race-neutral alternatives [were] available to achieve the important goals" of openness and diversity.[122]

The failure of the Bush II administration to take a hard-line position against affirmative action is telling. Previous Republican administrations (Reagan and Bush I) left federal affirmative action programs alone while allowing the Justice Department to attack affirmative action in Court. But pragmatists within the Bush II administration successfully fought off the efforts of Solicitor General Ted Olson and Attorney General John Ashcroft to file briefs condemning race preferences.[123] These pragmatists argued that an absolutist anti–affirmative action brief would make it harder for Bush to win over Hispanic and moderate suburban voters. In particular, with minority populations expanding, Bush's political advisors told him that his 2004 reelection bid may well hinge on his ability to reach out to more minority voters.[124]

Another contributing factor to both Bush's decision and the refusal of a single member of Congress to oppose the Michigan plan was the January 2003 ouster of Trent Lott as Senate majority leader. In December 2002 remarks, Lott appeared to embrace the segregationist appeals of Strom Thurmond's 1948 presidential campaign. Following these remarks, Lott was denounced by Bush and other Republicans for making statements that "do not reflect the spirit of our country."[125] Four Republican senators used the Lott episode as a springboard to urge Bush to support the University of Michigan's claim that racial diversity is a compelling government interest.[126]

The University of Michigan also benefited from amicus filings by Fortune 500 companies, a coalition of former high-ranking officers and civilian leaders of the military, other colleges and universities, and educational and psychological associations. These briefs argued that racial diversity was necessary, among other things, to allow college and law school graduates to succeed in a multiracial society, to allow American business to compete in a racially diverse global economy, and to enable the military to "fulfill its principal mission to provide national security."[127] In sharp contrast, affirmative action opponents received no support from business or mainstream educational interests.

Against this backdrop, it is little wonder that the Supreme Court would allow colleges and universities to take race into account. Indeed, the Court made numerous references to amicus briefs (including the Bush administration's brief) to establish that race diversity in education is a compelling governmental interest. To have concluded otherwise, the Court would have stood almost alone. At the same time, by rejecting the mechanical formula used by the undergraduate scheme, the Court signaled its discomfort with some race-conscious decisions.

State officials, members of Congress, and the Bush administration embraced the Court's decision. President Bush, for example, "applaud[ed]" the Court for "recognizing the value of diversity" and pledged to "promote policies that expand educational opportunities for Americans from all racial, ethnic, and economic backgrounds."[128] Not only did this middle-ground approach conform to elected government and interest group preferences, but it was generally consistent with public opinion. Although most Americans disapprove of race preferences in college admissions, opinion polls also reveal that Americans do not oppose affirmative action and think that colleges and universities should be racially diverse.[129]

Conclusions

Court decisions must operate within a political culture. Although they may affect this culture, social and political forces also shape the ultimate meaning of judicial action. For example, by narrowly interpreting *Adarand*, the Clinton administration was able to keep most federal affirmative action programs intact. Three decades earlier, Congress and White House support for *Brown* paved the way for meaningful school desegregation. The saga of voting rights likewise underscores the interactive nature of constitutional decision making. By allowing for numerically based proofs of discrimination, Congress was willing to correct the Court.

Beyond elected government responses to Court decisions, the Court often takes social and political forces into account when crafting an opinion. Chief Justice Warren's search for unanimity in *Brown* and the Burger Court's sensitivity to the *Swann* backlash are quintessential examples of this phenomenon. Along the same lines, Rehnquist Court school desegregation decisions are the outgrowth of opposition to mandatory assignments from both elected government and minority interests.[130]

School desegregation, voting rights, and affirmative action underscore how constitutional values are forged through a give-and-take process in which the courts, the people, and elected officials influence each other. Some critics condemn this process as producing middle-ground solutions insensitive to the needs of the minority community, yet it is often the case that elected officials are more responsive to minority interests than are the courts. For example, lawmaker efforts to expand voting rights protections in 1982, to countermand the Supreme Court's approval of the wartime internment of Japanese Americans, and to use the Civil Rights Act of 1991 to reverse the Court are a testament to the willingness of elected officials to correct Supreme Court decision making by expanding civil rights protections.

8

Speech

The commitment to individual conscience and free speech predates rulings by the Supreme Court and other judicial bodies. It was not until 1925 that the Court decided that the Free Speech Clause of the First Amendment was incorporated in the Due Process Clause of the Fourteenth Amendment, to be applied against the states.[1] Prior to that time, free speech was a matter decided by Congress, the President, and state and local communities. In his work on free speech, Zechariah Chafee Jr. counseled that the "victories of liberty of speech must be won in the mind before they are won in the courts."[2] Regardless of what courts decide or elected branches legislate, "the ultimate security for free and fruitful discussion lies in the tolerance of private citizens."[3]

Popular sentiment, not judicial edicts, explains the repudiation of the 1798 Alien and Sedition Act, the 1917 Espionage Act, and McCarthy-era restrictions on civil liberties. Likewise, social and political forces played a prominent role in the Warren Court's expansion of political speech and its liberalization of obscenity. Even Court decisions striking down the flag salute, indecency on the Internet, and much more are linked to the desires of the people and their elected officials. In other words, strong judicial protection of speech seems destined to continue—not because the Court wants it, but because the people embrace it.

Free Speech in the Early Republic

What does the First Amendment protect if not the freedom to criticize government? "Whatever differences may exist about interpretations of the First Amendment," the Supreme Court noted in 1978, "there is practically universal agreement that a major purpose of that Amendment was to protect the free discussion of governmental affairs."[4] In 1798, however, there was anything but universal agreement on this matter. That year, Congress enacted the repressive Alien and Sedition Acts, legislation that punished anyone who spoke or wrote anything "false, scandalous and malicious" against the federal government, either House of Congress, or the President, with intent "to defame" those governmental bodies.[5]

How could Congress enact and President John Adams sign such restrictive legislation? Equally troubling, by allowing the Sedition Act to be enforced, how could federal courts protect the power of government over individuals? The short answer is that, in 1798, it was unclear whether the First Amendment protected speech critical of the government. "The history of the framing and ratification of the First Amendment," according to a leading study, was controlled by individuals who "opposed a Bill of Rights" and, as such, almost certainly embraced Britain's practice of allowing seditious libel prosecutions.[6] Thanks to public resistance to the Alien and Sedition Acts, however, Justice Brandeis later spoke of the "freedom to think as you will and to speak as you think [as being] . . . indispensable to the discovery and spread of political truth."[7]

The Alien and Sedition Acts were a by-product of a bitter struggle between the Federalist and Republican Parties over the decision to go to war against France in 1798. The Federalist Congress decided to punish Republican critics of the administration. Indeed, having dubbed Republicans the "internal foe," Federalists saw seditious libel laws as a way to "express their view that the Republican party was a threat to the republic."[8] With Federalist prosecutors targeting critics of the Adams administration and Federalist judges quite willing to enforce the acts, three Republican newspapers were forced to cease publication.[9]

That Federalists sought to gain political advantage in approving and enforcing the Alien and Sedition Acts, however, does not explain how supporters defended the constitutionality of these measures both in Congress and the courts. Some members of Congress regarded the acts as a blatant violation of press freedoms protected by the First Amendment. Nathaniel Macon argued that Congress lacked the constitutional authority to pass the statute and "could only hope that the Judges would exercise the power placed in them of determining the law as unconstitutional law, if, upon scrutiny, they find it to be so."[10] "To restrict the press," said John Nicholas, "would be to destroy the elective principle, by taking away the information necessary to election."[11] Defenders of the measure countered by arguing that freedom of expression protected only against prior restraints, an argument grounded in England's practice of equating freedom of the press with freedom from prior restraints.[12]

Led by Thomas Jefferson and James Madison, Republicans also attacked the Alien and Sedition Acts as an infringement of state sovereignty. Claiming that seditious libel was a matter reserved to the states,[13] they drafted resolutions (Jefferson for Kentucky and Madison for Virginia) that challenged the authority of the federal government to enforce the two laws.

Finding that these laws infringed on the people's rights to freedom of speech and press, the Kentucky and Virginia resolutions appealed to other states to join them in protecting the prerogatives of the states and the people by declaring the Acts unconstitutional. Under this view, the states have the authority, when acting in concert, to nullify laws they consider unconstitutional.[14]

Kentucky and Virginia's pleas fell on deaf ears. No other state approved a similar resolution, and ten (of the sixteen) states expressed their disagreement with Virginia and Kentucky. But defeat of the resolutions hardly spelled victory for the Alien and Sedition Acts. Controversial prosecutions of prominent Republicans cost the Federalist Party. Witness, for example, the first prosecution under the Sedition Act, that of Matthew Lyon. Three weeks before the Act took effect, Lyon, a Republican congressman from Vermont, attacked Adams for his "unbounded thirst for ridiculous pomp, foolish adulation, and selfish avarice."[15] Although convicted (after an hour of jury deliberation), Lyon nonetheless was reelected while in prison. More telling, even though Sedition Act prosecutions put some Republican newspapers out of business, there was a substantial increase in the number of Republican newspapers by the time of the 1800 elections, "perhaps because of [the Act]."[16]

The Sedition Act expired by its own terms in 1801, the year Jefferson became President. After taking office, he invoked his pardon power to discharge "every person under punishment or prosecution under the sedition law, because I considered, and now consider, that law to be a nullity, as absolute and as palpable as if congress had ordered us to fall down and worship a golden image."[17] Indeed, the courts' failure to void the Sedition Act helped convince Jefferson that concerns over individual rights required the executive to play a more active role in constitutional interpretation. Forty years later, Congress followed suit, declaring the Sedition Act "unconstitutional, null, and void"[18] and reimbursing the fines against Lyon. Through these legislative and executive interpretations, the Supreme Court declared in 1964 that the Sedition Act had been invalidated not by a court of law but "by the court of history."[19]

The Rise of Political Speech

The Supreme Court was certainly correct in concluding that the 1798 Sedition Act had been repudiated politically, not judicially. Nevertheless, from the Civil War through the early 1950s anticommunist crusade led by Senator Joseph McCarthy, Congress and the courts were often hostile to the free speech claims of political dissidents. Indeed, contrary to the

Supreme Court's modern-day image as protector of First Amendment freedoms, the Court's record is quite mixed. Before the populist repudiation of the McCarthy era, the Justices almost always upheld elected branch efforts to limit political dissent. Since that time, the Court has been a vigilant defender of political speech claims. For its part, Congress has generally supported this contemporary judicial role. It rejected efforts to limit Court decision making and has used the confirmation process to defend political speech protections.

After the Sedition Act, the next major free speech issue involved slavery. Initially, abolitionists pointed to both the state and federal constitutions to attack restrictions on antislavery speech. They contended that "free enquiry and discussion is the corner stone of liberty; and the safeguard of truth . . . and that it is the RIGHT of American citizens to . . . express their opinions freely, and fully; privately, and openly."[20] Those who wanted to suppress abolitionist speech assumed the federal and state constitutions were not meant to safeguard it. Arguing that a publication that had the "direct tendency . . . to excite *rebellion against the laws* is libelous," pro-slavery forces dubbed abolitionists "firebrands of sedition" and "fanatical disturbers of the publick peace."[21] Under this "bad tendency test" (which courts used throughout the Civil War period), publications or speech could be suppressed if they tended to harm the public welfare.[22]

Public discussion of free speech and press remained quiet until 1837, when Elijah Lovejoy, an abolitionist editor, was killed while defending his printing press. As people began to realize that assaults on abolitionists could mean later aggression against other freedoms, the killing of Lovejoy was seen as "an attack on Northern liberty by the slave system of the South."[23] Ironically, following Abraham Lincoln's 1862 suspension of habeus corpus, pro-slavery forces embraced free speech principles. Specifically, in May 1863, federal officials arrested and tried pro-slavery Democrat Clement Vallandigham before a military tribunal; Vallandigham's offense was making an antiwar speech "discouraging volunteer enlistments [and encouraging resistance to] military drafts."[24] The Supreme Court concluded that it had no jurisdiction to review the Vallandigham case.[25] As such, the growing desire of the American people to ensure free speech proved to be the only meaningful check on the amount of suppression that occurred before and during the Civil War.

Following the Civil War and before World War I, there was widespread censorship of political ideas. Indeed, even before he asked Congress to declare war on Germany, President Woodrow Wilson informed lawmakers that "the gravest threats against our national peace and safety have been uttered within our own borders. There are citizens of the United States,

I blush to admit, born under other flags but welcomed under our generous naturalization laws . . . who have poured the poison of disloyalty into the very arteries of our national life."[26]

In June 1917, Congress enacted the Espionage Act. Under this statute, anyone who "shall willfully cause or attempt to cause insubordination, disloyalty, mutiny, or refusal of duty, in the military or naval forces of the United States" shall be subject to "a fine of not more than $10,000 or imprisonment for not more than twenty years."[27] Moreover, the statute deemed "nonmailable" any "letter, writing, circular, postal card, . . . newspaper, pamphlet, book, or other publication . . . advocating or urging treason, insurrection, or forcible resistance to any law of the United States."[28]

First Amendment concerns figured prominently in legislative debates about the Act. A provision that would have allowed the imprisonment of anyone publishing materials that the President deemed possibly useful to the enemy was rejected as an impermissible restraint on press freedoms. At the same time, there was little resistance to provisions banning the mailing of publications advocating opposition to the war and/or resistance to the draft. Lawmakers wanted an act that would regulate individual conduct, especially propaganda that might adversely affect the military.[29] Congress, moreover, wanted to send a message to immigrants: Shed your allegiance to foreign nations and ideas, or get out.

Between June 1917 and June 1920, over two thousand people were prosecuted under the Espionage Act, and over one thousand of these were convicted. Most courts, in upholding the Act, did not even refer to the First Amendment in their opinions; the few that did determined that the government's right to self-preservation trumped the individual's right to self-expression. For its part, a unanimous Supreme Court devoted one paragraph to First Amendment concerns when upholding the Espionage Act in *Schenck v. United States* (1919).[30] One year later, the Court divided 7 to 2 in affirming the conviction of Jacob Abrams, an anarchist who scattered leaflets calling on munitions workers to protest U.S. interference in the Russian Revolution.[31]

Abrams, however, was seen as a breakthrough by civil libertarians. For the first time, some members of the Court (Oliver Wendell Holmes and Louis Brandeis) invoked the First Amendment to limit governmental power. Holmes and Brandeis were influenced by an article written in the *Harvard Law Review* by Zechariah Chafee Jr., who argued strongly that free speech was important not only in time of peace but especially in time of war.[32] The extensive repression of free speech during World War I also prompted many Americans to take the First Amendment seriously. No longer viewing the government as benevolent, many came to value

First Amendment protections and, in so doing, embraced the then-emerging modern civil liberties movement.

With public support for First Amendment freedoms on the rise, government, too, became more accepting of civil liberties. During World War II, for example, Attorney General Francis Biddle resolved not to repeat the mistakes of his predecessors. As a result, there were hardly any civil liberties cases litigated during this period.[33] By 1945, however, the national mood had changed. Growing awareness of the "totalitarian threat" prompted a slew of laws and regulations designed to curb speech, especially that of communists.[34]

Following the Republicans' congressional sweep in 1946, President Truman responded to Republican criticism that he was soft on communism. In a 1947 executive order, Truman sought to quiet his critics by authorizing the investigation of federal employees by loyalty review boards.[35] But anticommunist sentiment continued to grow, reaching a fever pitch in the early 1950s. A number of events contributed to this cementing of anticommunist sentiment. In 1949, the Soviets exploded an atomic bomb, leading people to worry that spies had helped them get the technology. A few weeks later, China officially fell to the communists. In the immediate wake of China's fall, Justice Department prosecutors successfully tried former State Department official Alger Hiss for giving classified documents to communists. And in 1950, the United States sent troops to South Korea to defend it against communist North Korea. Against this backdrop, "anticommunism . . . became a staple of American politics and society."[36]

In the midst of this maelstrom, Congress, executive branch officials, and the Supreme Court joined forces in limiting free speech. The Immigration and Nationality Act of 1952 prohibited aliens from entering the United States if they advocated or taught communist doctrine, substantially expanding the power of existing government agencies to root out communism.[37] Government attorneys launched prosecutions against individuals who taught from books written by Stalin, Marx, Engels, and Lenin. The government accused these individuals of conspiring to organize the Communist Party and, as such, violating the Smith Act, which made it unlawful to "knowingly or willfully advocate, abet, advise, or teach the duty, necessity, desirability, or propriety of overthrowing or destroying any government in the United States by force or violence."[38] In upholding these prosecutions, the Supreme Court declined to invoke the First Amendment to limit Congress and White House efforts to deal with the "Red Scare"; instead, it would stand aside and let the elected branches sort out how they wanted to handle the problem of communist subversives.[39]

Public opinion supported this anticommunist crusade. Wisconsin Republican Joseph McCarthy, after accusing the State Department of harboring 205 communists, rose to national prominence in 1950. He smeared numerous Democrats for their "treason[ous]" support of communists and played an important role in the 1952 Republican sweep of the White House, Senate, and House of Representatives. Starting in 1953, however, support for McCarthy began to slide. The crisis atmosphere of the early 1950s eased with the death of Stalin and the end of the Korean War. By 1954, McCarthy himself had fallen into disrepute, publicly humiliated at hearings that investigated special favors he did for a staffer who had been drafted by the Army.

But Congress continued to beat the anticommunist drum, enacting legislation in 1954 to require the registration of members of the Communist Party.[40] Changes in the public mood opened the door to judges interested in championing First Amendment freedoms. With President Eisenhower's appointment of Earl Warren and William Brennan to the Supreme Court, anticommunist legislation was no longer rubber-stamped; instead, it was narrowly construed. In *Yates v. United States* (1957), the Court effectively overruled *Dennis* by holding that the government could not prosecute the advocacy and teaching of communism.[41] For journalist I. F. Stone, the Court, by making the "First Amendment a reality again," "reflect[ed] the steadily growing public misgivings and distaste for . . . [those] who have made America look foolish and even sinister during the last ten years."[42]

The public and their elected representatives, however, were not prepared to go as far as the Court. Congress and the White House disapproved of *Yates* and several other Court decisions limiting the government's ability to track down and prosecute communists. Legislation, for example, was introduced that would limit Supreme Court jurisdiction over matters that impacted the First Amendment rights of communists, such as the federal loyalty security program and state antisubversive statutes. In defending this measure, Senator William Jenner spoke of the need to counteract "[recent] decisions of the Supreme Court . . . [decisions in which] the Supreme Court has arrogated to itself [the power to legislate]."[43] Congress eventually rejected this proposal, but the Court responded to this attack by moderating its civil liberties campaign and, in so doing, prompted the *New York Times* to editorialize in 1960 that "what Senator Jenner was unable to achieve the Supreme Court has now virtually accomplished on its own."[44]

The retreat of the Warren Court proved to be "a tactical withdrawal, not a rout."[45] Well aware of intense Southern opposition to its civil rights decision making, especially *Brown v. Board of Education*, the Court understood that it could not dismantle existing anticommunist laws in the name of the First Amendment.[46] By 1964, the Court had weathered the storm of attacks that followed its decisions in *Brown*, *Yates*, and several other cases. Through the 1964 Civil Rights Act, Congress and the White House embraced *Brown* and, with it, federal solutions to race issues.

The Court quickly returned to the race issue, approving the public accommodations provisions of the 1964 Civil Rights Act, expanding the scope of its school desegregation decision making, and striking back at state efforts to limit the civil rights movement. In *New York Times v. Sullivan* (1964), for example, the Court expanded First Amendment protections in a case involving an advertisement signed by sixty-four civil rights leaders condemning alleged police misconduct in Montgomery, Alabama.[47] Even though some statements in the advertisement were false, the Court concluded that L. B. Sullivan, a city official, could not bring a defamation lawsuit unless he could show that those taking out the advertisement both knew that it was false and acted with "actual malice." Unlike World War I–era and McCarthy-era decision making, the Court wrote that all First Amendment cases must be considered "against the backdrop of a profound national commitment to the principle that debate on public issues should be uninhibited, robust, and wide-open."[48]

With a spate of Vietnam-era decisions the Court made clear that its support for free speech extended beyond the civil rights movement. Although ruling that the burning of a draft card was not protected speech, the Court upheld the rights of public school students, elected officials, and others to protest the war by, among other things, wearing black armbands or jackets that said "Fuck the Draft."[49] The Court also expanded First Amendment freedoms in the Pentagon Papers case, blocking government efforts to stop the *New York Times* and *Washington Post* from publishing excerpts of a secret report recounting the history of the Vietnam War.[50] And in a case far removed from the Vietnam War and the civil rights movement, the Court ruled that members of the Ku Klux Klan have nearly unlimited rights to send a political message. Specifically, in language that cannot be squared with any of its World War I–era or McCarthy-era rulings, the Court held that a state can punish only advocacy that "is directed to inciting or producing imminent lawless action and is likely to incite or produce such action."[51]

By 1987, these Vietnam-era precedents were well entrenched. When rejecting Reagan Supreme Court nominee Robert Bork, lawmakers formally embraced Court decisions limiting the power of government over speech—even of those who advocate the violent overthrow of the government. The Senate Judiciary Committee objected that Bork might seek to limit (if not overturn) Vietnam-era precedents: "Our system is built upon the precept that any political speech, short of that which will produce imminent violence, furthers public understanding and national progress—sometimes, by showing the virtues of the existing system."[52]

By embracing the Court this way, Congress has encouraged it to be a strong proponent of First Amendment freedoms. For this very reason, the Court's flag-burning decisions (discussed later in this chapter) can be linked to Congress's rejection of Bork.[53] In contrast, when Congress expressed disapproval of 1956 decision making expanding speech protections, the Court beat a hasty retreat, waiting until 1964 to reenter this fray. Unable "to maintain a position squarely opposed to a strong popular majority,"[54] Supreme Court decisions implicating political speech very much are products of the times.

Defending the Press

A 1978 Supreme Court decision provided Congress with another opportunity to support First Amendment freedoms. That year, the Court upheld the police search of a student newspaper, the *Stanford Daily*, to obtain photos of a clash between demonstrators and the police.[55] In rejecting the newspaper's claim that free press protections outweigh law enforcement needs, the Court approved state power to issue search warrants of newspapers. At the same time, the Justices invited the other two branches to participate in a constitutional dialogue on this issue, noting that the Fourth Amendment "does not prevent or advise against legislative or executive efforts to establish nonconstitutional protections against possible abuses of the search warrant procedure."[56]

Congress and the White House responded to this invitation and to newspaper claims that the decision was "a dire step toward a police state," an assault that "stands on its head the history of both the first and the fourth amendments," and a threat to the "privacy rights of the law-abiding."[57] The Senate Judiciary Committee concluded that the search warrant procedure approved by the Court "does not sufficiently protect the press and other innocent third parties and that legislation is called for."[58] For his part, President Carter proposed legislation "limiting police searches of newsrooms to deal with the problems created by the Supreme Court's *Stanford Daily* decision."[59]

The solution crafted by Congress and the White House required, with certain exceptions, a subpoena instead of a search warrant to obtain documentary materials from those who disseminate newspapers, books, broadcasts, or other similar forms of public communication.[60] Unlike search warrants, this subpoena-first policy would allow newspapers an opportunity to state their views in a court hearing. Moreover, assuming a subpoena is issued, newspapers would not be subjected to a disruptive search of their facilities; instead, the newspaper would simply turn over the document subpoenaed.

When debating this measure, lawmakers emphasized that the Justices had given Congress "an open invitation" to draw statutory lines that protect constitutional rights and, consequently, that the subpoena-first policy is "principally designed to protect the public's right to know."[61] For John Culver, "the threat of governmental intrusion into the unique independence of the American press is not to be taken lightly," for "a free society cannot endure without a free press."[62] Robert Kastenmeier, who managed the bill on the House floor, argued that the Court's decision has "thrown into doubt" a "longstanding principle of constitutional jurisprudence," and "rather than to await the results of many years of potential litigation" it is better "for Congress to step in to fill the void."[63] In so doing, Congress performed the identical task attempted by the Court—balancing the Fourth Amendment against other interests—and reached a strikingly different conclusion that gave greater protection to press freedoms.

Saving "Old Glory"

A 1989 Supreme Court decision striking down a Texas flag-burning decision prompted Congress to enact a flag protection statute of its own. But, in 1990, the Court found that statute unconstitutional. Although this decision unleashed a populist flurry against the Court, Congress has repeatedly turned down constitutional amendment proposals to limit the First Amendment's reach. Congress's failure to countermand the Court underscores both the difficulty of amending the Constitution and ever growing lawmaker acquiescence to the flag-burning decision.

Until the burning of an American flag during an April 1967 Vietnam War protest rally, flag protection was not a prominent issue. In 1968, Congress enacted legislation making it illegal to "knowingly cast contempt upon any flag of the United States by publicly mutilating, defacing, defiling, burning, or trampling upon it."[64] Dismissing arguments that the bill, by infringing on "one of the most basic freedoms, the freedom to dissent," "would do more real harm to the Nation than all the flag burners can possibly do,"[65] Congress overwhelmingly approved the measure (387 to 16 in the House and voice vote in the Senate). In debates that would foreshadow its consideration of flag-desecration proposals two decades later, lawmakers depicted the flag as a "beloved" and "sacred" "symbol of freedom and liberty"; spoke of flag burning as a "direct attack on the sovereignty of the United States," if not an act of treason; and dubbed flag burners "rabble," "anarchists," and "dirty, long-haired Communist-led beatniks."[66] Even lawmakers who traditionally defended the Bill of Rights, such as House Judiciary Chair Emanuel Celler, supported the bill. Although questioning the measure's constitutionality, Cellar explained, "Who can vote against something like this? It's like motherhood."[67]

Rather than end flag desecration, the 1968 law contributed to an explosion of antiwar flag desecration prosecutions. Commenting on this phenomenon, the *New York Times* noted that although the 1968 statute did not specify what constituted an "abuse" of the flag, police targeted "rebellious young people" whose beliefs "differ with prevailing ideas of patriotism."[68] Echoing this concern, the Supreme Court in 1974 recognized the dangers of selective prosecution. Nevertheless, although this and other Court decisions cast doubt on flag desecration measures, the Justices left the door open for subsequent legislation.[69]

In 1989 and again in 1990, the Court sought to close this door. At issue in the 1989 case was the arrest and conviction of Gregory Lee Johnson for his acts at a political protest held in Dallas during the 1984 Republican Convention. As a crowd of approximately a hundred demonstrators in front of City Hall chanted "America, the red, white, and blue, we spit on you," Johnson unfurled an American flag, doused it with kerosene, and ignited it. Ruling that free speech protections extend to expressive activities that most Americans find abhorrent, the Justices, by a 5–4 vote, contended that "the way to preserve the flag's special role is not to punish those who [burn it] . . . for in doing so, we dilute the freedom that this cherished emblem represents."[70] "If there is a bedrock principle underlying the First Amendment," the Court declared, "it is that the Government may not prohibit the expression of an idea simply because society finds the idea itself offensive or disagreeable."

One day after the Court issued its decision, the Senate passed by a 97 to 3 vote a resolution expressing its belief that "the act of desecrating the flag is clearly not 'speech' as protected by the first amendment" and calling for a study of possible ways to restore sanctions against flag burning.[71] The same day, in the House of Representatives, lawmakers took turns assailing the Court. Representative Doug Applegate said the Court had "humiliated" the flag, and Representative Tom Bevill spoke of "feel-[ing] disgusted and sickened that the highest court in our land would allow the American flag to be misused."[72]

One week later, on June 30, President George Bush I joined forces with congressional leaders. With the Iwo Jima Memorial as a backdrop, he spoke of the need to punish those who "dishonor" the flag, for "the surest way to preserve liberty is to protect the spirit that sustains it. And this flag sustains that spirit. . . . [It] reflects the fabric of our nation—our dreams, our destiny, our very fiber as a people."[73]

Public opinion polls meanwhile showed that only 28 percent of those polled agreed with the Court's decision, and roughly 70 percent supported a constitutional amendment reversing it.[74] With Congress, the White House, and the public pushing for action, there was little doubt that Congress would seek to override the Court's decision. The question remained, however, whether Congress would embrace a legislative solution or a constitutional amendment.

Pro-amendment forces had the early advantage. The Court's decision, according to Bush administration officials and several constitutional law scholars, could not be overturned by a statute. Noting that the Court found the governmental interest in protecting the flag's symbolic value insufficient, Office of Legal Counsel head (and later Attorney General) William Barr told the Senate Judiciary Committee that any statute based on protecting the flag as a symbol "will be dead on arrival."[75] For Robert Bork, an amendment was necessary. Otherwise, "Congress can overturn Supreme Court constitutional decisions by a straight majority vote and I don't think that is what our system of government imagines."[76]

But Congress's Democratic leadership opposed amending the Constitution. Don Edwards, House Judiciary Committee chair and one of a handful of members who voted against Congress's 1968 flag desecration law, vowed that he and other Democrats would "go to the wall" to stop a constitutional amendment.[77] For Edwards, the flag is "sturdy, flying proudly through every fierce battle of every war and through times of social upheaval." The Constitution, in contrast, is "fragile and can be amended by the votes of legislatures caught up in the emotional whirlwinds of the moment."[78] For Joseph Biden, chair of the Senate Judiciary Committee, "the flag deserves protection," but "amending the Constitution is a significant and solemn step and undertaking" and, consequently, should not be pursued "unless it was absolutely clear" that there was no constitutional way to "legislatively remedy a situation."[79] His solution: craft a content-neutral statute, one that focuses on the physical integrity of the flag, not the political message sent by those who desecrate it.

For several Republicans, the efforts of Biden and Edwards were deemed a "sham," an attempt to put off a constitutional amendment in the hopes that the flag desecration issue would eventually fade from view.[80] On this point, Chairman Edwards called his own motives into doubt by telling a reporter, "This statute gives Members cover. They can tell the American Legion, 'Look we are protecting the flag.'"[81] With several members expressing doubt about the statute's constitutionality,[82] Congress overwhelmingly approved the Flag Protection Act of 1989 (91–9 in the Senate; 380–38 in the House). President Bush, too, expressed "serious doubts" about whether the Act "can withstand Supreme Court review." Rather than veto the measure on constitutional grounds, however, Bush "decided to allow it to become law without [his] signature."[83]

Briefs filed by the Bush administration, the House of Representatives, and the Senate all argued that the statute was content-neutral and therefore distinguishable from the Texas law that the Court had struck down the year before. For Bush Solicitor General Kenneth Starr, "It is the physical assault and accompanying violation of the flag's physical integrity—not robust and uninhibited debate—that occasion the injury that our society should not be called upon to bear."[84] But the five Justices who invalidated the Texas law would have none of this. In striking down the Flag Protection Act, these Justices reasoned that the bill's content-neutral language was little more than a smoke screen for the government's true interest, namely, the suppression of free expression because of its content.[85]

Pro-amendment forces in Congress and the Bush White House, castigating the Court for "endanger[ing] the fabric of our country," wasted no time in voting for a flag amendment.[86] With Gallup polls showing 71 percent of the American people supporting a constitutional amendment, the House of Representatives boasted 169 amendment cosponsors. However, Democratic leadership undercut this drive for populist reform. A task force appointed by House Speaker Tom Foley shifted the debate to a referendum about the Bill of Rights.[87] Said Foley, "Every country has a flag. We are one of the few countries that has a Bill of Rights."[88] He reinforced this rhetoric with action. Contacting House Democrats (some of whom had previously signed on as amendment cosponsors), Foley and members of his flag task force succeeded in persuading fellow Democrats to vote against the amendment. When a vote was taken, 160 Democrats and 17 Republicans defeated the amendment.[89] The Senate also voted down the amendment, 58 to 42 (nine votes short). The time consumed by Congress in passing a law and having it tested in the courts was sufficient to take the steam out of the campaign to amend the Constitution.[90]

This defeat, however, did little to quiet the supporters of a flag-burning amendment. With the 1994 Republican takeover of Congress, a flag-burning amendment moved front and center among a host of amendments proposed by Republican leadership. Unlike the 1990 campaign, however, the White House opposed a flag amendment. Although Bill Clinton, when governor of Arkansas, called for legislation overturning the Court's 1989 decision, the Clinton administration felt that flag burning was not one of those "great and extraordinary occasions" that warrant a constitutional amendment.[91] Borrowing language from previous Solicitor General Charles Fried, Office of Legal Counsel head Walter Dellinger told the Senate Judiciary Committee, "We love the flag because it symbolizes the United States; but we must love the Constitution even more, because the Constitution is not a symbol. It is the thing itself."[92]

In 1995, 1998, 2000, and 2003, Congress considered but did not pass flag-burning amendments. Even though legislatures in every state but Vermont have passed resolutions favoring a constitutional amendment, pro-amendment forces have failed to punish lawmakers who oppose the amendment. This is especially true in the Senate. Thanks to a combination of safe Senate seats and six-year terms (so that a vote against the amendment is unlikely to become a campaign issue that very year), the Senate has consistently rejected flag-burning amendments. Consider, for example, the Senate's failure to debate such an amendment approved by the House in July 2001. Notwithstanding the nation's embrace of the flag following the September 11 terrorist attacks, the Senate let the amendment die a quiet death. For example, only two senators (amendment proponent Strom Thurmond and opponent Patrick Leahy) saw Flag Day as an occasion to talk about the amendment.[93]

Although Congress's failure to overturn the Court does not mean that lawmakers approve of the Court's action, there is little doubt that some lawmakers see the Court as a partner in protecting First Amendment freedoms when the political process cannot. For lawmakers who truly oppose the Court's decisions, the flag-burning saga calls attention to the difficulties of amending the Constitution. Absent overwhelming bipartisan support, there is little prospect of reversing the Court though the amendment process. This, of course, may simply signal the Court's practice of deciding cases that the public can tolerate (if not embrace). It also signals that one of Congress's most potent weapons to countermand the Court is rarely available to lawmakers.

Regulating Broadcasters

Government control over broadcasting dates back to 1927, when Congress created the Federal Radio Commission, and continues today under the watchful eye of the Federal Communications Commission (FCC) and its congressional overseers. Originally intended to remove "propaganda" stations from the air, the FCC later launched regulatory initiatives to, among other things, ensure fair coverage of public issues, promote racial diversity in broadcasting, and protect children from indecency.

Empowered to regulate the use of the airwaves in the "public interest, convenience, and necessity," the Commission has broad power to cabin broadcaster discretion through content-specific regulation. For this reason, broadcaster claims that FCC action oversteps the First Amendment are a critical weapon in the fight over the control of radio and television programming. Judicial rulings, of course, figure prominently in these broadcaster challenges. Of equal significance, broadcasters have advanced their deregulatory agenda by lobbying the White House and the FCC, sometimes convincing the President to make use of his veto power and the FCC to declare existing regulations unconstitutional.

Witness, for example, the saga of the FCC demand that "all sides of controversial public issues" be broadcast, the so-called fairness doctrine.[94] From 1949 until the early 1980s, the FCC heralded fairness as "the single most important requirement of operation in the public interest."[95] By 1987, however, the Commission concluded that its fairness doctrine was unconstitutional, the flawed product of a "New Deal dinosaur."[96]

In the shadow of the Commission's position stood a unanimous 1969 Supreme Court ruling that not only upheld the doctrine but defined the diminished constitutional freedom of broadcasters.[97] Broadcasters had argued in this case that the growth in the number of media outlets made "public trust" regulation unnecessary, and that broadcasters should, therefore, be accorded the same First Amendment freedoms as their brethren in the print media. But the Court agreed with FCC arguments that broadcasters may be forced to serve the public interest in exchange for the government's granting them one of a limited number of broadcast licenses.

There things stood until 1981, when Reagan's FCC appointees spoke of better, not bigger, government as part of the administration's "mandate for a leaner, less intrusive federal presence throughout the country."[98] In particular, arguing that "markets create the incentive" to give "consumers what consumers want as distinguished from what we, in Washington, think consumers should want," the Reagan FCC rejected the broadcast-print distinction championed by Congress and the Supreme Court.[99]

In August 1985, the FCC issued an elaborate 111-page *Fairness Report* condemning the fairness doctrine as "unnecessary and detrimental."[100] Pointing to the rapid growth of electronic media properties, the Commission concluded that market-inhibiting regulation actually reduced the discussion of controversial issues. For this reason, the FCC "questioned" the constitutionality of the doctrine, noting that "the complex constitutional issues presented by the doctrine" cannot be settled by "the mere recitation" of the 1969 decision.

Responding, however, to "intense" congressional pressure, the Commission determined that it would be "inappropriate" to repeal the fairness doctrine.[101] Instead, it encouraged the courts to find the doctrine both unconstitutional and contrary to the public interest. But the D.C. Circuit refused to grant the Commission the relief it requested. The obligation was now on the FCC to face the constitutional question. Ironically, by ordering the FCC to address the legality of the fairness doctrine, the decision gave the FCC the political cover it needed to formally reconsider the repeal of fairness.

Anticipating that the FCC would soon kill fairness, Congress took steps to statutorily mandate fairness obligations. For Congress, broadcasters are not part of the First Amendment press; instead, they are "licensees" subject to regulations, including content-based restrictions. More significant, pointing to the market's inability to compel broadcasters to fulfill their responsibilities as public trustees, Congress concluded that, without fairness requirements, "discussion of public affairs could become either one-sided or be reduced to a bland, uniform pablum as broadcasters react to economic pressures from commercial advertisers."[102] Like the Supreme Court's 1969 decision, Congress deemed broadcasters "public trustees with unique responsibilities" and, in June 1987, overwhelmingly approved fairness legislation (59–31 in the Senate and 302–102 in the House).

Congress's willingness to put the FCC in its place through fairness legislation did not end the issue. President Reagan, a former broadcaster who spoke proudly of "earning my living exercising my First Amendment rights," strongly opposed fairness and vetoed the bill as "antagonistic to the freedom of expression guaranteed by the First Amendment."[103] His veto message flatly rejected public trustee regulations in favor of full First Amendment rights for broadcasters. Following the veto (and Congress's inability to launch a serious override effort), the stage was set for the FCC's formal repeal of fairness. It did that one month later, on August 4, 1987.[104]

With the election of Bill Clinton, the prospects for the reinstatement of fairness seemed good. Congress continued to support fairness and Clinton's choice to head the FCC, Reed Hundt, signaled a willingness to reexamine fairness at his confirmation hearings. But, in 1993, Rush Limbaugh, G. Gordon Liddy, and other conservatives led a vitriolic and, ultimately, successful counteroffensive. Fearful that broadcasters would drop conservative talk shows rather than provide equal time for competing perspectives, conservative opponents to fairness waived the First Amendment banner, dubbing the fairness doctrine "today's application of political correctness."[105] More significant, by prompting fans of Limbaugh and other radio talkers to signal their opposition to fairness, Congress and the FCC no longer seemed interested in revitalizing fairness.

The demise of the fairness doctrine, however, had little impact on a corollary FCC rule requiring broadcasters who endorse candidates to provide reply time for their opponents. Although the FCC concluded in 1983 that broadcasters had made "a compelling case" that "political editorial rules do not serve the public interest,"[106] these rules remained in place until the D.C. Circuit, on October 11, 2000, directed the FCC to repeal them.[107] Rather than find the rules unconstitutional, however, the D.C. Circuit pointed to the FCC's repealed failure to justify the rules in light of the First Amendment infringement it imposes. With Bush II's victory over Al Gore (who called for reviving the fairness doctrine), there is little chance of the FCC revisiting this issue.

Indecency

Starting in 1948, Congress has prohibited broadcasters from uttering "any obscene, indecent, or profane language."[108] In 1978, the Supreme Court upheld the power of the FCC to regulate indecency;[109] since that ruling, the Justices have repeatedly considered the power of Congress to limit "obscene, lewd, indecent, filthy, or harassing communications."[110] From 1996 to 2003, the Court issued seven decisions, most of which have limited federal efforts to police indecency. Congress has generally accepted these decisions. There is no talk of curbing the Court or of using the confirmation process to pressure judicial nominees into approving indecency measures; instead, Congress seems content to take credit for passing legislation addressing the ills of child pornography, indecency on the Internet, and the like, while leaving it to the courts to sort out the constitutionality of such measures. This pattern seems destined to continue. Ever since the Warren Court liberalized obscenity law, elected officials have never launched a serious challenge to the Court's power to define this issue.

Before 1957, the year that the Court invalidated a Michigan law prohibiting the sale of books that have a potentially deleterious effect on youth,[111] state and federal regulators had near plenary power both to define obscenity and to limit the sale and distribution of "obscene materials." During this time, the postmaster general ruled D. H. Lawrence's *Lady Chatterly's Lover* nonmailable and censorship boards denied licenses to movies they considered obscene. However, by the end of the Warren era (1968), the

Supreme Court had effectively put censorship boards out of business and had approved movies featuring full nudity.[112]

Congress and the White House did relatively little to resist this liberalization of obscenity law. In 1967, Congress created a Commission on Obscenity and Pornography. Noting the lack of a clear "legal definition of what constitutes obscene materials," Congress set about to "explore methods of combating the traffic in obscene and noxious materials."[113] In 1970, the Commission issued a 1,000-page report in which it recommended that no restrictions be placed on material that adults could obtain. Although the report was condemned by both President Nixon and the Congress for "fail[ing] to carry out the mandate of Congress and its statutory duties by ignoring the potential effects of long-term exposure to obscene and pornographic materials,"[114] there was little reason for the Supreme Court to fear an elected government reprisal to its obscenity decisions. Instead, Congress and the President seemed content to make bully pulpit speeches.

By 1975, Congress and federal regulators had turned their attention to indecency, child pornography, and related issues. That year, the FCC (with all commissioners appointed by Presidents Nixon and Ford) concluded that a radio station ought not to broadcast satirist George Carlin's monologue on the "seven dirty words" before 10 P.M.[115] The Carter Justice Department challenged that FCC order as overbroad because the Commission did not consider the "context in which the offending words were used," but the Supreme Court agreed with FCC lawyers that their order appropriately protected "parental and privacy" interests.[116] Since Reagan's 1980 defeat of Carter, presidents and lawmakers have recognized that there is little to gain by opposing decency regulations.

The Reagan administration launched several modest antipornography initiatives. In 1985, a commission was formed to make recommendations "concerning ways in which the spread of pornography could be constrained."[117] Following this report, a National Obscenity Enforcement Unit was created to initiate and direct federal investigations and prosecutions of obscenity and child pornography.[118] At no time, however, did the administration seek to overturn Supreme Court obscenity decisions. Lawmakers reacted similarly; no effort has been made to push the Court to rethink its obscenity and indecency jurisprudence.

Congress's acquiescence is truly remarkable. Since 1989, there has been no backlash to the Supreme Court and lower federal courts striking down or narrowing the application of at least nine federal statutes, including efforts to prohibit indecent broadcasts,[119] to restrict the distribution of offensive materials on cable television and over the Internet,[120] to ban dial-a-porn,[121] to impose recordkeeping requirements for producers of sexually explicit content,[122] and to expand the federal prohibition of child pornography to computer-generated images of minors.[123]

Rather than attack the judiciary for limiting its anti-indecency campaign, lawmakers seem content to make speeches and enact new legislation. Indeed, on the question of Supreme Court authority to strike down these statutes, Congress has largely embraced judicial supremacy. When enacting dial-a-porn legislation, for example, lawmakers punted questions of the Act's constitutionality. Representative Dan Coats explained, "We are not elected in this body to stand here and make a constitutional decision, that is done across the street at the Supreme Court."[124] Likewise, Representative Ralph Hall argued that Congress "should make every assault upon pornography that we can"; as such, lawmakers should approve the bill and "send it to the courts . . . [who] get [the] last guess at whether the law is constitutional."[125]

The Communications Decency Act (CDA) tells a similar story. Public concern over the availability and marketing of pornography on the Internet (especially to children) exploded in the summer of 1995. *Time* and *Newsweek* ran stories, "Cyberporn: On a Screen Near You" and "A Parent's Guide to Sex on the Net," that fueled lawmaker interest in regulating the Internet. The "pro-family" CDA was quickly enacted by Congress. Although members had time to download graphic images from the Internet "to see how bad this is,"[126] there was no time for legislative hearings or serious discussion of the Act's constitutionality. Instead, by including an expedited Supreme Court review provision in the CDA, lawmakers delegated to the courts the responsibility of sorting out the Act's constitutionality. Correspondingly, after the Court struck down the CDA, Congress offered no challenge; it sought to "address the specific concerns raised by the Supreme Court" through new legislation, the 1998 Children's On-Line Protection Act.[127] Two years later, Congress set conditions on libraries who receive federal funds. This bill, the Children's Internet Pornography Act, requires participating libraries to make use of pornography filters when providing children access to the Internet.[128]

While accepting the Court's authority, Congress lashed out at the Clinton Justice Department efforts to limit the force of a 1984 child pornography law.[129] Arguing that the statute did not apply to young girls dressed in scanty apparel, the Justice Department sought to prevent the Supreme Court from ruling on this issue because its views and the criminal defendant's views were in sync.[130] In response, all one hundred senators voted for a resolution condemning the brief, and a 1994 crime bill formally embraced the "scanty apparel" standard.[131] Following this rebuke, the White House ordered the Justice Department to reverse course. Two years later, President Clinton signed the CDA, even though Justice had earlier concluded that the Act "threaten[s] important First Amendment and privacy rights."[132]

And so it goes. Congress and the White House have little to gain by defending "smut," especially "smut" that either depicts or is available to children. For that reason, lawmakers do not invoke the First Amendment when voting against anti-indecency measures; instead, they vote for the bill and leave it to the courts to sort out the permissible boundaries of indecency laws. Even though the courts often strike down these measures,[133] Congress and the White House have never led the charge to push the Court to reconsider its decisions. Rather, lawmakers are content to take their constitutional cues from the Court. In addition to refashioning the CDA to "address the [Court's] specific concerns," lawmakers have similarly recrafted dial-a-porn, virtual porn, and recordkeeping legislation.

Conclusions

For most of this nation's history, free speech protections have been tied more to popular sentiment than to judicial edicts. From the 1798 Alien and Sedition Acts through McCarthy-era attacks on communists, the Supreme Court either validated or steered away from citizen challenges to speech restrictions. During this period, the only meaningful check on government overreaching was the desire of the American people to be able to speak out—and hear others speak out—on controversial issues. Politically unpopular prosecutions of prominent Republicans under the Alien and Sedition Acts contributed to Thomas Jefferson's victory over John Adams and, with it, the repudiation of the Sedition Act. Likewise, post–World War I fears of totalitarianism helped fuel what has become the modern civil liberties movement. In contrast, during the Civil War, World War I, and the McCarthy era, the people often encouraged government suppression of speech.

Following the Warren Court's expansion of political speech freedoms and its liberalization of obscenity laws (events that can be linked to the end of the McCarthy era and rise of the civil rights movement), the Supreme Court has actively policed state and federal efforts to restrict speech. Rather than resist this judicial role, lawmakers have embraced it. Judicial confirmation hearings, if anything, point to the need for the Court to vigilantly defend First Amendment freedoms. Moreover, by including expedited review provisions in flag-burning and indecency legislation, Congress has signaled its willingness to abide by Supreme Court pronouncements.

Consequently, just as there is no dispute that the modern Court is a vigorous defender of First Amendment freedoms, there is also no dispute that Court decision making is moored to social and political forces. For this reason, the recent wave of Supreme Court indecency decisions is part and parcel of a political process that leaves it to the Court to establish constitutional standards on this issue. Within those standards, the burden remains on the elected branches to craft appropriate legislation and agency regulations. Correspondingly, though there are few instances of government officials expanding speech protections beyond Supreme Court norms (as they did with newspaper searches and the fairness doctrine), speech's emergence as "the people's privilege" owes as much to the rough and tumble of politics as it does to the opinions of the Supreme Court.

9

Religion

It is widely believed that courts are essential guardians in protecting religious liberty, particularly when majority rule threatens minority religions. Yet the Court barely began to sketch out a jurisprudence of religious freedom until 1940.[1] Thus, for a century and a half, the duty of protecting religious liberties was left to the regular political process. Individuals and private organizations, in their efforts to protect the rights of conscience, turned to nonjudicial bodies and the states for relief. Instead of the Court's serving as the exclusive guardian of individual rights, a powerful dialogue operates between judicial and nonjudicial bodies, with the courts often playing a secondary role. Courts can nudge society at times, but the judicial role is usually marginal rather than pivotal. Religious lobbies press their views on all three branches at the national level and on state governments. Often, they prefer to rely on Congress and state legislatures to advance their interests.

A study of these disputes shows why it is inaccurate to say, as a leading study of church-state relations once put it, "It advances the cause of realism in American constitutional law to say that the Constitution is what the judges say it is."[2] Even a casual review of American history reveals the inadequacy of that position. Instead of promoting realism, such statements advance the cause of illusion and deception.

The Religious Lobby

Individuals and private groups feel strongly about the rights of conscience and religious liberty. Rather than defer blindly to the judgments of courts, legislatures, administrative bodies, or experts, religious interests are not shy about testifying before legislative bodies and using other lobbying techniques, including litigation, to press their views. Religious organizations have participated in many volatile and emotionally charged issues in the United States, including military service, slavery, abortion, the Equal Rights Amendment, school prayer, and aid to parochial schools.[3]

In requiring citizens to serve in the militia, colonies and early state governments made exceptions for individuals who had religious objections. Massachusetts in 1661, Rhode Island in 1673, and Pennsylvania in 1757 passed legislation to allow conscientious objectors to perform noncombatant service.[4] On July 18, 1775, the Continental Congress created a militia while recognizing that some people, for religious reasons, could not bear arms.[5] After the Declaration of Independence, a number of state constitutions included language to protect the religious rights of conscientious objectors.[6] All of these accommodations to religious minorities were done through the regular legislative process.

Congress did not rely on conscription during the American Revolution, the War of 1812, or the Mexican War; the country depended on volunteers and state militia to do the fighting. The first national effort to draft soldiers came with the Civil War, when members of Congress debated language to excuse from military service persons who, from "scruples of conscience," were averse to bearing arms.[7] The Society of Friends (Quakers) led the way for statutory language that exempted certain conscientious objectors of "religious denominations" from combat service.[8] This protection for religious minorities did not come from the courts. Quakers and other religious groups turned instinctively to the President, executive officers, and members of Congress for relief.

Pressure mounted to recognize conscientious objection not merely for Quakers, Mennonites, and other established religions, but also for those who did not belong to any sect. Louis Fraina, convicted of conspiring to commit an offense against the United States by aiding and abetting others to evade military service during World War I, emphasized that conscientious objection related not to church membership but to individual conscience.[9] Quakers, agreeing with that position, lobbied Congress for a change in the statutory exemption. Instead of requiring conscientious objectors to belong to a "well-recognized religious sect," they insisted that consideration be "on the basis of conscience rather than on the basis of membership."[10] Under this pressure from religious groups, Congress changed the exemption in 1940 to cover individuals who, "by reason of religious training and belief," were "conscientiously opposed to participation in war in any form."[11]

Another example of successful religious lobbying for broader statutory language and legislative practice comes from the Civil War period. Prior to February 1, 1860, only Christians were selected to offer prayers in Congress. The House of Representatives changed that practice by inviting Dr. Morris J. Raphall of Congregation B'nai Jeshurun of New York City to give the first Jewish prayer.[12] Prayers are now routinely offered by Christians, Jews, Muslims, American Indians, and other religious groups.

Until the Civil War, only Protestants were chosen to serve as military chaplains. Regiments that were largely Jewish wanted someone from their own faith. President Lincoln and members of Congress recognized that the statutory language limiting military chaplains to ordained ministers from a "Christian denomination" was improper.[13] With Rabbi Arnold Fischel's personal lobbying, the statutory language "Christian denomination" was changed to "some religious denomination."[14]

Churches played a profound role in the fight against slavery. The first printed protest against slavery in America came from a Quaker publication in 1688.[15] George Keith, a Quaker, issued a broadside against slavery in 1693.[16] Quakers expelled slave-owning Friends in 1776.[17] In 1789, the General Committee of Virginia Baptists passed a resolution condemning slavery, and in 1800 the Methodist Conference called for the gradual emancipation of slaves.[18] In 1854, when the Kansas-Nebraska bill threatened to spread slavery into the territories, 3,050 clergy forwarded a protest to the U.S. Senate. A year later, from his position as minister of the Plymouth Church in Brooklyn, Henry Ward Beecher spoke out against the evils of slavery.[19]

Issues of religion and morality provoke people and groups to vigorously advocate their legal and constitutional positions. The Court accepts the legitimacy of lobbying by church groups: "Of course, churches as much as secular bodies and private citizens have that right."[20] The intensity of church lobbying on all three branches has increased dramatically. In 1950, there were approximately sixteen major religious lobbies in Washington, D.C.: ten Protestant, two Catholic, and four interdenominational.[21] By 1985 that number had climbed to "at least eighty and the list is growing."[22] In the 1990s, the estimate of the number of religious lobbies reached "at least one hundred."[23] A 1994 compilation of U.S. religious interest groups lists 120 organizations.[24]

These groups often coalesce to form a strikingly powerful political force, savvy and experienced in the ways of directing legislative, executive, and judicial agendas. Religious groups were part of the successful effort to enact the Civil Rights Act of 1964[25] and the Elementary and Secondary Education Act of 1965, which provided federal funds to both public and private schools.[26] The constitutional issue of church-state separation was surmounted by arguing that the funds would benefit children, not schools.

The growth in sophisticated lobbying by religious groups is reflected in amicus curiae filings with the Supreme Court. Religious groups successful in the legislative and executive arenas "realize that they must be participants in *every* major playing field, including the courts, if they are ever to count in America."[27] During the period from 1928 to 1940, amicus briefs were prepared for 14.3 percent of the church-state cases. For a more recent period, from 1986 to 1992, the participation rate is 100 percent.[28]

Religious organizations often oppose Court rulings and help enact legislation that codifies their disapproval. Religious interests, for example, spearheaded the movement to nullify *Roe v. Wade*. Religious concerns animate most antiabortion groups, including the National Right to Life Committee and the Christian Coalition. In the three decades since *Roe*, state and federal lawmakers have worked closely with these groups, enacting hundreds of abortion-related restrictions.[29]

Religious groups also mobilize their strength to defend Court decisions. In 1962, the Court held in *Engel v. Vitale* that a New York "Regents' Prayer" was unconstitutional because government should not compose an official prayer for minors in public schools.[30] The public outcry created pressure for a constitutional amendment to nullify the Court's ruling, but that movement stalled when congressional hearings revealed broad support by Protestant and Jewish organizations for the decision.[31]

Among religious groups, there has been a shift in attitudes about seeking relief in the courts for constitutional injuries. Battles over church-state relations in the United States, "historically the domain of the court, have moved in recent years to the Congress."[32] Instead of the "minoritarian politics" of the courts, religious groups engage in "the majoritarian or consensus-seeking politics of the Congress."[33]

Compulsory Flag Salute

In 1940 and 1943, the Supreme Court decided whether states could impose a compulsory flag salute on organizations that cited religious grounds in opposition. The first decision upheld the salute; the second struck it down. The opinion by Justice Jackson in 1943 is celebrated for its eloquent defense of religious minorities, but the primary safeguarding of constitutional rights belongs to the individuals and associations who denounced the 1940 ruling and refused to accept it as national policy.

A number of states in the 1930s passed legislation that compelled schoolchildren to salute the flag. The Jehovah's Witnesses, relying on a literal interpretation of the Bible, believed that saluting a secular symbol violated their religious beliefs.[34] The compulsory flag salute survived a number of early test cases, but in 1937 a federal district judge in Pennsylvania found this type of statute unconstitutional. Taking note of the religious intolerance that was "again rearing its ugly head in other parts of the world," as in Nazi Germany, he regarded it as "of the utmost importance that the liberties guaranteed to our citizens by the fundamental law be preserved from all encroachment."[35]

After this decision was upheld on appeal, the Supreme Court agreed to hear the case, *Minersville School District v. Gobitis*. In their brief, the plaintiffs pointed out that the "form of salute is very much like that of the Nazi regime in Germany."[36] Yet, instead of understanding the need for religious diversity and individual rights, many Americans turned with venom against minority sects. As the German army raced across Europe in the spring of 1940, American communities feared "Fifth Column" activities. On May 23, a mob in Del Rio, Texas, attacked three Witnesses thought to be Nazi agents. On June 2, a Gallup poll reported that 65 percent of the people believed that Germany would attack the United States.[37] In the midst of this emotional frenzy, the Court upheld the compulsory flag salute.

The Court seemed to give little thought to the political impact of their ruling. Studies on the behavior of the Justices in conference describe the flag salute decision as a "case study in judicial misperceptions and breakdown in communication."[38] Writing for an 8–1 majority, Justice Felix Frankfurter leaned heavily on two premises: Liberty requires unifying sentiments, and national unity promotes national security. Although the Witnesses urged the Court to embrace religious pluralism, Frankfurter advised them to present their case "in the forum of public opinion and before legislative assemblies rather than to transfer such a contest to the judicial arena."[39] Frankfurter's decision was excoriated by law journals, the press, and religious organizations. Thirty-one of thirty-nine law reviews that discussed the decision did so critically. Newspapers accused the Court of violating constitutional rights and buckling under popular hysteria.[40]

In at least thirty-one states, school authorities took legal steps against nonsaluting Witnesses.[41] Worse still, Frankfurter's decision was followed by a tidal wave of violence against Witnesses across the country. Within two weeks of the decision, hundreds of attacks were reported to the Justice Department. "In the two years following the decision," according to Justice Department officials, "an uninterrupted record of violence and persecution [persisted]. . . . Almost without exception, the flag and the flag salute can be found as the percussion cap that sets off these acts."[42]

Justices Black, Douglas, and Murphy decided to bolt from Frankfurter's 8–1 majority. A few months after the decision, Douglas told Frankfurter that Black was having second thoughts. Sarcastically, Frankfurter asked whether Black had spent the summer reading the Constitution. "No," Douglas replied, "he has been reading the papers."[43]

Some state courts also found Frankfurter's opinion unacceptable. Children of Jehovah's Witnesses in New Hampshire were suspended from public school because they refused to salute the flag; by so acting, they were judged delinquent, taken from their family, and placed in a state industrial school. In 1941, the Supreme Court of New Hampshire deplored the breaking up of a family for "no more than the conscientious acts of the children, based upon the religious teachings of their parents."[44] It urged legislative and administrative authorities to seek an accommodation that would not violate the religious scruples of the students. Similar decisions came from the Supreme Court of New Jersey and the Supreme Court of Kansas in 1942.[45]

This nationwide debate had a profound impact on the U.S. Supreme Court. In 1942, Justices Black, Douglas, and Murphy announced that *Gobitis* had been "wrongly decided."[46] Frankfurter bitterly remarked that his opinion was "okayed by those great libertarians until they heard from the people."[47] Deserted by his three colleagues, Frankfurter clung to a bare 5–4 majority. The margin was even shakier because two members of the *Gobitis* majority had been replaced by Wiley Rutledge and Robert H. Jackson. Opinions by Rutledge while serving on the D.C. Circuit suggested that he would likely vote to overturn *Gobitis*.[48]

Legislation that Congress passed in 1942 to codify existing rules and customs for the display and use of the American flag also shook the foundations of *Gobitis*. Language in the bill indicated a preference for avoiding rigidly enforced flag salutes. After stating that in pledging allegiance to the flag a citizen would extend the right hand, palm upward, toward the flag, the statute further provided, "However, civilians will always show full respect to the flag when the pledge is given by merely standing at attention, men removing the headdress."[49] The Justice Department interpreted this statute to undercut a compulsory flag salute because Jehovah's Witnesses were willing to stand at attention during the flag salute exercise.[50] The Justice Department instructed U.S. attorneys to advise local authorities of the more flexible standard adopted by Congress.[51]

When the flag salute issue returned to the Supreme Court, this time involving a West Virginia case, a brief by the ACLU noted that Congress had entered the field by passing legislation. Of "great importance," said the brief, "is the fact that Congress did not deem it wise, or see fit, to impose any penalties for failure to salute the flag."[52] During oral argument, counsel for the expelled students offered this remark about *Gobitis*: "There cannot be found in the law a more unstatesmanlike decision, except possibly the Dred Scott decision."[53]

The Supreme Court overruled *Gobitis* in 1943, almost three years to the day that it was announced. Writing for a 6–3 majority, Justice Robert

Jackson condemned efforts to coerce uniformity and reminded the nation that "no official, high or petty, can prescribe what shall be orthodox in politics, nationalism, religion, or other matters of opinion or force citizens to confess by word or act their faith therein."[54] Jackson's defense of religious freedom and the Bill of Rights was powerful and moving, but credit for the liberalized decision belongs to those who refused to accept the Court's 1940 pronouncements on the meaning of the Constitution, minority rights, and religious liberty.

School Prayer

In response to the 1962 Supreme Court's school prayer decision, *Engel v. Vitale*, members of Congress retaliated with constitutional amendments to overturn the Court, offered proposals to remove its jurisdiction to hear such cases, and drafted other restrictive measures. However, with most religious denominations lining up behind the Court, all of these court-curbing efforts failed.

The decision has been widely misinterpreted. The Court did not speak against prayer; it spoke against governmental efforts to draft an official prayer to be said by students who are compelled to attend school. During oral argument, the attorney for the plaintiffs opposing the Regents' Prayer strongly endorsed religion and prayer. He told the Justices, "I come here not as an antagonist of religion . . . my clients are deeply religious people . . . I say prayer is good. My clients say prayer is good."[55] Writing for the majority, Hugo Black took care to place religion in a positive light. Noting that "the history of man is inseparable from the history of religion," he explained that prayer is a "purely religious function [that should be left] to the people themselves and to those the people choose to look to for religious guidance."[56]

Members of Congress heaped scorn on the decision. Senator Sam J. Ervin Jr. announced that the Court "has held that God is unconstitutional." Thomas Abernathy urged legislative action against the Court "to calm the power grab of these power-drunken men." Mendel Rivers railed against "this bold, malicious, atheistic and sacrilegious twist of this unpredictable group of uncontrolled despots."[57] George William Andrews touched all the bases of the conservative community: "They put the Negroes in to the schools and now they have driven God out of them."[58]

Although President Kennedy implored those who disagreed with the ruling "to maintain our constitutional principle" and "support the Supreme Court decisions even when we may not agree with them,"[59] pressure mounted for a constitutional amendment to permit school prayer. One month after the Court's decision, the Senate Judiciary Committee held two days of hearings to explore the issue of prayer in public schools. The hearings allowed critics of the decision to fulminate and voice their disgust, but no steps were taken to challenge the Court.[60]

When the House Judiciary Committee finally held hearings in 1964 on a constitutional amendment to reverse the Court, most of the religious organizations testified in favor of the school prayer decision. Protestant and Jewish groups generally opposed the amendment; Catholic leaders were divided.[61] Dr. Edwin H. Tuller, speaking on behalf of the National Council of Churches (representing about 40 million Americans), told the committee that public institutions belong to all citizens, "whatever their religious beliefs or lack of them," and that it was not right for a majority to impose religious practices on the minority in public institutions.[62]

Over the next three decades, several hundred constitutional amendments were introduced to permit school prayer; none of them succeeded.[63] Notwithstanding the rhetoric of those who wanted to put "God back in the classroom," these amendments never disturbed *Engel's* fundamental principle that government should not compose school prayers and force students to recite them. For example, the Republican platform in 1964 offered constitutional language to permit individuals and groups "who choose to do so to exercise their religion freely in public places, provided religious exercises are not *prepared or prescribed* by the state or political subdivision thereof and no person's participation therein is coerced, thus preserving the traditional separation of church and state."[64]

In his 1980 presidential campaign, Ronald Reagan embraced school prayer, creationism, and tax breaks for religious schools. Through his appointments power, he sought to transform Supreme Court decision making. Attorney General Edwin Meese, Education Secretary William Bennett, and Supreme Court nominee Robert Bork all took issue with Court decisions limiting religious observance in the public schools. Reagan nominees sought to undo both the 1962 school prayer decision and a 1971 ruling that severely limited state efforts to facilitate religious instruction in the schools. Before the Supreme Court, as he did with abortion, Reagan Solicitor General Rex Lee called for the Court to "reapprais[e]" its precedents and "take a fresh look" at school prayer.[65]

In the midst of his administration's campaign to recalibrate judicial decision making, Reagan made several bully pulpit speeches to religious conservatives and, more important, embraced a school prayer amendment. In 1982, remarking that "God should [never] have been expelled from the classroom," he proposed this constitutional amendment: "Nothing in this Constitution shall be construed to prohibit individual or group prayer in public schools or other public institutions. No person shall be required by the United States or by any State to participate in prayer."[66] This language did not repudiate *Engel*; instead, it embraced its guiding principle.

Unlike earlier amendment proposals (only one of which, in 1971, reached the floor for a vote), the Reagan proposal prompted Congress to act. By a vote of 14 to 3, the Senate Judiciary Committee adopted a silent prayer amendment. Speaking of the need to "provide a formal, structured opportunity during the school-day when each student can silently speak to his creator," the Committee concluded that an "amendment is necessary to restore the historic meaning of the first amendment, abruptly altered by the Court's [school prayer] decision." [67] But when the Senate voted on this measure in March 1984, it fell eleven votes short of the two-thirds needed.

Continued disagreement among religious interests, in part, explains the amendment's defeat. For example, to counter lobbying by the Religious Right, a joint letter of opposition was submitted by a coalition of religious organizations, including American Baptist Churches, American Jewish Congress, Seventh-Day Adventists, Lutheran Church in America, Presbyterian Church in the USA, United Church of Christ, United Methodist Church, and United Presbyterian Church.[68] More significant, fearing a backlash from voters who thought the Senate's legislative work should focus on a skyrocketing deficit, not prayer, eighteen Republican senators broke ranks with the President and voted against the amendment.[69]

After this vote in 1984, only one other prayer amendment proposal reached the floor for a vote. In June 1998, the House of Representatives rejected a prayer amendment by a vote of 224 to 203, or sixty-one votes short. Congress also dismissed efforts to strip the federal courts of jurisdiction in school prayer cases. Starting in 1974 and ending in 1988, Congress debated the merits of the "Helms amendment," which would have returned state-sponsored prayer to the public schools by denying jurisdiction to the Supreme Court and lower federal courts in "any case arising out of any . . . State statute, ordinance, rule, or regulation, which relates to voluntary prayers in public schools and public buildings."[70] But Helms's proposal was too radical. For Attorney General–designee Edwin Meese, the Helms amendment undermined a core judicial function and therefore was constitutionally suspect.[71] Likewise, the Conference of Chief Justices of State Courts concluded that Helms and the other court-stripping proposals would leave pressing constitutional matters in the hands of state courts in the hope that state court judges "will not honor their oath to obey the United States Constitution."[72]

Congress's rejection of absolutist measures, such as court stripping and constitutional amendment, hardly signifies legislative acquiescence to the school prayer issue. In 1984, Congress responded to that issue by passing an "Equal Access" bill. Building on a Supreme Court decision in 1981 that upheld the right of student religious groups to have access to university buildings for their meetings, Congress gave students in public high schools the same right. The law prohibits any public secondary school receiving federal funds from denying equal access to students who wish to conduct a meeting devoted to religious objectives. Such meetings are to be voluntary, student-initiated, and without school sponsorship.

Sometimes referred to as the "son of school prayer," Congress enacted the Equal Access Act in response to perceived "state hostility toward religion."[73] For Jerry Falwell, "We knew we couldn't win on school prayer but equal access gets us what we wanted all along."[74] In particular, as act sponsor Jeremiah Denton observed, because of court rulings "there was a sealed door to keep any practice of religion out of the schools. Now that seal has been broken. This is not a foot in the door; this is an epic change."[75] The Supreme Court upheld equal access in 1990. The Justices recognized that so long as religious and secular groups had access to public school facilities, Congress had every right to conclude "that religious speech in particular was valuable and worthy of protection."[76]

The Court also turned back efforts by Alabama to bring prayer into the schoolroom. In 1981, when Governor Fob James began his first term, the legislature passed a statute authorizing a one-minute period of silence in public schools "for meditation or voluntary prayer." Another statute the following year authorized teachers to lead "willing students" in a prayer composed by the teacher or one specified by law. The Supreme Court struck down those statutes in 1984 and 1985 on the ground that their purpose was to advance religion.[77] Alabama responded with another statute in 1993, this time authorizing public school prayers that were nonsectarian, nonproselytizing, student-initiated, and voluntary. In 1997, after a federal district court held that statute to be unconstitutional, James took the issue to the Supreme Court but lost.[78]

The willingness of state officials to challenge the Court is telling. Over the years, local community compliance with the 1962 decision has figured prominently in the story of school prayer. Several studies at the end of the 1960s revealed that the Court's ruling had reduced the amount of school-sponsored prayer in public schools but had not eliminated it. Outright defiance was commonplace.[79] More than two decades after the Court's decision, some students in public schools were still beginning each day with a prayer.[80] School superintendents and teachers could safely ignore the Court's decision in many areas because local prosecutors, raised nearby, were unlikely to use their resources to force compliance with an unpopular decision.

State lawmakers, too, have sought to blunt the force of the 1962 ruling. More than twenty states, for example, encouraged religious exercise in the public schools by enacting "moment of silence" statutes.[81] A number of states, moreover, enacted voluntary prayer laws despite the fact that these statutes have always been declared unconstitutional.[82] States have filed amicus curiae briefs defending these and other laws. For example, in a 1985 case, attorneys general from Arizona, Delaware, Indiana, Louisiana, Oklahoma, and Virginia filed an amicus curiae brief in support of moment of silence laws.[83]

Much has changed since 1962. Because of the Equal Access Act and other initiatives, there are many opportunities for students to pray and study religion in public schools. In 1995, in an effort to take some of the steam out of a proposed school prayer amendment, President Clinton issued a memorandum to clarify the rights of public school children to religious expression. He said that nothing in the First Amendment "converts our public schools into religion-free zones, or requires all religious expression to be left behind at the schoolhouse door." Students have the right to engage in individual or group prayer and religious discussion during the schoolday. They may "read their Bibles or other scriptures, say grace before meals, and pray before tests to the same extent that they may engage in comparable non-disruptive activities." In informal settings, such as cafeterias and hallways, students may pray and discuss their religious views; they may attempt to persuade their peers about religious topics; they may participate in before and after school events with religious content.[84] Studies indicate that students in public schools are active in prayer clubs and other religious activities.[85]

The school prayer wars, like abortion, underscore the dynamic nature of constitutional decision making. While the Court has held steadfast to its 1962 decision, state and federal resistance to that decision has made possible some types of religious practice in the public schools. Moreover, nonacquiescence to the 1962 decision contributed to the appointment of Supreme Court Justices more accepting of state support of religious practices. As a result, although the Court may not revisit its school prayer decision, states now have greater freedom to acknowledge religion than any time in the past forty years.

The Yarmulke Case

Religious interests, more often than not, fare well in the political marketplace. A particularly vivid illustration of the power of religious interests to obtain religious practice exemptions is the congressional response to a 1986 Supreme Court decision upholding an Air Force regulation that had prohibited an observant Jew in the military from wearing a skull cap (yarmulke). The Court's opinion unleashed a political storm, prompting Congress to intervene within a year to repair the damage.

Simcha Goldman, an Orthodox Jew and ordained rabbi, served as a captain in the U.S. Air Force and was assigned to a mental health clinic, where he worked as a clinical psychologist. Over a three-and-a-half-year period, Goldman wore a yarmulke while in uniform without incident. On May 8, 1981, he was informed that wearing a yarmulke violated the Air Force's dress code and was threatened with court-martial if he continued to wear a yarmulke while in uniform. Why, after three and a half years, did Goldman's wearing of a yarmulke create a problem? In April 1981, the month before he was warned about wearing the yarmulke, he had appeared at a court-martial proceeding to testify on behalf of the defense (and therefore against the Air Force). The action against Goldman therefore appeared to have a retaliatory motive.[86]

After exhausting administrative remedies, Goldman's attorney went to court. But the D.C. Circuit sided with the Air Force, accepting its claim that an accommodation to Goldman would encourage other military personnel to offer religious reasons to use turbans, face and body paint, amulets, symbolic daggers, and the like.[87] The D.C. Circuit voted against a motion to rehear the case en banc. Three judges, with quite familiar names, dissented from this denial of a rehearing. Judge Kenneth Starr, later solicitor general in the Bush I administration and independent counsel for the Whitewater investigation, said that the panel's decision in the Goldman case "does considerable violence to the bulwark of freedom guaranteed by the Free Exercise Clause."[88] Judges Ruth Bader Ginsburg and Antonin Scalia, now on the Supreme Court, remarked that the military's order to Goldman not to wear his yarmulke suggested "callous indifference" to Goldman's religious faith and ran counter to the American tradition of accommodating spiritual needs.

Following the D.C. Circuit's decision but before the Supreme Court agreed to hear the case, Representative Stephen Solarz, whose Brooklyn district contained the largest block of Orthodox Jews outside of Israel, proposed that members of the armed forces may wear unobtrusive religious headgear, such as a skull cap, if religious observances or practices require the wearing of such headgear. Under this amendment, the Defense Department could prohibit the headgear if it interfered with the performance of military duties.[89] Although Representative William Dickinson warned that "we are flying in the face of a court decision just made," the amendment was accepted.[90]

House and Senate conferees eliminated the House amendment and merely required the Defense Department to report on changes in service regulations that would promote the free expression of religion to the greatest extent possible consistent with the requirements of military discipline.[91] Released in 1985, this lengthy study concluded, "Except where permitted in sharply limited and clearly defined circumstances . . . mandatory standards for accommodating of personal religious practice runs a grave risk of undermining esprit de corps, military discipline, and the military justice system."[92]

During oral argument before the Supreme Court in 1986, Kathryn Oberly of the Justice Department advised the Court to stay out of the battle and leave the dispute to the elected branches: "If Congress thinks that further accom[m]odation is either required or desirable it can legislate it," but if the Court tried to constitutionalize mandatory exceptions to the uniform requirements, it would be "far more difficult for what might turn out to be a mistake in judgment about the effect on discipline and morale to be corrected."[93]

The Supreme Court, divided 5 to 4, accepted the judgment of the Air Force that the outfitting of military personnel in standardized uniforms "encourages the subordination of personal preferences and identifies in favor of the overall group mission."[94] In dissent, Justice Brennan, although highly critical of the Court's abdication of its role "as principal expositor of the Constitution and protector of individual liberties," pointed to a political remedy. Acknowledging that "guardianship of this precious liberty is not the exclusive domain of federal courts," he called on Congress to "correct this wrong."

There was never any doubt about the authority of Congress to direct the Air Force to change its regulation. The Constitution provides that Congress shall "make rules for the Government and Regulation of the land and naval Forces."[95] Within two weeks of the decision, legislation was introduced to override *Goldman*. That effort failed, thanks in part to Senator Barry Goldwater, chair of the Senate Armed Services Committee. He warned of Hopi Indians wearing a red band around their head ("That is religion, too") and other Indians wearing feather headdresses. His blunt advice: "If you are not happy in uniform, get out of uniform. Join something else."[96]

The following year, the amendment resurfaced. To no one's surprise, the American Legion, with over 2.5 million members, and the Military Coalition, representing sixteen of the largest organizations for military personnel, opposed the amendment.[97] In a letter, Secretary of Defense Caspar Weinberger identified the reasons for rejecting the amendment, as did a document called a "20-star letter." The latter was signed by the chairman of the Joint Chiefs of Staff, the Army chief of staff, the Air Force chief of staff, the commandant of the Marine Corps, and the acting chief of Naval Operations: five officers with four stars each! A twenty-star letter against an amendment in a defense authorization bill is heavy artillery.[98]

Even so, with the strong support of religious lobbyists, the amendment passed both Houses and was enacted. As a result, unless the secretary of defense finds that the wearing of religious apparel interferes with military performance, service members can express their faith by wearing neat and conservative religious apparel.[99] Through passage of this statute, religious liberties that could not be obtained in court were protected by Congress.

Peyotism as a Religion

What began as a denial by Oregon of unemployment benefits to an American Indian who had ingested peyote during a religious ceremony led in time to a controversial decision by the Supreme Court in 1990. In sustaining the denial of benefits, the Court announced standards that many interpreted to be an alarming setback for religious liberty. Public opposition to the decision prompted hearings by Congress and the enactment of legislation in 1993 restoring religious freedom to its position before the Court's ruling. As one more round in the public dialogue over the meaning of religious freedom, in 1997 the Court declared the statute unconstitutional. In 2001, Congress responded with scaled-down legislation to add statutory protections for religious liberty.

The peyote religion among Indian tribes in the United States began at the end of the nineteenth century, although its use by Indians in other territories dates back 10,000 years. With its hallucinogenic properties, peyote offers a supernatural alternative to other religions by establishing an intermediate spirit (peyote, Jesus, or both) and a Supreme Being (the Great Spirit or God).[100] As practiced by the Native American Church (NAC) and interpreted by state courts, the drug is considered a sacrament (like bread and wine) and an object of worship.

Both Congress and the executive branch supported the religious use of peyote. The Drug Abuse Control Amendments of 1965, which brought peyote under federal control, expected the implementing regulation to exempt the religious use of peyote. In 1970 and 1978, Congress passed additional legislation offering protection for the peyote religion.[101] As anticipated by Congress, the implementing regulation issued in 1971 stated that the listing of peyote as a controlled substance "does not apply to the nondrug use of peyote in bona fide religious ceremonies of the Native American Church."[102]

Under Oregon law, however, the sacramental use of peyote was a crime. Unemployment benefits could be denied when an employee was discharged for misconduct, including the ingestion of peyote. For this reason, in 1984, unemployment benefits were denied to two NAC members, Alfred Smith and Galen Black, whose ingestion of peyote at a religious ceremony led to their dismissal.

The Oregon Supreme Court, first in 1986 and again in 1988, sided with Smith and Black. Pointing to constitutional judgments by Congress on this issue as well as exemption legislation approved by other states, the court held that this denial of benefits violated First Amendment religious liberty protections.[103] David Frohnmayer, attorney general of Oregon, took the case to the U.S. Supreme Court. He objected strongly to the reliance by the state supreme court on congressional interpretations of the Constitution: "The Oregon Supreme Court's holding is not a product of the court's independent assessment of what the first amendment requires. At most, it represents a choice to defer to congressional assumptions about the requirements of the federal constitution. . . . This process of canvassing congressional understanding to resolve an important first amendment question would be troubling under any circumstance."[104]

In 1990, the U.S. Supreme Court attempted to settle the matter by holding that the Free Exercise Clause permits a state to prohibit sacramental peyote use and to deny unemployment benefits to persons discharged for such use. In an opinion written by Justice Scalia, the Court in *Employment Division v. Smith* ruled that state law may prohibit the possession and use of a drug even if it incidentally prohibits a religious practice, provided that the state law is neutral and generally applicable to all individuals.[105] Under this test, the Court should ask only whether the government's action is rationally related to a legitimate state interest. Unlike earlier rulings, which placed a heavy burden on government to justify infringements on religious practice, the Court claimed that its role in overseeing democratic institutions was limited. Proclaiming that "it is horrible to contemplate that federal judges will regularly balance against the importance of general laws the significance of religious practice," Scalia acknowledged that his test would place religious minorities at the mercy of the political process, but discriminatory treatment was an "unavoidable consequence of democratic government."

With the Court offering no relief, interest groups turned their attention to Congress and the legislative process. Relying on Congress's Section 5 power to enforce the Fourteenth Amendment, religious interests helped draft the Religious Freedom Restoration Act (RFRA). Under this legislation, the government could not burden a person's free exercise of religion—even if the burden resulted from a rule of general applicability—unless the burden was "essential to further a compelling government interest and is the least restrictive means of furthering that interest."

While Congress considered this proposal, the Oregon legislature repaired some of the damage of the U.S. Supreme Court's decision by enacting a bill that protects the sacramental use of peyote by the NAC. As enacted in 1991, the bill states that in any prosecution for the manufacture, possession, or delivery of peyote, it is an affirmative defense that the peyote is being used or is intended for use (1) in connection with the good faith practice of a religious belief, (2) as directly associated with a religious practice, and (3) in a manner that is not dangerous to the health of the user or others who are in the proximity of the user.[106]

Legislative consideration of RFRA showcased representatives from "an unprecedented coalition" of religious and other interest groups.[107] At congressional hearings, few of the witnesses challenged the legislation and nearly all attacked *Smith*, often by demanding that Congress overturn the decision. Illustrative of this line of attack are comments from three members of the Coalition for the Free Exercise of Religion. Robert Dugan Jr., representing the National Association of Evangelicals, said that *Smith* "has deprived us of our birthright as Americans" and must be "overrule[d]."[108] Dallin H. Oaks, from the Church of Jesus Christ of Latter-Day Saints (the Mormon Church), regarded the statutory restoration of the compelling interest standard as "both a legitimate and a necessary response by the legislative branch to the degradation of religious freedom resulting from the *Smith* case."[109] Oliver S. Thomas, general counsel of the Baptist Joint Committee on Public Affairs, referred to *Smith* as "the Dred Scott of first amendment law."[110]

Lawmakers read from a nearly identical script. They were unwilling to cede, as Congressman Henry Hyde urged, that "Congress is institutionally unable to restore a prior interpretation of the first amendment once the Supreme Court has rejected that interpretation."[111] Most lawmakers condemned the Court for its "disastrous" and "devastating" decision, leading to "degradation" of religious liberty protections.[112] For his part, President Clinton, invoking "the power of God," spoke of his conviction that RFRA "is far more consistent with the intent of the Founders of this Nation than the [*Smith*] decision."[113] Lawmakers and the White House paid homage to RFRA's interest group sponsors, applauding the Coalition for the Free Exercise of Religion as "one of the broadest coalitions ever assembled to support a bill before Congress" and for spanning "ideological and religious lines."[114]

With no meaningful interest group resistance, the question of whether the Supreme Court would approve RFRA was barely touched on. For example, Congress did not engage in the type of fact-finding that would place RFRA within the ambit of the Court's (admittedly murky) Section 5 analysis. Instead of making specific findings of fact to support the legislation, Congress contented itself with doing precisely what RFRA's interest group sponsors clamored for: a repudiation of *Smith*.

When a constitutional challenge to RFRA made its way to the Supreme Court, a unanimous Court invalidated the statute. Invoking *Marbury v. Madison* for the proposition that the "powers of the legislature are defined and limited," the Court claimed that constitutional interpretation is a judicial monopoly: "Our national experience teaches that the Constitution is preserved best when each part of the government respects both the Constitution and the proper actions and determinations of the other branches. When the Court has interpreted the Constitution, it has acted within the province of the Judicial Branch, which embraces the duty to say what the law is."[115] Accordingly, "if Congress could define its own powers by altering the Fourteenth Amendment's meaning," the Court warned that "no longer would the Constitution be 'superior paramount law, unchangeable by ordinary means.'"[116]

There is nothing in two hundred years of constitutional practice and construction to support that position. It is obvious that all three branches have powers that are not expressly defined in the Constitution, for example, the power of Congress to investigate, the power of the President to recognize foreign governments, and the Court's own power (implied) to exercise judicial review, as in this case. More striking, the Court, through case law, is continually changing the meaning of the Constitution. Two days before the Court invalidated RFRA, it overruled a decision from 1985 that had limited federal assistance to parochial schools.[117]

Notwithstanding its bravado in striking down RFRA, the Court's decision shed little light on congressional authority to correct Supreme Court decisions. For example, although concluding that Congress's Section 5 enforcement powers are limited to "enforcement" and "remedial" actions, the Court readily conceded that "the line between measures that remedy or prevent unconstitutional actions and measures that make a substantive change in the governing law is not easy to discern."[118] Moreover, recognizing that "Congress must have wide latitude in determining" whether its corrective legislation is, in fact, remedial, the Court acknowledged that Congress does engage in constitutional dialogues. Indeed, a year after enacting RFRA, Congress passed legislation to permit the use of peyote by Native Americans during religious ceremonies.[119]

A separate question concerned the constitutionality of RFRA as applied not to the states but to the federal government. In 1998, the Eighth Circuit held that RFRA was constitutional as applied to federal law, it did not violate the separation of powers doctrine, and it did not violate the Establishment Clause.[120] In 2001, the Tenth Circuit ruled that RFRA was a legitimate congressional action under Article I to govern the conduct of federal prison officials.[121]

Following *City of Boerne v. Flores*, the House and Senate Judiciary Committees held hearings to explore legislative options.[122] The resulting legislation, the Religious Liberty Protection Act (RLPA), relied primarily on the commerce and spending powers.[123] The bill passed the House in 1999, supported by ninety-two religious and civil liberties groups, including Protestant, Catholic, Jewish, Muslim, and Native American organizations.[124] The vote was 306 to 118.[125]

By the time the bill (called "Son of RFRA") cleared both chambers in 2000, it had been restricted to provide two kinds of protections. First, it offers religious groups protection in land-use disputes, such as zoning issues (the kind that triggered *Boerne*). Second, the statute makes it easier for prisoners and other persons confined in state-run institutions to practice their faith. The statute applies to any organization that receives federal money, including state and local prisons that get federal construction and maintenance funds. Finally, the statute relies on congressional power over interstate commerce, because construction materials are shipped between states for the renovation of buildings owned by religious organizations.[126]

Home Schooling and Church Schools

Responding to restrictive court interpretations of both the federal and state constitutions, religious interests have had great success in convincing state lawmakers to expand religious liberty protections. One prominent example of this phenomenon is state regulation of religious schooling.

Controversies between state education officials and religious parents date back to the establishment of public schools and continue today. Early battles concerned state authority to outlaw private schooling altogether. In 1922, for example, Oregon voters, to ensure "the mingling together . . . of the children of all races and sects,"[127] passed an initiative outlawing religious and other private schools. Enacted at the urging of the Ku Klux Klan, the proposal was designed to frustrate the efforts of Catholics and immigrants to attend schools that reflect *their* values, not the values and beliefs of the dominant Protestant culture. The Supreme Court rejected such coerced uniformity and ruled that parents "have the right, coupled with the high duty, to recognize and prepare [their children] for additional obligations."[128]

Contemporary skirmishes center on the applicability of state regulations governing teacher certification, curriculum, and the like to religious parents and schools. On one side, religious parents and educators claim that state-prescribed "minimum standards" and licensing procedures would violate their religious beliefs. This claim is rooted in the Free Exercise Clause of the First Amendment and the implied Fourteenth Amendment right of parents to direct their children's upbringing. Over recent decades, this challenge to state authority has been championed by Christian educators and parents.

On the other side, state authorities assert their right to impose "reasonable" regulations on religious schools and religious home instruction. For the state, these regulations establish minimum criteria to protect children from the adverse consequences of an inadequate education. The state, moreover, asserts an independent interest in assisting the child in developing citizenship skills. Schools and parents that do not conform to these regulations violate compulsory school attendance laws and may be subject to criminal prosecution.

From 1975 to 1983, Christian educators and parents fought a holy war with state officials. With neither side especially interested in accommodating the other, lawsuits flourished in most states. Sometimes religious liberty claimants succeeded; most often, the state prevailed. But state victories came at a substantial price. Unwilling to comply with court-approved regulations, religious parents and ministers were jailed, churches were padlocked, and the state threatened to terminate parental rights.

Since 1983 this struggle, though far from dormant, has become subdued. Both sides seem more accepting of the other. More significant, the battleground has shifted from adversarial, winner-take-all litigation to legislative reform. Thirty-two states have adopted home-schooling statutes or regulations since 1982, and twenty-three of these states have repealed teacher certification requirements. In the end, rather than jailing parents and ministers for noncompliance, state officials have backed down from High Noon–style showdowns with fundamentalist Christian educators and parents. This is the lesson of North Carolina, Nebraska, and several other states.

The political process in North Carolina has been extraordinarily sensitive to the religious liberty concerns of its citizens. After a 1978 state trial court decision approved existing curriculum and teacher certification requirements as "based upon sound educational policy and logic,"[129] the legislature in 1979 specifically exempted church-affiliated schools from state compulsory education laws. The only obligations placed on religious schools were to keep attendance and disease immunization records, to comply with building codes, and to administer a nationally standardized achievement test, to be selected by the school and with no state-prescribed minimum score. These minimal demands were rooted in the belief that "in matters of education . . . no human authority shall interfere with the rights of conscience or with religious liberty."[130]

The 1979 law, however, did not satisfy religious liberty concerns. Home instruction was not mentioned in the law and the state's attorney general interpreted this omission to mean that home schools were unauthorized. The legislature "corrected" this interpretation in 1987, exempting home instruction from nearly all state oversight.[131] Religious liberty interests pushed this bill through the state house, 93 to 0. A competing proposal, advanced by North Carolina's Board of Education, never made it out of committee.

Home educators learned how to exploit religion. As explained by one reporter, "During the legislative process, home schoolers originally took a straightforward political approach. But this didn't take them anywhere. However, when the home schoolers added the religious angle, the legislature backed off quickly."[132] The legislature "simply wanted to avoid crossing swords with the Fundamentalists, so religion became the trump card that won the game for home schoolers."[133]

In Nebraska, a 1981 state supreme court decision involving Pastor Evert Sileven's unaccredited Faith Christian School triggered a bitter, controversial, and somewhat bizarre battle between the state and Christian educators.[134] After a three-year struggle with the state, Sileven, who publicly prayed for God to kill state education officials, proved the victor. That the state ultimately backed down suggests that enforcing state regulatory schemes may entail too great a cost to be practicable, despite court rulings upholding their constitutionality.

The events leading up to this collision date back to 1977, when Faith Baptist Church of Louisville, Nebraska, opened a school without state approval. The leadership of the church claimed that the school operated as "an extension of the ministry of the church," over which the state had no authority. Church officers refused to provide a list of the students enrolled in the school, seek approval for the educational program, employ certified teachers, or seek approval to operate the institution.

The state sought to close the school because of noncompliance with state regulations. The Nebraska Supreme Court supported that effort, characterizing Sileven's actions as an "arbitrary and unreasonable attempt to thwart the legitimate, reasonable, and compelling interests of the State in carrying out its educational obligations, under a claim of religious freedom."[135] Sileven responded first by operating out of a church in Iowa and an "underground" church in Nebraska. Within a year he had reopened the school at Faith Baptist. Refusing, for religious reasons, to close the institution, he was sentenced to four months in jail for contempt of court. When Faith Christian School reopened without state approval, Sileven was again arrested and returned to jail. To prevent continued operation of the school, the state padlocked the church on weekdays. After efforts at compromise failed, seven fathers of Faith Christian students were jailed for refusing to answer a judge's questions about the school. Their wives and children fled the state to avoid prosecution.

These struggles prompted U.S. Secretary of Education T. H. Bell to suggest that Nebraska might lose federal education funds if evangelicals could show that state education officials were practicing religious discrimination toward the Faith Christian School. The dispute attracted national publicity, much of it negative, for the jailing of individuals who acted on the basis of religious conscience.

In the midst of this confrontation, Nebraska governor (and later U.S. senator) Robert Kerrey established a four-member panel to examine and report on the questions surrounding Christian schools. On January 26, 1984, the panel concluded that existing procedures violated the First Amendment religious liberty protections and that some accommodations to the Christian schools had to be recognized.[136] The panel recommended that standardized tests be offered to students in place of teacher certification and curriculum requirements. In so doing, the panel ignored the state supreme court decision.

The state legislature enacted the panel's recommendations into law in April 1984.[137] The statute does not require Christian schools to provide any information to state officials. Instead, parents who elect to send their children to a school that does not apply for state approval must provide the state with information about the education their children are receiving. They submit an "information statement" that their children attend school for 175 days a year and are instructed in core curriculum subjects.

Nebraska's actions, like North Carolina's, speak to the ability of fundamentalist educators to succeed in accomplishing through elected officials what they failed to achieve in court. Indeed, the explicit and implicit compromises reached in North Carolina and Nebraska are not unusual.[138] On the question of state regulation of fundamentalist Christian schools, several states—including Alabama, Arizona, Pennsylvania, Vermont, and West Virginia—also exempt religious schools from licensing, teacher certification, and curriculum requirements. Other states, including Colorado and Iowa, adopted administrative compromises. Some states, including Kentucky, Maine, and Ohio, failed to respond to court decisions striking down state laws and procedures. Sometimes, as in North Carolina, these reforms respond to court rulings; sometimes they result from grassroots political pressure. Whatever the explanation, religious interests typically prevail in the legislative arena.

Conclusions

The Supreme Court has operated in the midst of majoritarian pressures for two hundred years, sometimes leading the charge for minority rights, but more often pulling up the rear. Interest groups mobilize to apply pressure to the branch most responsive to their needs. At times, the courts are more supportive of interest group claims; on other occasions, it is an elected branch. No single institution, including the judiciary, can lay claim to having the last word, certainly not in the volatile world of religious politics.

Religious sects have learned to consolidate their interests with other denominations to exert the maximum pressure and effectiveness. With ready access to parishioners, religious interests can mobilize more quickly and effectively than nearly any other interest group. Consequently, legislatures, supposedly rough institutions designed to satisfy the majority's interests, have shown a keen sensitivity and solicitude in protecting minority rights. For this reason, on matters of religious faith and observance, elected officials, more than judges, have played an integral role in defining the reaches of religious liberty protections.

10

The Ongoing Dialogue

This book explains how constitutional law is produced by many forces: political and legal, nonjudicial and judicial, national and local, public and private. All three branches are involved, not just one. Fifty-one constitutions are at play, not just one. The historical record of this constitutional dialogue is richly documented, and yet support for judicial supremacy remains strong. Why? Are we that resistant to facts and reality?

No doubt, powerful symbols help nourish the continuing belief that the U.S. Supreme Court alone decides the meaning of the Constitution (or at least has the last word). There is something reassuring about a blind-folded lady holding the scales of Justice, unswayed by politics. We sing praises to the "rule of law," impartiality, and judicial independence. We all yearn for even-handed justice. We like the idea of an institution that can right the wrong, protect embattled minorities, and come to the rescue of the isolated individual (who might be us).

Perhaps citizens look to the Court as a sort of parental figure, telling them what is right and wrong and guiding them to the true path. If that is the model, U.S. citizens have never played the obedient and respectful child, dazzled by the parent's wisdom and intelligence. Citizens rebel whenever they like, letting the Court know in blunt terms that it has bungled again in judging constitutional and national values. Moreover, the parental figure is likely to tell the child: The kind of question you just presented is one I don't answer. You figure it out.

In truth, we are at cross-purposes and destined to remain so. We want an independent court but hope that other forces are available to check the Court to make it reverse directions and adjust doctrines. As Robert Dahl noted, Americans are not quite willing to accept the fact that the Supreme Court "*is* a political institution and not quite capable of denying it; so that frequently we take both positions at once. This is confusing to foreigners, amusing to logicians, and rewarding to ordinary Americans who thus manage to retain the best of both worlds."[1]

217

For more than a century, the legal profession claimed that judges "found" the law rather than made it. No one takes that seriously any more, even if judges still begin their sentences "We find . . . " Writing in 2003, Justice Sandra Day O'Connor recognized the inextricable link between law and politics. Noting that when it comes to putting judicial interpretations "into practice, ultimately, the Court must rely on the other branches of the government," O'Connor acknowledged that if "one looks at the history of the Court, the country, and the Constitution over a very long period, the relationship appears to be more of a dialogue than a series of commands."[2]

In a perceptive essay, C. Herman Pritchett noted that the disciplines of law and political science drifted apart for semantic, philosophical, and practical reasons. "Law is a prestigious symbol, whereas politics tends to be a dirty word. Law is stability; politics is chaos. Law is impersonal; politics is personal. Law is given; politics is free choice. Law is reason; politics is prejudice and self-interest. Law is justice; politics is who gets there first with the most."[3] With the options drawn that crudely, it is hardly surprising that the courts look attractive. Many parents dream of their child's being a judge; they are less likely to want a son or daughter to be a politician. Yet we need government, in one form or another, and that means public officials (or "politicians") who are elected or serve as advisors and staff. Although some people hate to admit it, the judiciary is part of government and is simultaneously independent and interdependent.

The Case for Judicial Supremacy

Academics and public officials often defend judicial supremacy as essential to the rule of law. Law school casebooks and newspaper stories likewise treat Supreme Court decisions as final and dispositive. Why is this? As our analysis makes clear, each decision by a court is subject to scrutiny and rejection by private citizens and public officials. What is "final" at one stage of our political development may be reopened at some later date, leading to revisions, fresh interpretations, and reversals of Court doctrines.

If the Court is not the Constitution, what, then, explains the persistence of judicial supremacy? Perhaps the desire for finality is simply human nature. "There is a magnetic attraction to the notion of an ultimate constitutional interpreter," wrote Walter Murphy, "just as there is a magnetic pull to the idea of some passkey to constitutional interpretation that will, if properly turned, always open the door to truth, justice, and the American way."[4] However, finality is not our only value. Like the patient who gets bad news from the doctor, we like to get a second opinion. We like choices, not dead ends. And we need to participate in our own destiny, not simply be told the result.

Another explanation is that judicial supremacy is fueled by those who benefit from it. Needless to say, the Supreme Court is the principal beneficiary of the myth of judicial supremacy. Lacking the powers of purse and sword, the Court's status depends inescapably on public acceptance of its decisions. But the judicial supremacy myth benefits many others. The power and prestige of the Justice Department, for example, is often tied to the judicial supremacy myth. The Department's power to represent the United States in court is necessarily linked to the Supreme Court's power to bind the nation through its pronouncements. For similar reasons, members of the Senate Judiciary Committee often embrace judicial supremacy; the Committee's power over judicial nominations is directly tied to the power of the Court. The President and members of Congress also seek cover in Supreme Court rulings. When enacting item veto legislation, some members of Congress hoped that the Court would protect legislative prerogatives and "save this Congress from itself."[5] More telling, other members embraced an expedited Supreme Court review provision so that Congress could avoid having to determine the constitutionality of this politically popular bill. For their part, Presidents have long pointed to the Supreme Court as a way of ducking politically controversial issues; for example, John F. Kennedy and Dwight Eisenhower accepted the Court's power to authoritatively settle constitutional disputes.[6]

Even state and local officials see judicial supremacy as a useful rallying cry. Late 1960s voting rights decisions upholding congressional reforms gave cover to Southern officials willing to comply with the new policy but unwilling to take responsibility for it.[7] Likewise, many state officials hid behind the Supreme Court's decision in *Roe*. For example, when Idaho's pro-life governor Cecil Andrus staved off a threatened boycott of Idaho potatoes by vetoing antiabortion restrictions, he observed that "there is not the remotest chance of this legislation's being found constitutional by the Supreme Court."[8]

Judicial supremacy also benefits law professors and journalists covering the Supreme Court. For law professors, there are strong incentives to see the Court as a somewhat closed system (speaking the last word on constitutional issues). Specifically, this model communicates that they are expert in what matters the most: the teaching/practice of constitutional law. Perhaps for this reason, law professors make use of casebooks filled with Supreme Court decisions and academic commentary about those decisions—so that the language of lawyers becomes the language of constitutional law. In contrast, were the decisions of the Supreme Court seen as part of a broader sociopolitical mosaic, lawyer training and, with it, law professor expertise would matter less. For almost identical reasons, journalists do not want Court decisions to be seen as simply one volley in an ongoing dialogue over the Constitution's meaning. Like law professors, the power of Supreme Court journalists is tied to the power of the Court. In plain terms, the Supreme Court "beat" is only as important as the Court.

Judicial supremacy seems destined to survive—but only because elected officials find it convenient and only because it is a half-truth. Indeed, notwithstanding their continuing adherence to Court-centered casebooks, contemporary academics increasingly dismiss the Supreme Court as the leading (let alone ultimate) interpreter of the Constitution. Nevertheless, judicial supremacy still has its academic defenders. Writing in the *Harvard Law Review* in 1997, Larry Alexander and Frederick Schauer spoke of judicial supremacy as a necessary way of settling legal disputes, assuring doctrinal coherence, and promoting political stability.[9] We disagree, fundamentally, on each point. Nothing in America's experience supports the notion that concentrating power in the Court would settle political controversies, yield doctrinal coherence, or promote political stability. Quite the contrary.

Placing complete interpretive authority in the Court would create political instability and undermine the fragile foundation that supports and sustains judicial power. Instead of suggesting that the judiciary can settle in any decisive way such contentious issues as abortion, affirmative action, federalism, privacy, race districting, and religious freedom, the record of the past two centuries points to a more modest and circumscribed judicial role. If we were ever to grant the Court the last word on the Constitution's meaning, judicial exclusivity would marginalize the Constitution. For example, elected officials might ignore the Constitution, placing their policy-driven judgments ahead of the Court's constitutional judgments. Also, many of the issues that now go to the courts, with the understanding that they will be part of a national dialogue, would be kept within the elected branches, perhaps by stripping courts of jurisdiction. In effect, we would have two constitutions: one decided by the Court, the other decided by elected officials.

Preserving the Constitution

Can the Constitution be preserved and honored without "a final interpretive authority for choosing among competing [constitutional] interpretations?"[10] For its modern-day defenders, judicial supremacy is heralded as the only way to protect "a single written constitution" from "shifting political fortunes."[11] This conclusion, however, is not suggested in the text or structure of the Constitution, the framers' intent, historical development, or even Supreme Court declarations of its status as the ultimate and final interpreter of the Constitution.[12] Instead, the overriding value promoted by the framers was a system of checks and balances, with each branch asserting its own powers and protecting its own prerogatives. Moreover, "shifting political fortunes" obviously affect the judiciary as much as they do the elected branches. After all, courts are a part of government and their membership changes just as in the executive and legislative branches.

As we have already detailed, the Constitution's text, its original intent, and intervening practice support a limited form of judicial review. Indeed, at the time of *Marbury*, several Justices wondered whether the power of judicial review would reach to congressional and presidential actions. Likewise, starting with George Washington (whose first veto was on constitutional grounds), Presidents have maintained that Supreme Court rulings would extend only to "such influence as the force of their reasoning may deserve."[13] Prominent examples include Thomas Jefferson's pardoning every person convicted under the Alien and Sedition Acts, Abraham Lincoln's repudiation of *Dred Scott*, Franklin Delano Roosevelt's court-packing proposal, Richard Nixon's campaign to undo Warren Court liberalism, Ronald Reagan's attack on *Roe v. Wade*, and Bill Clinton's signing of the Religious Freedom Restoration Act.

For its part, Congress has launched numerous challenges to the Court. In response to *Dred Scott*, Congress passed a bill prohibiting slavery in the territories. Disagreeing with the Court's 1918 ruling that the commerce power could not be used to regulate child labor, Congress two decades later again based child labor legislation on the Commerce Clause. The public accommodations protections contained in the 1964 Civil Rights Act collided with the civil rights cases of 1883, which the Court had never repudiated. More recently, lawmakers have challenged Court rulings on abortion, busing, flag burning, religious freedom, voting rights, the independent counsel, and the legislative veto.

Judicial exclusivity, then, finds no support in congressional and White House practices, in the debates surrounding the drafting and ratification of the Constitution, or in the Constitution itself. To the extent that language and tradition matter, the argument for judicial supremacy is a nonstarter. Furthermore, without a scintilla of evidence to support the Court's "ultimate interpreter" status, advocates of judicial supremacy cannot pull off the impossible feat of demonstrating fidelity to the Constitution by disregarding its basic command about the separation of powers.

Settling Transcendent Values

What about the central question that animates the normative inquiry: "What . . . is law for?"[14] Even assuming that law's principal function is to settle matters authoritatively and promote stability, the argument for judicial supremacy falls flat. Without the powers of purse and sword, the Court "must take care to speak and act in ways that allow people to accept its decisions."[15] Rather than advance its institutional self-interest through claims of judicial supremacy, the Court understands its limited role in government.

On war powers, for example, the Court typically steers clear of presidential invocations of inherent commander in chief powers. Specifically, because the contemporary Congress hardly ever checks the President (preferring, instead, to dutifully follow presidential initiatives), Supreme Court Justices and other federal court judges are unwilling to fill the void left open by lawmakers. More to the point, without the cover provided by Congress, the courts are unwilling to risk either elected branch reprisals or presidential noncompliance with their orders. Instead, contemporary courts invariably conclude that they are without jurisdiction to resolve legal challenges to presidential war initiatives. From 1800 to 1952, courts regularly took these war powers cases.

The history of the Supreme Court has been a search for various techniques and methods that will permit the judiciary to limit and constrain its own power. Justices understand, either by instinct or experience, that the hazards are great when the Court attempts to settle political, social, and economic matters best left to the political process. Despite occasional utterances from the Court that it is the "ultimate interpreter," Justices by necessity adhere to a philosophy that is much more modest, circumspect, and nuanced. Court decisions, at best, momentarily resolve a dispute forced into court.

Marbury v. Madison nicely illustrates how political challenges to the Court's interpretive authority and vaunted claims of judicial supremacy are inextricably linked to each other. When *Marbury* was decided, the Supreme Court and its Chief Justice, John Marshall, were under attack. Court foe Thomas Jefferson had just been elected President and, at his urging, Secretary of State James Madison openly challenged the Court's authority to subject executive officers to court orders. Unwilling to engage in a head-to-head confrontation with the Jeffersonians, the Court's supposed war cry that "it is emphatically the province and duty of the judicial department to say what the law is" is window dressing for the Court's ultimately ducking the *Marbury* dispute on jurisdictional grounds.[16]

On those few occasions when the Court insists that it has the last word in interpreting the Constitution, such announcements make sense only in their political context. *Cooper v. Aaron* (1957) illustrates this practice. The Court's claim that federal court constitutional interpretations are "supreme" was made in the face of massive Southern resistance to *Brown v. Board of Education*, including Arkansas's enlistment of the national guard to deny black schoolchildren access to Little Rock's Central High School. Backed to the wall, the Court decided to underscore its authority, perhaps recalling that wishy-washy opinions (like *Brown II*) can invite noncompliance.

Planned Parenthood v. Casey similarly underscores the Court's belief that "a surrender to political pressure" would result in "profound and unnecessary damage" to the Court.[17] Moreover, although refusing to bend to the stated desires of the Presidents who appointed them and overrule *Roe* "under fire," the Court (by jettisoning the trimester standard) recognized that the nation had not accepted *Roe*.

The threat of resistance to the Court's orders likewise animated invocations of judicial supremacy in other cases, such as the reapportionment case of *Baker v. Carr*. At oral argument, counsel for Tennessee suggested that they might resist court-ordered reapportionment. The same lesson applies to the Court's declaration of judicial supremacy in *Powell v. McCormack*, which involved the refusal of the House of Representatives to seat Congressman Adam Clayton Powell. The House signaled to the Court that it might resist a judicial order requiring it to seat Powell.[18] Likewise, in the Watergate tapes case, Nixon's attorney James St. Clair equivocated on Nixon's willingness to accept the Court's judgment on executive privilege as binding on the President.[19] This put pressure on the Court to craft a unanimous decision (which it did).

The Supreme Court's practice of declaring itself the final word on the Constitution's meaning when it feels especially challenged by the other branches is anything but surprising. Invariably, the Court takes a bold stand because it fears that the political order will ignore its command. Perhaps for this reason, invocations of judicial supremacy often place few demands on the government (as in *Marbury*) or are linked with popular sentiment. With respect to *Cooper*, although Arkansas Governor Faubus's repudiation of *Brown* scored points with in-state voters, national public opinion favored President Eisenhower's decision to send federal troops into Little Rock.[20] The reapportionment case of *Baker v. Carr* risked ill will with state officials in order to reach an outcome popular in the national political arena; of sixty-three leading metropolitan daily newspapers, thirty-eight favored the Court's decision, ten opposed it, and the remainder were neutral or confused.[21] Public opinion strongly supported the Court's authority to compel President Nixon to release the Watergate tapes.[22] The "undue burden" standard announced in *Casey* closely matched public opinion.[23]

Lacking the power to appropriate funds or command the military, the Court understands that it must act in a way that wins public acceptance.[24] The Court realizes that its role as interpreter of the Constitution depends on public support and understanding of its decisions.[25] Court decisions cannot be divorced from a case's (sometimes explosive) social and political setting.

Promoting Political Stability

If Court decisions were viewed as final, democratic government would largely ignore those rulings and insist on their policy preferences. "Final" court decisions would hang in the air, isolated from public policy. This marginalization of the Constitution (and the Court) is directly at odds with the settlement function of law. Stability, instead, can be achieved only through a give-and-take process involving all of government as well as the people. Justice Brandeis observed that "the process of trial and error, so fruitful in the physical sciences, is appropriate also in the judicial function."[26]

In other words, what is constitutional or unconstitutional must be left for us to explore, ponder, and come to terms with. Through this process of dialogue and colloquy, the Court is able to recalibrate its decision making—taking social and political forces into account and, where appropriate, updating or reversing its decisions. In an interview in 1982, Justice Blackmun put it this way: "It may prove to be well in the long run that people do get disturbed and concerned and interested in what the Court does. I think on balance that this is a good thing for the country, because the Supreme Court of the United States belongs to the country."[27] More to the point, the Constitution belongs to the country. For Supreme Court interpretations of the Constitution to have meaning, elected officials and the public must accept those rulings or, at least, must accept the Court's power to make such rulings.

This process of trial and error does not mean that the Court should simply bend to popular opinion. The Court, however, does not promote political stability by issuing opinions that do little but trigger disobedience. Political stability can be achieved only when the Court's authority to bind the nation through its constitutional interpretations is generally accepted. For this reason, the Court must engage in a politically sensitive balancing act: To preserve its power, it cannot demand that *all* of its decisions (even those that the public considers outdated) be treated as final and definitive; it must sometimes reverse itself to conform to social and political forces. Indeed, recognizing the link between its authority and public acceptance, the Court is rarely out of step with prevailing mores.[28] Witness, for example, the collapse of the *Lochner* era under the weight of changing social conditions, economic structures, and hostile public reactions. Following Roosevelt's 1936 election victory in all but two states, the Court, embarrassed by public attacks against the Justices, announced several decisions upholding New Deal programs. In explaining this transformation, Justice Owen Roberts recognized the extraordinary importance of public opinion in undoing the *Lochner* era: "Looking back, it is difficult to see how the Court could have resisted the popular urge for uniform standards throughout the country—for what in effect was a unified economy."[29]

Social and political forces also played a defining role in the Court's reconsideration of decisions on sterilization and the eugenics movement,[30] state mandated flag salutes,[31] the *Roe* trimester standard,[32] the death penalty,[33] states' rights,[34] and much more.[35] It did not matter that some decisions commanded an impressive majority of 8 to 1.[36] Without popular support, those decisions settled nothing. Justice Robert Jackson instructed us that "the practical play of the forces of politics is such that judicial power has often delayed but never permanently defeated the persistent will of a substantial majority."[37] For a Court that wants to maximize its power and legitimacy, taking social and political forces into account is an act of necessity, not cowardice. When the Court gives short shrift to public values or concerns, its decision making is unworkable and destabilizing.

The Supreme Court may be the ultimate interpreter in a particular case, but not in the larger issue of which that case is a part. In the more than two centuries of rulings from the Supreme Court, it is difficult to locate a single decision that finally settled a transcendent question of constitutional law. When a decision fails to persuade or otherwise proves unworkable, elected officials, interest groups, academic commentators, and the press will speak their mind and the Court, ultimately, will listen.

Even in decisions that are generally praised, such as *Brown v. Board of Education*, the Court must calibrate its decision making against the sentiments of the implementing community and the nation. In an effort to temper Southern hostility to its decision, the Court did not issue a remedy in the first *Brown* decision, and *Brown II* a year later left broad scope to the timing and nature of desegregation decisions. On many occasions the Court has invoked the so-called passive virtues: procedural and jurisdictional mechanisms that allow the Court to steer clear of politically explosive issues. It is the practice of the Court not to "anticipate a question of constitutional law in advance of the need of deciding it," not to "formulate a rule of constitutional law broader than is required," nor "pass upon a constitutional question . . . if there is . . . some other ground," such as statutory construction, on which to dispose of the case.[38] Moreover, as our study of separation of powers and war powers makes clear, the Supreme Court sometimes concludes that it lacks jurisdiction to settle an issue, leaving it to Congress and the White House to bargain with each other. This deliberate withholding of judicial power reflects the fact that courts lack ballot box legitimacy and need to avoid costly collisions with the general public and other branches of government.

Assuring Doctrinal Coherence

It is sometimes argued that courts operate on principle, while the rest of government is satisfied with compromises. Chief Justice Earl Warren claimed that progress in politics "could be made and most often was made by compromising and taking half a loaf where a whole loaf could not be obtained. The opposite is true so far as the judicial process was concerned."[39] That argument is dishonest. A multimember Court, like other parts of government, gropes incrementally toward consensus and decision through compromise, expediency, and ad hoc actions. "No good society," as Alexander Bickel observed, "can be unprincipled; and no viable society can be principle-ridden."[40]

Indeed, because it is a multimember body, it is inevitable that the Court will issue fractured opinions. To start with, the Court focuses its energies on disputes in which the law is not settled and in which plausible arguments can be made on both sides of an issue. It therefore is to be expected that, in resolving hard cases, the Court will be sharply divided and that it will be difficult to forge a consensus around broad coherent principles.[41] Indeed, even proponents of judicial supremacy recognize (albeit with disappointment) the proliferation of divided judgments without a majority opinion, the desire of Justices to make their own points (rather than speak as a Court with a single voice), and the corresponding absence of clear rules.[42] Against this backdrop, there is no reason to think that judicial supremacy will yield doctrinal coherence.

What, then, of settling legal disputes? Would a system in which democratic government saw Supreme Court decisions as definitive achieve a degree of settlement and stability? Would it remove transcendent questions from majoritarian control? Of course not. If the Court viewed the

Constitution as its exclusive domain, it would not moderate its opinions to take account of social and political forces. For their part, policymakers would believe the Constitution to be irrelevant to their official duties, something to treat with indifference. Lawmakers would debate policy divorced from constitutional concerns.

The failings of judicial exclusivity, we think, are best illustrated by *Dred Scott*, a decision that cried out for disobedience. At the time the case was to be decided, the Court was so confident of its "high and independent character" that Justice John Catron informed President-elect James Buchanan that the Court was prepared to "decide & settle" the slavery controversy "which has so long and seriously agitated the country."[43] Happy to duck the controversy, Buchanan took the Court at its word. In his inaugural address, he assured the nation that the issue before the Court would be "speedily and finally settled."[44] The judicial settlement was certainly speedy but not final. Two days later, the Court's *Dred Scott* decision helped propel the nation into a bloody civil war that, out of a population of about 30 million, left more than 600,000 dead and another 400,000 wounded.

Abraham Lincoln, through words and deeds, challenged the legitimacy and reasoning of *Dred Scott*. To Lincoln, judicial decisions were binding on the parties to a particular case but did not bind elected officials to judicially imposed policies. What if Lincoln had treated *Dred Scott* as settling the constitutionality of slavery? Would he have seen his repudiation of the decision, his issuance of the Emancipation Proclamation, and the Civil War itself as illegitimate? Hardly. As proponents of judicial supremacy recognize, even if Lincoln thought he had an "obligation to follow *Dred Scott* because [the Supreme Court is] its source," he almost certainly would have seen the decision as an "overridable obligation"— legally binding but appropriately subject to civil disobedience.[45] In this way, judicial supremacy seems an empty concept; it inevitably yields to "overriding" social and political forces.

Proponents of judicial supremacy argue that *Dred Scott* is aberrational and, consequently, that a "decision procedure" ought not to be grounded in "one case that might never be repeated."[46] But *Dred Scott* was not aberrational. The Supreme Court regularly confronts divisive, emotional issues, issues where lawmakers and the public may well find "overriding values" that warrant civil disobedience. If policymakers accept Supreme Court rulings as final, some outlet will have to be found for expressing discontent with the consequences of disfavored Court rulings. If unable to engage in constitutional dialogues with the Court, elected officials will not be content to wait a decade or two in the hopes that the Court will change its membership and orientation; instead, elected officials may choose civil disobedience when the voters disapprove of a judicial ruling. Rather than "aberrations," such challenges may become an important part of public life.

Consider, for example, the willingness of democratic institutions to resist Court rulings on abortion, affirmative action, busing, child labor, the death penalty, flag burning, gay rights, the legislative veto, school prayer, voting rights, and religious liberty. Today, these challenges take place in the framework of give-and-take dialogues among the Court, elected officials, and the public. Were judicial supremacy to rule the day, some or all of these challenges might become occasions for disobedience. With Supreme Court decisions on states' rights, the minimum wage, abortion, and religious liberty already analogized to *Dred Scott*,[47] there is good reason to think that such challenges will, in fact, take place. Whether or not they succeed, it is difficult to see how judicial exclusivity will either promote stability or nullify majoritarian control of transcendent questions. Indeed, rather than assure doctrinal coherence, judicial supremacy simply creates occasions for civil disobedience. By encouraging Supreme Court Justices and elected officials to go their own way rather than engage in constitutional dialogues with each other, judicial supremacy is more apt to yield politically unworkable decisions than anything else.

How Not to Marginalize the Constitution

Judicial exclusivity is likely to marginalize the Court and, with it, the Constitution. Democratic institutions will take the Constitution seriously only if they have some stake in it. Correspondingly, with elected officials having no reason to engage in politicized constitutional discourse, the Court's educative function will be severely limited, as will the enduring values of the Constitution itself.

Proponents of judicial supremacy are hardly troubled by this state of affairs. To "generate a single conception of what the Constitution require[s]," for example, Alexander and Schauer would encourage lawmakers *not* to expand constitutional protections beyond the floor set by the Supreme Court.[48] By this interpretation, they would then disapprove of legislation authorizing disparate-impact proofs in voting rights and employment discrimination legislation; legislation and regulation authorizing the assignment of women to combat aircraft; legislation and regulation allowing federal employees, including members of the armed services, to wear an item of religious apparel; and other initiatives launched by democratic government in the face of Supreme Court decisions that narrow individual rights.

By stifling public discourse in this way, the Constitution becomes less relevant. Constitutional arguments will no longer be used as a roadblock to stymie progressive reforms or, alternatively, to expand constitutional protections beyond the floor set by the Supreme Court. Elected officials would be discouraged from adopting public policies that implicate constitutional values and from discussing the fundamental values that underlie the Constitution and, with it, the United States itself. The virtues of "settlement for settlement's sake" pale in relation to these costs.

These costs are particularly acute in two categories of cases that are outside the radar of judicial supremacy proponents. One involves "underenforced" constitutional norms: matters that for one reason or another are not likely to make their way into court.[49] Here, it is left to democratic government to define the Constitution's meaning. But if elected officials do not engage in constitutional dialogues with the courts, there is little reason to think that the constitutional dimensions of these issues will be given serious treatment; instead, consistent with the judicial supremacy model, elected officials will focus their energies on policy—not the constitutional dimensions of their policy choices.

The second category involves instances in which the Court sees itself as a partner with government in shaping constitutional values. As a way of minimizing error, miscalculation, and needless conflict with society and its coequal branches, the Court sometimes enlists the help of elected government. School desegregation is a particularly telling example of this practice. More than a decade after *Brown*, the percentage of African American children in all-black schools in the South stood at 98.[50] Through the 1964 Civil Rights Act and other federal initiatives, that figure dropped to 25 percent by 1968.[51] With the President, congressional leadership, and the public committed to undoing Jim Crow laws, the Court was emboldened to attack discrimination and segregation "root and branch."[52]

Herein lies the real danger of judicial exclusivity. In rejecting constitutional decision making by other branches, judicial exclusivity does little to promote stability. It encourages acrimony, not cooperation. Instead of engaging the Court in a constitutional dialogue, democratic government will give short shrift to the Court and the Constitution. For its part, the Court will neither enlist democratic government's help nor look to public opinion as a measure of its legitimacy. No longer constrained by its responsibilities as educator (why educate if the public is not involved in constitutional discourse?), and certain of its status as final constitutional arbiter, the Court will see little value in calibrating its decisions against social and political forces.

Pragmatism and political judgment must balance legal theory. The argument that judicial exclusivity will have a stabilizing effect is unconvincing. To be stabilizing, court decisions must command respect and be generally acceptable and understandable. Judges must weigh the risks of noncompliance. There must be a dialogue. It is not enough for the Court to release rulings with the self-anointed claim that it speaks the final voice.

Rethinking the Last Word Debate

Judicial supremacy yields unworkable solutions, not a more equitable world. "Government by lawsuit," as Justice Robert Jackson warned, "leads to a final decision guided by the learning and limited by the understanding of a single profession—the law."[53] Alexander Bickel put the matter more directly by doubting the Court's capacity to develop "durable principles" and therefore doubting "that judicial supremacy can work and is tolerable."[54]

We list here ten basic qualifications of the "last word doctrine":

1. The fact that the Supreme Court upholds the constitutionality of a measure, as when it sustained the U.S. Bank in *McCulloch* or the independent counsel in *Morrison*, places no obligation on executive and legislative branches to adopt that legislation in the future. Congress, for example, was free at any time to discontinue the independent counsel statute (something it did in 1999). Likewise, President Jackson was well within his rights to veto legislation renewing the Bank. A decision by the Supreme Court did not relieve the other branches of their duty or freedom to reach independent interpretations. *McCulloch* and *Morrison* stood for the proposition that if the two branches wanted to create a U.S. Bank or an independent counsel, the Court saw nothing in the Constitution to stop them. If Congress and the President subsequently came to have constitutional doubts about the Bank or an independent counsel, it was within their power to repeal the statute or not extend the statutory authority about to expire.

2. A decision by the Supreme Court that a certain practice is not prohibited by the Constitution does not prevent the other branches from passing legislation to prohibit or restrict these practices. Rights unprotected by the courts may be secured by Congress, the President, and the states. President Jefferson's pardoning of individuals convicted under the Sedition Act; Congress's decisions to expand voting rights, speech, and religious

liberty protections; and state enactments extending religious liberty and disability rights protections are all examples of this phenomenon.

3. When the Supreme Court concludes that an action has no constitutional protection in the federal courts, the states are not inhibited in any way from protecting these actions by interpreting their own constitution. Decisions by the Court set a floor, or minimum, for constitutional rights. States may find the floor set too low and can add supplemental rights through independent interpretations of their own constitutions and unique cultures. State courts, for example, have interpreted their own constitutions to provide broader protections of abortion rights, gay rights, and religious liberty than Supreme Court interpretations of the U.S. Constitution.

4. Many constitutional issues are resolved through rules of evidence, statutes, customs, and accommodations—a common-law method of settling disputes. With these techniques, institutions outside the courts play a decisive role in shaping constitutional values and constitutional doctrines. And on several other occasions, the Court has looked to executive and legislative debate to inform decisions, "drawing their inspiration and authority from, but not required by, various constitutional provisions."[55]

5. The Supreme Court sometimes steers clear of constitutional questions by concluding that it has no jurisdiction to hear the case. On war powers and executive privilege disputes, for example, the Court typically invokes standing or political question limitations to avoid resolving conflicts between lawmakers and the executive. Also, by refusing to grant a writ of certiorari, the Court can duck important constitutional issues, sometimes forever.

6. There are occasions when Supreme Court rulings strike such a discordant note in the body politic that they will be tested again and again with new variations on the same theme. Court decisions are entitled to respect, not adoration. When the Court issues its judgment, we should not suspend ours. Witness, for example, the New Deal Congress's success in prevailing over judicial roadblocks on child labor, economic regulation, and other Commerce Clause matters. Likewise, public dissatisfaction with its initial ruling explains the Court's hasty retreat on the flag salute issue. *Planned Parenthood v. Casey*'s substitution of the "undue burden" test for the *Roe* trimester standard is another illustration of this phenomenon. Many other examples

could be cited. These challenges and collisions keep the constitutional dialogue open and vigorous. In the search for harmony between constitutional law and self-government, we must all participate.

7. It is unrealistic to expect the Court to "settle" an important issue at a single stroke. Typically, the Court tackles one slice at a time, leaving the rest for subsequent court decisions and nonjudicial actions. Justice Ginsburg has explained that adjudication often involves "a continuing dialogue" with other branches of government, the states, and the private sector.[56] For example, before declaring segregated schools unconstitutional, the Court issued several narrow rulings concerning segregation in universities and law schools. Likewise, before invalidating antimiscegenation laws, the Court waited for the *Brown* principle to be accepted by federal and (most) state officials.

8. The Court generally announces broad guidelines: "undue burden" for abortion; "compelling governmental interest," "narrowly tailored," "all deliberate speed" for desegregation; and "prurient" for obscene material. It is up to elected officials and juries to translate those general principles and rules and apply them to particular cases. The Court defines the edges; nonjudicial actors fill in the important middle.

9. In some cases, the Court does have finality, but the impact is tightly confined. When it decides that Florida election officials cannot recount so-called undervotes or that President Truman cannot seize the steel mills, that is the end of it. Yet those decisions depend on legal doctrines that may have to be implemented in future disputes. More significant, the ultimate meaning of Court decision making may well hinge on the willingness of elected officials to abide by the Court's decision. Consider, for example, Chief Justice Rehnquist's decision to turn down a White House effort to prevent the Office of Independent Counsel from questioning Secret Service agents about Monica Lewinsky's visits to President Clinton. Finality occurred here, but Congress may reopen the issue by enacting legislation that gives Secret Service agents greater privilege not to testify about presidential activities. Also, elected officials may treat the Court's order as binding only on the parties to the dispute. Thus, *INS v. Chadha* (legislative veto) settled only the issue of Chadha's deportation; Congress and the White House have found the decision impractical and have ignored it in many respects.

10. Judicial decisions are not pure creative acts. They build on precedents and values established by nonjudicial actors. Long before the Court decided *Miranda* the FBI gave warnings to the accused. Long before *Gideon v. Wainwright* many states had decided that due process required that attorneys be appointed by the court to represent indigent defendants. The Court regularly looks to state practices when sorting out whether physician-assisted suicide, homosexual sodomy, and much more is protected by the right to privacy. Beyond instances in which courts look to elected officials to establish constitutional standards, the Court often moderates its decision making to take into account elected government preferences.

Judicial review fits our constitutional system because we like to fragment power. We feel safer with checks and balances, even when an unelected Court tells an elected legislature or elected President that they have overstepped. This very preference for fragmented power denies the Supreme Court an authoritative and final voice for deciding constitutional questions. We do not accept the concentration of legislative power in Congress or executive power in the President. For the same reason, we cannot permit judicial power and constitutional interpretation to reside only in the courts. We reject supremacy in all three branches because of the value placed on freedom, discourse, democracy, and limited government.

Taking the Constitution Away from the Courts

Throughout this book, we have called attention to the critical role that nonjudicial actors play in shaping constitutional values. In this chapter, we have also shown that populist disagreement with the Court makes the Constitution more stable and more enduring. The question remains: What value does judicial review serve? For some scholars, interest groups ought not to pursue court-ordered reform because judicial review is either inconsequential or counterproductive.[57] There is some appeal to these arguments, although we disagree with them.

To start with, there is reason to doubt the efficacy of judicial review. Its effectiveness is often hinged on elected government's willingness to implement court edicts. For example, the legislative veto decision was widely ignored and hence largely inconsequential; in contrast, Congress and the White House made school desegregation a reality through mid-1960s reforms.[58] Furthermore, inherent limits in judicial factfinding suggest that courts are apt to be poorly informed and mistaken in their judgments. Specifically, with judges and advocates relying on precedent-based legal arguments, courts simply cannot engage in thorough cost-benefit analysis. Courts are also hamstrung in that they decide cases at a moment in time, so that a changed understanding of the underlying facts can be corrected only through a reversal. Moreover, the Court often relies on the arguments made by the parties before it, and the parties before it frequently frame the issues that the Court will consider.

Perhaps more troubling, judicial review sometimes distorts elected branch consideration of constitutional questions. In some cases, judicial review encourages policymakers to delegate constitutional issues to the court instead of struggling over possible constitutional infirmities in their handiwork. Expedited Supreme Court review provisions are an example of this phenomenon. Also, when lawmakers talk about the Constitution, they frequently mimic the Supreme Court. In particular, rather than develop their own distinctive interpretive methodologies, lawmakers sometimes focus their energies on whether the Court will uphold their actions.

Nevertheless, we think that judicial review is necessary, not counter-productive. Courts sometimes get out in front of an issue and, in so doing, set in motion a constructive interbranch dynamic that otherwise wouldn't take place. Southern resistance to *Brown v. Board of Education*, for example, eventually prompted Congress to place nondiscrimination requirements on the distribution of federal funds. Likewise, the pro-choice movement looked to judicial remedies. In particular, although the abortion reform movement predates *Roe*, the legislative battles leading up to *Roe* suggest that state lawmaker resistance to fundamental abortion rights was quite entrenched—so much so that most pro-choice activists did not even seek repeal of criminal abortion statutes.

Just as courts have institutional weaknesses, they have institutional strengths. For example, because courts must offer justifications for their decisions, judges are especially interested in making reasoned arguments. Judges can also play an important role in sorting out the complex social policy issues endemic to constitutional decision making. Judges and politicians, by sometimes reacting differently to social and political forces, each have a unique perspective on constitutional controversies. Because special interest group pressures affect courts and elected officials in different ways, a full-ranging consideration of the costs and benefits of different policy outcomes is best accomplished by a governmentwide decision-making process. For this reason, courts as well as elected officials should be activists in shaping constitutional values.

There is another reason that courts should participate in constitutional dialogues. In particular, even when the principles that courts identify are wrongheaded, their efforts at being "a voice of reason . . . articulating and developing impersonal and durable principles"[59] can be salutary. By sometimes invoking high-sounding principles when striking down elected government action, courts are well positioned to validate governmental decision making. Charles L. Black Jr. has explained the way this works: "What a government of limited power needs, at the beginning and forever, is some means of satisfying the people that it has taken all steps humanly possible to stay within its powers. . . . The Court, through its history, has acted as a legitimator of government."[60] By speaking about right and wrong, judges can perform their most important task: affirming and legitimating the actions of elected government.

Shaping Constitutional Values

Complex social policy issues are ill suited to the winner-take-all nature of litigation. As our case studies have shown, hydraulic pressures within the political system make the Constitution more enduring and stable.[61] In particular, absolutist and often rigid judicial pronouncements accomplish very little; instead, emotionally charged and highly divisive issues are best resolved through political compromises that yield middle-ground solutions. Consider, for example, abortion and school desegregation. Here, courts and elected officials influenced each other, resulting in a constitutional standard that successfully (if not perfectly) balanced competing interests.

On abortion rights, *Roe v. Wade* served both as a critical trigger to judicial recognition of abortion rights and a rallying call to pro-life interests. From 1973 to 1989, 306 abortion-restricting measures were passed by forty-eight states. Likewise, abortion played a prominent, if not decisive, role in Supreme Court appointments. In 1992, after decades of elected government resistance and the appointment of new Supreme Court Justices, the Court carved out a middle-ground approach: reaffirming abortion rights but rejecting *Roe*'s stringent trimester test. This decision, *Planned Parenthood v. Casey*, did not trigger an antiabortion revolution. Although the Court signaled its increased willingness to uphold abortion regulations, state lawmakers (fearing a backlash from pro-choice voters) have typically steered clear of the abortion issue. In particular, with the exception of partial-birth abortion, abortion-restricting regulations adopted since *Casey* typically involve restrictions approved by the Court: waiting periods, informed consent, and parental notification.

To a pro-choice advocate, *Casey*'s balance sells out important interests of women. To a pro-lifer, it permits moral outrages to continue. But there is no realistic alternative to the Court's balancing of pro-life and pro-choice interests. The political upheaval that followed *Roe* reveals the unworkability of a strident pro-choice jurisprudence. But a jurisprudence allowing the prohibition of abortions is equally unworkable. In the years before *Roe*, when nontheraputic abortions were prohibited in nearly every state, abortion rates were nearly identical to rates in the years following the *Roe* decision. Ultimately, abortion is too divisive for either pro-choice or pro-life absolutism to rule the day. Absent the dialogue that followed *Roe*, however, the politically unworkable trimester standard would have remained in place.

Supreme Court efforts to end racial segregation in education likewise exemplify the reaches and limits of the judiciary's ability to transform society. Although *Brown v. Board of Education* proved critical to the eradication of dual school systems in Southern states, the Supreme Court allowed its perception of elected government preferences to shape its decision making in this area. For example, in an effort to temper Southern hostility to its decision, the Court did not issue a remedy in the first *Brown* decision.

Social and political forces, especially federal government efforts to enforce *Brown* during the 1960s, also figured prominently in the Supreme Court's approval of mandatory busing remedies in *Swann v. Charlotte-Mecklenburg Board of Education*. *Swann*, however, went well beyond elected government preferences. During the Nixon and Reagan administrations, the Court and elected government fought a pitched battle over busing—a battle that has now abated. Specifically, by allowing district court judges to take local conditions into account in deciding whether a school system has satisfied its desegregation obligations, the Court has returned the desegregation issue to local judges—many but not all of whom have terminated long-standing desegregation injunctions.

Attaining an equilibrium with regard to school desegregation and abortion required all branches and all levels of government to do battle with one another. This dynamic process yielded a very nuanced, very delicate compromise. That this interactive process may too closely resemble the making of sausage helps to explain Barbara Craig and David O'Brien's characterization of the abortion dispute as an "illustrative . . . [and] disappointing reflection" of the American system.[62] Nevertheless, as Justice Ginsburg rightly observed at her confirmation hearing, our system is one in which courts "do not guard constitutional rights alone. Courts share that profound responsibility with Congress, the president, the states, and the people."[63]

That courts sometimes initiate these constitutional dialogues is indisputable. Without *Brown* or *Roe*, equal educational opportunity and abortion rights would mean very different things today. But it is equally indisputable that workable approaches to school desegregation and abortion rights required elected government participation, sometimes supporting and at other times opposing Court action.

Brown and *Roe* are revealing for other reasons. The *Brown* Court pursued radical social change while taking into account inherent limits in its authority. *Roe*, in contrast, is a case study in judicial hubris. In an effort to end the abortion dispute, Justice Harry Blackmun put forth a trimester test intended to limit future governmental efforts to sidestep the decision. As a result, the political upheaval that followed *Roe* was especially nasty and disruptive. Had the Court issued a less ambitious decision in *Roe*, it is possible that the ensuing constitutional dialogue would have been more civil and more constructive. For example, a decision limited to the issue at stake in *Roe* (that a rape victim could not obtain an abortion) would have held open the possibility that the Court might approve other types of abortion restrictions. As such, pro-life interests would not have seen the overruling of *Roe* as the only way to advance their agenda; for their part, pro-choice interests would have looked to lawmakers as well as judges (instead of looking only to courts to advance their agenda). Although pro-choice and pro-life interests might not have reached a political accommodation with each other, it is hard to imagine that this process would not have worked as well as the *Roe*-driven constitutional dialogue.

The lesson here is simple: Courts do not resolve contentious social questions once and for all in a single decision. Rather, Court decision making ought to leave room for democratic deliberation, including populist resistance. Complex social policy issues, especially those that implicate constitutional values, are best resolved through "the sweaty intimacy of creatures locked in combat."[64] No doubt, this politicization of constitutional discourse will contribute to partisan, value-laden constitutional analysis. Any other process, however, will not allow for the give and take needed to make the Constitution relevant to all parts of government and the people as well. Likewise, any other process will likely yield solutions that are unacceptable to the people, their representatives, or the Court. For this reason, courts, elected officials, and the people should be activist in shaping government policy, including the interpretation of the Constitution.

Conclusion: Continuing Colloquies

The belief in judicial supremacy imposes a burden that the Court cannot carry. It sets up expectations that invite disappointment, if not disaster. The Supreme Court is (and should remain) a critical player in shaping popular attitudes toward constitutional questions, but constitutional decision making is not well served by making challenges to Court decision making "difficult," if not "futile."[65] As this book urges, courts cannot be separated from the social and political influences that permeate all aspects of constitutional decision making. Perhaps more fundamental, we think that the dialogue that takes place among the Court, elected government, and the American people is as constructive as it is inevitable. Because each part of government has unique strengths and weaknesses, constitutional interpretation is improved by broad and vigorous participation. Furthermore, the Constitution is made more vibrant and more stable by these constitutional dialogues—because the courts, elected officials, and the people all see themselves as stakeholders.

We reach these conclusions for institutional reasons, not for political, partisan, or policy ends. Some scholars share our views, but do so because the Court has become too conservative for their tastes. They therefore advocate a more active role by the elected branches, believing that the results will be better. If the Court changed and looked more like the Warren Court, they would switch allegiance and back the judiciary. Our position is independent of the Court's makeup and predilections. The views we advance apply to current conditions and to every decade, and century, before it.

Political realities and constitutional values require the judiciary to share with other political institutions and society at large the complex task of interpreting the Constitution. Constitutions do not govern by text alone or solely by judicial interpretation. They draw their life from forces outside the courts: from ideas, customs, society, and statutes. Through this rich and dynamic political process, the Constitution is regularly adapted to seek a harmony between legal principles and the needs of a changing society. Bickel described the courts as engaged in a "continuing colloquy" with political institutions and society at large, a process in which constitutional principle is "evolved conversationally not perfected unilaterally."[66]

The chief alternative to judicial exclusivity is not "interpretive anarchy,"[67] with each public official at every level of government making independent judgments about the Constitution. The main purpose of the Constitution was not to vest a final interpretive authority in a single branch. The overriding value of the framers was a system of checks and balances that is antithetical to vesting in any branch a monopoly on constitutional values. The result, from the start, was "coordinate construction," with each branch capable of making independent constitutional interpretations and willing to do so. That system has endured for more than two centuries without deteriorating into interpretive anarchy.

No single institution, including the judiciary, has the final word on constitutional questions. The Court is a key player, but it is not the only game in town. It is this process of give and take and the mutual respect the branches have for one another that permits the unelected Court to function in a democratic society. By agreeing to an open exchange among the branches, all three institutions are able to expose weaknesses, hold excesses in check, and gradually forge a consensus on constitutional values. By participating in this process, the public has an opportunity to add legitimacy, vitality, and meaning to what might otherwise be an alien and short-lived document. Therein lies true stability. Therein lies respect for and understanding of the Constitution.

Notes

Preface

1. *See, e.g.*, Gerald N. Rosenberg, The Hollow Hope (1991) (suggesting that courts have not played a significant role in defining race, abortion, etc.); Cass R. Sunstein, One Case at a Time (1999) (defending judicial minimalism).

2. See Bruce Ackerman, We the People: Foundations (1991); Mark Tushnet, Taking the Constitution Away from the Courts (1999).

3. For recent defenses of vigorous judicial review (that tie into themes explored in this volume), *see* Terri Jennings Peretti, In Defense of a Political Court (1999) (defending politically motivated constitutional decision making); Louis Michael Seidman, Our Unsettled Constitution (2001) (judicial review encourages all those who participate in the political process to bargain with each other); Christopher Eisgruber, Constitutional Self Government (2001) (highlighting ways that courts educate other parts of government and the people).

4. Books that focus on subject areas include Michael Kent Curtis, Free Speech: The People's Darling Privilege (2000); Lee Epstein & Joseph F. Kobylka, The Supreme Court and Legal Change: Abortion and the Death Penalty (1992); Michael J. Glennon, Constitutional Diplomacy (1990); Barbara Hickson Craig & David M. O'Brien, Abortion and American Politics (1993). Books that focus on historical periods include Wayne D. Moore, Constitutional Rights and Powers of the People (1996); Keith E. Whittington, Constitutional Construction: Divided Power and Constitutional Meaning (1999). For an extended historical argument, *see* Robert G. McCloskey The American Supreme Court (revised by Sanford Levinson, 2d ed. 1994) (calling attention to how the Court preserves its status in government by issuing decisions that match social norms).

5. *See, e.g.*, Robert A. Burt, The Constitution in Conflict (1992) (defending three-branch interpretation as consistent with democratic theory); Robert F. Nagel, Constitutional Cultures: The Mentality and Consequences of Judicial Review (1989) (arguing that the political Constitution is superior to the legal Constitution and therefore cautioning against excessive reliance on judicial review); Stephen M. Griffin, American Constitutionalism (1996) (arguing that theories of constitutional interpretation must take political institutions into account); Sanford Levinson, Constitutional Faith (1988) (looking, among other things, to Protestant-Catholic disputes to examine who should interpret the Constitution).

6. Some constitutional law casebooks include a significant number of concrete examples. These include Paul Brest et al., *Processes of Constitutional Decisionmaking* (4th ed. 2000); Louis Fisher, *American Constitutional Law* (5th ed. 2003); James C. Foster & Susan M. Leeson, *Constitutional Law: Cases in Context* (2d ed. 1998); and Walter F. Murphy et al., *American Constitutional Interpretation* (2d ed. 1995).

Introduction

1. Ruth Marcus, *Constitution Confuses Most Americans; Public Ill-Informed on U.S. Blueprint*, Washington Post, Feb. 15, 1987, at A13.
2. Edwin J. Meese, *The Law of the Constitution*, 61 Tul. L. Rev. 979, 983 (1987). This episode is recounted in chapter 1.
3. Louis Fisher, Constitutional Dialogues: Interpretation as Political Process (1988); Neal Devins, *The Constitution between Friends*, 67 Tex. L. Rev. 213 (1988).
4. Chapter 7 examines *Brown* and its aftermath.
5. The *Steel Seizure* case is considered in chapter 5.
6. Chapter 3 examines public accommodations legislation.
7. Chapter 7 details this episode.
8. *Garcia* and its aftermath are discussed in chapter 3.
9. This story is detailed in chapter 4.
10. For additional discussion, see chapter 7.
11. Chapter 3 details the court-packing controversy.
12. Chapter 9 examines this controversy.
13. For additional discussion, *see* chapters 6 (abortion) and 7 (school desegregation). Chapter 6 also explains how elected branch disapproval of *Roe* contributed to Court rulings on homosexual sodomy and physician-assisted suicide.
14. This episode is discussed in chapter 3.
15. For additional discussion, *see* chapters 3 (sovereign immunity), 4 (independent counsel), 6 (sodomy), 7 (voting rights), 8 (freedom of press and fairness doctrine), and 9 (religious liberty).
16. Impeachment and executive privilege are considered in chapter 4; war power is considered in chapter 5.
17. Examples include abortion (chapter 6), gay rights (chapter 6), and religious schooling (chapter 9).
18. Learned Hand, *The Spirit of Liberty*, *in* The Spirit of Liberty 189, 190 (3d ed. 1960).

Chapter 1

1. For an inventory of these challenges, *see* our preface.
2. W. Michael Reisman, *International Incidents: Introduction to a New Genre in the Study of International Law*, 10 Yale J. Int'l L. 1, 8 n.13 (1984).

3. Brown v. Allen, 344 U.S. 443, 540 (1953) (Jackson, J., concurring).

4. Welsh v. United States, 398 U.S. 333, 370 (1970) (White, J., dissenting).

5. Addresses and Papers of Charles Evans Hughes 139 (1908).

6. *Id.* at 141–42. *See also* Hughes's later reflection on his Elmira address; The Autobiographical Notes of Charles Evans Hughes 143–44 (David J. Danelski & Joseph S. Tulchin eds., 1973).

7. Robert H. Bork, The Tempting of America: The Political Seduction of the Law 3 (1990).

8. Ronald Dworkin, Law's Empire 356 (1986).

9. 143 Cong. Rec. S12024 (daily ed. Nov. 7, 1997).

10. For a general treatment of this topic, emphasizing that lawmakers sometimes support judicial invalidation of unpopular laws, *see* Mark A. Graber, *The Nonmajoritarian Difficulty: Legislative Deference to the Judiciary*, 7 Studies in American Political Development 35 (1993).

11. The Gramm-Rudman-Hollings Act of 1985, the Flag Protection Act of 1989, the Line Item Veto Act of 1996, and the Communications Decency Act of 1996.

12. 5 A Compilation of the Messages and Papers of the Presidents 431 (James D. Richardson ed., 1897).

13. Public Papers of the Presidents, 1957, at 690.

14. *See* Gerald M. Boyd, *Goals for Hiring to Stay in Place*, N.Y. Times, Aug. 25, 1986, at A1 (discussing Reagan-era affirmative action initiatives).

15. Joan Biskupic, *The Shrinking Docket*, Washington Post, Mar. 18, 1996, at A15.

16. Joan Biskupic, *In June, Rulings Move with Supreme Speed*, Washington Post, May 26, 1998, at A15 (emphasis in original).

17. Marbury v. Madison, 5 U.S. (1 Cranch) 137, 177 (1803).

18. 10 The Works of James Buchanan 106 (John Bassett Moore ed.,1910).

19. Cooper v. Aaron, 358 U.S. 1, 18 (1958).

20. Baker v. Carr, 369 U.S. 186, 211 (1962); Powell v. McCormack, 395 U.S. 486, 521 (1969).

21. Planned Parenthood of Southeastern Pennsylvania v. Casey, 505 U.S. 833, 866 (1992).

22. City of Boerne v. Flores, 521 U.S. 507, 535–36 (1997).

23. Planned Parenthood of Southeastern Pennsylvania v. Casey, 505 U.S. 833, 869, 867 (1992).

24. 2 The Records of the Federal Convention 46, 132–33, 146, 172, 186 (M. Farrand, ed. 1937) [hereinafter Farrand].

25. *Id.* at 430.

26. *Id.*

27. 3 The Debates in the Several State Conventions on the Adoption of the Federal Constitution 532 (J. Elliot ed. 1836) [hereinafter Elliot]. *See* statement by Madison on June 20, 1788); The Federalist No. 80, at 503 (B. Wright ed., 1961).

28. 2 Farrand 27.

29. *Id.* at 92. *See also* comment by Madison at 93. For further details on the framers' intent about judicial review, *see* Louis Fisher, *The Curious Belief in Judiciary Supremacy*, 25 Suffolk U. L. Rev. 85, 87–92 (1991).

30. 5 The Writings of James Madison 294 (Gaillard Hunt ed., 1904).

31. 1 Stat. 143–45, ch. 11 (1792); 1 Stat. 324–25, ch. 17 (1793); Hayburn's Case, 2 U.S. (2 Dall.) 409 (1792).

32. Hylton v. United States, 3 U.S. (3 Dall.) 171 (1796).

33. *Id.* at 175 (emphasis in original).

34. Hollingsworth v. Virginia, 3 U.S. (3 Dall.) 378 (1798).

35. Calder v. Bull, 3 U.S. (3 Dall.) 386, 399 (1798).

36. Cooper v. Telfair, 4 U.S. (4 Dall.) 14, 19 (1800).

37. 5 U.S. (1 Cranch) 137, 177 (1803).

38. Warren E. Burger, *The Doctrine of Judicial Review: Mr. Marshall, Mr. Jefferson, and Mr. Marbury, in* Views from the Bench 14 (Mark W. Cannon & David M. O'Brien ed., 1985).

39. 3 Albert J. Beveridge, The Life of John Marshall 177 (1919). Marshall dated the letter January 23, 1804. From the context, scholars now conclude that he misdated the note; it should have been a year later. 6 The Papers of John Marshall 348 n.1 (Charles F. Hobson ed., 1990). *See also* David E. Engdahl, *John Marshall's "Jeffersonian" Concept of Judicial Review*, 42 Duke L. J. 279 (1992).

40. Walter F. Murphy, *Why Marbury Matters*, 1 Constitution 62, 68 (1989). For a close analysis of *Marbury*, concluding that it did not vest in the Court the final authority to interpret the Constitution, *see* Robert Clinton, *Marbury v. Madison* and Judicial Review (1989).

41. William G. Andrews, Coordinate Magistrates: Constitutional Law by Congress and the President 1–20 (judicial review), 21–43 (Bank), 44–64 (slavery), 65–95 (interstate commerce), 109–30 (removal power), 131–44 (war powers) (1969). For early debate on internal improvements, *see* A Documentary History of American Economic Policy since 1789 53–84 (William Letwin ed., 1961). *See also* James Hart, The American Presidency in Action 78–111 (treaties and foreign relations), 152–248 (removal power) (1948); Charles Miller, The Supreme Court and the Uses of History 52–70, 205–10 (removal power) (1969); Donald G. Morgan, Congress and the Constitution 49–57 (removal power), 101–18 (investigative power), 140–59 (interstate commerce) (1966); Abraham D. Sofaer, War, Foreign Affairs and Constitutional Power (1976) (discussing constitutional deliberations by Congress from 1789 to 1829).

42. David P. Currie, The Constitution in Congress 296 (1997).

43. 1 Annals of Congress 500 (Joseph Gales ed., 1834).

44. Letter from Thomas Jefferson to Mrs. John Adams (July 22, 1804), *in* 11 The Writings of Thomas Jefferson 42, 43 (Andrew A. Lipscomb ed., 1905). For a detailed treatment of this episode, *see* chapter 8.

45. 3 A Compilation of the Messages and Papers of the Presidents 1145 (James D. Richardson ed., 1897). For a detailed discussion of the politics surrounding *McCulloch* and its aftermath, *see* chapter 3 and Paul Brest et al., Processes of Constitutional Decisionmaking 1–59 (4th ed. 2000).

46. S. Rept. No. 711, 75th Cong., 1st Sess. 20 (1937).

47. Dred Scott v. Sandford, 60 U.S. 383, 451 (1856).

48. Charles Warren, Congress, the Constitution, and the Supreme Court 135 (1925).

49. 2 Collected Works of Abraham Lincoln 516 (Roy Basler ed., 1953).

50. 6 A Compilation of the Messages and Papers of the Presidents 9 (James D. Richardson ed., 1897).

51. 10 Op. Att'y Gen. 382. Bates said that what Chief Justice Taney had said about citizenship was pure dictum and "of no authority as a judicial decision." *Id.* at 412.

52. 12 Stat. 432, c. 111 (1862).

53. Baker v. Carr, 369 U.S. 186, 217 (1962).

54. Louis Fisher, Constitutional Dialogues 103 (1988).

55. Alexander M. Bickel, *The Passive Virtues*, 75 Harv. L. Rev. 40, 49 (1961).

56. Gerald Gunther, *The Subtle Vices of the "Passive Virtues"—A Comment on Principle and Expediency in Judicial Review*, 64 Colum. L. Rev. 1, 25 (1964).

57. Oliver Wendell Holmes, The Common Law 36 (1963 ed.).

58. The White House: Organization and Operations 94 (R. Gordon Hoxie ed., 1971).

59. Brown v. Board of Education, 347 U.S. 483 (1954); Brown v. Board of Education, 349 U.S. 294 (1955). Chapter 6 details the history of Southern resistance to *Brown.*

60. INS v. Chadha, 462 U.S. 919 (1983). For further discussion, *see* chapter 4.

61. David Adamany & Joel B. Grossman, *Support for the Supreme Court as a National Policymaker*, 5 Law & Policy Qtly. 405, 407 (1983) (citing studies).

62. Linda Greenhouse, *Telling the Court's Story: Justice and Journalism at the Supreme Court*, 105 Yale L. J. 1537, 1542–43 (1996).

63. Witness, for example, Justice Stephen Breyer's attempt to recast Justice Sandra Day O'Connor's concurrence in the 1997 physician-assisted suicide decision: "I believe that Justice O'Connor's views, which I share, have greater legal significance than the Court's opinion suggests. I join her separate opinion, except insofar as it joins the majority." Washington v. Glucksberg, 521 U.S. 702, 789 (1997).

64. Ruth Bader Ginsburg, *Communicating and Commenting on the Court's Work*, 83 Geo. L. J. 2119, 2128 (1995).

65. Jack W. Peltason, Federal Courts in the Political Process 14 (1955).

66. Sotirios A. Barber, On What the Constitution Means 3 (1984); Tom Goldstein, *In Rare Attack, Justice Marshall Says Court Erred*, N.Y. Times, May 28, 1979, at A1, A11.

67. Oregon v. Elstad, 470 U.S. 298, 320 (1985) (dissenting opinion).

68. *Id.* at 346.

69. United States v. Butler, 297 U.S. 1, 79 (1936).

70. *See* Stuart S. Nagel, *Court-Curbing Periods in American History*, 18 Vand. L. Rev. 925 (1965). For a review of proposals to remedy judicial activism, *see* Charles Grove Haines, The American Doctrine of Judicial Supremacy 467–99 (1932).

71. Richard Funston, *The Supreme Court and Critical Elections*, 69 Am. Pol. Sci. Rev. 795 (1975); David Adamany, *Legitimacy, Realigning Elections, and the Supreme Court*, 1973 Wisc. L. Rev. 790 (1973).

72. The Federalist No. 78, at 465 (B. Wright ed. 1961).

73. Walter F. Murphy & Joseph Tannenhaus, *Publicity, Public Opinion, and the Court*, 84 Nw. U. L. Rev. 985, 992 (1990).

74. Cong. Globe, 38th Cong., 1st Sess. 1480 (1864).

75. *Id.* at 1482.

76. The Eleventh Amendment (prohibiting suits against a state by "Citizens of Another State"), the Sixteenth Amendment (approving a federal income tax), and the Twenty-sixth Amendment (granting eighteen-year-olds the right to vote in both federal and state elections).

77. Jane Mansbridge, Why We Lost the ERA 13 (1986). *See also* David A. Strauss, *The Irrelevance of Constitutional Amendments*, 114 Harv. L. Rev. 1457, 1476–78 (2001) (pointing to ERA in arguing that constitutional amendments have not been an important way to change the Constitution's meaning).

78. The newspaper case is discussed in chapter 8. The yarmulke case is discussed in chapter 9. Another, more controversial example of this phenomenon involves congressional invocations of its authority under Section 5 of the Fourteenth Amendment. Examples of this practice include voting rights legislation (discussed in chapter 7) and the Religious Freedom Restoration Act (discussed in chapter 9).

79. John R. Schmidhauser & Larry L. Berg, The Supreme Court and Congress at 141–42 (1972).

80. For an assessment of the 1979–1987 period, *see* William N. Eskridge Jr., *Overriding Supreme Court Statutory Interpretation Decisions*, 101 Yale L. J. 331 (1991).

81. S. Rept. No. 711, 75th Cong., 1st Sess. 14 (1937). For additional discussion of FDR's court-packing plan, *see* chapter 3.

82. *Limitation of Appellate Jurisdiction of the United States Supreme Court: Hearings on S. 2646 before the Subcommittee to Investigate the Administration of the Internal Security Act and Other Internal Security Laws of the Senate Committee on the Judiciary*, 85th Cong., 1st Sess. 22 (1957).

83. *Limitation of Appellate Jurisdiction of the United States Supreme Court (Part 2): Hearings on S. 2646 before the Subcommittee to Investigate the Administration of the Internal Security Act and Other Internal Security Laws of the Senate Committee on the Judiciary*, 85th Cong., 2nd Sess. 574 (1958).

84. Abram Chayes, *Public Law Litigation and the Burger Court*, 96 Harv. L. Rev. 4, 4 (1982).

85. *Nomination of Edwin Meese III: Hearing before the Senate Committee on the Judiciary*, 98th Cong., 2d Sess. 185–86 (1984).

86. Edwin Meese, *The Law of the Constitution*, 61 Tul. L. Rev. 981, 982 (1987).

87. *Id.* at 985–86.

88. *Id.* at 983.

89. James Vicini, *Meese Scoured for Saying High Court Rulings Not Law of Land*, N.Y. Times, Oct. 24, 1986, at A17.

90. *Id.*

91. *Id. See also Mr. Meese's Contempt of Court*, N.Y. Times, Oct. 26, 1986, at

E22; Anthony Lewis, *Law or Power?*, N.Y. Times, Oct. 27, 1986, at A23; *and* Michael Kinsley, *Meese's Stink Bomb*, Washington Post, Oct. 29, 1986, at A19.

92. The Washington Post, Oct. 29, 1986, at A18.

93. *Nomination of Justice William Hubbs Rehnquist: Hearing before the Senate Committee on the Judiciary*, 99th Cong., 2d sess. 187 (1986).

94. William H. Rehnquist, Grand Inquests: The Historic Impeachments of Justice Samuel Chase and President Andrew Johnson 278 (1992).

95. *Nomination of Anthony M. Kennedy: Hearing before the Senate Committee on the Judiciary*, 100th Cong., 1st sess. 222–23 (1987).

96. Ruth Bader Ginsburg, *Speaking in a Judicial Voice*, 67 N.Y.U. L. Rev. 1185, 1198 (1992).

97. S. Exec. Rept. 103–6 (Part 2), 103d Cong., 1st Sess. (1993).

98. Lamb's Chapel v. Center Moriches Union Free School Dist., 508 U.S. 384, 398–99 (Scalia, J., concurring in the judgment).

99. *Id.*

Chapter 2

1. Benjamin N. Cardozo, The Nature of the Judicial Process 168 (1921).

2. South Carolina v. United States, 199 U.S. 437, 448 (1905).

3. Max Lerner, *Constitution and Court as Symbols*, 46 Yale L. J. 1290 (1937).

4. Morris R. Cohen, Law and the Social Order 380–81 n.86 (1933).

5. Lord Radcliffe, The Law & Its Compass 92–93 (1960).

6. James G. Wilson, *The Role of Public Opinion in Constitutional Interpretation*, 1993 B.Y.U. L. Rev. 1037. The examples that follow are drawn from Wilson.

7. The Federalist No. 84 at 535 (Benjamin Fletcher Wright ed., 1961).

8. The Federalist No. 46 at 330.

9. People v. Anderson, 493 P.2d 880 (Cal. 1972), cert. denied, 406 U.S. 958 (1972); Cal. Const., Art. I, § 27.

10. Furman v. Georgia, 408 U.S. 238 (1972).

11. *Id.* at 329 n.37 (Marshall, J., concurring). In *Woodson v. North Carolina*, a plurality of the Court likewise referred to "public sentiment." 428 U.S. 280, 293 n.27 (1976).

12. Gregg v. Georgia, 428 U.S. 153 (1976).

13. *See* Stuart Banner, *The Changing Debate over the Death Penalty*, N.Y. Times, June 22, 2002 at A27.

14. Atkins v. Virginia, 536 U.S. 304 2002 (2002); Ring v. Arizona, 536 U.S. 584 (2002).

15. Atkins, 536 U.S. at 316. In so ruling, the Court overturned Penry v. Lynaugh, 492 U.S. 302 (1989).

16. Robert A. Dahl, *Decision-making in a Democracy: The Supreme Court as a National Policy-maker*, 6 J. Pub. L. 279 (1957); David Adamany, *Legitimacy, Realigning Elections, and the Supreme Court*, 1973 Wisc. L. Rev. 790 (1973); Richard Funston, *The Supreme Court and Critical Elections*, 69 Am. Pol. Sci. Rev. 795

(1975). *See also* Jonathan D. Casper, *The Supreme Court and National Policy Making*, 70 Am. Pol. Sci. Rev. 50 (1973); William Mishler & Reginald S. Sheehan, *The Supreme Court as a Countermajoritarian Institution? The Impact of Public Opinion on Supreme Court Decisions*, 87 Am. Pol. Sci. Rev. 87 (1993).

17. Alexis de Tocqueville, 1 Democracy in America 151–52 (Phillip Bradley ed., 1951).

18. William Howard Taft, *Criticisms of the Federal Judiciary*, 29 Am. L. Rev. 641, 642 (1895).

19. *Id.* at 643.

20. William M. Wiecek, The Sources of Antislavery Constitutionalism in America, 1760–1848 (1977).

21. Howard M. Hyman, A More Perfect Union: The Impact of the Civil War and Reconstruction on the Constitution 6 (1975).

22. Herbert M. Kritzer, *Federal Judges and Their Political Environment*, 23 Am. J. Pol Sci. 194 (1979); Herbert M. Kritzer, *Political Correlates of the Behavior of Federal District Judges: A "Best Case" Analysis*, 40 J. Pol. 25 (1977); Gerald L. Clore, *Judicial Activity and Public Attitude: A Quantitative Study of Selective Service Sentencing in the Vietnam War Period*, 23 Buff. L. Rev. 465 (1974).

23. 35 F.R.D. 398 (1964).

24. Alpheus T. Mason, Harlan Fiske Stone: Pillar of the Law 614–15 (1968).

25. William H. Rehnquist, *Constitutional Law and Public Opinion*, 20 Suffolk U. L. Rev. 751, 768 (1986).

26. *Id.* at 768–69.

27. Rogers v. Bellei, 401 U.S. 815, 837 (1971).

28. Robert H. Jackson, *Maintaining Our Freedoms: The Role of the Judiciary*, Vital Speeches, No. 24, Vol. XIX, Oct. 1, 1951, at 761.

29. Charles L. Black Jr., The People and the Court 52 (1960) (emphasis in original).

30. Thurgood Marshall, *Group Action in the Pursuit of Justice*, 44 N.Y.U. L. Rev. 661, 662 (1969).

31. 2 Notable American Women, 1607–1950, at 414 (1971); 20 Stat. 292 (1879).

32. For typical court rulings, denying women the right to practice law, *see In re* Bradwell, 55 Ill. 535 (1869); Bradwell v. State, 83 U.S. (16 Wall.) 130 (1873); *In re* Goodell, 39 Wis. 232 (1875).

33. 8 Cong. Rec. 1084 (1879).

34. Clement E. Vose, *National Consumers League and the Brandeis Brief*, 1 Midwest J. Pol. Sci. 267, 277 (1957).

35. Clement E. Vose, *Litigation as a Form of Pressure Group Activity*, 319 The Annals 20 (1958).

36. Alfred Kelly, *The School Desegregation Case*, *in* Quarrels That Have Shaped the Constitution 307 (John A. Garraty ed., 1964).

37. *See* Peter Irons, The Courage of their Convictions 396 (1990). For additional discussion of this case, *Bowers v. Hardwick, see* chapter 6.

38. *See* William B. Rubenstein, *Divided We Litigate: Addressing Disputes among*

Group Members and Lawyers in Civil Rights Campaigns, 106 Yale L. J. 1623, 1639–44 (1997).

39. 103 Cong. Rec. 16160 (1957).

40. *Id.* at 16167 (statement by Prof. Louis B. Schwartz).

41. Chester A. Newland, *The Supreme Court and Legal Writing: Learned Journals as Vehicles of an Anti-Antitrust Lobby*, 48 Geo. L. J. 105, 140 (1959). *See also* Chester A. Newland, *Legal Periodicals and the United States Supreme Court*, 3 Midwest J. Pol. Sci. 58 (1959).

42. Samuel Krislov, *The Amicus Curiae Brief: From Friendship to Advocacy*, 72 Yale L. J. 694, 695 (1963).

43. Lucius J. Barker, *Third Parties in Litigation: A Systemic View of the Judicial Function*, 29 J. Pol. 41, 62 (1967).

44. Krislov, *The Amicus Curiae Brief*, at 704.

45. Lee Epstein, *Interest Group Litigation during the Rehnquist Court Era*, 9 J. Law & Pol. 639, 645 (1993).

46. *Id.* (discussing 1990 Supreme Court term).

47. *See id.* at 651. *See also* Lee Epstein & C. K. Rowland, *Interest Groups in the Courts: Do Groups Fare Better?*, in Allan J. Cigler and Burdett A. Loomis, Interest Group Politics 275 (2d ed. 1986) (arguing that interest group participation affects Court decision making); Joseph D. Kearney and Thomas W. Merrill, *The Influence of Amicus Briefs on the Supreme Court*, 148 U. Pa. L. Rev. 744 (2000) (arguing that amicus briefs affect Court decision making).

48. *See* Susan Behuniak-Long, *Friendly Fire: Amici Curiae and Webster v. Reproductive Health Services*, 74 Judicature 261 (1991).

49. *See* Lawrence Lessig, *Fidelity and Constraint*, 65 Fordham L. Rev. 1365, 1397–99 (1997).

50. The pivotal role that interest groups play before elected officials is detailed in most of this book's case studies. Chapter 8 (religion), in particular, traces the power of interest group participation.

51. Chapter 3 details efforts by state and local officials to shape federalism discourse.

52. 144 Cong. Rec. S8747–49, S8769 (daily ed. July 22, 1998).

53. David S. Broder, *White House to Rewrite Federalism Order, Now with State-Local Input*, Washington Post, July 29, 1998, at A19; David S. Broder, *Clinton "Suspends" Federalism Order to Assuage Local, State Officials*, Washington Post, Aug. 2, 1998, at A5.

54. Jeffrey Abramson, We, the Jury (1994).

55. 2 The Works of John Adams 254–55 (Charles Francis Adams ed., 1850).

56. 15 The Papers of Thomas Jefferson 283 (Julian P. Boyd ed., 1958).

57. Francis Wharton, State Trials of the United States during the Administrations of Washington and Adams 84–85, 88 (1849); 2 John Marshall, The Life of George Washington 273 (1832).

58. Mark DeWolfe Howe, *Juries as Judges of Common Law*, 52 Harv. L. Rev. 582, 582 (1939) (emphasis in original). There is good reason to think that the

framers saw juries as a critical democratic check on government action. *See* Akhil Reed Amar, *The Bill of Rights as a Constitution*, 100 Yale L. J. 1131 (1991); Akhil Reed Amar, *Reinventing Juries: Ten Suggested Reforms*, 28 U.C. Davis L. Rev. 1169 (1992).

59. Woodson v. North Carolina, 428 U.S. 280, 289–91 (1976); The Death Penalty in America 27–28 (Hugo Adam Bedau ed., 1968).

60. Harry Kalven, Jr. & Hans Zeisel, The American Jury 286–97 (1966).

61. *Id.* at 319.

62. Miller v. California, 413 U.S. 15 (1973).

63. Paul Butler, *Racially Based Jury Nullification: Black Power in the Criminal Justice System*, 105 Yale L. J. 677, 700 (1995).

64. *Id.* at 679.

65. Andrew D. Leipold, *Rethinking Jury Nullification*, 82 Va. L. Rev. 253, 324 (1996).

66. W. John Moore, *In Whose Court?*, National Journal, Oct, 5, 1991, at 2400.

67. National Abortion Rights Action League (NARAL) Supreme Court Alert, June 27, 1991.

68. Robin West, *The Aspirational Constitution*, 88 Nw. U. L. Rev. 241, 241 (1993).

69. Owen M. Fiss, *The Forms of Justice*, 93 Harv. L. Rev. 1, 10 (1979).

70. Abner J. Mikva, *How Well Does Congress Support and Defend the Constitution?*, 61 N.C. L. Rev. 587, 609–10 (1983).

71. Paul Brest, *Congress as Constitutional Decisionmaker and Its Power to Counter Judicial Doctrine*, 21 Ga. L. Rev. 57, 59 (1986).

72. Louis Fisher, *Constitutional Interpretation by Members of Congress*, 63 N.C. L. Rev. 707, 708, 746 (1985) (citing Alexander Bickel).

73. Chapter 3 details this story.

74. Raines v. Byrd, 521 U.S. 811 (1997).

75. Kennedy v. Sampson, 364 F.Supp. 1075 (D.D.C. 1973), aff'd, Kennedy v. Sampson, 511 F.2d 430 (D.C. Cir. 1974).

76. Northern Pipeline Co. v. Marathon Pipe Line Co., 458 U.S. 50 (1982); INS v. Chadha, 462 U.S. 919 (1983).

77. 117 Cong. Rec. 32323 (1971).

78. Reed v. Reed, 404 U.S. 71 (1971).

79. Leslie Friedman Goldstein, *The ERA and the U.S. Supreme Court*, 1 Law & Policy Stud. 145, 145 (1987).

80. United States v. Miller, 425 U.S. 435 (1976); 92 Stat. 3617 (1978)

81. David A. Strauss, *Presidential Interpretation of the Constitution*,15 Cardozo L. Rev. 113, 114 (1993).

82. Jeremy Rabkin, *At the President's Side: The Role of the White House Counsel in Constitutional Policy*, 56 Law & Contemp. Prob. 63, 97 (1993).

83. Public Papers of the Presidents, 1989, II, at 1403.

84. Public Papers of the Presidents, 1985, II, at 1472.

85. Chapter 5 details both the rise and persistence of the legislative veto.

86. Rust v. Sullivan, 500 U.S. 173 (1991).

87. 1 Op. Off. Legal Counsel 228, 231 (1977).

88. H. W. Perry, Deciding to Decide 128 (1991).

89. Philip Elman & Norman Silber, *The Solicitor General's Office, Justice Frankfurter, and Civil Rights Litigation, 1946–1960: An Oral History*, 100 Harv. L. Rev. 817, 842 (1987).

90. For one account, *see* Joseph Califano, Governing America 237–43 (1987); for a slightly different account, *see* Griffin Bell & Ronald J. Ostrow, Taking Care of the Law 28–32 (1992).

91. Brief for the United States, at 14, FCC v. Pacifica Found., 438 U.S. 726 (1978). For further discussion, *see* chapter 9.

92. Brief for the FCC, at 16; 199 Landmark Briefs 217. Brief for the United States as Amicus Curiae, at 8; 199 Landmark Briefs 293.

93. Metro Broadcasting, Inc. v. FCC, 497 U.S. 547 (1990).

94. Michael A. Kahn, *The Politics of the Appointment Process: An Analysis of Why Learned Hand Was Never Appointed to the Supreme Court*, 25 Stan. L. Rev. 251, 283 (1973).

95. Fred Rodell, Woe Unto You, Lawyers! 36 (1939).

96. Hepburn v. Griswold, 8 Wall. (75 U.S.) 603 (1870); Legal Tender Cases, 12 Wall. (79 U.S.) 457 (1871).

97. Sidney Ratner, *Was the Supreme Court Packed by President Grant?*, 50 Pol. Sci. Q. 343 (1935).

98. William O. Douglas, The Court Years, 1939–1975, at 113 (1980).

99. Elman & Silber, *The Solicitor General's Office*, 100 Harv. L. Rev. at 840.

100. Rogers v. Bellei, 401 U.S. 815, 837 (1971).

101. Mitchell v. W.T. Grant Co., 416 U.S. 600, 636 (1974).

102. George S. Hellman, Benjamin N. Cardozo: American Judge 200–201 (1940).

103. Stephen J. Wermiel, *Confirming the Constitution: The Role of the Senate Judiciary Committee*, 56 Law & Contemp. Prob. 121, 121–22 (1993).

104. *Id.* at 122. *Stare decisis* calls on the Court to respect precedent to ensure stability in our legal system and, with it, to distinguish precedent-based judicial decision making from elected government policymaking.

105. *See* Leo Pfeffer, Church, State, and Freedom (1967); Neal Devins, *Fundamentalist Christian Educators v. State: An Inevitable Compromise*, 60 G.W. L. Rev. 818 (1992).

106. Michigan v. Long, 463 U.S. 1032 (1983).

107. Shirley S. Abrahamson, *Reincarnation of State Courts*, 36 Sw. L. J. 951, 965 (1982). For a fuller treatment of this topic, *see* James A. Gardner, *Southern Character, Confederate Nationalism, and the Interpretation of State Constitutions: A Case Study in Constitutional Argument*, 76 Tex. L Rev. 1219 (1998); Robert A. Schapiro, *Identity and Interpretation in State Constitutional Law*, 84 Va. L Rev. 389 (1998).

108. Davenport v. Garcia, 834 S.W.2d 4, 16 (Tex. 1992).

109. Ravin v. State, 537 P.2d 494, 504 (Alaska 1975).

110. Gideon v. Wainwright, 372 U.S. 335 (1963); Webb v. Baird, 6 Ind. 13 (1854); Carpenter v. Dane, 9 Wis. 249 (1859); 27 Stat. 252 (1892).

111. PruneYard Shopping Center v. Robins, 447 U.S. 74, 81 (1980).

112. William J. Brennan Jr., *Special Section*, Natl. L. J. Sept. 29, 1986 at S-1; William J. Brennan Jr., *The Bill of Rights and the States: The Revival of State Constitutions as Guardians of Individual Liberties*, 61 N.Y.U. L. Rev. 535, 548 (1986).

113. Wisconsin v. Constantineau, 400 U.S. 433, 440 (1971) (Burger, dissenting).

114. State v. Chrisman, 619 P.2d 971 (Wash. 1980); Washington v. Chrisman, 455 U.S. 1 (1982); State v. Chrisman, 676 P.2d 419 (Wash. 1984). For an overview of these and other decisions, *see* Louis Fisher, *How the States Shape Constitutional Law*, 14 State Legislatures 37 (1989).

115. *Developments in State Constitutional Law: 1992*, 24 Rutgers L. J. 1101 (1993).

116. Ronald K. L. Collins & Peter J. Galie, *Models of Post-Incorporation Judicial Review: 1985 Survey of State Constitutional Individual Rights Decisions*, 55 U. Cin. L. Rev. 317 (1986).

117. Earl Warren, The Memoirs of Earl Warren 6 (1977).

118. Potter Stewart, *The Road to Mapp v. Ohio and Beyond: The Origins, Development and Future of the Exclusionary Rule in Search and Seizure Cases*, 83 Colum. L. Rev. 1365, 1366 (1983).

119. Robert H. Jackson, The Supreme Court in the American System of Government 10 (1955).

Chapter 3

1. Gibbons v. Ogden, 22 U.S. (9 Wheat.) 1 (1824).

2. 20 Journals of the Continental Congress, 1774–1789, at 519, 530–31, 542, 545–48.

3. 9 The Writings of James Madison 419–21 (Gaillard Hunt ed., 1910); 4 The Papers of James Madison 18–19, 21 n.7 (William T. Hutchison & William M. E. Rachal eds., 1965).

4. 2 Farrand 615–16.

5. 2 Annals of Cong. 2082–112 (report of Dec. 13, 1790).

6. *Id.* at 1945–46, 1955, 1960.

7. *Id.* at 1977.

8. Walter Dellinger & H. Jefferson Powell, *The Constitutionality of the Bank Bill: The Attorney General's First Constitutional Law Opinions*, 44 Duke L. J. 110 (1994).

9. 19 The Papers of Thomas Jefferson 276 (Julian P. Boyd ed., 1974).

10. 1 Annals of Cong. 761 (Aug. 18, 1789).

11. 8 The Papers of Alexander Hamilton 97–103, 107 (Harold C. Syrett ed. 1965).

12. 1 Stat. 191 (1791).

13. Pennsylvania v. Wheeling &c. Bridge Co., 13 How. (54 U.S.) 518 (1852); 10 Stat. 112, § 6 (1852); Pennsylvania v. Wheeling and Belmont Bridge Co., 18 How. (59 U.S.) 421 (1856).

14. Pennsylvania v. Wheeling and Belmont Bridge Co., 18 How. (59 U.S.) at 440.

15. Prudential Ins. Co. v. Benjamin, 326 U.S. 408, 425 (1946).

16. United States v. Lopez, 514 U.S. 549, 580 (1995). *See also* Northeast Bancorp v. Board of Governors, FRS, 472 U.S. 159, 174 (1985).

17. United States v. Cruikshank, 92 U.S. 542, 550 (1876).

18. Leisy v. Hardin, 135 U.S. 100, 125 (1890).

19. 21 Cong. Rec. 4954 (1890).

20. *Id.* at 4964.

21. 26 Stat. 313 (1890).

22. *In re* Rahrer, 140 U.S. 545 (1891).

23. Woodrow Wilson, Constitutional Government in the United States 178–79 (1908) (paper ed. 1964). William Howard Taft, Popular Government 142–43 (1913). For an examination of why Taft, as Chief Justice, was willing to put into effect his present beliefs about the "public interest," *see* Robert Post, *Federalism in the Taft-Court Era: Can It Be "Revisited"?*, 51 Duke L. J. 1512 (2002).

24. 1 National Party Platforms 194, 199, 204, 207 (1978).

25. H. Rept. No. 46 (Part 1), 64th Cong., 1st Sess. 7 (1916).

26. 37 The Papers of Woodrow Wilson 429 (1981). Although women, nationwide, would have to await the Nineteenth Amendment (1920) to vote in federal elections, in a number of states they were already voting in both state and federal elections. M. Margaret Conway et al., Women and Political Participation 8–9 (1997).

27. Hammer v. Dagenhart, 247 U.S. 251 (1918).

28. 56 Cong. Rec. 8341, 11560 (1918).

29. *Id.* at 7432.

30. *Id.* at 7433.

31. 57 Cong. Rec. 621, 3035 (1918–19); 40 Stat. 1138 (1919).

32. Brief on Behalf of Appellants and Plaintiff in Error, Bailey v. Drexel Furniture Co., Nos. 590, 657, U.S. Supreme Court, October Term, 1921, at 47, 544–55; 21 Landmark Briefs 52, 59–60.

33. Child Labor Tax Case, 259 U.S. 20, 37 (1922).

34. The prohibition on child labor did not apply to children employed in agriculture, in motion pictures, or in theatrical productions. H. Rept. No. 2738, 75th Cong., 3d Sess. 8–9 (1938).

35. United States v. Darby, 312 U.S. 100 (1941).

36. Prudential Ins. Co. v. Benjamin, 328 U.S. 408, 415 (1946).

37. Schechter Corp. v. United States, 295 U.S. 495 (1935).

38. 4 Public Papers and Addresses of Franklin D. Roosevelt (1935 volume), at 221. *See also* 200–222.

39. S. Rept. No. 711, 75th Cong., 1st Sess. 38–40 (1937).

40. Barry Cushman, Rethinking the New Deal Court, 13–14 (1998); Barry Friedman, *The History of the Countermajorian Difficulty, Part Four: Law's Politics*, 148 U. Pa. L. Rev. 971 (2000).

41. William E. Leuchtenburg, The Supreme Court Reborn: The Constitutional Revolution in the Age of Roosevelt 142 (1995).

42. Robert H. Jackson, The Struggle for Judicial Supremacy 207–13 (paper ed. 1941).

43. Steward Machine Co. v. Davis, 301 U.S. 548 (1937); NLRB v. Jones & Laughlin Steel Corp., 301 U.S. 1 (1937).

44. Jackson, The Struggle for Judicial Supremacy, at 235.

45. S. Rept. No. 711, 75th Cong., 1st Sess., at 23.

46. *Id.* at 14.

47. 50 Stat. 24 (1937).

48. 6 Public Papers and Addresses of Franklin D. Roosevelt (1937 vol.), at lxvi, lxx [signed by Roosevelt on June 3, 1941].

49. Owen Roberts Jr., The Court and the Constitution 61 (1951).

50. 18 Stat. 335 (1875).

51. 3 Cong. Rec. 940 (1875).

52. *Id.*

53. 109 U.S. 3, 10 (1883).

54. *Id.* at 19.

55. Public Papers of the Presidents, 1963, at 485–87.

56. *Civil Rights—Public Accommodations (Part 1): Hearings before the Senate Committee on Commerce*, 88th Cong., 1st Sess. 23 (1963).

57. *Id.* at 23, 26, 28, 90.

58. S. Rept. No. 872, 88th Cong., 2d Sess. 12–14 (1964).

59. *Civil Rights—Public Accommodations (Part 1): Hearings before the Senate Committee on Commerce*, 88th Cong., 1st Sess., at 193.

60. H. Rept. No. 914, 88th Cong., 1st Sess. 2–3, 20–22, 98–101 (1963); H. Rept. No. 914 (Part 2), 88th Cong., 1st Sess. 1–2, 7–9 (1963).

61. Heart of Atlanta Motel v. United States, 379 U.S. 241, 250 (1964); Katzenbach v. McClung, 379 U.S. 294 (1964).

62. Maryland v. Wirtz, 392 U.S. 183 (1968).

63. Public Papers of the Presidents, 1969, at 638.

64. Public Papers of the Presidents, 1973, at 749.

65. 88 Stat. 58 (1974).

66. Oral argument in National League of Cities v. Usery, March 2, 1976, at 23–24; 86 Landmark Briefs 899–900.

67. National League of Cities v. Usery, 426 U.S. 833, 852 (1976).

68. *E.g.*, Hodel v. Virginia Surface Mining & Recl. Assn., 452 U.S. 264 (1981); FERC v. Mississippi, 456 U.S. 742 (1982); United Transportation Union v. Long Island R. Co., 455 U.S. 678 (1982); EEOC v. Wyoming, 460 U.S. 226 (1983).

69. Linda Greenhouse, *Court Takes the Glow Off the 10th Amendment*, N.Y. Times, Mar. 13, 1983, at E9.

70. 44 Fed. Reg. 75628–30 (1979).

71. Letter from Coleman to Goldschmidt, Apr. 15, 1980.

72. Letter from Goldschmidt to Attorney General Benjamin R. Civilitti, May 15, 1980.

73. Memorandum from John M. Harmon, Assistant Attorney General, Office of Legal Counsel, to Associate Attorney General John H. Shenefield, June 16, 1980.

74. Dove v. Chattanooga Area Reg. Transp. Auth., 701 F.2d 50 (6th Cir. 1983); Alewine v. City Council of Augusta, Ga., 699 F.2d 1060 (11th Cir. 1983); Kramer v. New Castle Area Transit Auth., 677 F.2d 308 (3d Cir. 1982); Francis v. City of Tallahassee, 424 So.2d 61 (Fla. App. 1982).

75. Douglas W. Kmiec, The Attorney General's Lawyer 136–37 (1992).

76. 159 Landmark Briefs 912–13.

77. Mark Tushnet, *Why the Supreme Court Overruled National League of Cities*, 47 Vand. L. Rev. 1623, 1628 (1994).

78. 99 Stat. 787 (1985).

79. 131 Cong. Rec. 28984 (1985).

80. Gregory v. Ashcroft, 501 U.S. 452 (1991).

81. New York v. United States, 505 U.S. 144, 175 (1992).

82. Brief for the United States, State of New York v. United States, Nos. 91–543, 91–558, and 91–563, at 20–21; 213 Landmark Briefs 314–15.

83. Brief for the United States, United States v. Lopez, No. 93–1260, at 9.

84. United States v. Lopez, 514 U.S. 549 (1995).

85. *Guns in Schools: A Federal Role?: Hearing before the Subcommittee on Youth Violence of the Senate Committee on the Judiciary*, 104th Cong., 1st Sess. 4, 10 (1995).

86. 110 Stat. 3009–369, § 657 (1996).

87. Printz v. United States, 521 U.S. 898, 912 (1997) (emphasis in original).

88. *Id.* at 935.

89. United States v. Morrison, 529 U.S. 598 (2000).

90. Reno v. Condon, 528 U.S. 141 (2000).

91. Alden v. Maine, 527 U.S. 706 (1999); College Savings Bank v. Florida Prepaid Postsecondary, 527 U.S. 666 (1999); Florida Prepaid Postsecondary v. College Sav., 527 U.S. 627 (1999).

92. City of Boerne v. Flores, 521 U.S. 507 (1997); Kimel v. Fla. Bd. of Regents, 528 U.S. 62 (2000); Bd. of Trustees of the Univ. of Alabama v. Garrett, 531 U.S. 356 (2001). Chapter 9 provides an extended discussion of *Boerne v. Flores*, the decision invalidating the Religious Freedom Restoration Act.

93. Bush v. Gore, 531 U.S. 98, 115 (2000) (emphasis in original).

94. Linda Greenhouse, The Supreme Court: Federalism; States Are Given New Legal Shield by Supreme Court, N.Y. Times, June 24, 1999, at A22.

95. *See generally* Christopher H. Schroeder, *Causes of the Recent Turn in Constitutional Interpretation*, 51 Duke L. J. 307 (2001).

96. 141 Cong. Rec. 9748 (1995).

97. This episode is recounted in chapter 2.

98. Michael Grunwald, *In Legislative Tide, State Power Ebbs*, Washington Post, Oct. 24, 1999, at A1; Ron Eckstein, *Federalism Bills Unify Usual Foes*, Legal Times, Oct. 18, 1999, at 1.

99. Stuart Taylor Jr., *The Tipping Point*, National Journal, June 10, 2000, at 1811.

100. *See* Neal Devins, *Congress as Culprit: How Lawmakers Spurred on the Court's Anti-Congress Crusade*, 51 Duke L. J. 435 (2001).

101. *See id.* at 447.

Chapter 4

1. United States v. Nixon, 418 U.S. 683, 707 (1974).
2. *Id.*
3. *Id.* at 707–13.
4. Nixon v. Administration of Gen. Serv., 433 U.S. 425, 441–42 (1977) (quoting Humphrey's Executor v. United States, 295 U.S. 602, 629 (1935)).
5. 433 U.S. at 442.
6. Nixon v. Fitzgerald, 457 U.Sl 731, 754 (1982).
7. 462 U.S. 919, 944 (1983).
8. *Id.* at 951.
9. Bowsher v. Synar, 478 U.S. 714, 722 (1986).
10. *Id.* at 733–34.
11. The congressional power to investigate is implied in the power to legislate wisely. McGrain v. Daugherty, 273 U.S. 135 (1927). Congress has the power to issue subpoenas. Eastland v. United States Servicemen's Fund, 421 U.S. 491, 505 (1975). Congress also has the power to punish contempt. Anderson v. Dunn, 19 U.S. (6 Wheat.) 204, 228 (1821).
12. Morrison v. Olson, 487 U.S. 654, 691 (1988).
13. *Id.*
14. *Id.* at 693–94 (quoting United States v. Nixon, 418 U.S. 693, 707 (1974)).
15. Mistretta v. United States, 488 U.S. 361, 380 (1989).
16. *Id.* at 381.
17. U.S. Const., art. I, § 9, cl. 7.
18. 2 Elliot 345.
19. 3 Farrand 150.
20. 3 Joseph Story, Commentaries on the Constitution of the United States 214 (1833).
21. Richardson v. United States, 465 F.2d 844, 853 (3d Cir. 1972).
22. United States v. Richardson, 418 U.S. 166 (1974).
23. *Id.* at 200–201.
24. Halperin v. CIA, 629 F.2d 144 (D.C. Cir. 1980). For another CIA case that denied the plaintiff standing, *see* Harrington v. Bush, 553 F.2d 190 (D.C. Cir. 1977).
25. United States v. Richardson, 418 U.S. at 179.
26. Harrington v. Bush, 553 F.2d at 194.
27. Aftergood v. CIA, Civ. No. 98–2107 (TFH) (D.D.C. 1999).
28. Nixon v. United States, 506 U.S. 224 (1993).
29. Constitutional Grounds for Presidential Impeachment: Report by the Staff of the Impeachment Inquiry, House Committee on the Judiciary, 93d Cong., 2d Sess. 26 (Feb. 1974).
30. Louis Fisher & Neal Devins, Political Dynamics of Constitutional Law 151–52 (3d ed. 2001).
31. 144 Cong. Rec. H11822 (daily ed. Dec. 18, 1998) (remarks of Rep. Edward Markey (D-Mass.)).
32. 145 Cong. Rec. S1470 (daily ed. Feb. 12, 1999) (remarks of Sen. Kent Conrad

(D-N.D.)); 144 Cong. Rec. H11792 (daily ed. Dec. 18, 1998) (remarks of Rep. John Dingell (D-Mich.)).

33. 3 Richardson 1289, 1291.

34. Eric Pianin, *Speaker-Elect's Vow Imperils His Hope to Pacify House*, Washington Post, Dec. 14, 1998, at A14.

35. U.S. Const., art. I, § 6, cl. 2.

36. 1 Farrand 379–82, 386–90; 2 Farrand 283–84, 489–92.

37. Reservists Comm. to Stop the War v. Laird, 323 F.Supp. 833, 835–37 (D.D.C. 1971), aff'd mem., 495 F.2d 1075 (D.C. Cir. 1972), rev'd, 418 U.S. 208 (1974).

38. *Id.* at 834.

39. Schlesinger v. Reservists to Stop the War, 418 U.S. 208 (1974).

40. *Id.* at 227.

41. 1 Op. O.L.C. 242 (1977).

42. 17 Op. Att'y Gen. 365 (1882); 17 Op. Att'y Gen. 522 (1883); 21 Op. Att'y Gen. 211 (1895).

43. 43 Cong. Rec. 2205 (1909).

44. *Id.* at 2392.

45. *Id.* at 2415.

46. 35 Stat. 626 (1909).

47. *Ex parte* Levitt, 302 U.S. 633 (1937).

48. McClure v. Carter, 513 F.Supp. 265 (D. Idaho 1981), aff'd sub nom. McClure v. Reagan, 454 U.S. 1025 (1981).

49. *Id.* at 270.

50. 3 Op. O.L.C. 298 (1979).

51. 119 Cong. Rec. 37689 (1973) (statement of Robert G. Dixon, Assistant Attorney General, Office of Legal Counsel).

52. *Id.* at 38315–48.

53. *Id.* at 39234–45; 87 Stat. 697 (1975).

54. 94 Stat. 343 (1980).

55. 107 Stat. 4 (1993).

56. Michael Stokes Paulsen, *Is Lloyd Bentsen Unconstitutional?*, 46 Stan. L. Rev. 907 (1994).

57. 3 Annals of Cong. 539, 541 (1792).

58. 6 Annals of Cong. 2326–32 (1797).

59. 22 Annals of Cong. 984, 997–98 (1811).

60. Cong. Globe, 23d Cong., lst–2d Sess. 326 (1835).

61. Cong. Globe, 24th Cong., 1st Sess. 435, 469 (1836).

62. Louis Fisher, *Separation of Powers: Interpretation outside the Courts*, 18 Pepperdine L. Rev. 57, 66–67 (1990).

63. 4 Hinds' Precedents § 3537–38 n.2 (1907).

64. 7 Cannon's Precedents § 1111 (1935).

65. *Id.*

66. Missouri Pac. Ry. Co. v. Kansas, 248 U.S. 276 (1919).

67. E. I. Renick, *The Power of the President to Sign Bills after the Adjournment of Congress*, 32 Am. U. L. Rev. 208 (1898).

68. 32 Op. Att'y Gen. 225 (1920); 36 Op. Att'y Gen. 403, 406 (1931).

69. Edwards v. United States, 286 U.S. 482 (1932).

70. U.S. Const., art. I, § 7.

71. The Pocket Veto Case, 279 U.S. 655 (1929).

72. Wright v. United States, 302 U.S. 583 (1938).

73. Kennedy v. Sampson, 511 F.2d 430 (D.C. Cir. 1974); Kennedy v. Sampson, 364 F.Supp. 1075 (D.D.C. 1973).

74. Barnes v. Kline, 759 F.2d 21 (D.C. Cir. 1985); Barnes v. Carmen, 582 F.Supp. 163 (D.D.C. 1984).

75. Burke v. Barnes, 479 U.S. 361 (1987).

76. Public Papers of the Presidents, 2000–2001, II, 1564.

77. *Id.* at 1742–43.

78. 146 Cong. Rec. H7240 (daily ed. Sept. 6, 2000).

79. *Id.* at H7335 (daily ed. Sept. 7, 2000).

80. *Id.* at H7509–20 (daily ed. Sept. 13, 2000).

81. U.S. Const., art. II, § 2, cl. 3.

82. 1 Op. Att'y Gen. 631 (1823); 2 Op. Att'y Gen. 525 (1832); 4 Op. Att'y Gen. 523 (1846); 10 Op. Att'y Gen. 356 (1862); 12 Op. Att'y Gen. 32, 38 (1866); 12 Op. Att'y Gen. 455, 457 (1868); 16 Op. Att'y Gen. 522, 524 (1880); 18 Op. Att'y Gen. 29 (1884); 19 Op. Att'y Gen. 261, 262 (1889); 30 Op. Att'y Gen. 314, 315 (1914); 33 Op. Att'y Gen. 20, 23 (1921); 41 Op. Att'y Gen. 463, 465–66 (1960). *See also In re* Farrow, 3 F. 112, 113–15 (C.C.N.D. Ga. 1880) (concurring with the Attorney's General opinions from 1823 to 1880).

83. S. Rept. No. 80, 37th Cong., 3d Sess. 5 (1863).

84. *Id.* at 6.

85. 12 Stat. 642, 646 (1863).

86. 39 Stat. 801 (1916).

87. 54 Stat. 751 (1940).

88. Staff of House Committee on the Judiciary, *Recess Appointments of Federal Judges*, 86th Cong., lst Sess. (Committee Print 1959). *See also* Note, *Recess Appointments to the Supreme Court—Constitutional But Unwise?*, 10 Stan. L. Rev. 124 (1957).

89. 106 Cong. Rec. 12760–62, 18130–45 (1960).

90. United States v. Allocco, 305 F.2d 704 (2d Cir. 1962), cert. denied, 371 U.S. 964 (1963).

91. United States v. Woodley, 751 F.2d 1008 (9th Cir. 1985), cert. denied, 475 U.S. 1048 (1986).

92. Annals of Cong., 2d Cong., 1–2 Sess. 490 (1792).

93. *Id.* at 491.

94. *Id.* at 493.

95. 1 The Writings of Thomas Jefferson 303–5 (Mem. ed. 1903).

96. 273 U.S. 135 (1927).

97. *E.g.*, Watkins v. United States, 354 U.S. 178 (1957); Christoffel v. United States, 338 U.S. 84 (1949).

98. Eastland v. United States Servicemen's Fund, 421 U.S. 491, 509 (1975); Barenblatt v. United States, 360 U.S. 109 (1959).

99. United States v. AT&T, 567 F.2d 121, 127 (D.C. Cir. 1977).

100. Louis Fisher, The Politics of Executive Privilege 112–14, 121–23 (2004).

101. *Contempt of Congress: Hearings before the House Committee on Energy and Commerce*, 97th Cong., 2d Sess. 385–94 (1982).

102. 128 Cong. Rec. 31746–76 (1982).

103. United States v. House of Representatives, 556 F.Supp. 150 (D.D.C. 1983).

104. *Justice Dept. Avoids Collision with House over FBI Opinion*, Washington Post, Aug. 1, 1991, at A13. For further details on congressional subpoena and contempt powers, *see* Louis Fisher, The Politics of Executive Privilege (2003).

105. Edward M. Kennedy, *Rehnquist: No Documents, No Senate Confirmation*, L.A. Times, Aug. 5, 1986, Part II, at 5.

106. Al Kamen, Howard Kurtz, *Rehnquist Told in 1974 of Restriction in Deed*, Washington Post, Aug. 6, 1986, at A1.

107. *Senators Are Given More Rehnquist Data*, Washington Post, Aug. 8, 1986, at A3.

108. Bill Gertz, *CIA Offer of Help on Nominee Frees Up Authorization Bill*, Washington Times, Nov. 5, 1993, at A5.

109. Sen. Chuck Grassley, *Holds Practice Needs Big Changes* (letter to the editor), Roll Call, Aug. 2, 1999, at 4.

110. United States v. AT&T, 551 F.2d 384, 394 (D.C. Cir. 1976). *See also* United States v. AT&T, 567 F.2d 121 (D.C. Cir. 1977).

111. *See generally* Neal Devins, *Congressional-Executive Information Access Disputes: A Modest Proposal—Do Nothing*, 48 Admin. L. Rev. 109 (1996); Louis Fisher, *Congressional Access to Information: Using Legislative Will and Leverage*, 52 Duke L. J. 323 (2002).

112. Public Papers of the Presidents, 1929, at 432.

113. 47 Stat. 382, 413–15, §§ 401–8 (1932).

114. 83 Cong. Rec. 4487 (1938).

115. *Id.* at 5003–4.

116. 53 Stat. 561, 562–63, § 5 (1939).

117. 63 Stat. 203, 207, § 202 (1949).

118. 54 Stat. 670, 672, § 20(c) (1940); 66 Stat. 162, 216, §244(b) (1952).

119. Harvey C. Mansfield, *The Legislative Veto and the Deportation of Aliens*, 1 Pub. Admin. Rev. 281 (1941).

120. William French Smith, Law and Justice in the Reagan Administration: Memoirs of an Attorney General 221 (1991).

121. Public Papers of the Presidents, 1984, II, at 1056–57.

122. NASA Administrator James M. Beggs to House and Senate Appropriations Committee, Aug. 9, 1984, *reprinted in* Fisher and Devins, Political Dynamics of Constitutional Law 126 (3rd ed. 2001).

123. Ashwander v. TVA, 297 U.S. 288, 347 (1936) (Brandeis, J., concurring), quoting from Liverpool, N.Y. & P.S.S. Co. v. Emigration Commissioners, 113 U.S. 333 (1885).

124. Louis Fisher, *The Legislative Veto: Invalidated, It Survives*, 56 Law & Contemp. Prob. 273 (Autumn 1993).

125. *Provision for Special Prosecutor: Hearings before the House Comm. on the Judiciary*, 94th Cong., 2d Sess. 33–34 (1976).

126. *Watergate Reorganization and Reform Act of 1975: Hearings before the Senate Comm. on Government Operations*, 94th Cong., 1st Sess. 3 (1975).

127. 96 Stat. 2039, 2042 (1983); *see* Katy J. Harriger, The Special Prosecutor in American Politics 74–77 (2d ed. 2000).

128. Charles Fried, Order and Law 137 (1991).

129. Paul Gewirtz, *Congress, As Well as Courts, Must Make Constitutional Law*, Hartford Courant, July 24, 1988, at C3.

130. *The Future of the Independent Counsel Statute: Hearings before the Senate Committee on the Judiciary*, 106th Cong., 1st Sess. 243 (1999).

131. *Id.* at 245.

132. *Id.* at 423.

133. *Id.* at 424.

134. *Id.* at 243.

Chapter 5

1. 15 The Papers of Thomas Jefferson 397 (Julian P. Boyd ed., 1958).

2. David Gray Adler, *Foreign Policy and the Separation of Powers: The Influence of the Judiciary, in* Judging the Constitution: Critical Essays on Judicial Lawmaking 158 (Michael W. McCann & Gerald L. Houseman eds., 1989).

3. *E.g.*, John C. Yoo, *The Continuation of Politics by Other Means: The Original Understanding of War Powers*, 84 Cal. L. Rev.167 (1996).

4. John Locke, Second Treatise of Government, §§ 146–48 (1690).

5. 2 William Blackstone, Commentaries on the Laws of England 238, 239, 251, 258, 262.

6. The statements in this paragraph and the next appear in 1 Farrand 64–66.

7. 6 The Writings of James Madison 312 (Gaillard Hunt ed., 1900–1910) (letter of Apr. 2, 1798 to Thomas Jefferson).

8. William Michael Treanor, *Fame, the Founding, and the Power to Declare War*, 82 Corn. L. Rev. 695, 740 (1997).

9. The statements in this paragraph and the next appear in 2 Farrand 318–19.

10. 2 Elliot 528.

11. 4 Elliot 107.

12. *Id.* at 287.

13. 10 Op. Att'y Gen. 74, 79 (1861).

14. 1 Stat. 96, § 5 (1789).

15. 1 Stat. 121, § 16 (1790); 1 Stat. 222 (1791).

16. 4 The Territorial Papers of the United States 195 (Clarence Edwin Carter ed., 1936).

17. 33 The Writings of George Washington 73.

18. 1 Stat. 264, § 1 (1792).

19. *Id.*, § 2.

20. 1 Richardson 150–52.

21. 54 Dep't of State Bull. 474, 484 (1966).

22. 1 Richardson 226.

23. 8 Annals of Congress 1519 (1798). *See* 1 Stat. 547–611 (1798) for statutes authorizing the quasi-war.

24. Bas v. Tingy, 4 U.S. 37, 43 (1800); Talbot v. Seeman, 5 U.S. 1, 28 (1801).

25. 4A O.L.C. 187 (1980); 140 Cong. Rec. 19808 (1994) (statement by Senator McCain). The opinion by the Office of Legal Counsel was placed in the *Congressional Record* in 1993: 139 Cong. Rec. 25702 (1993).

26. 2 Stat. 129 (1802); 2 Stat. 206 (1803); 2 Stat. 291 (1804); 2 Stat. 391 (1806); 2 Stat. 436 (1807); 2 Stat. 456 (1808); 2 Stat. 511 (1809); 2 Stat. 614 (1811); 2 Stat. 675 (1812); 2 Stat. 809 (1813); 3 Stat. 230 (1815).

27. 1 Richardson 315.

28. *See* Abraham D. Sofaer, War, Foreign Affairs and Constitutional Power: The Origins 209–14 (1976).

29. 15 Annals of Cong. 19 (1805).

30. 2 Richardson 479.

31. 2 Stat. 671, 676, 683, 685, 695, 699, 704 (1812).

32. 2 Richardson 490.

33. 5 Richardson 2292.

34. Cong. Globe, 30th Cong., 1st Sess. 95 (1848).

35. 1 The Collected Works of Abraham Lincoln 451–52 (Roy Basler ed., 1953) (emphasis in original).

36. 7 Richardson 3225.

37. Cong. Globe, 37th Cong., 1st Sess. 393 (1861) (Senator Howe); 12 Stat. 326 (1861).

38. *Ex parte* Merryman, 17 Fed. Case 9,487 (1861), at 153.

39. The Prize Cases, 67 U.S. (2 Black) 635, 668, 669 (1863).

40. *Id.* at 660 (emphasis in original).

41. 299 U.S. 304, 320 (1936).

42. Annals of Congress, 6th Cong., 613 (1800).

43. For broad-delegation arguments, *see Ex parte* Endo, 323 U.S. 283, 298 n.21 (1944); Zemel v. Rusk, 381 U.S. 1, 17 (1965); *and* Goldwater v. Carter, 444 U.S. 996, 1000 n.1 (1979). Inherent powers are discussed in United States v. Pink, 315 U.S. 203, 229 (1942); Knauff v. Shaughnessy, 338 U.S. 537, 542 (1950); United States v. Mazurie, 419 U.S. 544, 566–567 (1975); and Dames & Moore v. Regan, 453 U.S. 654, 661 (1981).

44. 9 Public Papers and Addresses of Franklin D. Roosevelt 267 (1940 volume).

45. *Id.* at 391.

46. 39 Op. Att'y Gen. 484, 486–87 (1940).

47. Louis Fisher, *The Korean War: On What Legal Basis Did Truman Act?*, 89 Am. J. Int'l L. 21 (1995).

48. 91 Cong. Rec. 8185 (1945).

49. 59 Stat. 621, § 6 (1945).

50. 96 Cong. Rec. 9229 (1950) (statement of Senator Scott Lucas).

51. Edward S. Corwin, *The President's Power*, New Republic, Jan. 29, 1951, at 16.

52. 98 Cong. Rec. 3956 (1952).

53. *Id.* at 4029–30, 4033–34.

54. Public Papers of the Presidents, 1952, at 273.

55. *Id.* at 284.

56. H. Doc. No. 534, 82d Cong., 2d Sess. 255–58, 362–63, 371–72 (1952).

57. Youngstown Sheet & Tube Co. v. Sawyer, 103 F.Supp. 569, 577 (D.D.C. 1952).

58. Maeva Marcus, Truman and the Steel Seizure Case 130 (1994 ed.)

59. Youngstown Co. v. Sawyer, 343 U.S. 579 (1952).

60. William H. Rehnquist, The Supreme Court 95 (1987).

61. 1 Stephen E. Ambrose, Eisenhower: Soldier, General of the Army, President-Elect 569 (1983).

62. Dwight D. Eisenhower, Mandate for Change 82 (1963).

63. Public Papers of the Presidents, 1954, at 306.

64. Foreign Relations of the United States [FRUS], 1952–1954, vol. XIII, part 1, at 1242.

65. FRUS, 1952–1954, vol. XIV, part 1, at 611.

66. *Id.* at 618.

67. Public Papers of the Presidents, 1955, at 209.

68. 69 Stat. 7 (1955).

69. Public Papers of the Presidents, 1957, at 11. *See also* 12, 15.

70. 71 Stat. 5 (1957).

71. Dwight D. Eisenhower, Waging Peace 179 (1965).

72. Public Papers of the Presidents, 1962, at 806.

73. *Id.* at 674.

74. 2 Memoirs by Harry S. Truman, Years of Trial and Hope 337, 339, 519 (1956).

75. 2 Stephen Ambrose, Eisenhower: The President 175–76 (1984).

76. Public Papers of the Presidents, 1964, II, at 926.

77. Edwin E. Moïse, Tonkin Gulf and the Escalation of the Vietnam War (1996).

78. Public Papers of the Presidents, 1964, II, at 926.

79. 78 Stat. 384 (1964).

80. 110 Cong. Rec. 18427 (1964).

81. 84 Stat. 1943, § 7(a) (1971).

82. Department of State Bulletin, No. 1871, 72 (May 5, 1975): 562.

83. Public Papers of the Presidents, 1973, at 893.

84. Representatives Bella Abzug, Robert Drinan, John Duncan, John James Flynt Jr., William Harsha, Ken Hechler, Elizabeth Holtzman, William Hungate, Phillip Landrum, Trent Lott, Joseph Maraziti, Dale Milford, William Natcher, Frank Stubblefield, and Jamie Whitten.

85. *E.g.*, 119 Cong. Rec. 36220 (1973) (Rep. Elizabeth Holtzman).

86. *Id.* at 33870.

87. *Id.* at 36221.

88. Thomas F. Eagleton, War and Presidential Power 213–20 (1974).

89. 119 Cong. Rec. 36204 (1973).

90. *Id.* at 36207 (Rep. Thomson); *id.* at 36208 (Rep. Eckhardt); *id.* at 36220 (Rep. Dellums).

91. *Id.* at 36177.

92. *Id.* at 36953.

93. *Id.* at 36178.

94. 141 Cong. Rec. S17863 (daily ed. Nov. 30, 1995); *id.* at 17529 (daily ed. Nov. 27, 1995); 144 Cong. Rec. H11722 (daily ed. Dec. 17, 1998).

95. Crockett v. Reagan, 558 F.Supp. 893 (D.D.C. 1982), aff'd, Crockett v. Reagan, 720 F.2d 1355 (D.C. Cir. 1983); Conyers v. Reagan, 578 F.Supp. 324 (D.D.C. 1984), dismissed as moot, Conyers v. Reagan, 765 F.2d 1124 (D.C. Cir. 1985); Sanchez-Espinoza v. Reagan, 568 F.Supp. 596 (D.D.C. 1983); Sanchez-Espinoza, 770 F.2d 202 (D.C. Cir. 1985); Lowry v. Reagan, 676 F.Supp. 333 (D.D.C. 1987), aff'd, No. 87–5426 (D.C. Cir. 1988).

96. Sanchez-Espinoza, 770 F.2d at 211.

97. Dellums v. Bush, 752 F.Supp. 1141 (D.D.C. 1990).

98. *Id.* at 1145.

99. Campbell v. Clinton, 52 F.Supp. 2d 34, 43 (D.D.C. 1999).

100. Campbell v. Clinton, 203 F.3d 19 (D.C. Cir. 2000).

101. *Id.* at 24–25.

102. *Id.* at 40–41.

103. Mike Allen and Juliet Eilperin, *Bush Aides Say Iraq War Needs No Hill Vote*, Washington Post, Aug. 26, 2002, at A1.

104. *Bush Rejects Hill Limits on Resolution Allowing War*, Washington Post, Oct. 2, 2002, at A12.

105. 112 Stat. 3181, § 8 (1998).

106. Louis Fisher, *The Road to Iraq*, Legal Times, Sept. 2, 2002, at 34.

107. Robert C. Byrd, *Congress Must Resist the Rush to War*, N.Y. Times, Oct. 10, 2002, at A35.

108. 116 Stat. 1498 (2002).

109. Doe v. Bush, 240 F.Supp.2d 95, 96 (D. Mass. 2002).

110. *Id.*

111. *Id.*

112. Doe v. Bush, 323 F.3d 133, 140 (1st Cir. 2003).

113. *Id.* at 139.

114. *Id.* at 142 (quoting Massachusetts v. Laird, 451 F.2d 26, 31–32 (1st Cir. 1971)).

115. *Id.* at 143.

116. Louis Fisher, *Deciding on War Against Iraq: Institutional Failures*, 118 Pol. Sci. Q. 389 (2003).

117. Louis Fisher, *Sidestepping Congress: Presidents Acting under the UN and NATO*, 47 Case W. Res. L. Rev. 1237 (1997).

118. Harold Hongju Koh, The National Security Constitution 132 (1990).

119. Congressman Lee H. Hamilton, *The Role of the Congress in U.S. Foreign Policy*, delivered to the Center for Strategic and International Studies, Nov. 19, 1998, at 1.

120. Joseph A. Califano Jr., *When There's No Draft*, Washington Post, Apr. 6, 1999, at A23.

121. Eugene Robinson, *U.S. Halts Attacks on Iraq after Four Days*, Washington Post, Dec. 20, 1998, at A1; Eugene Robinson, *Iraq Remains Defiant as U.S. Ends Attacks*, Washington Post, Dec. 20, 1998, at A48.

122. 144 Cong. Rec. E1668 (daily ed. Sept. 9, 1998).

Chapter 6

1. Alexander M. Bickel, The Least Dangerous Branch 21 (1962).

2. *See* Robert G. McCloskey, The American Supreme Court 150–74 (1960).

3. Lochner v. New York, 198 U.S. 45 (1905).

4. As explained in chapter 3, his plan was rejected by Congress but contributed to changes in the Court's personnel and, with that, changes in judicial doctrines.

5. 381 U.S. 479, 484–85 (1965).

6. David J. Garrow, Liberty and Sexuality: The Right to Privacy and the Making of *Roe v. Wade* 17 (1994).

7. 61 Landmark Briefs and Arguments of the Supreme Court of the United States 452 (1975). Emerson, however, did suggest in a 1965 *Michigan Law Review* symposium on *Griswold* that the Court might be willing to recognize abortion rights. Thomas Emerson, *Nine Justices in Search of a Doctrine*, 64 Mich. L. Rev. 219 (1965).

8. Bernard Schwartz, The Unpublished Opinions of the Warren Court 239 (1985).

9. 410 U.S. 113 (1973).

10. John Hart Ely, *The Wages of Crying Wolf: A Comment on Roe v. Wade*, 82 Yale L. J. 920, 939 (1973).

11. 1984 Republican Party Platform, reprinted in 1984 CQ Almanac, 55-B, 56-B.

12. William French Smith, *Urging Judicial Restraint*, 68 A.B.A. J. 59, 61 (1982) (quoting Griswold v. Connecticut, 381 U.S. 479, 521 (1965)).

13. Public Papers of the President, 1982, II, at 1104, 1105.

14. Edward Walsh, *Court Change Elevates Biden's Profile*, Washington Post, July 12, 1987, at A7.

15. Robert Bork, *Neutral Principles and Some First Amendment Problems*, 47 Ind. L. J. at 9.

16. Michael Pertschuk & Wendy Schaetzel, The People Rising: The Campaign against the Bork Nomination 257 (1989).

17. Washington Post, advertisement, Sept. 14, 1987, at A9.

18. *Nomination of Robert H. Bork to be Associate Justice of the Supreme Court of the United States (Part I): Hearings before the Senate Comm. on the Judiciary*, 100th Cong., 1st Sess. 115, 150–51 (1987).

19. S. Exec. Rept. No. 7, 100th Cong., 1st Sess. 20 (1987).

20. *Nomination of Anthony M. Kennedy to be Associate Justice of the Supreme Court of the United States: Hearings before the Senate Comm. on the Judiciary*, 100th Cong., 1st Sess. 164 (1987) (emphasis supplied).

21. *Nomination of David H. Souter to be Associate Justice of the Supreme Court of the United States: Hearings before the Senate Comm. on the Judiciary*, 101st Cong., 2d Sess. 54 (1990).

22. *Nomination of Judge Clarence Thomas to be Associate Justice of the Supreme Court of the United States (Part I): Hearings before the Senate Comm. on the Judiciary*, 102d Cong., 1st Sess., 127 (1997).

23. Telephone interview of Charles Fried by Carolyn Kimbler, Nov. 16, 1990.

24. Gerald Rosenberg, The Hollow Hope 180 (1991).

25. *See* Susan B. Hansen, *State Implementation of Supreme Court Decisions: Abortion Rates since Roe v. Wade*, 42 J. Pol. 372, 379 (1980).

26. Ruth Bader Ginsburg, *Speaking in a Judicial Voice*, 67 N.Y.U. L. Rev. 1185, 1198, 1208 (1992) (emphasis added).

27. *See generally* Robert J. Blendon et al., *The Public and the Controversy over Abortion*, 270 JAMA 287 (1993).

28. The precise terms of the Hyde Amendment change from year to year, sometimes allowing for abortions where the mother's life is in jeopardy, at other times providing funds for the victims of rape and incest, and one year also authorizing the funding of abortions when there is a risk of "severe and long-lasting physical health damage."

29. 42 U.S.C. §§ 300z-10 (2000).

30. 108 Stat. 694 (1994), nullifying Bray v. Alexandria Women's Health Clinic, 506 U.S. 263 (1993).

31. Brief of Rep. Jim Wright (and other Members of Congress), at 14, Harris v. McRae, 448 U.S. 297 (1980).

32. Brief of Sen. Robert Packwood et al., at 3, Thornburgh v. American College of Obstetricians and Gynecologists, 476 U.S. 747 (1986).

33. 122 Cong. Rec. 20410–12, 30898, 27672–75 (1976).

34. *Reauthorization of the Adolescent Family Demonstration Projects Act of 1981: Hearings before the Subcommittee on Family and Human Services of the Senate Committee on Labor & Human Resources*, 98th Cong. 2d Sess. 4 (1984).

35. *The Child Custody Protection Act: Hearings before the Senate Committee on the Judiciary*, 105th Cong. 2d Sess. (1998); *The Child Custody Protection Act: Hearings before the Subcommittee on the Constitution of the House Committee on the Judiciary*, 105th Cong. 2d Sess. (1998).

36. Partial Birth Abortion Ban Act of 2003, H. Rept. No. 58, 108th Cong., 1st Sess. 35 (2003).

37. *See* Laurence H. Tribe, Abortion: The Clash of Absolutes 147–50 (1990).

38. Barbara Hinkson Craig & David M. O'Brien, Abortion and American Politics 157 (1993).

39. Charles Fried, Order and Law 72 (1991).

40. On this point, *see* Reagan's remarkable Human Life Review article reprinted in Ronald Reagan, Abortion and the Conscience of the Nation 15 (1984).

41. 84 Stat. 1504, 1508 (1970).

42. Rust v. Sullivan, 500 U.S. 173, 184 (1991).

43. 1989 CQ Almanac 757–60.

44. 37 Weekly Comp. Pres. Doc. 216 (Jan. 22, 2001).

45. Dana Milbank, *Bush Signs Ban on Late-Term Abortions Into Effect*, Washington Post, Nov. 6, 2003, at A4.

46. Craig & O'Brien, Abortion and American Politics, at 77.

47. *See* Lynn D. Wardle & Mary Ann Q. Wood, A Lawyer Looks at Abortion 43 (1982).

48. *See* Glen Halva-Neubauer, *Abortion Policy in the Post-Webster Age*, 20 Pubilus 27 (1990).

49. Ely, *The Wages of Crying Wolf*, 82 Yale L. J. (1973) at 947.

50. Webster v. Reproductive Health Services, 492 U.S. 490 (1989).

51. 135 Cong. Rec. 18170 (1989) (statement of Rep. AuCoin).

52. 505 U.S. 833 (1992).

53. Alan Guttmacher Institute, Legislative Proposals and Actions, State Reproductive Health Monitor, Dec. 1993 at i.

54. Stenberg v. Carhart, 530 U.S. 914 (2000).

55. *Survey of Abortion Law*, 1980 Ariz. St. L. J. 67, 106–11 (1980); Eva R. Rubin, Abortion, Politics, and the Courts: *Roe v. Wade* and Its Aftermath 31–57 (1987).

56. Right to Choose v. Byrne, 450 A.2d 925, 931 (N.J. 1982). *See also* Committee to Defend Reprod. Rights v. Myers, 625 P.2d 779 (Cal. 1981); Doe v. Maher, 515 A.2d 134 (Conn. Super. 1986); Moe v. Secretary of Administration, 417 N.E.2d 387 (Mass. 1981); Planned Parenthood Ass'n v. Dept. of Human Res., 663 P.2d 1247 (Or. App. 1983).

57. American Academy of Pediatrics v. Lundgren, 940 P.2d 797, 809 (Cal. 1997) (emphasis in original).

58. *See* Philip Hager, *Court Again Rejects Curbs on Abortions*, L.A. Times, Nov. 17, 1989, at A3; American Academy of Pediatrics v. Van de Kemp, 263 Cal. Rptr. 45 (1989).

59. Sandra Day O'Connor, The Majesty of the Law: Reflections of a Supreme Court Justice 45 (2003).

60. *See* Anne B. Goldstein, *History, Homosexuality, and Political Values: Searching for the Hidden Determinants of Bowers v. Hardwick*, 97 Yale L. J. 1073, 1082–83 (1988).

61. Exec. Order No. 10450, 18 Fed. Reg. 2491 (1953).

62. Peter Irons, The Courage of Their Convictions 384 (1988).

63. *Id.* at 385.

64. Hardwick v. Bowers, 760 F.2d 1202 (11th Cir. 1985).

65. John C. Jeffries Jr., Justice Lewis F. Powell, Jr. 524 (1994).

66. Bowers v. Hardwick, 478 U.S. 186, 194 (1986).

67. 132 Cong. Rec. 19943 (1986); 135 Cong. Rec. 13950–51 (1989).

68. Earl M. Maltz, *The Court, the Academy, and the Constitution*, 1989 BYU L. Rev. 59, 60.

69. Charles Fried, Order and Law, at 82–83.

70. Jeffries, Justice Lewis F. Powell, Jr., at 530.

71. David Lauter, *Complex Issues Still Unresolved on Gay Rights*, National Law Journal, Apr. 14, 1986, at 1.

72. William N. Eskridge Jr., *Outsider-Insiders: The Academy of the Closet*, 71 Chi.-Kent L. Rev. 977 (1996).

73. 1993 Statutes of Nevada 236 at 518; R.I. Gen. Law § 11–10-1 (1998); D.C. Act. 10–23 (D.C. Code Supp. 1994).

74. Powell v. State, 510 S.E.2d 18, 24 (Ga. 1998).

75. Jegley v. Picado, 80 S.W.3d 332 (Ark. 2002); Kentucky v. Wasson, 842 S.W.2d 487 (Ky. 1992); Michigan Organization for Human Rights v. Kelley, No. 88–815820 CZ (Mich. Cir. Ct. July 6, 1999); Gryczan v. State, 942 P.2d 112 (Mont. 1997); Campbell v. Sundquist, 926 S.W.2d 250 (Tenn. Ct. App. 1996).

76. Louisiana v. Baxley, 663 So.2d 142 (La. 1994); Missouri v. Walsh, 713 S.W.2d 508 (Mo. 1986).

77. Public Papers of the Presidents, 1993, I, at 510.

78. Public Papers of the Presidents, 1998, I, at 849.

79. Public Papers of the Presidents, 1993, I, at 1111.

80. Pub. L. No. 103–160, 107 Stat. 1547, 1670, § 571 (1993).

81. Jim Weiner, *Military Discharges of Homosexuals Soar*, N.Y. Times, Apr. 7, 1998, at A24; Dana Priest, *Number of Recruits Discharged for Being Gay Increase for Fifth Year*, Washington Post, Jan. 23, 1999, at A5.

82. Public Papers of the Presidents, 1999, II, at 2293.

83. Pub. L. No. 104–199, 110 Stat. 2419 (1996).

84. H. Rept. No. 104–664, 104th Cong., 2d Sess. 12 (1996) (the latter quote comes from Murphy v. Ramsey, 114 U.S. 15, 45 (1886).

85. Frank Newport, *Six Out of Ten Americans Say Homosexual Relations Should Be Recognized as Legal*, Gallup News Service, May 15, 2003.

86. Matt Murray, *Walmart Shift Shows Job Sites Welcome Gays*, Wall Street Journal, July 7, 2003, at A9.

87. Lawrence v. Texas, 123 S.Ct. 2472, 2484 (2003).

88. Dana Milbank, *White House Pushes to Reshape California GOP*, Washington Post, Feb. 21, 2002, at A8.

89. Pam Belluck, *Massachusetts Gives New Push to Gay Marriage*, N.Y. Times, Feb. 5, 2004, at A1.

90. Amanda Paulson, *Debate on Gay Unions Splits along Generations*, Christian Science Monitor, July 7, 2003, at 1.

91. Cruzan v. Director, Missouri Dept. of Health, 497 U.S. 261 (1990).

92. Washington v. Glucksburg, 521 U.S. 702 (1997); Vacco v. Quill, 521 U.S. 793 (1997).

93. Washington v. Glucksburg, 521 U.S. at 735.

94. Derek Humphrey & Ann Wickett, The Right to Die: Understanding Euthanasia 4 (1986).

95. Pub. L. No. 101–508, 104 Stat. 1388–115, 1388–117, § 4027 (1990).

96. *See* Robert Suro, *States to Become Forum for Fight over Assisted Suicide*, Washington Post, June 27, 1997 at, A19.

97. Jeffrey Rosen, *What Right to Die?*, New Republic, June 24, 1996, at 28.

98. Pub. L. No. 105–12, 111 Stat. 23 (1997).

99. Brief for the American Medical Association et al., Vacco v. Quill, 521 U.S. 793 (1997) at 1, 2.

100. Brief of Amicus Curiae States of California et al., Washington v. Glucksberg, 521 U.S. 702 (1997), at 1–3. In *Cruzan*, state attorneys general did not support Missouri, in large part because most states allow family members to speak the voice of their loved ones.

101. Brief for the United States, Washington v. Glucksberg, 521 U.S. 702 (1997), at 9.

102. Don Colburn, *Study Puts Face on Patients in Assisted Suicide*, The Oregonian, June 12, 2003, at A1.

103. Sam Howe Verhovek, *U.S. Acts to Stop Assisted Suicides*, N.Y. Times, Nov. 7, 2000, at A1.

104. *Id.* For a detailed analysis, *see* Nelson Lund, *Why Ashcroft Is Wrong on Assisted Suicide*, Commentary, Feb. 2002, at 50.

105. Oregon v. Ashcroft, 192 F. Supp. 2d 1077 (D. Ore. 2002).

106. Kathryn L. Tucker, *The Death with Dignity Movement: Options after Glucksberg and Quill*, 82 Minn. L. Rev. 931, 933–35 (1998).

107. Michael W. McConnell, *Supreme Humility*, Wall Street Journal, July 2, 1997, at A14.

108. Joan Biskupic, *Ginsburg's Graduation*, Washington Post, July 21, 1993, at A6.

Chapter 7

1. Remarks of Justice Thurgood Marshall, Annual Seminar of the San Francisco Patent and Trademark Law Association, in Maui, Hawaii (May 6, 1987).

2. U.S. Const., art. IV, § 2 (removed by the Thirteenth Amendment).

3. Karen Arrington, *The Struggle to Gain the Right to Vote: 1787–1965, in* Voting Rights in America (Karen McGill & William Taylor eds., 1992).

4. *Nomination of Judge Clarence Thomas to be Associate Justice of the Supreme Court of the United States (Part 1 of 4 Parts): Hearings before the Senate Committee on the Judiciary*, 102d Cong., 1st Sess. 35 (1991) (statement of Sen. Kennedy); *id.* at 52 (statement of Sen. Leahy).

5. 60 U.S. (19 How.) 393 (1857). For additional discussion of *Dred Scott* and its aftermath, *see* chapter 1.

6. 12 Stat. 432, c.111 (1862).

7. 10 Op. Att'y Gen. 382 (1862).

8. There is good reason to think that both the framers of the Fourteenth Amendment and Reconstruction-era legislators thought that benign color-conscious laws were constitutional. *See* Andrew Kull, The Color-Blind Constitution 53–87 (1992); Stephen A. Siegel, *The Federal Government's Power to Enact Color-Conscious Laws: An Originalist Inquiry*, 92 Nw. U. L. Rev. 477 (1998).

9. Cong. Globe, 39th Cong., 1st Sess. 544 (1866) (statement of Rep. Taylor).

10. *Id.* at 401 (statement of Sen. McDougall).

11. *Id.* at 588 (statement of Rep. Donnelly); *id.* at 939 (statement of Sen. Trumbull); *id.* at 632 (statement of Rep. Moulton).

12. 3 Cong. Rec. 940 (1875) (statement of Rep. Butler).

13. The Civil Rights Cases, 109 U.S. 3 (1883). For a detailed treatment of this topic, *see* chapter 3.

14. 163 U.S. 537, 552 (1896). *See also* Pace v. Alabama, 106 U.S. 583 (1883) (upholding Alabama's prohibition of miscegenation).

15. Commission on Wartime Relocation and Internment of Civilians, Personal Justice Denied 28–29 (1982).

16. *See* Roger Daniels, The Politics of Prejudice 1–19 (1962).

17. Personal Justice Denied at 33 (quoting school board).

18. G. Edward White, Earl Warren: A Public Life 69 (quoting Associated Press news release) (1982).

19. *National Defense Migration (Part 29): Hearings before the House Select Committee Investigating National Defense Migration,* 77th Cong., 2d Sess. 11015 (1942).

20. Personal Justice Denied, at 6 (quoting DeWitt's recommendation).

21. William H. Rehnquist, *When the Laws Were Silent,* American Heritage 77, 78 (Oct. 1998) (quoting Biddle).

22. Executive Order 9066, 7 Fed. Reg. 1407 (1942).

23. 56 Stat. 173 (1942).

24. 88 Cong. Rec. 2723 (1942) (remarks of Sen. Reynolds). *See generally id.* at 2722–26, 2729–30.

25. Brief for the United States, Korematsu v. United States, 42 Landmark Briefs 213 n.2. For a detailing of why the Justice Department did not alert the Court to War Department misrepresentations, *see* Peter Irons, Justice at War 186–218 (1983).

26. Amicus Curiae Brief for the American Civil Liberties Union, Korematsu v. United States, 42 Landmark Briefs 302.

27. *Id.* at 332 (quoting a memo contained in Box 133 of Murphy's papers).

28. Korematsu v. United States, 323 U.S. 214, 218, 219 (1944).

29. Earl Warren, *The Bill of Rights and the Military,* 37 N.Y.U. L. Rev. 181, 192 (1962).

30. Public Papers of the Presidents, 1988–89, II, at 1054–55 (signing the Civil Rights Liberties Act of 1988, 102 Stat. 903 (1988)). In 1998, an apology was issued to and restitution paid to Latin Americans of Japanese descent who were deported to and interned by the United States during World War II. *See* Lena H. Sun, *U.S. Apologizes for Internment,* Washington Post, June 13, 1998, at A-4.

31. In 1984 and again in 1987, the judiciary partially redeemed itself by voiding the criminal convictions of Fred Korematsu and Gordon Hirabayashi, two of the Japanese Americans whose challenges to the interment and an earlier curfew policy were turned down by the Supreme Court. Korematsu v. United States, 584 F. Supp. 1406 (N.D. Cal. 1984); Hirabayashi v. United States, 828 F.2d 591 (9th Cir. 1987). In vacating these convictions, the courts found that the government deliberately misled the Supreme Court.

32. Rehnquist, *When the Laws Were Silent*, American Heritage, at 89.

33. One notable exception is Buchanan v. Warley, 245 U.S. 60 (1917), holding that residential segregation laws violate an individual's right to acquire, use, and dispose of property. For a perceptive treatment of the case, *see* David E. Bernstein, *Philip Sober Controlling Philip Drunk: Buchanan v. Warley in Historical Perspective*, 51 Vand. L. Rev. 797 (1998).

34. Richard Kluger, Simple Justice 274 (1976).

35. For a description of these cases, *see* Louis Fisher, American Constitutional Law 803–4 (5th ed. 2003).

36. *See* Kluger, Simple Justice; Jack Greenberg, Crusaders in the Courts (1994). For a competing perspective, *see* Mark V. Tushnet, The NAACP's Legal Strategy against Segregated Education, 1925–1950 (1987) (suggesting that the NAACP frequently changed strategy and, as such, its campaign against segregation was not meticulously planned).

37. 347 U.S. 483, 495 (1954).

38. Mary L. Dudziak, *Desegregation as a Cold War Imperative*, 41 Stan. L. Rev. 61, 103 (1988) (discussing Shelley v Kraemer, 334 U.S. 1 (1948)). *See also* Mary L. Dudziak, Cold War Civil Rights: Race and the Image of American Democracy (2000).

39. Brief for the United States as Amicus Curiae, Brown v. Board of Education, 49 Landmark Briefs 122 (quoting letter from the Secretary of State).

40. William O. Douglas, The Court Years 113 (1980).

41. 349 U.S. 294, 301 (1955).

42. *Id.* at 299–300.

43. Bernard Schwartz, Super Chief 89 (1983).

44. 102 Cong. Rec. 4515 (1956).

45. 2 Stephen E. Ambrose, Eisenhower 126–27 (1984).

46. Phillip Elman, *The Solicitor General's Office, Justice Frankfurter, and Civil Rights Litigation, 1946–1960: An Oral History*, 100 Harv. L. Rev. 817, 842 (1987).

47. Ambrose, Eisenhower, at 338.

48. Public Papers of the Presidents, 1957, at 689–94.

49. Cooper v. Aaron, 358 U.S. 1, 18 (1958). For a detailed look of the politics surrounding the *Cooper* decision, *see* Mary L. Dudziak, *The Little Rock Crisis and Foreign Affairs: Race, Resistance, and the Image of American Democracy*, 70 S.Cal. L. Rev. 1641 (1997).

50. Reed Sarratt, The Ordeal of Desegregation 200 (1966) (quoting a southern attorney).

51. Naim v. Naim, 87 S.E. 2d 749, 756 (Va. 1955).

52. Del Dickson, *State Court Defiance and the Limits of Supreme Court Authority: Williams v. Georgia Revisited*, 103 Yale L. J. 1423, 1475–76 (1994). *See also* Schwartz, Super Chief, at 158–162. For a defense of the Court's action, *see* Alexander M. Bickel, The Least Dangerous Branch 174 (1962). For a critique, *see* Herbert Weschler, *Toward Neutral Principles in Constitutional Law*, 73 Harv. L. Rev. 1, 34 (1959).

53. 110 Cong. Rec. 6814 (1964) (remarks of Sen. Douglas).

54. Griffin v. County School Bd., 377 U.S. 218, 229 (1964).

55. United States v. Jefferson County Board of Education, 372 F.2d 836, 847 (5th Cir. 1966) (emphasis in original).

56. Griffin v. County School Bd., 377 U.S. at 234.

57. Thomas Byrne Edsall & Mary D. Edsall, Chain Reaction 47 (1991).

58. Leon Daniel, *Troopers Rout Selma Marchers*, Washington Post, Mar. 8, 1965, at A1.

59. Public Papers of the Presidents, 1965, I, at 284.

60. U.S. Commission on Civil Rights, The Voting Rights Act: Ten Years After 40, 49 (1975).

61. South Carolina v. Katzenbach, 383 U.S. 301 (1966); Katzenbach v. Morgan, 384 U.S. 641 (1966).

62. Allen v. State Board of Elections, 393 U.S. 544 (1969).

63. Loving v. Virginia, 388 U.S. 1, 12 (1967).

64. Gary Orfield, The Reconstruction of Southern Education 39 (1969).

65. Gary Orfield, Public School Desegregation in the United States, 1968–1980, at 5 (1983). The percentage change is so dramatic that it no doubt overstates the progress, reflecting changes to "all-black" schools and nothing else.

66. 80 Stat. 1209, § 181 (1966).

67. Public Papers of the Presidents, 1970, at 309.

68. James M. Naughton, *Nixon Disavows HEW Policy on Busing*, N.Y. Times, Aug. 4, 1971, at A15.

69. 402 U.S. 1 (1971).

70. *Id.* at 25, 28.

71. Public Papers of the Presidents, 1972, at 428.

72. H.R. 13915, 92d Cong., 2d Sess. (1972).

73. 86 Stat. 372, § 802(b) (1972).

74. *See* Louis Fisher and Neal Devins, Political Dynamics of Constitutional Law 261–63 (3d ed. 2001).

75. Milliken v. Bradley, 433 U.S. 267 (1977).

76. San Antonio v. Rodriguez, 411 U.S. 1, 58 (1973).

77. Griggs v. Duke Power Co., 401 U.S. 424 (1971). For an exhaustive account of how *Griggs* misinterpreted employment discrimination legislation, *see* Hugh Davis Graham, The Civil Rights Era (1990).

78. Washington v. Davis, 426 U.S. 229 (1976); Mobile v. Bolden, 446 U.S. 55 (1980).

79. Graham, The Civil Rights Era, at 387.

80. Bernard Schwartz, The Ascent of Pragmatism: The Burger Court in Action 13–14, 257 (1990).

81. Board of Education v. Dowell, 498 U.S. 237, 248 (1991).

82. Public Papers of the Presidents, 1965, II, at 636.

83. President's Advisory Council of Minority Business Enterprise, Blueprint for the 70's, at 5 (1971).

84. Graham, The Civil Rights Era, at 325.

85. Neal Devins, *The Civil Rights Hydra*, 89 Mich. L. Rev. 1723 (1991).

86. 1980 CQ Almanac 105-B.

87. *Id.* at 62-B.

88. *Oversight Hearings on Equal Employment Opportunity and Affirmative Action (Part 1): Hearings before the Committee on Education and Labor*, 97th Cong., 1st Sess. 137 (1981) (statement of William Bradford Reynolds, Assistant Attorney General for Civil Rights).

89. I.R.S. News Release, Jan. 8, 1982.

90. Chester E. Finn Jr., *Affirmative Action under Reagan*, Commentary, Apr. 1982, at 27.

91. *See President Fires Three Members of U.S. Commission on Civil Rights*, Daily Lab. Rep. (BNA), at A-1 (Oct. 25, 1983); Public Papers of the Presidents, 1983, II, at 1508.

92. Bob Jones University v. United States, 461 U.S. 574 (1983).

93. Berry v. Reagan, Civil Action No. 83–3182 (D.D.C. Nov. 14, 1983); Louis Fisher, Constitutional Conflicts between Congress and the President 76 (1997).

94. 96 Stat. 131 (1982).

95. S. Rept. No. 417, 97th Cong., 1st Sess. 16 (1982).

96. Of equal significance, race-conscious districting "pack[ed] blacks into a few districts," making the surrounding districts "whiter, less Democratic, and fertile soil for GOP candidates." Matthew Cooper, *Beware of Republicans Bringing Voting Rights Suits*, Washington Monthly, Feb. 1987 at 11. Indeed, the 1994 Republican takeover of Congress is partially attributable to the ability of Republicans to win districts that were more white than before.

97. Oral Arguments in Shaw v. Reno, 221 Landmark Briefs 582.

98. Shaw v. Reno, 509 U.S. 630, 657 (1993).

99. Hunt v. Cromartie, 526 U.S. 541, 551 (1999) (emphasis in original).

100. Wygant v. Jackson Board of Education, 476 U.S. 267 (1986); City of Richmond v. J.A. Croson Co., 488 U.S. 469 (1989).

101. Memorandum from Assistant Attorney General Walter Dellinger to General Counsels, Re: *Adarand* (June 28, 1995), *reprinted in* 1995 Daily Lab. Rep. (BNA) No. 125, at D-33 (June 29, 1995).

102. *Id.*

103. Al Kamen, *High Court Ruling Signals Support for Affirmative Action*, Washington Post, May 20, 1986, at A1; Philip Hager & Michael Wines, *Layoff Plan Favoring Blacks Voided by the Court*, L.A. Times, May 20, 1986, at A1. *See also* Stuart Taylor Jr., *High Court Bars a Layoff Method Favoring Blacks*, N.Y. Times, May 20, 1986, at A1, A20.

104. MacNeil/Lehrer News Hour (PBS television broadcast, Mar. 31, 1986).

105. *See* Gary L. McDowell, *Affirmative Inaction*, Policy Review, Spring 1989, at 32, 34.

106. *See* Gerald M. Boyd, *Goals for Hiring to Stay in Place*, N.Y. Times, Aug. 25, 1986, at A1.

107. Nathan Glazer, *The Affirmative Action Stalemate*, Public Interest, Winter 1988, at 107.

108. Public Papers of the Presidents, 1989, I, at 29.

109. *See* Brief for Federal Communications Commission, Metro Broadcasting, Inc. v. FCC, 199 Landmark Briefs 190–251.

110. *See generally Symposium, The Civil Rights Act of 1991: Theory and Practice*, 68 Notre Dame L. Rev. 911 (1993); *Symposium, Civil Rights Legislation in the 1990s*, 79 Cal. L. Rev. 591 (1991).

111. 515 U.S. 200, 237 (1995).

112. Jeremy A. Rabkin, *The Color of California*, American Spectator, May 1995, at 24.

113. *See* Kevin Merida, *Senate Rejects Gramm Bid to Bar Affirmative Action Set Asides*, Washington Post, July 21, 1995, at A13; Gerald F. Seib, *GOP Congress Debates an Attack on Affirmative Action*, Wall Street Journal, Dec. 10, 1996, at A24.

114. *See* Juliet Eilperin, *House Defeats Bill Targeting College Affirmative Action*, Washington Post, May 7, 1998, at A4; James Dao, *Senate Stops Bid to End Road-Work Set Asides*, N.Y. Times, Mar. 7, 1998, at A9.

115. Public Papers of the Presidents, 1995, II, at 1112.

116. Text of *Affirmative Action Review* Report to President Clinton Released July 19, 1995, *reprinted in* 1995 Daily Lab. Rep. (BNA) No. 139, at Special Supplement (July 20, 1995).

117. Bill Stall, *Wilson Steps Up Affirmative Action Attack*, L.A. Times, July 19, 1995, at A3. *See also* Pete Wilson, *Equal Rights, Not Special Privileges*, L.A. Times, June 1, 1995, at A11. Unlike Wilson, most Republican governors are uninterested in leading the charge against affirmative action. *See* David S. Broder & Robert A. Barnes, *Few Governors Join Attack on Racial Politics*, Washington Post, Aug. 2, 1995, at A1.

118. Coalition for Economic Equity v. Wilson, 110 F.3d 1431, 1437 (9th Cir. 1997).

119. *See* Sam Howe Verhovek, *In a Battle over Preferences, Race and Gender Are at Odds*, N.Y. Times, Oct. 20, 1998, at A1. Affirmative action opponents are also waging their war against preferences before lower federal court judges. Yet, while lower federal courts seem increasingly willing to invalidate preferential treatment programs, the significance of these program-by-program challenges pales in comparison to initiatives that eliminate *all* affirmative action programs throughout a particular state.

120. Alex Fryer, *Affirmative-Action Fight Shifts from Ballot Box to Courtroom*, Seattle Times, Nov. 25, 2002, at A1.

121. 539 U.S. 306 (2003).

122. Brief for the United States, Grutter v. Bollinger, 9, 10.

123. Peter Schmidt, *Bush Asks Supreme Court to Strike Down U. of Michigan's Affirmative Action Policy*, The Chronicle of Higher Education, Jan. 24, 2003, at 20.

124. Adam Nagourney, *Bush and Affirmative Action: The Context; With His Eye on Two Political Prizes, the President Picks His Words Carefully*, N.Y. Times, Jan. 16, 2003 at A26.

125. Adam Nagourney & Carl Hulse, *Divisive Words: The Republican Leader; Bush Rebukes Lott over Remarks on Thurmond*, N.Y. Times, Dec. 13, 2002, at A1.

126. Letter from Arlen Specter, Olympia Snow, Susan Collins, and Lincoln Chafee to President George W. Bush, Jan. 14, 2003.

127. Brief of Lt. Gen. Julius W. Becton Jr. et al. as Amici Curiae in Support of Respondents, Grutter v. Bollinger, 5.

128. 39 Weekly Compilation of Presidential Documents 802 (2003).

129. David Von Drehle, *Court Mirrors Public Opinion*, Washington Post, June 24, 2003, at A1.

130. *See* Christine H. Rossell, *The Convergence of Black and White Attitudes on School Desegregation Issues*, *in* Equality Redefined 120 (Neal Devins & Davison M. Douglas eds., 1998); Drew S. Days III, *Brown Blues: Rethinking the Integrative Ideal in id.* at 133; Matthew Richer, *Busing's Boston Massacre*, Policy Review, Nov.–Dec. 1998, at 42.

Chapter 8

1. Gitlow v. New York, 268 U.S. 652, 666 (1925).

2. Zechariah Chafee Jr., Free Speech in the United States 325 (1941).

3. *Id.* at x.

4. Landmark Communications, Inc. v. Virginia, 435 U.S. 829, 838 n. 11 (1978) (citing Mills v. Alabama, 384 U.S. 214, 218 (1966)).

5. 1 Stat. 596, ch. 74, § 1 (1798).

6. Leonard W. Levy, Freedom of Speech and Press in Early American History: Legacy of Suppression 233 (1960). For a competing assessment of the historical record, *see* David Anderson, *The Origin of the Press Clause*, 30 U.C.L.A. L. Rev. 455 (1983).

7. Whitney v. California, 274 U.S. 357, 375 (1927) (concurrence).

8. Lucas A. Powe Jr., The Fourth Estate and the Constitution: Freedom of the Press in America 59 (1991).

9. *See id.* at 60; Wayne D. Moore, *Reconceiving Interpretive Autonomy: Insights from the Virginia and Kentucky Resolutions*, 11 Const. Com. 315, 317 (1994).

10. 8 Annals of Cong. 2152 (1798).

11. *Id.* at 2144.

12. *See* David P. Currie, The Constitution in Congress 260–61 (1997). For a famous defense of this position, *see* Levy, Freedom of Speech and Press in Early American History.

13. Levy, Freedom of Speech and Press in Early American History, at 258.

14. *See* Moore, *Reconceiving Interpretative Autonomy. But see* Currie, The Constitution on Congress, at 269–70 (depicting the resolutions as an appeal to Congress). Differences between Madison's and Jefferson's views are detailed in Wayne D. Moore, Constitutional Rights and Powers of the People 239–62 (1996).

15. H. Rept. No. 86, 26th Cong., 1st Sess. 1 (1840).

16. Leonard W. Levy, Freedom in Turmoil, Era of the Sedition Act: The Crisis of 1797–1800, at 164 (1962).

17. 11 The Writings of Thomas Jefferson 43–44 (Mem. ed. 1904) (letter to Mrs. John Adams, July 22, 1804).

18. H. Rept. No. 86, 26th Cong., 1st Sess. 2 (1840); 6 Stat. 802, c. 45 (1840).

19. New York Times Co. v. Sullivan, 376 U.S. 254, 276 (1964).

20. Michael Kent Curtis, *Free Speech: "The People's Darling Privilege"* 209 (2000) (quoting Proceedings of the New York Anti-Slavery Convention Held at Utica, Oct. 21, and New York Anti-Slavery State Society Held at Petersboro, Oct. 22, 1835, at 3).

21. *Id.* at 196 (quoting *The Law of Libel and the Abolitionists*, Evening Post (N.Y.), Aug. 31, 1835, at 2) (emphasis in original).

22. Curtis, *Free Speech: "The People's Darling Privilege,"* at 385–89.

23. *Id.* at 217.

24. William H. Rehnquist, All the Laws but One 60 (1998).

25. *Ex parte* Vallandigham, 68 U.S. 243 (1864).

26. 53 Cong. Rec. 99 (1915).

27. 40 Stat. 219, sec. 3 (1917).

28. *Id.* at 230, sec. 2.

29. For a summary of the Act's legislative history, *see* Rabban, Free Speech in Its Forgotten Years at 249–55.

30. 249 U.S. 47, 51–52 (1919).

31. Abrams v. United States, 250 U.S. 616 (1919).

32. Zechariah Chafee Jr., *Freedom of Speech in War Time*, 32 Harv. L. Rev. 932 (1919); *see also* Louis Fisher, American Constitutional Law 462–63 (5th ed. 2003).

33. Litigation involving the federal government's internment of Japanese Americans and state laws mandating that schoolchildren salute the American flag are notable exceptions to this pattern. For discussion of these cases, *see* chapters 7 (internment) and 9 (flag salute). Another important exception is United States v. Lovett, 328 U.S. 303 (1946). In *Lovett*, the Court concluded that Congress could not deny federal salaries to government employees because of their political opinions. The Roosevelt administration, which refused to defend the statute in court, also thought the law an unconstitutional bill of attainder. *See* Louis Fisher, Constitutional Dialogues 88–89 (1988).

34. *See* Robert G. McCloskey, The American Supreme Court 131–32 (2d ed. 1994, revised by Sanford Levinson).

35. Exec. Order No. 9835 *reprinted in* 5 U.S.C. § 631 (1952).

36. *See* Lucas A. Powe Jr., The Warren Court and American Politics 14–15 (2000). *See also* Albert Fried, McCarthyism: The Great American Red Scare 70–71 (1997).

37. 66 Stat. 163 (1952). President Truman vetoed the bill, arguing that some of the provisions were "worse than the infamous Alien Act of 1798." Public Papers of the Presidents, 1952–53, at 445. Congress, however, overrode Truman's veto.

38. 54 Stat. 671, sec. 2(a)(1) (1940).

39. Dennis v. United States, 341 U.S. 594 (1951). To the Court, the harms of overthrowing the government were so great that the government should have a free hand in punishing those who advocated such teachings.

40. 68 Stat. 775 (1954).

41. 354 U.S. 298 (1957) (concluding that the Smith Act is limited to speech that "incites" illegal action).

42. I. F. Stone, The Haunted Fifties 203 (1963).

43. 104 Cong. Rec. 4423 (1958).

44. Walter F. Murphy, Congress and the Court 245 (1962) (quoting Mar. 2, 1960 editorial).

45. *Id*. at 246.

46. Chapter 7 details both Southern resistance to *Brown* and the Court's cautious response to it.

47. 376 U.S. at 270. Other First Amendment cases implicating civil rights concerns include NAACP v. Button, 371 U.S. 415 (1963) (invalidating a Virginia statute regulating the solicitation of funds to support litigation) and Bond v. Floyd, 385 U.S. 116 (1966) (concluding that Georgia legislature cannot refuse to seat an African American legislator for statements he made in opposition to the Vietnam war).

48. 376 U.S. at 270.

49. *See* Bond v. Floyd, 385 U.S. 116 (1966) (upholding right of elected officials to protest War); United States v. O'Brien, 391 U.S. 367 (1968) (burning of draft card subject to criminal sanction); Tinker v. Des Moines School District, 393 U.S. 503 (1969) (upholding right of public school students to protest War); Cohen v. California, 403 U.S. 15 (1971) (political protesters can make use of profanities to express their message).

50. New York Times v. United States, 403 U.S. 713 (1971). For a detailed recounting of this case, *see* David Rudenstine, The Day the Presses Stopped (1996).

51. Brandenburg v. Ohio, 395 U.S. 444, 447 (1969).

52. S. Exec. Rep. No. 7, 100th Cong., 1st Sess. 54 (1987).

53. It is noteworthy that Anthony Kennedy, who was confirmed to the seat that Bork was nominated to fill, supplied the critical fifth vote in tossing out state and federal statutes banning flag burning.

54. McCloskey, The American Supreme Court at 132 (discussing speech cases).

55. The newspaper was not charged by the police. Instead, it was a "third party" in possession of photographs that might identify the demonstrators.

56. Zurcher v. Stanford Daily, 436 U.S. 547, 567 (1978).

57. S. Rept. No. 874, 96th Cong., 2d Sess. 4–5 (1980).

58. *Id*.

59. Public Papers of the Presidents, 1980–81, I, at 157.

60. 94 Stat. 1879 (1980).

61. S. Rept. No. 874, at 5; 126 Cong. Rec. 26567 (1980) (remarks of Rep. Hyde).

62. 126 Cong. Rec. at 16341.

63. *Id*. at 26562.

64. 82 Stat. 291 (1968).

65. H. Rept. No. 350, 90th Cong., 1st Sess. 17 (1967) (minority views by Rep. Conyers and Rep. Edwards).

66. *Desecration of the Flag: Hearings before the House Committee on the Judiciary*,

90th Cong., 1st. Sess. at 32 (remarks of Rep. Quillen), at 55 (remarks of Rep. Roudebush), at 29 (remarks of Rep. Quillen), at 46 (remarks of Rep. Kelley), at 133 (remarks of Rep. Berry), at 185 (remarks of Rep. Watson); *Hot Summers and Short Tempers*, 205 Nation 36, 37 (1967) (quoting Rep. Baring). *See generally* Robert Justin Goldstein, Saving Old Glory 118–37 (1995).

67. *Flag Burning Ban Advances in House*, N.Y. Times, June 7, 1967, at 29.

68. Anthony Ripley, *The American Flag: A Center of Dispute on Birthday of U.S.*, N.Y. Times, July 5, 1971, at 1; Fred P.Graham, *The Flag: Chaos over the Issue of Its Abuse*, N.Y. Times, Jan. 10, 1971, at 4–10.

69. Smith v. Goguen, 415 U.S. 566, 581–82 (1974).

70. Texas v. Johnson, 491 U.S. 397, 419–20 (1989).

71. 135 Cong. Rec. 13005 (1989).

72. *Id.* at 12849, 12851.

73. Public Papers of the Presidents, 1989, I, at 832.

74. *See Americans Disagree with Supreme Court on Flag Burning Poll*, Reuters, June 24, 1989; Michelle Battle, *Poll: 69% Want Flag Protected*, USA Today, June 23, 1989, at A1.

75. *Hearings on Measures to Protect the Physical Integrity of the American Flag: Hearings before the Senate Committee on the Judiciary*, 101st Cong., 1st Sess. 66 (1989).

76. *Statutory and Constitutional Responses to the Supreme Court Decision in Texas v. Johnson: Hearings before the House Committee on the Judiciary*, 101st Cong., 1st Sess. 202 (1989).

77. Joseph Mianowany, *House Panel Ignores Bush, Passes Flag Bill*, UPI, July 27, 1989.

78. *Statutory and Constitutional Responses to the Supreme Court Decision in Texas v. Johnson: Hearings before the House Committee on the Judiciary*, at 2.

79. 135 Cong. Rec. 23122 (1989).

80. 135 Cong. Rec. 20105–6 (1989) (remarks of Rep. Douglas).

81. *Id.* at 20106 (citing an article in USA Today). *See also* Richard Wolf, *Topic: The Flag Amendment; Don't Let Hysteria Hurt Flag's Meaning*, USA Today, July 12, 1989.

82. *See, e.g.*, Cong. Rec. 23123–24 (remarks of Sen. Thurmond) *and* 23132–33 (remarks of Sen. Dixon).

83. Public Papers of the Presidents, 1989, II, at 1403.

84. Brief for the United States, United States v. Eichman, 194 Landmark Briefs 408.

85. United States v. Eichmann, 496 U.S. 310 (1990).

86. Joan Biskupic, *Congress Snaps to Attention over New Flag Proposal*, CQ Weekly Report, June 16, 1990, at 1877 (quoting President Bush); Public Papers of the Presidents, 1990, I, at 812.

87. *See* Daniel H. Pollitt, *The Flag Burning Controversy: A Chronology*, 70 N.C. L. Rev. 553, 598–99 (1992).

88. Biskupic, *Congress Snaps to Attention over New Flag Proposal*, at 1877.

89. The final vote was 254 to 177, 34 votes short of the two-thirds needed.

90. Charles Tiefer, *The Flag-Burning Controversy of 1989–90: Congress' Valid Role in Constitutional Dialogue*, 29 Harv. J. on Legis. 357 (1992).

91. *Proposing a Constitutional Amendment Authorizing the States and Congress to Prohibit the Physical Desecration of the Flag: Hearings before the Senate Committee on the Judiciary*, 104th Cong., 1st Sess. 33 (1995) (statement by Walter Dellinger).

92. *Id.* at 34.

93. *See* 148 Cong. Rec. S5529 (daily ed. June 13, 2002) (remarks of Sen. Leahy); 148 Cong. Rec. S5581 (daily ed. June 14, 2002) (remarks of Sen. Thurmond).

94. Editorializing by Broadcast Licenses, 13 F.C.C. 1246 (1949).

95. Committee for the Fair Broadcasting of Controversial Issues, 25 F.C.C. 2d 283, 292 (1970).

96. Mark S. Fowler, *The Federal Communications Commission 1981–1987: What the Chairman Said*, 10 Hastings Comm/Ent L. J. 409, 411 (1988); *In re* Complaint of Syracuse Peace Council, 2 F.C.C.R. 5043 (1987).

97. Red Lion Broadcasting v. FCC, 395 U.S. 367 (1969).

98. Fowler, *The Federal Communications Commission 1981–1987*, at 410.

99. FCC Chairman Dennis Patrick, cited in *Broadcast Deregulation: The Reagan Years and Beyond*, 40 Admin. L. Rev. 345, 353 (1988).

100. Inquiry into Section 73.1910 of the Commission's Rules and Regulations Concerning the General Fairness Obligations of Broadcast Licensees, 102 F.C.C. 2d 143 (1985).

101. *Id.* at 246–47.

102. *Codification of Fairness Doctrine Appears Imminent*, Broadcasting, Apr. 13, 1987, at 78 (quoting John Dingell, chair of the FCC's oversight committee). *See also* Edward J. Markey, *Congress to Administrative Agencies: Creator, Overseer, and Partner*, 1990 Duke L. J. 967.

103. Public Papers of the Presidents, 1987, I, at 690. *See The President vs. the Fairness Doctrine*, Broadcasting, June 29, 1987, at 29.

104. *In re* Complaint of Syracuse Peace Council Against WTVH, 2 F.C.C.R. 5043, 5057 (1987).

105. Rush Limbaugh, *It's an Attempt to Make Talk Radio PC*, Electronic Media, Sept. 27, 1993, at 13.

106. Repeal of Modification of the Personal Attack and Political Editorial Rules, 48 Fed. Reg. 28,295, 28,298 (1983).

107. Radio-Television News Directors Association et al. v. Federal Communications Commission et al., 229 F.3d 269 (D.C. Cir. 2000).

108. 62 Stat. 769, sec. 1464 (1948).

109. FCC v. Pacifica Foundation, 438 U.S. 726 (1978).

110. Jim Exon, *We Can't Allow Smut on the Internet*, Washington Post, Mar. 9, 1995, at A20.

111. Butler v. Michigan, 352 U.S. 380, 383 (1957) (concluding that the law would "reduce the adult population of Michigan to reading only that which is fit for children").

112. Powe, The Warren Court and American Politics at 336–57.

113. 113 Cong. Rec. 12211 (1967) (statement of Sen. Mundt); *id.* at 12212 (reprinting the Senate Resolution that created the Commission).

114. 116 Cong. Rec. 36459 (1970) (reprinting a Senate resolution criticizing the Report).

115. 56 F.C.C. 2d 94, 99 (1975).

116. FCC v. Pacifica Foundation, 438 U.S. 726 (1978); Brief for the United States, 101 Landmark Briefs 525 (1977); Petitioner's Reply Brief, 101 Landmark Briefs 504 (1977).

117. Final Report of the Attorney General's Commission on Pornography 1957 (1986).

118. United States Department of Justice, Beyond the Pornography Commission: The Federal Response 43 (1988). A clearinghouse for legal resources and information about pornography, the Obscenity Law Center, was also created. *Id.*

119. *See* Action for Children's Television v. FCC, 932 F.2d 1504 (D.C. Cir. 1991).

120. *See* Denver Area Educ. Telecom. Consortium v. FCC, 518 U.S. 727 (1996) (cable); Reno v. ACLU, 521 U.S. 844 (1997) (Internet); ApolloMedia Corp. v. Reno, 526 U.S. 1061 (1999) (e-mail); American Library Ass'n et al. v. United States et al., 201 F. Supp. 2d 401 (E.D. Pa. 2002) (Internet).

121. *See* Sable Communications of Cal. v FCC, 492 U.S. 115 (1989).

122. American Library Ass'n v. Thornburgh, 713 F. Supp. 469 (D.D.C. 1989); American Library Ass'n v. Barr, 794 F. Supp. 412 (D.D.C. 1992).

123. Ashcroft v. Free Speech Coalition, 535 U.S. 234 (2002).

124. 134 Cong. Rec. 7337 (1988) (statement of Rep. Coats).

125. *Id.* at 7336 (1988) (statement of Rep. Hall).

126. 141 Cong. Rec. 15504 (1995) (statement of Senator Exon).

127. H. Rept. No. 105–775, 105th Cong., 2d Sess. 12 (1998). In Ashcroft v. ACLU, 535 U.S. 564 (2002), the Supreme Court, after concluding that "contemporary community standards" were relevant to identifying materials harmful to minors, sent the case back to a federal appellate court to sort out other constitutional objections to the statute.

128. In United States v. American Library Association, the Supreme Court rejected a facial challenge to the statute. 123 S. Ct. 2297 (2003). The Justices, however, signaled that the law could be subject to a new First Amendment challenge if it proved unduly burdensome to adult access to the Internet.

129. 98 Stat. 204 (1984).

130. *See* Linda Greenhouse, *Supreme Court Roundup; Child Smut Conviction Vacated after U.S. Shift,* N.Y. Times, Nov. 2, 1993, at B7.

131. *See* Linda Greenhouse, *Court Rejects Appeal of Man Convicted in Child Smut Case with Political Overtones,* N.Y. Times, Jan. 18, 1995, at D20.

132. Letter from Acting Assistant Attorney General Kent Markus to Hon. Patrick J. Leahy *reprinted in* 141 Cong. Rec. 16022 (1995) (statement of Sen. Leahy).

133. One important exception is Congress's power to set conditions on the receipt of federal grants and subsidies. *See* National Endowment for Arts v. Finley, 524 U.S. 569 (1998) (upholding Congress's power to take "general standards of decency" into account when making arts-related grants); United States v. Ameri-

can Library Association, 123 S. Ct. 2297 (2003) (rejecting facial challenge to Children's Internet Protection Act).

Chapter 9

1. Cantwell v. Connecticut, 310 U.S. 296 (1940).
2. Frank J. Sorauf, The Wall of Separation: The Constitutional Politics of Church and State 3 (1976).
3. Allen D. Hertzke, Representing God in Washington: The Role of Religious Lobbies in the American Polity 5 (1988).
4. U.S. Selective Service System, Conscientious Objection (Special Monograph No. 11, Vol. I) 30 (1950).
5. 2 Journals of the Continental Congress 189 (1905).
6. Pa. Const. of 1776, VIII; Vt. Const. of 1775, Ch. I, IX; N.H. Const. of 1784, Art. I, XIII; Me. Const. of 1819, Art. VII, Sec. 5; *reproduced in* Sources and Documents of United States Constitutions (William F. Swindler ed., 1973–1979): 8 Swindler 278; 9 Swindler 490; 6 Swindler 345; 4 Swindler 323.
7. Cong. Globe, 37th Cong., 3d Sess. 994 (1863) (statement by Senator Ira Harris). *See also* debate at 1261, 1292, 1389–90.
8. Edward Needles Wright, Conscientious Objectors in the Civil War 15–16, 69–72 (1931); 13 Stat. 9, § 17 (1864).
9. Fraina v. United States, 255 F. 28, 31 (2d Cir. 1918).
10. National Service Board for Religious Objectors, Congress Looks at the Conscientious Objector 15 (1943).
11. 54 Stat. 889, § 5(g) (1940). For further details on the statutory history of conscientious objectors, *see* Louis Fisher, Religious Liberty in America: Political Safeguards 82–104 (2002).
12. Cong. Globe, 36th Cong., 1st Sess. 648–49 (1860); Bertrum Wallace Korn, Eventual Years and Experiences 107 (1955).
13. 12 Stat. 270, § 9 (1861); 12 Stat. 288, § 7 (1861); Bertrum Wallace Korn, American Jewry and the Civil War 58–60, 65–68, 70 (1951); Jonathan D. Sarna & David G. Dalin, Religion and State in the American Jewish Tradition 130 (1997).
14. 12 Stat. 595, § 8 (1862).
15. 2 Anson Phelps Stokes, Church and State in the United States 121 (1950).
16. Luke Eugene Ebersole, Church Lobbying in the Nation's Capital 2 (1951).
17. Robert Booth Fowler & Allen D. Hertzke, Religion and Politics in America: Faith, Culture, and Strategic Choices 18 (1995).
18. Ebersole, Church Lobbying in the Nation's Capital, at 3.
19. *Id.* at 4–5.
20. Walz v. Tax Commission, 397 U.S. 664, 670 (1970).
21. Ebersole, Church Lobbying in the Nation's Capital, at 24–56. Also descriptive of church lobbies, in 1968, is Richard E. Morgan, The Politics of Religious Conflict: Church and State in America 48–68 (1968).

22. Allen D. Hertzke, *The Role of Religious Lobbies, in* Religion in American Politics 123 (Charles W. Dunn ed., 1989).

23. Fowler & Hertzke, Religion and Politics in America, at 54.

24. Paul J. Weber & W. Landis Jones, U.S. Interest Groups: Institutional Profiles (1994).

25. A. James Reichley, Religion in American Public Life 246–50 (1985).

26. James L. Adams, The Growing Church Lobby in Washington 89–106 (1970).

27. Fowler & Hertzke, Religion and Politics in America, at 202 (emphasis in original).

28. Lee Epstein, *Interest Group Litigation during the Rehnquist Court Era*, 9 J. Law & Pol. 639, 685 (1993). *See also* Leo Pfeffer, *Amici in Church-State Litigation*, 44 Law & Contemp. Prob. 83 (Spring 1981).

29. A summary of lawmaker initiatives can be found in chapter 6.

30. Engel v. Vitale, 370 U.S. 421 (192).

31. Louis Fisher, American Constitutional Law 647–48 (5th ed. 2003).

32. Hertzke, Representing God in Washington, at 161.

33. *Id.*

34. "Thou shalt not make unto thee any graven image, or any likeness of any thing that is in heaven above, or that is in the earth beneath, or that is in the water under the earth. Thou shalt not bow down thyself to them, nor serve them" (Exodus 20:4–5).

35. Gobitis v. Minersville School Dist., 21 F.Supp. 581, 586 (E.D. Pa. 1937).

36. Respondents' Brief, Minersville School Dist. v. Gobitis, at 3; 37 Landmark Briefs 375.

37. Francis H. Heller, *A Turning Point for Religious Liberty*, 29 Va. L. Rev. 440, 447 (1943).

38. Alice Fleetwood Bartee, Cases Lost, Causes Won 53 (1984).

39. Minersville School District v. Gobitis, 310 U.S. 586, 600 (1940).

40. David R. Manwaring, Render unto Caesar: The Flag-Salute Controversy 149–60 (1962); John T. Noonan Jr., The Believer and the Powers That Are 250–51 (1987); Heller, *A Turning Point for Religious Liberty*, 29 Va. L. Rev. at 452–53.

41. Manwaring, Render unto Caesar, at 187.

42. Victor W. Rotnem & F. G. Folson Jr., *Recent Restrictions upon Religious Liberty*, 36 Am. Pol. Sci. Rev. 1053, 1062 (1942).

43. H. N. Hirsch, The Enigma of Felix Frankfurter 152 (1981).

44. State v. Lefebvre, 20 A.2d 185, 187 (N.H. 1941).

45. *In re* Latrecchia, 26 A.2d 881, 882 (N.J. 1942); State v. Smith, 127 P.2d 518, 522 (Kans. 1942).

46. Jones v. Opelika, 316 U.S. 584, 624 (1942).

47. Joseph P. Lash, From the Diaries of Felix Frankfurter 70 (1975).

48. Busey v. District of Columbia, 129 F.2d 24, 38 (D.C. Cir. 1942).

49. 56 Stat. 380, § 7 (1942).

50. Rotnem & Folsom, *Recent Restrictions upon Religious Liberty*, 36 Am. Pol. Sci. Rev. at 1064.

51. Manwaring, Render unto Caesar, at 188–89.

52. Brief for American Civil Liberties Union, Amicus Curiae, West Virginia State Board of Education v. Barnette; 40 Landmark Briefs 177–78.

53. 11 LW 3279 (1943).

54. West Virginia State Board of Education v. Barnette, 319 U.S. 624, 640–41, 642 (1943).

55. 56 Landmark Briefs 1038.

56. 370 U.S. at 433–35.

57. 108 Cong. Rec. 11709, 11718, 11732 (1962).

58. Philip B. Kurland, *The Regents' Prayer Case:"Full of Sound and Fury, Signifying . . . ,"* 1962 Sup. Ct. Rev. 1, 3.

59. Public Papers of the Presidents, 1962, at 510–11.

60. *Prayers in Public Schools and Other Matters: Hearings before the Senate Committee on the Judiciary*, 87th Cong., 2d Sess. (1962).

61. 1964 CQ Almanac 399.

62. *School Prayers (Part I): Hearings before the House Committee on the Judiciary*, 88th Cong., 2d Sess. 656 (1964).

63. John R. Vile, Encyclopedia of Constitutional Amendments, Proposed Amendments, and Amending Issues 237–39 (1996).

64. 2 Donald Bruce Johnson, National Party Platforms 683 (1978) (emphasis added).

65. Brief for the United States as Amicus Curiae, Wallace v. Jaffree, 155 Landmark Briefs 124–25 (1985). The Court rejected this invitation, ruling in 1985 that Alabama acted unconstitutionally when it authorized a period of silence for "meditation or voluntary prayer." Wallace v. Jaffree, 472 U.S. 38 (1985).

66. Public Papers of the Presidents, 1982, I, at 603, 647–48.

67. S. Rept. No. 98–347, 98th Cong., 2d Sess. 38 (1984).

68. *See* James E. Wood Jr., *Equal Access: A New Direction in American Public Education*, 27 J. Church & State 5, 8 (1985).

69. *See* Helen Dewar, *Reelection Agendas Differ: GOP Senators Don't Dance to Reagan Tune*, Washington Post, Mar. 27, 1984, at A4.

70. S. 450, 96th Cong., 1st Sess. (1979).

71. *Nomination of Edwin Meese III: Hearings before the Senate Committee on the Judiciary*, 98th Cong. 2d Sess. 185–88 (1984).

72. 128 Cong. Rec. 689 (1982).

73. S. Rept. 98–347, 98th Cong., 2d Sess., at 12.

74. Quoted in 130 Cong. Rec. 20934–35 (1984) (statement of Rep. Schumer).

75. Quoted in Wood, *Equal Access*, 27 J. Church & State, at 10.

76. Westside Community Bd. of Ed. v. Mergens, 496 U.S. 226, 249 (1990).

77. Wallace v. Jaffree, 466 U.S. 924 (1984); Wallace v. Jaffree, 472 U.S. 38 (1985).

78. *In re* James, 524 U.S. 936 (1998).

79. Kenneth M. Dolbeare & Phillip E. Hammond, The School Prayer Decisions: From Court Policy to Local Practice (1969); Ben A. Franklin, *Pennsylvanians Lead School Prayer Revolt*, N.Y. Times, Mar. 26, 1969, at 1; H. Frank Way Jr., *Survey*

Research on Judicial Decisions: The Prayer and Bible Reading Cases, 21 West. Pol. Q. 189 (1968).

80. David E. Rosenbaum, *Prayer in Many Schoolrooms Continues Despite '62 Ruling,* – N.Y. Times, Mar. 11, 1984, at 1.

81. *See* Note, *The Unconstitutionality of State Statutes Authorising Moments of Silence in the Public Schools,* 96 Harv. L. Rev. 1874, 1874 n.1 (1983).

82. *See* David Z. Seide, *Daily Moments of Silence in Public Schools: A Constitutional Analysis,* 58 N.Y.U. L. Rev. 364, 367 n.19 (1983).

83. *See* Brief of the States' Attorneys General as Amici Curiae, Wallace v. Jaffree, 155 Landmark Briefs 559 (1995).

84. Public Papers of the Presidents, 1985, II, at 1078–81.

85. Caryle Murphy, *At Public Schools, Religion Thrives,* Washington Post, May 7, 1998, at A1.

86. Goldman v. Weinberger, 475 U.S. 503, 511 (1986) (concurrence by Justice Stevens, joined by Justices White and Powell).

87. Goldman v. Secretary of Defense, 734 F.2d 1531, 1539 (D.C. Cir. 1984).

88. Goldman v. Secretary of Defense, 739 F.2d 657, 658 (D.C. Cir. 1984).

89. 130 Cong. Rec. 14295 (1984).

90. *Id.* at 14298.

91. H. Rept. No. 98–1080, 98th Cong., 2d Sess. 293–94 (1984); 98 Stat. 2532–33, sec. 554 (1984).

92. Joint Service Study on Religious Matters xi–xii (Mar. 1985).

93. Oral argument, Goldman v. Weinberger, U.S. Supreme Court, Jan. 14, 1986, at 45.

94. Goldman v. Weinberger, 475 U.S. 503, 508 (1986).

95. U.S. Const., art. I, sec. 8, cl. 14.

96. 132 Cong. Rec. 19802, 19803 (1986).

97. 133 Cong. Rec. 25251 (1987) (statement by Senator Murkowski).

98. *Id.* at 25256.

99. 101 Stat. 1086–87, § 508 (1987).

100. George de Verges, *Freedom of Religion: Peyote and the Native American Church,* 2 Am. Ind. L. Rev. 71 (1974); H. Rept. No. 103–675, 103d Cong., 2d Sess. 3 (1994).

101. Smith v. Employment Division, 763 P.2d 146, 149 (Ore. 1988).

102. 21 CFR § 1307.31.

103. Smith v. Employment Div., 721 P.2d 445 (Ore. 1986); Smith v. Employment Div., 763 P.2d 146 (Ore. 1988).

104. Petition for Writ of Certiorari to the Supreme Court of the State of Oregon, Employment Division v. Smith; 196 Landmark Briefs 425.

105. 494 U.S. 872 (1990).

106. Oregon Laws, Chap. 329, § 1 (June 24, 1991); *reprinted in* 1995 Oregon Revised Statutes 475.992, § 5 (v. 9, p. 80).

107. 139 Cong. Rec. 9680 (1993) (statement of Rep. Brooks).

108. *Religious Freedom Restoration Act of 1991: Hearings on H.R. 2797 before the House Committee on the Judiciary,* 102d Cong., 2d Sess. 10, 14 (1992).

109. *Id.* at 25.

110. *The Religious Freedom Restoration Act: Hearings before the Senate Committee on the Judiciary,* 102d Cong., 2d Sess. 4 (1992).

111. *Religious Freedom Restoration Act of 1991: Hearings before the House Committee on the Judiciary,* 102d Cong., 2d Sess. 7 (1992).

112. 139 Cong. Rec. 9683 (1993) (statement of Rep. Nadler); *id.* at 9684 (statement of Rep. Schumer); *id.* at 9685 (statement of Rep. Orton).

113. Public Papers of the President, 1993, II, at 2000.

114. 139 Cong. Rec. (1993) (statement of Senator Hatch); Public Papers of the President, 1993, II, at 2000.

115. Boerne v. Flores, 521 U.S. 507, 535–36 (1997).

116. *Id.* at 529.

117. Agostini v. Felton, 524 U.S. 203 (1997), reversing Aguilar v. Felton, 473 U.S. 402 (1985).

118. Boerne v. Flores, 521 U.S. at 519.

119. 108 Stat. 3124 (1994).

120. *In re* Young, 141 F.3d 854 (8th Cir. 1998), cert. denied, sub nom. Christians, Trustee v. Crystal Evangelical Free Church, 525 U.S. 811 (1998).

121. Kikumura v. Hurley, 242 F.3d 950 (10th Cir. 2001).

122. *Protecting Religious Freedom after Boerne v. Flores: Hearing before the House Committee on the Judiciary,* 105th Cong., 1st Sess. (1997); *Congress' Constitutional Role in Protecting Religious Liberty: Hearings before the Senate Committee on the Judiciary,* 105th Cong., 1st Sess. (1997).

123. 144 Cong. Rec. S5791 (daily ed. June 9, 1998).

124. 145 Cong. Rec. H5583 (daily ed. July 15, 1999).

125. *Id.* at 5608.

126. 114 Stat. 803 (2000). For further details on Peyotism, *see* Fisher, Religious Liberty in America, at 147–201.

127. Pierce v. Society of Sisters, 268 U.S. 510, 525 (1925).

128. *Id.* at 535. This period is treated well in William G. Ross, Forging New Freedoms: Nativism, Education, and the Constitution, 1917–1927 (1994).

129. State v. Columbus Christian, No. 78 CVS 1978, slip op. at 14 (N.C. Super. Ct. September 1, 1978). This decision was vacated after the North Carolina legislature amended its education statute.

130. 1979 N.C. Sess. Laws 505, codified at N.C. Gen. Stat. §§ 115, 547–54 (1991).

131. 1987 N.C. Sess. Laws 891, codified at N.C. Gen. Stat. § 115C-563 (1991).

132. Telephone interview with Tim Simmons, Education Reporter, Raleigh News and Observer, Oct. 10, 1991.

133. Telephone interview with Simmons, Oct. 17, 1991.

134. State v. Faith Baptist Church, 301 N.W.2d 571 (Neb. 1981), appeal dismissed, 454 U.S. 803 (1981).

135. *Id.* at 580.

136. The Report of the Governor's Christian School Panel, Jan. 26, 1984, at 27.

137. Nebraska Revised Statutes, §§ 79–1701 (1990).

138. *See* Neal Devins, *Fundamentalist Christian Educators v. State: An Inevitable Compromise*, 60 G.W. L. Rev. 818 (1992).

Chapter 10

1. Robert A. Dahl, *Decision-Making in a Democracy: The Supreme Court as a National Policy-Maker*, 6 J. Pub. L. 279 (1957) (emphasis in original).

2. Sandra Day O'Connor, The Majesty of Law: Reflections of a Supreme Court Justice 43, 44 (2003).

3. C. Herman Pritchett, *The Development of Judicial Research*, in Frontiers of Judicial Research 31 (Joel B. Grossman and Joseph Tanenhaus eds.,1969).

4. Walter F. Murphy, *Who Shall Interpret? The Quest for Ultimate Constitutional Interpreter*, 48 Review of Politics 401, 417 (1981).

5. 142 Cong. Rec. H3010 (daily ed. Mar. 28, 1996) (statement of Rep. Marge Roukema (R-N.J.)).

6. *See* chapters 7 (school desegregation), 9 (school prayer).

7. *See* Walter F. Murphy & Joseph Tannenhaus, *Publicity, Public Opinion, and the Court*, 84 Nw. U. L. Rev. 985, 1017 (1990).

8. Cecil Andrus, Text of Speech, Idaho Statesman, Mar. 29, 1990 at A-9.

9. Larry Alexander & Frederick Schauer, *On Extrajudicial Constitutional Interpretation*, 110 Harv. L. Rev. 1359 (1997).

10. *Id.* at 1381.

11. *Id.* at 1376.

12. On Court declarations of its last word status, *see* Louis Fisher, *The Curious Belief in Judicial Supremacy*, 25 Suffolk U. L. Rev. 85 (1991).

13. 3 Richardson 1145. This quote comes from Andrew Jackson's veto of legislation rechartering the Bank of the United States.

14. Alexander & Schauer, *On Extrajudicial Constitutional Interpretation*, 110 Harv. L. Rev. at 1370, 1371.

15. Planned Parenthood v. Casey, 505 U.S. 833, 865 (1992).

16. 5 U.S. at 177. As we explain in chapter 1, Marshall also feared that, had he ruled against President Jefferson, his political enemies would push for his impeachment.

17. 505 U.S. 833, 867, 869 (1992).

18. Robert B. McKay, *Comments on Powell v. McCormack*, 17 UCLA L. Rev. 117, 125–29 nn. 42–44 (1969).

19. 79 Landmark Briefs 861, 871–72, 879.

20. Gerald N. Rosenberg, The Hollow Hope 78 (1991).

21. Richard C. Cortner, The Apportionment Cases 144–47 (1970).

22. Louis Harris, *President Should Obey Order to Give Up Tapes*, The Harris Survey, July 29, 1974.

23. Neal Devins, Shaping Constitutional Values 73–74 (1996).

24. Planned Parenthood v. Casey, 505 U.S. at 965–96 (recognizing the connection between the Court's "legitimacy" and "public acceptance").

25. Tom R. Tyler & Gregory Mitchell, *Legitimacy and Empowerment of Discretionary Legal Authority: The United States Supreme Court and Abortion Rights*, 43 Duke L. J. 703, 715 (1994).

26. Burnet v Coronado Oil & Gas Co., 285 U.S. 393, 408 (1932) (Brandeis, dissenting).

27. *A Justice Speaks Out: A Conversation with Harry A. Blackmun*, Cable News Network, Inc., Dec. 4, 1982, at 20.

28. Richard Funston, *The Supreme Court and Critical Elections*, 69 Am. Pol. Sci. Rev. 795 (1975); Walter F. Murphy & Joseph Tanenhaus, *Publicity, Public Opinion, and the Court*, 84 Nw. U. L. Rev. 985 (1990); Robert A. Dahl, *Decision-Making in a Democracy: The Supreme Court as National Policy-Maker*, 6 J. Pub. L. 279 (1957); David Adamany, *Legitimacy, Realigning Elections, and the Supreme Court*, 1973 Wisc. L. Rev. 790 (1973).

29. Owen J. Roberts, The Court and the Constitution 61 (1951). For additional discussion, *see* chapter 3.

30. Louis Fisher, *Social Influences on Constitutional Law*, 15 J. Pol. Sci. 7, 11–15 (1987).

31. *See also* David R. Manwaring, Rendering unto Caeser: The Flag Salute Controversy 154–60 (1962); H. N. Hirsch, The Enigma of Felix Frankfurter 152–53 (1981).

32. *See also* Devins, Shaping Constitutional Values, at 56–77, 139–48.

33. Louis Fisher, Constitutional Dialogues 75–76 (1987).

34. Chapter 3 examines the Rehnquist Court's revitalization of states' rights. *See also* Mark Tushnet, *Living in a Constitutional Moment: Lopez and Constitutional Theory*, 46 Case W. Res. L. Rev. 845 (1996).

35. For a useful summary of instances where the Court overturned earlier precedent, *see* Michael J. Gerhardt, *The Role of Precedent in Constitutional Decisionmaking and Theory*, 60 G.W. L. Rev. 68, 147–59 (1991).

36. Minersville School District v. Gobitis, 310 U.S. 586 (1940) (upholding mandatory flag salute), overruled three years later by West Virginia State Board of Education v. Barnette, 319 U.S. 624 (1943).

37. Robert H. Jackson, *Maintaining Our Freedoms: The Role of the Judiciary*, 19 Vital Speeches 759, 761 (1953).

38. Ashwander v. TVA, 297 U.S. 288, 346–48 (1936) (Brandeis, J., concurring).

39. Earl Warren, The Memoirs of Earl Warren 6 (1977). For the classic academic statement of this position, *see* Herbert Wechsler, *Towards Neutral Principles of Constitutional Law*, 73 Harv. L. Rev. 1, 14–15 (1959).

40. Alexander M. Bickel, *The Supreme Court, 1960 Term—Foreword: The Passive Virtues*, 75 Harv. L. Rev. 40, 49 (1961).

41. For a more comprehensive treatment of this subject (including an explanation of why the Supreme Court cannot decide issues in a coherent way whenever there are more than two possible rules of decision), *see* Frank H. Easterbrook, *Ways of Criticizing the Court*, 95 Harv. L. Rev. 802 (1982).

42. Larry Alexander & Frederick Schauer, *Defending Judicial Supremacy: A Reply*, 17 Const. Comm. 455, 479 (2000).

43. 10 The Works of James Buchanan 106 n. 1 (John B. Moore ed., 1910).

44. 7 Richardson 2962.

45. Alexander & Schauer, *On Extrajudicial Constitutional Interpretation*, 110 Harv. L. Rev. at 1382.

46. *Id.* at 1383.

47. *E.g.*, Ronald Reagan, Abortion and the Conscience of the Nation 15, 19–21 (1984); *The Religious Freedom Restoration Act: Hearings before the Senate Committee on the Judiciary*, 102d Cong., 2d Sess. 4 (1992) (statement of Oliver S. Thomas).

48. Alexander & Schauer, *On Extrajudicial Constitutional Interpretation*, 110 Harv. L. Rev. at 1385.

49. The best treatment of this topic is Lawrence Gene Sager, *Fair Measure: The Legal Status of Underenforced Constitutional Norms*, 91 Harv. L. Rev. 1212 (1978).

50. Gary Orfield, Public School Desegregation in the United States, 1968–1980, at 5 (1983).

51. *Id.*

52. Green v. County School Bd., 391 U.S. 430, 438 (1968).

53. Robert H. Jackson, The Struggle for Judicial Supremacy 291 (1941).

54. Alexander M. Bickel, The Supreme Court and the Idea of Progress 99 (1970).

55. Henry P. Monaghan, *The Supreme Court 1975 Term—Foreword: Constitutional Common Law*, 89 Harv. L. Rev. 1, 3 (1975).

56. Ruth Bader Ginsburg, *Communicating and Commenting on the Court's Work*, 83 Geo. L. J. 2119, 2125 (1995).

57. Prominent examples include Gerald N. Rosenberg, The Hollow Hope: Can Courts Bring About Social Change? (1991) (inconsequential); Mark Tushnet, Taking the Constitution Away from the Courts (2000) (counterproductive). Needless to say, Tushnet's book is the source of the heading for this section.

58. See chapters 4 (legislative veto), 6 (school desegregation).

59. Henry M. Hart, *Foreword: The Time Chart of the Justices*, 73 Harv. L. Rev. 84, 99 (1959).

60. Charles L. Black Jr., The People and the Courts 52 (1960).

61. For this very reason, we think our study explains what the rejection of judicial supremacy means "in practice." *See* Larry D. Kramer, *The Supreme Court 2000 Term, Foreword: We the Court*, 115 Harv. L. Rev. 4, 8 n.12; *id.* at 7–8 (critiquing us and other scholars who reject judicial supremacy).

62. Barbara H. Craig & David M. O'Brien, Abortion and American Politics 15 (1993).

63. Joan Biskupic, *Ginsburg Stresses Value of Incremental Change*, Washington Post. July 21, 1993, at A6.

64. Bickel, The Least Dangerous Branch, at 261.

65. Alexander & Schauer, *On Extrajudicial Constitutional Interpretation*, 110 Harv. L. Rev. at 1386.

66. Bickel, The Least Dangerous Branch, at 240, 244.

67. Alexander & Schauer, *On Extrajudicial Constitutional Interpretation*, 110 Harv. L. Rev. at 1379.

Case Index

Case name followed by cite and page number(s)

Bob Jones University v. United States, 461 U.S. 574 (1983), 163, 272
Boerne v. Flores, 521 U.S. 507 (1997), 12, 72, 211, 212, 243, 255, 284
Bond v. Floyd, 385 U.S. 116 (1966), 180, 276
Bowers v. Hardwick, 478 U.S. 186 (1986), 131, 139–43, 266
Bowsher v. Synar, 478 U.S. 714 (1986), 78–79, 98, 256
Bradwell v. State, 83 U.S. (16 Wall.) 130 (1873), 34, 248
Brandenburg v. Ohio, 395 U.S. 444 (1969), 180, 276
Bray v. Alexandria Women's Health Clinic, 506 U.S. 263 (1993), 133, 265
Brown v. Allen, 344 U.S. 443 (1953), 9, 243
Brown v. Board of Education, 347 U.S. 483 (1954), 4, 6, 11, 20, 35, 45, 47,
    49, 154–57, 159, 170, 179–80, 223, 225, 229, 232, 234, 236–37, 242, 245,
    270
Brown v. Board of Education, 349 U.S. 294 (1955), 20, 155–56, 225, 245, 270
Buchanan v. Warley, 245 U.S. 60 (1917), 154, 270
Burke v. Barnes, 479 U.S. 361 (1987), 258
Burnet v. Coronado Oil & Gas Co., 285 U.S. 393 (1932), 224, 286
Busey v. District of Columbia, 129 F.2d 24 (D.C. Cir. 1942), 200, 281
Bush v. Gore, 531 U.S. 98 (2000), 72–73, 255
Butler v. Michigan, 352 U.S. 380 (1957), 189, 278

Calder v. Bull, 3 U.S. (3 Dall.) 386 (1798), 15, 244
Campbell v. Clinton, 203 F.3d 19 (D.C. Cir. 2000), 122, 263
Campbell v. Clinton, 52 F.Supp. 2d 34 (D.D.C. 1999), 122, 263
Campbell v. Sundquist, 926 S.W.2d 250 (Tenn. Ct. App. 1996), 141, 267
Cantwell v. Connecticut, 310 U.S. 296 (1940), 195, 280
Carpenter v. Dane, 9 Wis. 249 (1859), 50, 251
Child Labor Tax Case, 259 U.S. 20 (1922), 60, 253
Christians, Trustee v. Crystal Evangelical Free Church, 525 U.S. 811 (1998), 212, 284
Christoffel v. United States, 338 U.S. 84 (1949), 92, 258
City of Richmond v. J. A. Croson Co., 488 U.S. 469 (1989), 164, 272
Coalition for Economic Equity v. Wilson, 110 F.3d 1431 (9th Cir. 1997), 168, 273
Cohen v. California, 403 U.S. 15 (1971), 180, 276
College Savings Bank v. Florida Prepaid Postsecondary, 527 U.S. 666 (1999), 72, 255
Committee to Defend Reprod. Rights v. Myers, 625 P.2d 779 (Cal. 1981), 138, 266
Conyers v. Reagan, 578 F.Supp. 324 (D.D.C. 1984), 121, 263
Conyers v. Reagan, 765 F.2d 1124 (D.C. Cir. 1985), 121, 263
Cooper v. Aaron, 358 U.S. 1 (1958), 12, 156, 223, 243, 270
Cooper v. Telfair, 4 U.S. (4 Dall.) 14 (1800), 15, 244
Crockett v. Reagan, 558 F.Supp. 893 (D.D.C. 1982), 121, 263
Crockett v. Reagan, 720 F.2d 1355 (D.C. Cir. 1983), 121, 263
Cruzan v. Director, Missouri Dept. of Health, 497 U.S. 261 (1990), 144, 145, 267

Dames & Moore v. Regan, 453 U.S. 654 (1981), 111, 261
Davenport v. Garcia, 834 S.W.2d 4 (Tex. 1992), 50, 251
Dellums v. Bush, 752 F.Supp. 1141 (D.D.C. 1990), 122, 263

Lochner v. New York, 198 U.S. 45 (1905), 128–29, 140, 264
Louisiana v. Baxley, 663 So.2d 142 (La. 1994), 141, 267
Loving v. Virginia, 388 U.S. 1, 12 (1967), 159, 271
Lowrey v. Reagan, 676 F.Supp. 333 (D.D.C. 1987), aff'd No. 8705426 (D.C. Cir. 1988), 121, 263

Marbury v. Madison, 5 U.S. (1 Cranch) 137 (1803), 5, 12, 14–16, 18, 211, 221–22, 243, 244
Maryland v. Wirtz, 392 U.S. 183 (1968), 66, 254
Massachusetts v. Laird, 451 F.3d 26 (1st Cir. 1971), 124, 263
McClure v. Carter, 513 F.Supp. 265 (D. Idaho 1981), 85, 257
McClure v. Reagan, 454 U.S. 1025 (1981), 85, 257
McCulloch v. Maryland, 17 U.S. 316 (1819), 4, 17, 55–57, 230
McGrain v. Daugherty, 273 U.S. 135 (1927), 78–79, 92, 256
Metro Broadcasting v. FCC, 497 U.S. 547 (1990), 46, 251
Michigan v. Long, 463 U.S. 1032 (1983), 49, 251
Michigan Organization for Human Rights v. Kelley, No. 88-815820 (Mich. Cir. Ct. July 6, 1999), 141, 267
Miller v. California, 413 U.S. 15 (1973), 39, 250
Milliken v. Bradley, 433 U.S. 267 (1977), 160, 271
Mills v. Alabama, 384 U.S. 214 (1966), 174, 274
Minersville School District v. Gobitis, 310 U.S. 586 (1940), 199–200, 225, 281, 286
Missouri v. Walsh, 713 S.W.2d 508 (Mo. 1986), 141, 267
Missouri Pac. Ry. Co. v. Kansas, 248 U.S. 276 (1919), 257
Mistretta v. United States, 488 U.S. 361 (1989), 79, 256
Mitchell v. W.T. Grant Co., 416 U.S. 600, (1974), 47, 251
Mobile v. Bolden, 446 U.S. 55 (1980), 161, 271
Moe v. Secretary of Administration, 417 N.E.2d 387 (Mass. 1981), 138, 265
Morrison v. Olson, 487 U.S. 654 (1988), 79, 230, 256
Murphy v. Ramsey, 114 U.S. 15 (1886), 142, 267

NAACP v. Button, 371 U.S. 415 (1963), 180, 276
Naim v. Naim, 87 S.E. 2d 749 (Va. 1955), 156, 270
National Endowment for Arts v. Finley, 524 U.S. 569 (1968), 192, 279
National League of Cities v. Usery, 426 U.S. 833 (1976), 67, 254
New York v. United States, 505 U.S. 144 (1992), 70, 255
New York Times v. United States, 403 U.S. 713 (1971), 180, 276
New York Times Co. v. Sullivan, 376 U.S. 254 (1964), 175, 180, 275
Nixon v. Administration of Gen. Serv., 433 U.S. 425 (1977), 78, 256
Nixon v. Fitzgerald, 457 U.S 731, 754 (1982), 78, 256
Nixon v. United States, 506 U.S. 224 (1993), 81, 256
NLRB v. Jones & Laughlin Steel Corp., 301 U.S. 1 (1937), 62, 254
Northeast Bancorp v. Board of Governors, FRS, 472 U.S. 159 (1985), 253
Northern Pipeline Co. v. Marathon Pipe Line Co., 458 U.S. 50 (1982), 42, 250

Sanchez-Espinoza v. Reagan, 568 F.Supp. 596 (D.D.C. 1983), 121, 263
Sanchez-Espinoza v. Reagan, 770 F.2d 202 (D.C. Cir. 1985), 121, 263
Schechter Corp. v. United States, 295 U.S. 495 (1935), 61, 253
Schenck v. United States, 249 U.S. 47 (1919), 177
Schlesinger v. Reservists to Stop the War, 418 U.S. 208 (1974), 83, 84, 257
Shaw v. Reno, 509 U.S. 630 (1993), 164, 272
Smith v. Employment Division, 494 U.S. 872 (1990), 208–9
Smith v. Employment Division, 721 P.2d 445 (Ore. 1986), 208–9, 283
Smith v. Employment Division, 763 P.2d 146 (Ore. 1988), 208–9, 283
Smith v. Goguen, 415 U.S. 566 (1974), 183, 277
South Carolina v. Katzenbach, 383 U.S. 301 (1966), 158, 271
South Carolina v. United States, 199 U.S. 437 (1905), 29, 247
State v. Chrisman, 619 P.2d 971 (Wash. 1980), 50, 252
State v. Chrisman, 676 P.2d 419 (Wash. 1984), 50, 252
State v. Columbus Christian, No. 78 CVS 1978, slip op. at 14 (N.C. Super. Ct. September 1, 1978), 213, 284
State v. Faith Baptist Church, 301 N.W.2d 571 (Neb. 1981), 214, 284
State v. Faith Baptist Church, 454 U.S. 803 (1981), 214, 284
State v. Lefebvre, 20 A.2d 185 (N.H. 1941), 200, 281
State v. Smith, 127 P.2d 518 (Kans. 1942), 200, 281
Stenberg v. Carhart, 530 U.S. 914 (2000), 137, 266
Steward Machine Co. v. Davis, 301 U.S. 548 (1937), 62, 254
Swann v. Charlotte-Mecklenburg, 402 U.S. 1 (1971), 160–61, 170, 236

Talbot v. Seeman, 5 U.S. 1 (1801), 108, 261
Texas v. Johnson, 491 U.S. 397 (1989), 183, 277
The Pocket Veto Case, 279 U.S. 655 (1929), 87, 258
Thornburgh v. American College of Obstetricians and Gynecologists, 476 U.S. 747 (1986), 133, 265
Tinker v. Des Moines School District, 393 U.S. 503 (1969), 180, 276

United States v. Allocco, 305 F.2d 704 (2d Cir. 1962), 258
United States v. Allocco, 371 U.S. 964 (1963), 258
United States v. American Library Association, 123 S. Ct. 2297 (2003), 191, 192, 279–80
United States v. AT&T, 551 F.2d 384, 394 (D.C. Cir. 1976), 94, 259
United States v. AT&T, 567 F.2d 121 (D.C. Cir. 1977), 92, 94, 259
United States v. Butler, 297 U.S. 1 (1936), 22, 245
United States v. Cruikshank, 92 U.S. 542 (1876), 57, 253
United States v. Curtiss-Wright Corp., 299 U.S. 304 (1936), 111–12, 261
United States v. Darby, 312 U.S. 100 (1941), 60, 253
United States v. Eichmann, 496 U.S. 310 (1990), 185, 277
United States v. House of Representatives, 556 F.Supp. 150 (D.D.C. 1983), 92, 259
United States v. Jefferson County Board of Education, 372 F.2d 836 (5th Cir. 1966), 157, 271

United States v. Lopez, 514 U.S. 549 (1995), 57, 70, 253, 255
United States v. Lovett, 328 U.S. 303 (1946), 178, 275
United States v. Mazurie, 419 U.S. 544 (1975), 111, 261
United States v. Miller, 425 U.S. 435 (1976), 43, 250
United States v. Morrison, 529 U.S. 598 (2000), 72, 255
United States v. Nixon, 418 U.S. 683 (1974), 77–78, 256
United States v. O'Brien, 391 U.S. 367 (1968), 180, 276
United States v. Pink, 315 U.S. 203 (1942), 111, 261
United States v. Richardson, 418 U.S. 166 (1974), 80, 81, 256
United States v. Woodley, 751 F.2d 1008 (9th Cir. 1985), 90, 258
United States v. Woodley, 475 U.S. 1048 (1986), 90, 258
United Transportation Union v. Long Island R. Co., 455 U.S. 678 (1982), 67, 254

Vacco v. Quill, 521 U.S. 793 (1997), 144, 267

Wallace v. Jaffree, 466 U.S. 924 (1984), 204, 282
Wallace v. Jaffree, 472 U.S. 38 (1985), 203, 204, 282
Walz v. Tax Commission, 397 U.S. 664 (1970), 197, 280
Washington v. Chrisman, 455 U.S. 1 (1982), 50, 252
Washington v. Davis, 426 U.S. 229 (1976), 161, 271
Washington v. Glucksberg, 521 U.S. 702 (1997), 21, 144, 245, 267
Watkins v. United States, 354 U.S. 178 (1957), 92, 258
Webb v. Baird, 6 Ind. 13 (1854), 50, 251
Webster v. Reproductive Health Services, 492 U.S. 490 (1989), 137, 266
Welsh v. United States, 398 U.S. 333 (1970), 4, 13, 243
West Virginia State Board of Education v. Barnette, 319 U.S. 624 (1943), 201,
    225, 282, 286
Westside Community Bd. of Ed. v. Mergens, 496 U.S. 226 (1990), 204, 282
Whitney v. California, 274 U.S. 357 (1927), 174, 274
Wisconsin v. Constantineau, 400 U.S. 433 (1971), 50, 252
Woodson v. North Carolina, 428 U.S. 280 (1976), 31, 39, 247, 250
Wright v. United States, 302 U.S. 583 (1938), 87, 258
Wygant v. Jackson Board of Education, 476 U.S. 267 (1986), 164, 272

Yates v. United States, 354 U.S. 298 (1957), 179–80, 276
Youngstown Co. v. Sawyer, 343 U.S. 579 (1952), 4, 114, 242, 262
Youngstown Sheet & Tube Co. v. Sawyer, 103 F.Supp. 569 (D.D.C. 1952), 114,
    262

Zemel v. Rusk, 381 U.S. 1 (1965), 111, 261
Zurcher v. Stanford Daily, 436 U.S. 547 (1978), 181, 276

Subject Index

Brest, Paul, 41
Breyer, Stephen, 48, 131
broadcasting rights, 186–92
Brock, Bill, 165
Buchanan, James, 11, 12, 227
Burford, Anne Gorsuch, 92
Burger, Warren, 16, 47, 50, 67, 159, 161
Bush, George H. W., 20, 44, 45, 53, 88, 120, 121, 165–66, 183–84, 185
Bush, George W., 20, 45, 73, 91, 122–24, 136, 143–44, 169, 170
Bush, Jeb, 168
busing, school, 159–61, 223, 236
Butler, Benjamin, 64
Butler, Pierce, 63, 106
Byrd, Robert C., 42, 123

Califano, Joseph, 125
Campbell, Tom, 122
Cardozo, Benjamin, 29, 35, 48, 62
Carlin, George, 190
Carter, Jimmy, 87–88, 90, 92, 98, 120, 134, 181
Catron, John, 12, 227
Celler, Emanuel, 183
censure, 82–83
Central Intelligence Agency, 79–81
Chafee, Zechariah, Jr., 173, 177
chaplains, military, 197
Chase, Samuel, 14–15, 16, 108
Chayes, Abram, 26
child labor, 47, 58–61, 221
Churchill, Winston, 112
citizenship, 47
civil rights, 25, 41–42, 140, 157–59, 166, 179–80, 197, 221, 229
Civil War, 110, 196–97
Clark, James B. (Champ), 84, 86
Cleveland, Grover, 87
Clinton, Bill, 20, 37, 45, 48, 82, 85, 88, 90–91, 99, 120–21, 122, 141–42, 167, 185, 188, 191, 205, 210, 221, 232

Coats, Dan, 191
Cohen, Morris Raphael, 30
Coleman, William T., Jr., 68
commerce power, 42, 54–55, 57, 58–61, 61–66, 70–71, 72, 212, 221
Communications Decency Act, 191–92
Congress, participation of, 40–43
Congressional Budget Office, 74
conscientious objection, 196
consumers, 34–35
contempt, power of, 79, 92
Continental Congress, 104, 196
contraceptives, 128–29
Contract with America, 73–74, 167
Corcoran, Thomas, 20
Corwin, Edward S., 113
council of revision, 14
counsel, assistance of, 39, 50
court curbing, 22–26
court packing, 18, 25, 60, 61–63, 128, 221
covert actions, 115
covert spending, 79–81
Cox, Archibald, 98, 119
Craig, Barbara, 236
Cruzan, Nancy, 145–146
Cuban missile crisis, 116
Culver, John, 182

Dahl, Robert, 217
Dana, Richard Henry, Jr., 110
death penalty, 30, 31, 38–39, 225
Deaver, Michael, 98
Declaration of Independence, 32, 63, 196
Defense of Marriage Act (DOMA), 142
Dellinger, Walter, 71, 186
Denton, Jeremiah, 204
desegregation, 11, 20, 21, 35, 45, 47, 49, 225, 229, 232, 234, 235–37
DeWitt, John L., 152, 153
dial-a-porn, 190–91, 192
Dickinson, William, 206
Dole, Bob, 121, 131, 167

Donovan, Raymond, 98
Douglas, William O., 47, 63, 80, 128, 199, 200
Dugan, Robert, Jr., 210
Dulles, John Foster, 115
Duncan, Charles W., Jr., 92
Dworkin, Ronald, 10

Eagleton, Tom, 119
Edgerton, Henry W., 18
Edmunds, George, 58
Edwards, Don, 184
Edwards, James B., 92
Eisenhower, Dwight D., 11, 45, 47, 90, 114–16, 140, 156, 179, 219, 223
Eleventh Amendment, 72
Ely, John Hart, 129, 136
Emancipation Proclamation, 227
Emerson, Thomas, 128–29
Equal Access Act, 204
Equal Rights Amendment, 23–24, 43
Ervin, Sam J., Jr., 201
Espionage Act, 177
eugenics, 225
exclusionary rule, 51–52
executive branch interpretations, 43–46
executive privilege, 77–78, 91–94, 223, 231
expedited procedures, congressional, 11, 191, 192, 219, 234

fairness doctrine, 187–89
Falwell, Jerry, 204
Faubus, Orval, 12, 156, 223
federalism, 37, 53–75, 174–75
fetal tissue research, 135
Fischel, Arnold, 197
Fiske, Robert B., Jr., 99
Fiss, Owen, 41
flag protection legislation, 44, 182–85
flag salute, compulsory, 198–201, 225, 231
Foley, Tom, 185

Ford, Gerald, 87–88, 120, 121, 134, 153
Fraina, Louis, 196
Frankfurter, Felix, 32–33, 47, 62, 199, 200
free speech, 50
Freedom of Access to Clinic Entrances Act, 133, 134
Freedom of Choice Act, 132, 134
Freedom of Information Act, 80, 81
Fried, Charles, 99, 131, 133, 134–35, 141, 186
Frist, Bill, 143
Frohnmayer, David, 209

gag rule, 135
gay rights. See homosexuality
Gerry, Elbridge, 106
Gewirtz, Paul, 99
Gillespie, Oscar W., 84
Gingrich, Newt, 121
Ginsburg, Ruth Bader, 21, 28, 121, 131, 132, 147, 206, 232, 236
Goldman, Simcha, 206
Goldschmidt, Neil, 68
Goldwater, Barry, 207
Gramm, Phil, 167
Gramm-Rudman bill, 44, 78, 98, 99
Grant, Ulysses S., 46–47
Grassley, Charles, 93
Green, William, 119
Greenberg, Jack, 154
Greenhouse, Linda, 67, 73
Gregory, Roger, 90–91
Grier, Robert, 57, 110
Griffiths, Martha, 43
gun control, 71
Gunther, Gerald, 20

Haiti, 120
Hall, Ralph, 191
Halperin, Morton, 93
Hamilton, Alexander, 13, 22–23, 30, 54, 55–56, 105
Hamilton, Lee, 125–26

Livingston, Robert, 80
lobbying, individual and group, 34–
   37, 195–98, 203, 208, 209–11,
   212, 214, 216, 225, 233
Locke, John, 104
Lockwood, Belva, 34
Lott, Trent, 169
Lovejoy, Elijah, 176
Lyon, Matthew, 175

Macon, Nathaniel, 174
Madison, James, 13, 14, 16, 17, 30,
   54, 55–56, 78, 86, 103, 105, 106,
   109, 174, 222
Marbury, William, 16, 18
Marshall, John, 12, 15–16, 17–18, 22,
   54–55, 56, 60, 108, 111, 222
Marshall, Thurgood, 21, 34, 44, 149,
   154
Mason, George, 106
McCain, John, 121
McCarthy, Joseph, 175, 176, 179
McCormack, John, 116
McHenry, James, 80
McKellar, Kenneth, 112
McLean, John, 57
media, 21
Meese, Edwin, 26–27, 98, 99, 202, 203
Merryman, John, 110
Metzenbaum, Howard, 69
Mikva, Abner, 41, 85
minimum wages, 66–69
miscegenation, 156, 159, 232
Mitchell, John, 98
Montesquieu, 54
Morris, Gouverneur, 14
Morris, Robert, 55
Morse, Wayne, 117
Murphy, Frank, 63, 153, 199, 200
Murphy, Walter, 16, 218–19
Muskie, Ed, 85, 119

Neutrality Act, 38
neutrality proclamation, 38
Nicholas, John, 174

Nixon, Richard M., 66–67, 78, 82,
   85, 87, 98, 117, 118, 119, 159,
   160, 161, 162, 190, 221, 223, 224
Nixon, Walter, 81
noncompliance, 20–21, 204, 214–15,
   223, 230
North Atlantic Treaty Organization
   (NATO), 124
Nunn, Sam, 142
Nussbaum, Bernard, 93

Oaks, Dallin H., 210
Oberly, Kathryn, 207
obiter dicta, 21
O'Brien, David, 236
obscenity, 39, 232
O'Connor, Sandra Day, 48, 57, 70,
   133, 139, 218
Office of Legal Counsel, 44, 45, 68,
   71, 184, 186
Olson, Ted, 169
Owen, Robert L., 59

pardon power, 175, 221, 230
partial-birth abortion, 136, 137, 235
Patient Self-Determination Act, 145
Patman, Wright, 35
Pentagon Papers, 180
peyotism, 208–12
Pickering, John, 16
Pinckney, Charles, 104, 106
Pine, David A., 114
Polk, James, 109, 110
pornography, 39
Powell, Adam Clayton, 12, 223
Powell, Lewis F., Jr., 67, 130, 140,
   141, 161
prayer, school, 21, 27, 198, 201–5
press freedoms, 181–82
Pritchett, C. Herman, 218
privacy, 50, 127–47
   banking, 43
Prohibition, 39
public accommodations, 63–66, 151,
   180, 221